SURVIVAL?

SURVIVAL?

Death as a Transition

by

DAVID LORIMER

www.whitecrowbooks.com

Survival?
Death as a Transition

For information, contact White Crow Books
at 3 Hova Villas, Hove, BN3 3DH United Kingdom,
or e-mail info@whitecrowbooks.com.

Cover Design by Astrid@Astridpaints.com
Interior design by Velin@Perseus-Design.com

Paperback ISBN 978-1-78677-035-6
eBook   ISBN 978-1-78677-036-3

Non Fiction / Body, Mind & Spirit / Death & Dying / Parapsychology

www.whitecrowbooks.com

Open up the second shutter,
so that more light may come in

~ GOETHE, *DYING WORDS*, 1832

PRAISE FOR
SURVIVAL? DEATH AS A TRANSITION

A scholarly and highly readable work that is sure to achieve the status of a classic in its field.

~ COLIN WILSON, AUTHOR OF *SUPER CONSCIOUSNESS*

By far the best book I have read on this subject.

~ SIR JOHN ECCLES, FRS

ABOUT THE AUTHOR

David Lorimer, MA, PGCE, FRSA is a writer, lecturer and editor who is Programme Director of the Scientific and Medical Network. He has also been President of Wrekin Trust and of the Swedenborg Society and was founding Chief Executive of Character Education Scotland. Originally a merchant banker then a teacher of philosophy and modern languages at Winchester College, he is the author and editor of over a dozen books, most recently The Protein Crunch (with Jason Drew) and A New Renaissance (edited with Oliver Robinson) He has a long-standing interest in the perennial wisdom and has translated and edited books about the Bulgarian sage Peter Deunov. His edited book *Prophet for our Times* was republished in 2015 with a foreword by Wayne Dyer.

He is also a founding member of the International Futures Forum and was editor of its digest, *Omnipedia - Thinking for Tomorrow*. His book on the ideas and work of the Prince of Wales – Radical Prince - has been translated into Dutch, Spanish and French. He is the originator of the Inspiring Purpose Values Poster Programmes, which have reached over 300,000 young people. See www.inspiringpurpose.org.uk and www.character-scotland.org.uk

He lives in France with his partner Marianne van Mierlo. Personal website: www.davidlorimer.co.uk

CONTENTS

ACKNOWLEDGMENTS

The author and publishers gratefully acknowledge permission to include the following:

Excerpts from *The Golden Bough* (copyright 1936) arid *The Belief in Immortality* (copyright 1913), by Sir J. G. Frazer. Reprinted by permission of Trinity College, Cambridge.

Excerpts from *Life After Death*, by Neville Randall. Copyright 1975 by Neville Randall. Reprinted by permission of the author, Robert Hale Ltd and Watson, Little Ltd.

Excerpt from *Life in the World Unseen*, by Anthony Borgia. Copyright 1974 by Anthony Borgia. Reprinted by permission of Psychic Press Ltd.

Excerpt from *Life at Death*, by Kenneth Ring. Reprinted by permission of Coward, McCann & Geoghagan, Inc. from Life at Death by Kenneth Ring. Copyrights © 1980 by Kenneth Ring.

Excerpts from *To Die is Gain* by J. C. Hampe published and copyright 1979 by Darton, Longman & Todd Ltd, London, and used by permission of the publishers.

Excerpts from *Immortals at my Elbow*, by Rosemary Brown. Copyright Rosemary Brown 1974. Reprinted by permission of Bachman & Turner Ltd.

Excerpts from *What Happens When you Die*, by Robert Crookall. Copyright Robert Crookall 1978. Reprinted by permission of Colin Smythe Ltd.

Excerpts from *Beyond Death's Door*, by Maurice Rawlings. Copyright Maurice Rawlings 1979. Reprinted by permission of Sheldon Press.

Excerpts from *Life after Life* by Raymond Moody. Copyright Raymond Moody 1975. Reprinted by permission of Mockingbird Books Inc.

I am most grateful to my colleagues Stephan Hopkinson, James Sabben Clare, David Conner and Paul Williams for kindly reading parts of the manuscript and offering many helpful and constructive suggestions. Needless to say, the final version is my responsibility.

D. L.

INTRODUCTION
TO THE NEW EDITION

I t is now 35 years since I wrote *Survival*, mainly over the summer holiday of 1982. I was 30 then, now I am 65 – in a different phase of life. Writing the book was an intense process, and much harder work than with modern word-processing equipment. I produced the first draft in 8 weeks on a manual typewriter and got up early for several months over the autumn and winter to retype two pages a day of a manuscript that ran to 240 pages. I had met Eileen Campbell of Routledge and Kegan Paul at the Mystics and Scientists conference in 1982 and she said she might be interested in publishing the book when I had finished it. I did not know then that I would take over the running of these conferences in the late 1980s, and the series, beginning in 1978, has just celebrated its 40th anniversary in 2017. I duly sent the manuscript to Eileen and she sent it to Colin Wilson, who enthusiastically recommended its publication. This led to meeting Colin Wilson at his house in Cornwall along with his library of some 25,000 volumes. There were books in every nook and cranny and he offered £10 to visitors for any ideas of where to put another bookcase!

Survival – now sub-titled *Death as Transition* - is the first book of two and lays the groundwork for *Resonant Mind*, where I formulate an ethic of interconnectedness, partly based on the life review in the NDE. During the life review we re-experience events multidimensionally, not just from our own viewpoint. Thus we feel what it was like to be another person experiencing that event. In *Survival* I survey the history of ideas about the nature of death in the first part. Then I consider the status of evidence, recommending that a legal rather than a scientific approach is more appropriate to the kinds of case histories presented in this book. Experiments are repeatable, while our experiences are unique. So one has to establish the validity and internal coherence of these related psychic experiences, experiences that should not be possible if the tenets of scientific materialism are correct. However, as Lawrence LeShan has pointed out, impossible facts don't happen – it is just that theories may not be able to account for them. We can't change the facts, so we have to modify our theories so that they are capable of explaining these phenomena rather than dismissing them or explaining them away.

No developments over the last thirty years have fundamentally modified my analysis and conclusions in this book. The basic issues remain the same: is consciousness just a local by-product of the brain? If so, then near-death experiences should not happen during cardiac arrest; nor should children's memories of previous lives; and even less so should there be any verifiable communications with the deceased. Yet all these things do happen, therefore a paradigm shift in our understanding of consciousness is urgently required. Scientific materialists continue to maintain their sceptical position mainly by collectively ignoring the evidence. In my view, this is intellectually disreputable. It is like Nelson at the Battle of Copenhagen putting the telescope to his blind eye and saying: "I see no ships."

It is five years since the publication of a landmark book by the brilliant 'heretical' biologist Rupert Sheldrake: *The Science Delusion: Freeing the Spirit of Enquiry.* In this book he discusses a number of scientific dogmas and turns them into questions. These include the propositions that nature is essentially mechanical, that matter is unconscious, that brains produce consciousness, that memories are stored as material traces in the brain, that minds are confined to the head and that unexplained phenomena like telepathy are illusory. None of these propositions is true, as Rupert convincingly demonstrates; yet they are dogmatically adhered to in spite of over 100 years of evidence to the contrary. This shackles the spirit of enquiry and stifles the real progress that might be made if mainstream scientists had more courage in questioning these dogmas, defying the peer pressure of their colleagues. As Nikola Tesla, another neglected genius, put it: 'the day science begins to study nonphysical phenomena, it will make more progress in one decade than in all the previous centuries of its existence.'

David Lorimer, St Colombe sur l'Hers, France, August 2017

Note: *extensive footnotes from the original publication have been removed from this edition but all the references are listed in the bibliography.*

INTRODUCTION: DEATH AS A 'MORBID' SUBJECT

The greatest part of what we say and do is unnecessary.

MARCUS AURELIUS

Presque toute notre vie est employée à des curiosités niaises. En revanche il y a des choses qui devraient exciter la curiosité des hommes au plus haut degré, et qui, à en juger par leur train de vie ordinaire, ne leur en inspirent aucune.

Où sont nos amis morts?

Pourquoi sommes-nous ici?

Venons-nous de quelque part?....

[Almost our whole life is used up in idiotic trifles. By contrast there are things that should excite our curiosity to the highest degree and which, judging from people's everyday lives, excite no curiosity at all:

Where are our dead friends?

Why are we here?

Do we come from somewhere?

CHARLES BAUDELAIRE

The answer to human life is not to be found within the limits of human life.

C. G. JUNG

Man has not basically changed. Death is still a fearful, frightening happening, and the fear of death is a universal fear even if we think we have mastered it on many levels.

ELISABETH KÜBLER-ROSS

Medical advances may postpone death, but no degree of scientific sophistication is able to eliminate it altogether. Sooner or later each of us has to confront the prospect of the death of the physical body. Then what? The annihilation of a dreamless sleep, or might conscious existence continue in some sense? If so, what might be the nature of such a continued existence? Might my present conduct and attitudes influence its quality?

The decline in infant mortality has made us less familiar with death in the immediate family. We may see disasters on the television news, we may read of murders in the newspapers, but such events rarely touch us directly: this kind of thing could never happen to us, we remain insulated and apart. Our old people are often carefully segregated in institutions out of contact with the rest of society, and when they fall ill they are discreetly transported to clockwork hospitals. Here they become patients, further isolated from their normal environments, and are often cloaked in a conspiracy of silence regarding the real nature and gravity of their illness. Kübler-Ross constructs a scenario of what may ensue at this stage:

Our imaginary patient has now reached the emergency ward. He will be surrounded by busy nurses, orderlies, interns, residents, a lab technician perhaps who will take some blood, another technician who takes the electrocardiogram. He may be moved to X-ray and he will overhear opinions of his condition and discussions and questions to members of his family. Slowly but surely he is beginning to be treated like a thing. He is no longer a person. Decisions are made often without taking his opinion. If he tries to rebel he will be sedated, and after hours of waiting and wondering whether he has the strength, he will be wheeled into the operating room or intensive treatment unit and become an object of great concern and great financial investment. He may cry out for rest, peace, dignity, but he will get infusions, transfusions, a heart machine, or a tracheotomy.

The alienation is exacerbated. For medicine death is the ultimate symbol of failure and defeat: life must be prolonged where possible. Death is to be evaded and denied. Such evasion and denial surrounding the terminal patient may temporarily prop up the medical staff and relatives, but it is liable to elicit feelings of horror and revulsion towards the dying person at the very moment when he most needs human sympathy and comfort. People are afraid of identifying themselves too closely. But one day it will be their turn.

Toynbee traces the modern Western fear of death back to the general loss of faith in Christianity during the seventeenth century. Broadly speaking he argues that fear of death is inversely proportional to religious faith, although there are some people of strong convictions who are terrified of death, or perhaps of hell. He amplifies on the modern fear of death as follows:

This more and more prevalent post-17th century fear of death in the West reveals itself in various ways. The typical modern Western man or woman has allowed one of the most characteristic and most noble faculties of human nature to atrophy; or, if it is not atrophied, he or she tries deliberately to suppress it. This is the faculty – cultivated so earnestly and so effectively in India – of communing with oneself and, through oneself, not with oneself alone but with the Ultimate Spiritual Reality behind the universe. This faculty of spiritual contemplation is one of the features of human nature that makes us human. We turn subhuman if we lose this faculty or destroy it. Yet the average modern Westerner becomes uneasy if he is by himself. Science, applied with sensational success to technology, has substituted the physical conquest of non-human nature for the spiritual conquest of himself as Western man's ideal paramount objective. Modern Western man is therefore inclined to spend the maximum possible amount of his time and energy on work, except in so far as he curbs this inclination by restrictive practices for protecting his work from being exploited unduly for other people's profit; and the time and energy that is not consumed in working, feeding, and sleeping is occupied by some form of 'entertainment'. If gregarious entertainment is not obtainable, he turns on the television set or the radio or the gramophone. Anything and everything is acceptable that will preclude 'the flight of the alone to the alone (sic)'. Confronted by death without belief, modern man has deliberately been clipping his spiritual wings.

As a topic of conversation, death is taboo: don't be so morbid, let's talk about more cheerful subjects. The man of experience scorns the youthful seeker for being more concerned with the significance of death than his elders and betters, such matters being beyond our capacity to ascertain: we are not intended to discover anything about death. Schiller imagines the following paternalistic homily if the man of experience is unusually sympathetic and candid:

> My boy, I can well remember the time when I, too, felt about it just as you do now, and would have given worlds to know. So I read a number of books on the subject and even went to a séance or two. But I got very little out of it, and when I found that my friends were beginning to express serious concern for my sanity, and that I was endangering my professional reputation, I very wisely dropped the matter. Be sensible, therefore, and take my word for it, we are not meant to know about such things. Suppress your morbid craving for truth. You will soon get over it and think as everyone else does.

In other words, hardly think at all. Schiller detects a certain ambiguity in attitudes towards establishing survival of bodily death as a fact. He contends that the great majority of men, instead of thinking of death tempered with immortality, prefer not to think of death at all. The subject is depressing and distasteful because men are for the most part at home in the world. They do not want to hear about it and, above all, they do not want to know about it. Schiller continues:

> For if once they knew, it would be most inconvenient. They would have to act on their knowledge, and that would upset the habits of a lifetime. And the older one gets, the less one likes that. What the decision was would not much matter; whether science decided for immortality or annihilation, the blissful ignorance that enabled one to ignore the subject in everyday life would be gone for ever. Hence an uncertainty, to which we have grown adapted, is instinctively or deliberately preferred to a knowledge that would involve the readjustment of ingrained habits.

He goes on to say that religion has submitted to this preference, having renounced attempts to prove immortality as a matter of fact supported by evidence. This is not entirely true. There are those who regard psychical research as a supplement to faith while others, such as William Temple, treat it as a dangerous threat. Doctrines of immortality are kept tantalisingly vague – 'a vision which floats before the eye of faith, not a brutal fact to be thrust upon a reluctant attention'. Matters of faith, Schiller argues, are accepted at a large discount from their face value, and their acceptance scarcely affects the value of the hard-money facts of everyday life. Hell is reserved for people a great deal worse than oneself. The case for the acceptance of doctrines of immortality is summed up as follows: 'they yield a vague, remote guarantee against annihilation which may be summoned up or dismissed at pleasure, and does not involve any immediate practical consequences.'

But is such a complacent ignorance adequate, relying as it does on an apparently unsigned life assurance policy? The history of man's attitude towards body, mind and the possibility of post-mortem existence will be surveyed in the first part of this work. We shall find that the wide variety of conceptions of the mind-body relationship lead to two divergent twentieth-century views: identity theory materialism, and interactionism. The first theory is incompatible with any form of post-mortem experience, as it claims that the mind corresponds to processes in the brain and therefore perishes with it. (In this work we shall use the term 'conscious self' to denote the individual centre of consciousness and identity.) Interactionism, on the other hand, while not denying that mind and brain are very closely correlated in normal experience, asserts that the conscious self is a distinct entity operating through the brain: in other words that the brain does not produce consciousness but transmits it. Even if all the exponents of this theory do not state as much, this position is compatible with the continued existence of the conscious self after death.

In the second part we shall be investigating four clues, which enable us to reach some tentative conclusions about the possibility of such post-mortem existence: apparitions, out-of-the-body experiences, near-death experiences, and post-mortem descriptions of the death experience. All four of these clues suggest that some of our everyday assumptions about the conscious self and perception may be misleadingly superficial. We are used to our sense of identify, perception and thought being located in the head and associated with the functioning of the physical brain; and we take it for granted that the material space in which we move is 'reality', even if we realise that many things lie beyond the immediate spectrum of perception. Yet people do have experiences, which contravene these assumptions, and suggest a different interpretation of material reality. Some experiences of apparitions are such realistic duplicates of physical appearance that the perceiver only realises that he has seen an apparition when it moves through the furniture or vanishes into thin air; the apparition moving through apparently solid objects is a reminder that matter is only solid in terms of objects of the same frequency. Although the apparition has a physical appearance, it seems to be operating in a space which interpenetrates normal physical space but is not identical to it. This point will be elaborated in Chapter 8.

In a typical out-of-the-body experience (OBE) the subject finds that his conscious self has shifted out of the brain and the physical body, and yet is able to perceive the physical body from the outside. Frequently the physical appearance of the location seems unaltered: in other words the subject simply sees the scene as if he were, say, looking down from the top of a ladder. For the materialist, the paradox is inexplicable except as a delusion: the conscious self is perceiving and thinking outside the physical brain. More curious still are reciprocal cases of OBE and apparition: the OBE subject, aware that he is operating in some kind of duplicate body, travels to a distant location where he sees a person and is aware of being seen by that person; this person then confirms that he saw an apparition of the OBE subject at the time that the OBE subject claimed to be in his presence. Thus the two experiences corroborate each other.

The physical aspects of near-death experiences are an extension of OBEs, only the circumstances are all the more extraordinary, since the subject is frequently in a coma, perhaps undergoing surgery or heart attack resuscitation procedures. Yet reports suggest that the conscious self's awareness outside the body is not only unimpaired but enhanced: events which occurred during the period of unconsciousness events which occurred during the period of unconsciousness are described in accurate detail and confirmed by those present. The subject sometimes 'hears' the doctor pronouncing him dead when he feels intensely alive and free from physical pain, but finds himself returning unwillingly to the constrictions of the physical body. If OBEs showed the capacity of the conscious self to have experiences and perceptions outside the physical body, the near-death experience suggests that this capacity still obtains when the physical body is totally unconscious.

If the materialist is right in his assumption that consciousness is produced by the brain and perishes with it, there should be no such thing as a post-mortem description of the death experience. And yet such reports do exist. What is striking is their close correspondence to some of the features noted by near-death experiencers, so that one cannot help speculating that substantially the same experience is being described, and that the conscious self, which can operate outside the body during physical life, can operate completely independently of it after separation at bodily death.

However, since the above phenomena are of an anecdotal rather than an experimental nature, they cannot be said to constitute proof one way or the other; but might it not be rash to consign them to the rubbish heap? If the experiences are genuine, it is natural to attempt to formulate some kind of coherent explanatory hypothesis. Since no evidence is necessarily coercive, the reader may find the hypothesis of survival unconvincing, in which case he has set himself the challenge of finding a more comprehensive and adequate explanation.

Part One:

Historical

I.

THE ANIMISTIC OUTLOOK

The mystery of creation is like the darkness of night – it is great.
Delusions of knowledge are like the fog of the morning.

TAGORE

Man is not come into the world to solve the problems of the universe,
but to find out where the problem begins, and, as a consequence, to
keep within the bounds of the accessible.

GOETHE

Man almost everywhere, when confronted with the fact of death, has
refused to accept it as the ultimate term of human existence and has
persisted in believing, often in the face of a lively appreciation of the
evidence to the contrary, in some form of survival.

BRANDON

Primitive man is a plain unsophisticated practical person living in a precarious environment and continually confronted with perplexing situations which he endeavours to meet as well as he is able by natural and supernatural means.

WILLIAM JAMES

Because we are self-conscious we know that we shall die, even if we find this hard to imagine. We see around us the birth and death of many forms of physical life. The physical world is in a state of perpetual flux and transformation: the leaves of one year become the fertiliser of the next. Every day our bodies process matter in the form of food and drink, while the matter of the body itself is constantly being renewed or destroyed; at physical death this matter will be reconstituted in other forms. Such self-conscious understanding, however, is acquired rather than innate. We shall see how the development of a child's mentality and his growing understanding of the significance of death shed some light on the primitive's outlook.

Nagy highlights three stages in the child's understanding of the nature of death. In the first stage, characterising children from the ages of three to five, death is not envisaged as final or universal. It is seen as a temporary departure, separation or absence. Most children want to know where and how the person continues his existence after his disappearance:

> The child knows itself as a living being. In his egocentric way he imagines the world after his own fashion; so in the outside world he also imagines everything, lifeless things and dead people alike, as living. Living and lifeless he has not yet distinguished. He extends his animism to death, too.

Hence the dead are imagined as breathing, eating and knowing if someone thinks of them. However these children do see limitations in a life in the grave, and some even consider this diminished life to consist exclusively of sleep.

The second stage, typifying children between five and nine, indicates a personification of death, either in the form of a symbol such as a skull or scythe, or else as an animated skeleton or cold invisible messenger. Those carried off by the 'death-man' will die. Death is an eventuality, but not yet applies to oneself. It is only at the third stage, emerging at nine or ten, that death is recognised as inevitable and universal, resulting in the dissolution of the physical body. The conception now corresponds to the physical facts, and is reflected in the development of the child's overall picture of the world.

Piaget explains that the child does not initially differentiate himself from the world; the whole content of consciousness is put on the same plane, and the 'I' is not distinguished from the 'not-I'. There is no separate sense of the self, since the external world is vivified and the internal universe materialised. Take, for example, a child's explanation of dreams. Initially they are thought to be pictures of light or air coming before the eyes from the outside; they could be seen entering or leaving the room. They are then recognised to be internal, but proceeding from the head or stomach and appearing before the child. Finally reality is distinguished from appearance: the dream is localised in the eyes and then inside the head. Piaget comments that the initial non-differentiation (or realism as he terms it) is not simply due to ignorance of the internal world, but to confusion and absence of objectivity, and that 'it is through a progressive differentiation that the internal world comes into being and is contrasted with the external. Neither of these two terms is given at the start.'

The process that applies to this differentiation of the internal and external worlds applies equally to knowledge. In order to have 'objective' knowledge one must be aware of the subjective, or 'I'. A mind ignorant of itself would inevitably tend to classify things in accordance with its own prejudices; this applies to the domains of reasoning, immediate judgement and even perception. Piaget cites the notion of air or wind as an example of this con-fusion (literally melting together)

> During the earliest stages, air is conceived as participating with thought: the voice is air, and, in return, the wind takes notice of us, obeys us, and is 'good at making us grow', comes when we move our hands, and so on. When thought proper is localised in the self, and the participations between air and thought are broken, the nature of air changes by virtue of this fact alone. Air becomes independent of men, sufficient to itself, and living its own life. But, owing, to the fact that it is held to participate with the self, it retains at the very moment when it is severing these bonds, a certain number of purely human aspects: it still has consciousness, of a different kind perhaps than formerly, but its own nevertheless. Only very gradually will it be reduced to a mere thing.

The child thus becomes progressively more able to distinguish himself from the phenomenon observed. He invests the external world with fewer of his own qualities. By withdrawing these projections he is better able to understand nature itself as well as his own viewpoint: his sense of individuality is developed, and nature is understood in terms of its own laws which operate independently of the individual. Piaget does stress, however, that there is no such thing as complete objectivity in perception: some fragments of experience still cling to the outside world and colour our interpretations.

Neumann uses terms similar to those of Piaget when he refers to our dreams taking place in an interior world where all the images and symbols are projections of interior processes. In talking of primitive man's picture of the world he comments:

> The world of the dawn man is very largely an interior world experienced outside himself, a condition in which inside and outside are not discriminated from one another. The feeling of oneness with the universe, the ability of all contents to change shape and place in accordance with the laws of similarity and symbolic affinity ... the world of dreams shares with the dawn period of mankind.

At a distance Neumann states that it is easy to see as a transparent case of projection the animism (anima = soul) that endows trees with indwelling spirits or human beings with magical powers:

> We know that trees, idols, holy places, and human beings are recognisable objects of the external world, into which early man projected his inner psychic contents. By recognising them, we withdraw such 'primitive projections', we diagnose them as autosuggestion or something of the sort, and thus the fusion effected by participation between man and the objects of the external world is nullified.

Awareness dissipates the illusion of projection. Neumann goes on to point out that it is a much trickier operation to divest ourselves of our own unquestioned preconceptions, whether they concern the sanctity of our country, the devilish intentions of a superpower, or even the bad character of those we dislike. The objects of projection may change, but the ability and propensity to project qualities remains intact.

As the distinction between the outer and the inner, between the self and the other, becomes more clear-cut, so there emerges a principle

4

to organise, integrate and co-ordinate the various awarenesses and sensations. Without such an integrating principle, experience would be chaotic and without any real centre; this centre is filled by the ego, which differentiates perceptions of things and places, organises them into an abstract system, and controls adaptive behaviour in the environment. The ego experiences itself as different from the world and is able, gradually, to divide the world into subject and object (the word divide means 'see as two'); correspondingly, notions of space and time become less indefinite. Such a process of differentiation is symbolically represented in hero myths.

Neumann indicates that the ego's assessment of its relation to the body has important consequences for man's view of nature. The ego has its 'seat' or centre in the head and experiences the nether regions of the body as something strange to it. Then it discovers that parts of the body are subject to its will, so that thought is able to control the physical 'mechanism'; hand and foot are at the beck and call of the ego. The extension of the hand, as Bronowski pointed out in his lectures on the ascent of man, is the tool and then the machine, both of which enable man's will to impinge on nature. Initially, attempts to control nature were through magic, whose modern equivalent is technology. Neumann takes this line of thought a little further when he asserts that the development of ego-consciousness is paralleled by a tendency to wish to free itself from dependence on the body. In its more extreme form this leads to ascetic mortification of the body, especially in masculine initiation tests, where the pains and fears of the body must be overcome by the ego.

In his celebrated but much maligned work *Primitive Mentality*, Lévy-Bruhl analyses the ways in which our modes of thought differ from those of primitive man:

> The primitive makes no distinction between this world and the other, between what is actually present to sense, and what is beyond. He actually dwells with invisible spirits and intangible forces. To him it is these, which are real and actual.

Another authority, Schmidt, concludes:

> The uncivilised man knows but one world, embracing all experience; his apprehension of it resembles that of young children. For him the outward and visible world is one and the same with the world of the

imagination, including the life in dreams. His outlook sees but one plane, compounded in his adventure in both these regions.

These passages present us with the now familiar pattern of undifferentiated or only partially differentiated consciousness projecting the internal onto the external and drawing no distinction between the visible and the invisible. When it is argued that the external and internal worlds are 'one and the same reality', it should not be assumed that primitive man cannot distinguish between states of wakefulness and sleep; but simply that external and internal are equally significant. He does not consider the one to be illusory and the other real. This point will become clearer when we come to the question of causality.

Tylor's epoch-making work *Primitive Culture* appeared in 1871 and was the first to redefine the term 'Animism' with reference to primitive man. He divides animism into two great dogmas, each of which forms part of one consistent doctrine.

> First, concerning souls of individual creatures, capable of continued existence after the death or destruction of the body; second, concerning other spirits, upwards to the rank of deities. Spiritual beings are held to affect or control the events of the material world, and man's life here and hereafter.

He goes on to argue that, given the possibility of communication between these spirits and men, reverence and propitiation will soon arise, thus pointing to emergence of religion from a combination of ancestor-worship and worship of elemental forces. This view has been contested by, *inter alia*, Evans-Pritchard but a discussion of the issues falls outside the scope of this work. Whatever the controversy over the actual sequence of beliefs, it is generally recognised that the primitive outlook is characterised by the kind of animism formulated by Tylor.

This view does not limit the possibility of continued post-mortem existence to man. Frazer states that:

> The explanation of life by the theory of an indwelling and practically immortal soul is one which the savage does not confine to human beings but extends to the animate creation in general ... he commonly believes that animals are endowed with feelings and intelligence like those of men, and that, like men, they possess souls which survive the

death of their bodies either to wander about as disembodied spirits or to be born again in animal form.

The assumption that animals were also animated by souls had two important consequences. First, that the hunter who killed an animal believed himself thereby exposed to the vengeance of its disembodied spirit, or at least that the ensuing blood feud might be pursued by an animal of the same species. Accordingly the hunter will feel uneasy at the prospect of killing an animal, all the more so if the animal or reptile, for instance the crocodile, the snake, the tiger, or the wolf, is known to have killed men in the past. Some tribes, like the Dyaks of Borneo, are said only to kill a crocodile if the crocodile has first killed a man in the past; thus only as an act of vengeance. Other will perform elaborate rituals to propitiate the dead animal's spirit, in order to ward of the possible unpleasant consequences of the death, for instance the Koryak of north-eastern Siberia are reported to have propitiated a whale.

The second consequence is the doctrine of transmigration. Frazer comments that the primitive:

> arguing apparently from his own sensations ... conceives of life as an indestructible kind of energy, which when it disappears in one form must necessarily reappear in another, though in the new form it need not be immediately perceptible by us: in other words he infers that death does not destroy the vital principle nor even the conscious personality, but that it merely transforms them into other shapes, which are not less real because they commonly elude the evidence of our senses.

Some of the new forms, however, are conceived of as perceptible; the belief in transmigration is closely linked to the respecting and sparing of certain species of animal, as outlined above. In Sumatra it is supposed that the souls of the dead frequently transmigrate into tigers, so that the killer of the tiger can never be certain of not having caused one of his ancestors to vacate his latest form of incarnation. At this stage the idea of transmigration from human to animal form is not considered degrading for, as Jung points out: 'Primitive man does not dream of regarding himself as the lord of creation. His zoological classification does not culminate in *homo sapiens*, but in the elephant. Next comes the lion, then the python or the crocodile ... ' It is only when the essence of man comes to be regarded as something divine and immaterial that transmigration implies stepping down the ladder of creation. Thus, according to Plato, the souls of robbers will become wolves and hawks, those of poets swans or nightingales, and that of the buffoon an ape.

Frazer observes that rituals connected with rice in Indonesia:

> are founded on the simple conception of the rice as animated by a soul like that which these people attribute to mankind. They explain the phenomena of reproduction, growth, decay and death in the rice on the same principles on which they explain the corresponding phenomena in human beings. They imagine that in the fibres of the plant, as in the body of a man, there is a certain vital element, which is so far independent of the plant that it may for a time be completely separated from it without fatal effects ... this vital yet separable element is what, for want of a better word, we must call the soul of a plant, just as a similar vital and separable element is commonly supposed to constitute the soul of man.

The same animistic view of life is extended to the plant and animal kingdoms, and even, somewhat less logically, to the inanimate as well. We must now look more closely at man's idea of himself.

The presence or absence of the animating principle in the human body is used to account for a variety of natural phenomena: sleep, dreams, trance, disease and death. Tylor is particularly anxious to trace the origins of what he terms the apparition-soul or ghost-soul, and speculates on the possible associations that might occur to the so-called 'savage philosopher'. While it is impossible wholly to dismiss the jibe that any investigator of remote antiquity is bound to fall foul of the 'If I were a horse fallacy', Tylor's postulations do give a coherent account of the primitive view of the relationship between the animating life-principle and the occurrence of dreams and visions. It is supposed that the animating principle is temporarily absent in sleep and permanently so in death. If, therefore, the figures appearing in dreams are considered real, but known to be physically dead, it is inferred that the person still exists and that the phantom/image has left the body and taken the animating principle with it. Tylor reasons that both the animating principle and the phantom/image belong to the body, so that there is no reason why they should not belong to each other and be manifestations of one and the same soul: hence the conception of the ghost-soul. Crawley advances a rival theory to account for the origin of the idea of the soul. He argues that it originated as a 'mental repetition of a sensation – a mental replica – a thought of the thing or percept'. In other words he explains subject/object dualism in terms of the distinction between outer and inner worlds, between the thing itself and the idea we have of it in our minds. He equates the world of spirits with the private mental world. This theory does scant justice to the presence of phantoms in dreams and the connection of the phantom with the life principle. Nevertheless memory and imagination clearly contribute to primitive concepts of immortality.

Tylor gives a useful and comprehensive definition of his understanding of the primitive conception of the soul or spirit:

> It is a thin unsubstantial human image, in its nature a sort of vapour, film, or shadow; the cause of life and thought in the individual it animates; independently possessing the personal consciousness and volition of its corporeal owner, past or present; capable of leaving the body far behind, to [sic] flash swiftly from place to place; mostly impalpable and invisible, yet also manifesting physical power, and especially appearing to men awake or asleep as a phantasm separate from the body of which it bears the likeness; continuing to exist and appear to men after the death of that body; able to enter into, possess and act in the bodies of other men, of animals and even things.

The essence of this definition comes close to the *Shorter Oxford Dictionary*'s second definition of the soul as 'the principle of thought and action in man, commonly regarded as an entity distinct from the body; the spiritual part of man in contrast to the purely physical part'. Of course the second half of this definition implies a degree of refinement of thought, which had not yet been attained at the primitive stage of development.

The location of the soul was variously conceived: sometimes as being in the blood, or the heart, or inside the head. If it was regarded as co-extensive with the body and identified with the principle of vitality and strength, the result was sometimes cannibalism. The *mana* or vitality of the man, or indeed of an animal, was appropriated by the man through eating the body – a symbol of sharing and participation which some trace through Mithraism to the Eucharist. The two commonest sets of etymological associations with the word soul are shadow, shade and reflection, or the idea of wind or breath. Firth points out that the Tikopians call the body *tino* when alive, and *penu* when dead; the word *ata* is used to denote the recognisable ethereal image or semblance,

9

but also means reflection or shadow. Frazer cites the natives of British New Guinea as using the same word *arugo* for shadow and reflection; and with the Gilbert Islanders the word *tamuna* serves the same dual purpose. Tylor provides other instances: the Quiche language uses *natub* for shadow, soul; the Arawak *ueja* means shadow, soul, echo, image. Associations of soul and breath are to be found in the Maori culture where the word *hau* denotes wind, breath, soul (their other term *wairua* means shadow). West Australians use one word *waug* for breath, spirit, soul; in the Netela language of California *piuts* means life, breath, soul, while certain Greenlanders reckoned that man had two souls – his shadow and his breath. In Genesis 'The Lord God formed man out of the dust of the ground, and breathed into his nostrils the breath of life; and man became a living soul.' The Greek *pneuma* and the Latin *animus, anima,* and *spiritus* all carry the association of breath. Frazer relates that the Marquesans supposed that at death the soul left the body via the mouth or nose 'hence in order to delay its departure and so to prolong the life of its owner, affectionate relatives used to stop his mouth and nostrils, thus accelerating the event which they wished to retard'. The English word expire still has a double meaning. It can be seen that these linguistic associations are extremely widespread.

During sleep it is supposed that the soul wanders away from the body and actually performs the actions, visits the places and converses with the people encountered in the dream; it is sometimes imagined to assume the form of a bird, for instance by the Bororos of Brazil. The natives of British New Guinea believed that the dead often appear to the living in dreams to give them advice on the cultivation of their gardens and the practice of witchcraft. Among the Shilluks of the White Nile a dead king will appear in a dream and demand a sacrifice if the millet crop threatens to fail. If a man wants advice from his dead parents he will dig up their skulls and sleep beside them, and in case of a slow response he will sometimes provide himself with a cudgel with which he threatens to smash their skulls. Some dreams may be precognitive, although the primitive would not himself use our term; for him the events of his dream have already happened, so that his surprise is less when he sees the event occurring in the physical world. Lévy-Bruhl recounts an experience of the Rev. W.B. Grubb. One day an Indian, who had travelled 150 miles to see him, and was accused of stealing three of his pumpkins, accosted Grubb. It turned out that the Indian had dreamt that Grubb had stolen his pumpkins and had come to demand compensation. The fact that the Indian knew that Grubb had not so much as set foot in his garden did not in his view weaken his case; the intention apparent in the dream was the crucial factor.

If a man's soul should temporarily leave the body during waking hours, the result is thought to be sickness or insanity (for which we have the idiom to take leave of one's senses). It may be thought that the soul has been abducted by demons or sorcerers, in which case after consultation with the local sorcerer, an expedition will be mounted for the retrieval of the soul. Where the soul is associated with the shadow, a man may suffer through injury to his shadow, on the principle of sympathetic magic. In some Australian aboriginal tribes where the mother-in-law must always keep her face covered in the presence of her son-in-law, it is a curious fact that the son-in-law's shadow falling on her is regarded as sufficient grounds for divorce. Some other peoples fear losing their soul in their reflection in the water, or in a likeness drawn of them; while the Siknin called the camera 'the evil eye of the box', considering it to be an instrument for the imprisonment and abduction of their souls.

We have seen that the soul is considered to be semi-material, and that it is capable of leaving the body temporarily without causing death. Excursions from the body are sometimes regarded as dangerous, but equally it may be thought safer to deposit the soul somewhere outside the body. If it is maintained intact in a box or jar, then the person cannot be harmed, but equally if it is damaged or destroyed the person will be injured or die; meanwhile it is thought able to animate the body at a distance. This theory of the so-called external soul plays an important part in explaining the rationale of certain initiation ceremonies where the candidates undergo a ritual death and resurrection. The soul is extracted and transferred to the candidate's totem, which infuses him with new life; meanwhile the temporary absence of the soul throws the youth into a trance. When he revives it may well be in the 'form' of his totem, say a bear or wolf, which explains why he has lost his memory and has to relearn many things he formerly knew. The word initiation has connotations of beginning, training and instructing. The candidate is separated from his family both physically and by his ritual death, which gives him an opportunity to acquaint himself with the spiritual world; he is then reborn regenerated, and receives sacred instruction; finally he is reintegrated into the community in his new identity by means of various disciplines and food taboos. There are many variations on this basic pattern but the ritual of symbolic death and rebirth is common to them all.

While modern western medicine grapples with the problem of determining the exact moment of brain death, primitive man has a much more straightforward explanation. Death is regarded as a permanent absence of the soul, which is imagined to continue its existence elsewhere. Mbiti explains:

> Death is conceived of as a departure and not a complete annihilation of the personality. He moves on to join the company of the departed, and the only major change is the decay of the body, but the spirit moves on to another state of existence.

We shall take one example from Frazer's extensive selection of beliefs about the departure of the soul from the body; such ideas of departure and separation have already been encountered in young children's understanding of death:

> All the Central Melanesians believe that man is composed of a body and a soul, that death is the final parting of the soul from the body, and that after death the soul continues to exist as a conscious and more or less active being ... they imagine that as soon as the soul quits the body at death, it mounts into a tree where there is a bird's nest fern, and sitting there among the ferns it laughs and mocks at the people who are crying and making great lamentations over the deserted tabernacle. There he sits, wondering at them and ridiculing them. 'What are they crying for ... whom are they sorry for? Here am I' for they think that the real thing is the soul, and that it has gone away from the body just as a man throws off his clothes and leaves them, and the clothes lie by themselves with nothing in them.

The primitive conception of death does not identify the conscious self with the body, as can be seen from the above extract. The conscious self operates through the body during physical life (although we have seen how it can separate itself temporarily), and shifts its focus permanently out of the body at death.

In the conclusion of his Gifford lectures on the belief in immortality, and after indicating the way in which ancestor worship necessarily implies belief in the survival and power of human souls, Frazer comments as follows:

It is impossible not to be struck by the strength, and perhaps we may say the universality, of the natural belief in immortality among the savage races of mankind. With them a life after death is not a matter of speculation and conjecture, of hope and fear; it is a practical certainty which the individual as little dreams of doubting as he doubts the reality of his own existence. He assumes it without inquiry and acts upon it without hesitation, as if it were one of the best-ascertained truths within the limits of human experience.

His surveys in the other two volumes give no grounds for altering this conclusion.

As a foretaste of the wish-fulfilment explanation of man's belief in immortality, it is worth quoting at this stage the views of Malinowski, who speculates about the sources of religious belief and regards death as the event which most upsets and disorganises man's calculations. He states:

> The affirmation that death is not real, that man has a soul and that he is immortal, arises out of a deep need to deny personal destruction, a need which is not a psychological instinct but is determined by culture and by the growth of human sentiments ... the rituals before death ... confirm the emotional outlook [that of hope] ... of the individual who faces death.

In other words the ritual before death confirms society's need for reassurance about its own continuity, as well as reinforcing the individual's emotional expectation. In common with other wish-fulfilment theories this account presents only a pseudo-explanation of the issue. The phenomena of dreams and phantoms are not treated at their face value but side-stepped and explained away in terms of the author's own standpoint, in this case that of functionalism.

If there is unanimity about the nature of death among primitive societies, there is an almost equally universal belief that it is not natural, that people 'would not die at all if it were not for the maleficent arts of the sorcerer'; nor, for that matter, are diseases and accidents considered natural. They are also thought to originate with the wiles of the sorcerer, who must be identified in order that appropriate revenge may be exacted. An understanding of this mode of thought requires a closer look at the primitive idea of causality. Lévy-Bruhl calls the primitive's mental framework of reference a 'représentation collective', by which Jung understands 'widely current ideas whose truth is held to be self-evident'. Such ideas are axioms of judgment and are never called into question, since, with a little Procrustean stretching, they can be made to account for any set of facts; in the parlance of modern philosophy of science they are 'unfalsifiable'.

We have already suggested that the function of the ego is to order and integrate the stream of consciousness. Lévi-Strauss suggests that all thought, including the primitive, is founded on the demand for order; and he quotes a scientist as stating that the most basic postulate of science is that nature itself is orderly, although the vexed question of whether the order lies in the facts themselves or more in our interpretation of them remains unsolved. Malinowski points out that knowledge and foresight help to render the world more predictable and, hence, perhaps more controllable, but 'however much knowledge and science can help man in allowing him to obtain what he wants, they are unable to control chance, eliminate accidents, to foresee the unexpected turn of natural events'. Man therefore needs to combat the inevitable uncertainty involved in such dangerous pursuits as sailing and hunting, and to endeavour to control the waywardness of wind and weather or avert the calamity of sudden natural disaster by means of magical propitiation and sacrifice. But when a fatal accident or disaster supervenes, how does he account for it?

Lévy-Bruh cites a revealing incident. Three Cabinda women had been down to the river with their pots to fetch water. All three of them were filling them from the stream together when the middle one was snapped up by an alligator, carried away under the surface of the water, and drowned. The tabloid newspaper headline would have run 'Alligator Tragedy ...'; it might have commented on the stupidity or otherwise of collecting water from that particular spot, etc., but would probably have concluded that the event had occurred by chance, and that the other two women were extremely fortunate to escape. The primitives viewed the incident quite differently. The relatives of the dead women accused the other two of bewitching her; there could be no question of pure accident, as every similar occurrence originates in sorcery. Alligators would not have attacked the woman of their own accord; therefore someone must have incited this one to do so. Thus the alligator knew exactly which woman to drag away; it picked the middle one. This fact in itself was considered sufficiently weighty evidence to imply that the other two women were responsible, or else they, too, would have been seized; in this case the search for the culprit would have begun elsewhere. In the event the women had to take casca, an ordeal poison, which is almost certain to have been fatal. Lévy-Bruhl points out that the primitive knows nothing of the physiological processes of the internal organs, and still less of their interaction with the poison. So the chain of cause and effect is not seen to be physical but magical – a sort of divination through the human body. It was also important for the primitive to believe that the sorcery had been neutralised or eliminated, so that it could produce no further injury. Jung sums up the significance of the incident by saying that whereas we would interpret the events in terms of chance, the primitive attributes everything to some form of complex calculated intention; human motivation theory is extended to the animal.

'Experience fashions reason, and reason fashions experience.' This pithy formulation by Piaget illustrates the interdependence of these two factors. His researches into causality as envisaged by children throw some light on primitive formulations of intention and chance. He explains that the conception of causality 'is at the start neither purely moral nor purely physical. A given event is explained straight away by the intention or motive at the back of it, but the child does not ask itself how this intention worked itself into action.' Lévy-Bruhl makes the same point about primitive mentality when he contends that the particular content of the processes does not interest it because it considers only the beginning and the end. Bühler cites a six-year old's explanation of the forces of a magnet: 'The magnet has a soul and tiny little hands, so tiny that we cannot see them, and it is with them that he pulls the iron to himself.' The magnet is animistically personified. Piaget explains that:

> every movement is supposed by the child to contain an element of spontaneity. An internal motor is necessary if the object is to be moved by an external motor. If dead leaves 'move with the wind' it is because they are alive, even if driven by the wind.

Gradually, from this primal confusion of the self with the universe, which we have already observed with respect to original attitudes to reality, there emerges an objectification and a consequent appreciation of causal sequences; however, up to the age of eight, the concept of moral intention behind phenomena predominates. There is no room for chance, everything has a reason, indeed must have a reason, as many parents will know; the child even wants to know the reason for facts that we consider inexplicable because due to chance, for 'chance is banished from nature, for everything admits of justification or of motivation since everything in nature has been willed'. After the age of eight the child begins to grasp the idea of generality in the laws of nature; in proportion as he does so, the ascribing of moral intention fades away, and the concept of chance is admitted in greater measure. Chance, of course, is not an explanation, but the denial of explanation; reason concedes that it can discern no pattern in the event. At the same time moral or dynamic necessity in explanation – clouds move because they have been told to or want to – is replaced by logical and mechanical necessity: water flows downhill because of gravity, or the clock runs because the spring is wound up.

In his last reflections on the difference between our outlook and that of the primitive, Lévy-Bruhl modifies his original contentions on their lack of logic. He found that 'at certain moments these minds followed paths which we do not take, and, reciprocally, that they had extreme difficulty in following ours.' We have noted that the same holds for the child's outlook. This suggested to him a different orientation and different mental habits which were not at first glance as rigorously logical as his own. But the essential difference is not a logical one; it is rather a divergence of the premises or presuppositions on which the reasoning is based, as in the interpretations of chance above. Nor should we smugly assume that we ourselves are immune to superstition; what hostess would not have slight qualms if she knew that her guests might be driving home on black ice after being thirteen at the dinner table? Or, as Russell put it, what man would not feel uneasy if he were committing adultery in a tent during a thunderstorm? Besides, some coincidences may display a logic of meaning rather than of causality; but a discussion of Jung's concept of synchronicity falls outside the scope of the present chapter.

After examining primitive and child causality we are in a better position to understand the primitive's notion that death is caused by sorcery. Frazer relates that the Maoris held an inquest after every death in order to discover the wretch who had brought about the demise. Under the direction of a presiding sage, the culprit was detected, tracked down and exterminated. One can imagine that the scope for intrigue under such a 'system' would be almost boundless; indeed the sage himself would have a vested interest in remaining in the chair if he himself was not to be 'detected' by an aspiring successor. Occasionally, as among the Indians of Guiana, death is attributed to demonic intervention by ghosts or spirits; because it was by definition impossible to pin down the culprit, this theory did at least have the merit of precluding further bloodshed. More extensive loss of life was likely to result from a number of suspects having to undergo an ordeal. Frazer cites only two tribes, the Melanesians and the Caffees of Southern Africa, who extend the possible causes to disease pure and simple; but even they do not dispense with the other categories of explanation.

So the overall picture remains: that the vast majority of individual deaths are considered due to sorcery. This explanation does not account for the origin of death itself. Eliade explains how man was created from a *materia prima*: clay, stone or wood depending on the structure of the particular culture. Such *materia prima* symbolises perenniality: 'when man was made (or extracted) from stone, he partook of the mode of being of rock. He endured; he did not know death.' This idea of the primordial absence of death has to be reconciled with the ever-present fact of mortality. To this end various myths emerged; myth is defined by Eliade as 'before all else a tale ... it has no other function than to reveal *how something came into being*' (his italics). He goes on to say that the absurdity of the cause which introduced death is a mythical expression of the incomprehensibility of the fact of death; some of the narratives below lend support to this contention.

For the westerner, probably the most familiar account of the origin of death is to be found in Genesis. Man was created immortal on condition that he on no account ate of the tree of the knowledge of good and evil 'for in the day that thou eatest thereof thou shalt surely die'. Then along came the serpent with his bland assurances about the harmlessness of the fruit. Eve succumbed out of curiosity, Adam followed suit, and in the ensuing recriminations the buck is passed back to the serpent. The result of the act of disobedience is death, 'for dust thou art, and unto dust thou shalt return'.

A number of other stories contain the elements of curiosity and disobedience:

> Among various tribes of New South Wales it is said that the people were meant to live forever. But they were forbidden to approach a certain hollow tree. The wild bees made a nest in the tree, and the women coveted the honey. In spite of warnings by the men, a woman attacked the tree with her tomahawk, and out flew a huge bat. The bat was Death which was henceforth free to roam the world and claim all that it could touch with its wings.

In this case a woman was the culprit, but against the advice of the perhaps self-righteous men; in Genesis Adam is not consulted. Fijians account for the origin of death by disobedience: a god passed by when the first man was buried, and told the bystanders to dig him up, at the same time promising that he would live. The people refused to do so on the grounds that he stank, so that instead of being dug up like a banana after four days and being ripe, in future men would die and rot. This myth is curiously inconsistent in its assumption that the first man had actually died (unless he was just 'ripening') before the promise of immortality was given. One more instance of curiosity and disobedience:

> A certain man had received the gift of immortality in a small packet from a magician named Messou, who repaired the world after it had been seriously damaged by a great flood. In bestowing on the man this valuable gift the magician strictly enjoined him on no account to open the packet. The man obeyed, and so long as the packet remained unopened he remained immortal, but his wife was both curious and incredulous; she opened the packet to see what was in it, the precious contents flew away, and mankind has been subject to death ever since.

Patriarchal chauvinism almost invariably incriminates women for the blunder of originating mortality; men are pictured as the repositories of wisdom and restraint, while women are reckoned to have been rash and impulsive – or enterprising, depending on your point of view.

Frazer distinguishes four other structures of myth, which we shall now briefly illustrate. Among the commonest themes is that of the incompetent or lazy messenger. The Zulus describe how the Old Old One sent out a chameleon with a message of immortality for men. The chameleon was in no hurry so he stopped on the way to eat purple berries. He then climbed a tree to bask in the sun, filled his belly with flies, and fell asleep. Meanwhile the Old Old One had changed his mind and sent out a lizard with the message of mortality; the lizard arrived first – neither animal enjoys much popularity as a result. Sometimes the messengers are dogs and frogs, or sheep and goats, but the outcome is the same.

Another theme uses the symbolism of the waxing and waning moon. In the Caroline Islands it was said that death used to be a short sleep between the last day of the waning moon and the first day of the new moon; but an evil spirit somehow contrived that they should no longer wake up. The Hottentots tell another story, which contains elements of the messenger theme:

Once the moon charged the hare to go to men and say 'As I die and rise to life again, so shall you die and rise to life again'. So the hare went to men, but either out of forgetfulness or malice he reversed the message and said 'As I die and do not rise to life again, so shall you also die and not rise to life again'. Then he went back to the moon and she asked him what he had said. He told her, and when she heard that he had given the wrong message, she was so angry with him that she threw a stick at him and split his lip, which is the reason why the hare's lip is still split ... before he fled he clawed the moon's face, which still bears the marks of his scratching, as anybody can see for himself on a clear moonlit night.

This myth is notable for its economy in explaining at one stroke the origin of death, the hare's lip, and the man in the moon.

A third theme, that of the serpent and his cast skin, has a tenuous connection with the Genesis story. Some Melanesians say that a messenger was entrusted with the message of immortality for men, provided that they shed their skins every year; but serpents were to be mortal. Unfortunately the secret was betrayed to the serpents and the message reversed. In another case in Annam the messenger was entrusted with the same message but was intimidated by a group of serpents and obliged to repeat the message in reverse. It is interesting that both myths assume that the serpent somehow expropriated a privilege originally accorded to man. Another Sumatran story tells of a certain being who was sent down from heaven to put the finishing touches on creation. He was supposed to fast for a month, but could not resist eating a few bananas. This turned out to be a fatal mistake, for had he eaten river-crabs instead, men would have cast their skins like river-crabs and never died.

Frazer calls the fourth group the 'Banana Type' – its structure has something in common with the story just related. The natives of Poso in Central Celebes say that in the beginning the Creator used to lower his gifts to men on the end of a rope. One day he lowered a stone, but the first mother and father did not think very highly of it and asked for something else. So up went the rope; presently it reappeared, this time with a banana on the end. This was considered to be much more palatable, but the choice was a fatal error of judgment. The Creator pronounced:

Because ye have chosen the banana, your life shall be like its life. When the banana tree has offspring, the parent stem dies; so shall ye die and your children shall step into your place. Had ye chosen the stone, your life would have been like that of the stone, changeless and immortal.

In summing up the significance of these stories Frazer comments that:

they all imply a belief that death is not a necessary part of the order of nature, but that it originated in a pure mistake of some sort on somebody's part, and that we should all have lived happy and immortal if it had not been for that disastrous blunder or crime.

Perhaps because he is so convinced of immortality, primitive man seems to display little of modern western man's anxiety in the face of death. A corroboration of this attitude could be found in Benin: when the king died and was about to be lowered into the earth, his favourites and servants used to compete with each other for the privilege of being buried alive with his body in order to attend on him in the next world. Each subsequent day there would be an enquiry as to whether any of them had gone to serve their king; at first the answer would be 'no, not yet', but after four or five days all was silent. The heir was informed, and signalled the inauguration of his reign by roasting flesh on the tomb of his predecessor. At this point one might add that it has been customary from time immemorial to bury a man's implements, accessories and some food with his body in the grave; it is from this custom that earliest man's belief in immortality has been inferred.

Mbiti states that in Africa, immediately after death, the soul becomes a 'living-death', and may communicate with his relatives through a trance medium. However he points out that this 'personal immortality' lasts only as long as the memory of the last surviving man who knew the dead person; subsequently he passes to an anonymous collective immortality (or is reincarnated). Thus a time limit is imposed on personal immortality. This post-mortem existence represents an extension of the present life; there is as yet no conception of future rewards and punishments on a moral basis. Nor is the soul considered immaterial, and at war with its physical form. We shall see how the conceptions of eternity, rewards and punishments, and immateriality gradually evolve. However we have ascertained that the primitive man has a notion of a soul distinct from the body, that he identifies the conscious self with his soul, and that the life of the soul continues after the death and decay of the physical body.

2.

DEATH AND SURVIVAL IN TIBET, ANCIENT EGYPT AND GREEK CIVILISATION

We do not know anything about life; what can we know about death?

CONFUCIUS

The lord who is at the oracle at Delphi neither utters nor hides his meaning but shows it by a sign.

HERACLITUS

A great work of art, like a great scientific theory, is a cosmos imposed on chaos.

POPPER

Who knows if death be life, and life be death, and breath be mutton broth, and sleep a sheepskin?

ARISTOPHANES
(PARODYING EURIPIDES)

The Tibetan Book of the Dead

The Tibetan Book of the Dead, or Bardo Thodol (meaning Liberation by Hearing on the After-Death Plane) was first committed to writing in the eighth century AD, although the editor, Dr W.Y. Evans-Wentz, has no doubt that it represents 'the record of belief of innumerable generations in a state of existence after death'. We shall therefore discuss it in this section. It is thought that its teachings were initially handed down orally, then finally compiled and recorded by a number of individuals. This book is used as a funeral ritual, and is read out as a guide to the recently deceased. It contains an elaborate description of the moment of death, the states of mind experienced by the deceased at various stages of post-mortem existence (when he has dream-like encounters with the material contents of his own consciousness), and the path to liberation or rebirth, as the case may be. The reader may wonder how such information could be gleaned, short of shameless imposture. The translator thought that certain learned lamas had described the process of their own deaths to their devotees; or else that the event and intermediary states may have been 'remembered' from a previous existence.

The supposition that previous existences might be remembered raises the question of the book's philosophical and religious background. In the west we tend to think of time as irreversible, and life as a linear process that travels along between two points of time; the individual has one life between a unique birth and death. But, in the east, the conceptions of time and life are more cyclical, the individual undergoing a series of births and deaths. The idea probably originated in contemplation of the cycle of death and rebirth in nature, but was extended to cover human life as well. In Vedantic philosophy it also acquired a metaphysical dimension: the world of phenomena, flux, becoming (Samsara) was regarded as unreal and illusory except in relation to the samsaric (i.e. material) mind which perceived it. The Buddha's philosophy is based on the transience of the phenomenal world and the suffering associated with it. He diagnosed the source of this suffering as craving or desire; so long as the craving remained unabated, the cycle of death and rebirth would continue inexorably and externally. The craving could only be overcome by the attainment of enlightenment, which brings with it the realisation of the unreality of samsaric existence. Yogic control of the thinking processes will, it is hoped, lead the aspirant to emancipation or liberation from the samsaric wheel of rebirth. In the Bardo Thodol it is hoped that the deceased will attain liberation, but, if his karmic slate is not clean, his cravings and thoughts will draw him into another earthly incarnation.

Death is considered 'the reverse of the birth process, birth being the incarnating, death the discarnating of the consciousness-principle; but in both alike there is a passing from one state to another'. The term 'consciousness-principle' is also rendered as 'life-flux' or 'compound of consciousness' (similar in some ways to Jung's term 'ego-complex'). The word 'soul' is avoided, as Buddhist metaphysics, like that of Hume, denies the existence of such an unchanging personal conscious entity. The consciousness-principle is regarded as part of the world of transient samsaric phenomena, therefore illusory, or at best temporary. Immediately after death, the deceased is informed that his own consciousness is 'in reality void ... not formed into anything ... thine own consciousness, shining, void, and inseparable from the Great Body of Radiance, hath no birth, no death, and is the Immutable Light'. The deceased is urged to realise his identity and union with this 'Clear Light'; this will enable him to pass beyond the limitations of separate individual consciousness into formlessness, thus attaining liberation and perfect enlightenment. The aim is full realisation that the essence of individual consciousness is divine, and real only in so far as it identifies itself with the divine; thus the state of Nirvana is at once the transcendence, the extinction, and the fulfilment of individual being.

The three chief symptoms of death are described as (1) bodily sensation of pressure: 'earth sinking into water'; (2) a bodily sensation of clammy coldness as though the body were immersed in water, which gradually merges into that of feverish heat: 'water sinking into fire'; and (3) a feeling as though the body were being blown to atoms: 'fire sinking into air'. Each symptom is accompanied by visible changes in the body, such as loss of control over the facial muscles, loss of hearing, loss of sight, and the breath coming in gasps just before loss of consciousness. During this process the dying person should if at all possible remain conscious in the body so as to enable the thoughts to be focused on love and compassion, and then on the 'Clear Light', when it appears. It is also considered important that the consciousness-principle should pass out of the 'brahmanic aperture', or crown of the head. Ideally there should be no break in consciousness during the separation of the 'Bardo body' from its 'Human-plane envelope'.

The Bardo body, also referred to as the desire- or propensity-body, is:

> formed of matter in an invisible and ethereal-like state ... is an exact duplicate of the human body, from which it is separated in the process of death. Retained in the Bardo body are the consciousness-principle and the psychic nervous system (the counterpart, for the psychic or Bardo body, of the physical nervous system of the human body).

Death, then, is the separation from the physical body of the consciousness-principle, which is identified with the Bardo body. The fact that this Bardo body is an exact duplicate of the physical body implies that the person retains his recognisable individual form. But the consciousness-principle in the Bardo body is said to be endowed with two faculties which we should term supernormal: the intellect (consciousness-principle, or in our terms conscious self) is not now operating in a body of gross matter, 'so that now thou hast the power to go right through any rock-masses, hills, boulders, earth, houses, and Mount Meru itself without being impeded': this is described as the power of unimpeded motion. Secondly there is the power of 'miraculous action':

> Thou art able in a moment to traverse the four continents around Mount Meru. Or thou canst instantaneously arrive in whatever place thou wishest; thou hast the power of reaching there in the time which a man takes to bend or stretch forth his hand.

Thus the refined nature of the Bardo body enables it to pass through matter, which is only solid and impenetrable to the senses, not to modern physics; and the fact that the conscious self is not embedded in matter enables it to travel instantly where it desires. Flights of the imagination become objectively real; the wish comes true.

The first reaction of the consciousness-principle on being released from the body is one of bewilderment. It is still conscious but probably associates death with unconsciousness:

> When the consciousness-principle getteth outside the body, it sayeth to itself 'Am I dead or am I not dead?' It cannot determine. It seeth its relatives and connexions as it had been used to seeing them before. It even heareth the wailings.

A little later

> he can see that the body is being stripped of its garments ... can hear
> all the weeping and wailing of his friends and relatives, and, although
> he can see them and can hear them calling upon him, they cannot
> hear him calling upon them, so he goeth away displeased.

Still later

> Thou seest thy relatives and connexions and speakest to them, but
> receivest no reply. Then, seeing them and thy family weeping, though
> thinkest 'I am dead, what shall I do?', and feelest great misery, just like
> a fish cast out of water.

The fact that the Bardo body is able to pass through matter means
that it can have no sense of material touch and therefore no direct interaction with what we know of as matter. Furthermore the above extracts make it clear that the Bardo body is invisible to the bereaved
relatives. But on the other hand the deceased himself seems to have retained in some recognisable form his senses of sight and hearing; thus
he is in the frustrating position of not being able to communicate in
spite of the fact that he is able to see and hear what is going on. He is
unable to reassure his relatives and friends of his continued conscious
existence; there is perception without interaction. The significance of
these attributes of the Bardo body will become clear when we consider the phenomenon of apparitions and out-of-the-body experiences.
Although the Buddhist is decidedly less frivolous and more perplexed
than his Melanesian counterpart, he, too, asserts that the conscious
self persists after the death of the physical body.

Ancient Egypt

The Investigator of ancient Egyptian beliefs and practices might be
compared with a naturalist who arrives in a strange land with a logically arranged and illustrated catalogue of the specimens that he expects
to encounter there. At first he is delighted to find a few which seem to
correspond to his expectations; but, on consulting a local expert, he is
informed not only that the live specimen does not correspond to the
illustration, but also that specimens, which he took to be identical, are

called by different names. The more experts he consults, the greater the proliferation of opinions, and the more inextricable his confusion. However, there are good reasons for the complexities encountered. In his introduction to *The Egyptian Book of the Dead* Wallis Budge points out that its chapters 'are a mirror in which are reflected most of the beliefs of the various races which went to build up the Egyptians of history' – hence the difficulty of framing a coherent account of the beliefs at any one stage. In addition, one has to reckon with the immense period of time covered by the ancient Egyptian civilisation: the earliest pyramid texts date back to around 2425 BC, while the Book of the Dead covers a period extending roughly to 1090 BC. The intense conservatism of the masses made them cling reverently to precedent and tradition, but, at the same time, they did tolerate new settings of old thoughts; thus they 'kept both the old *and* the new'. Despite these ramifications our task is not impossible, for, as Petrie indicated:

> The idea of immortality was an axiom to the minds of the Egyptians; their notions might be confused, might be rebuffed by pessimism, might develop in various ways, yet from the first burial, with its regular offerings, the belief was always acting until it was expanded in the conversion to Christianity.

As all commentators have hastened to indicate, the Book of the Dead is not a unity but a collection of chapters of varying lengths and dating from different ages. A selection of these would be made for the deceased, and would be copied on the walls of the tomb or inscribed on the sides of the sarcophagi; or they might even be written on scrolls of papyri, which were then laid within the folds of the body cloths. The extracts were meant to benefit the deceased in a variety of ways:

> They were intended to give him the power to have and enjoy life everlasting, to give him everything he required in the Other World, to ensure his victory over his foes, to procure for him the power of ingratiating himself with friendly beings in the other World, and of going whithersoever he pleased and when and how he pleased, to preserve his mummified remains intact and uninjured, and finally to enable his soul to reach the kingdom of Osiris.

The book clearly contained a great deal of information that would be regarded as essential and indispensable. 'The Book of the Dead' is not a literal translation of the Egyptian, which is generally rendered 'The Chapters of Coming Forth by Day'. Naville translates the second part of the title as 'coming out from the day', and adds his own ingenious supporting commentary. Like Oedipus answering the Sphinx, he explains that the life of man is his day, with a morning and evening and that 'to come out from the day' is 'to be delivered from the decreed and determined duration of time pertaining to every earthly life, and to have an existence, with neither beginning nor end, and without limits in time and space'. The analysis has some symbolic neatness, but it does seem to display an Orphic/Platonic streak with its use of the word 'deliver', suggesting that the Egyptians considered life a form of bondage; this is hardly consistent with what is known of their zestful outlook on life.

Contrary to popular supposition, the Egyptians did not at the outset mummify their dead. The earliest excavations show that the body was buried whole in an embryonic position, as if to prepare it for rebirth; implements and food accompanied it, as we have found in other places. Later, there is evidence of disposal of the dead by burning, and also of dismemberment; it is speculated that this was practised partly in order to scatter the spirit of the deceased and thus prevent him from returning to haunt his old village, although there may also be links with the Osiris legend. Coinciding with the transfer of the seat of royal power from Thebes to Memphis, there emerged a completely new and contradictory approach to burial: dismemberment gave way to embalmment and mummification.

The body must now be kept intact at all costs, and an elaborated procedure was developed to this end. Petrie describes it in detail: the body was split from the ribs to the hips and all viscera except the heart were removed; these were stored separately in jars. The interior was coated with resin and perfumes before being sewn up again; then the whole body was soaked in a brine bath for some weeks; this was meant to remove water from the tissues and prevent decomposition. The brain was removed for separate storage, while the mouth and nose were padded with a soft soap of butter and soda. Any muscle bulk lost during the brine soaking was made good by sawdust, mud, or linen, and then the body was wrapped in linen. At a later stage short cuts crept in, and any loss of bulk was compensated for in the bandaging; there were even fraudulent practitioners who saved themselves trouble by wrapping up a skull and a thigh bone and pretending that it was the corpse of a child. One other interesting custom recalls the West African servants who volunteered to be buried with their dead chief. The Egyptian version is somewhat more refined and less gruesome: instead of slaves or servants being buried alive, stone or wooden figures (*ushabtiu*) of men were substituted; up to seven hundred of these might be found in one tomb. They were inscribed with the name of the deceased and were destined as a labour-saving stratagem; the deceased addressed them as follows:

> If I be called or if I be adjudged to do any work whatsoever of the labours which are to be done in the underworld ... let the judgement fall upon thee instead of me always, in the matter of sowing the fields, or filling the water courses with water, and of bringing the sands of this east to the west.

The shabti figure duly acknowledged his obligation, and the affair was settled.

In the *Book of the Dead* Osiris holds the key position of the Lord of the Dead. Frazer has established that in one of his aspects Osiris was a personification of the corn, like Adonis and Attis. This immediately links him to the annual cycle of birth, growth, and death, but there is a separate legend about how he became God of the Dead, with power to resurrect men from the dead as well as corn from the ground. Osiris was of divine origin, and reigned as a king of earth; he reclaimed the Egyptians from savagery and cannibalism, then gave them laws. He introduced the cultivation of the vine and corn, travelling far and wide in order to spread their benefits. At length he returned with divine acclaim to Egypt, but his brother Set plotted against him with seventy-two accomplices. Set stealthily took Osiris' measurements, and constructed a highly decorated coffer the same size as his brother. Then in the middle of a drinking session he jestingly promised the coffer to the man whom it fitted exactly. Osiris was the last to try it, and no sooner had he stretched himself out in it than the conspirators all rushed forward, slammed down the lid, nailed it, soldered it with molten lead and flung it into the Nile. The coffer floated out to sea and finally drifted ashore at Byblus, where an erica tree sprang up suddenly and enclosed the chest in its trunk. Isis, the sister and wife of Osiris, heard of this and travelled to Byblus in order to request the coffer. She recovered it after many tribulations and hid it while she went to visit her son Horus. As luck would have it, Set came upon the coffer while hunting, recognised the body, cut it into fourteen pieces, and scattered them around. Isis now set out to recover the limbs; with the help of the gods she reconstituted the body of the murdered Osiris, swathed it in linen bandages and performed all the other necessary rites. She then fanned the cold body with her wings, whereupon Osiris revived and thenceforth reigned over the land of the dead. It is the hope of the deceased Egyptian to reenact this resuscitation by identifying himself with Osiris: 'I have knit myself together; I have made myself whole and complete; I have renewed my youth; I am Osiris, the lord of eternity.'

In order to understand the rituals, incantations and processes described in the Book of the Dead, it is necessary to have some knowledge of the terms used by the Egyptians to denote the various aspects of man. The contradictions in the text caused one exasperated commentator to exclaim: 'Here, as in everything relating to the region of ideas or thought among the Egyptians, there is an absolute want of system or logic.' We must, nevertheless, make some attempt to come to grips with the problem, and shall follow the enumeration used by Wallis Budge. The perishable physical body, preservable only by mummification, is called the *khat* – there are no arguments about this. Next comes the *ka*, which is generally translated as 'double', and is defined by Wallis Budge as:

> an abstract individuality or personality which possessed the form and attributes of the man to whom it belonged, and, though its normal dwelling place was in the tomb with the body, it could wander about at will; it was independent of the man and could go and dwell in any statue of him.

It was not only independent but sometimes even multiple; a man might have as many as fourteen *kas* (the number of pieces into which Osiris was hacked), each of which might dwell in a separate statute. The *ka* in the tomb required food and drink, or else it would be obliged to wander about in search of any sustenance it could find, and might be defiled. Although the *ka* is described as 'lying prostrate within the body', it can, as indicated above, travel about. Petrie cites the story of the *ka* of Ahura, who was buried at Koptos, being able to visit the tomb of her husband in Memphis; he concludes that the *ka* contains 'the inner mental consciousness and hereditary powers of thought, as apart from the influence of the senses, and continued without the use of bodily actions'. By way of contrast, Breasted, another early authority, contends emphatically that the *ka* 'is not an element of personality ... but a superior genius intended to guide the fortunes of the deceased *in the hereafter*' (his italics); as such he awaited his earthly companion after death. Wallis Budge's view is closer to Petrie's but by no means coincides with it; and his use of the word 'abstract' is perhaps misleading in view of the elementary stage of conceptualisation. So we are obliged to return to the original idea of the double, which is a likeness of the man and normally dwells with the body in the tomb.

The *ba*, or heart-soul, is depicted as a bird and is often translated as 'soul'. It is sometimes conceived of as an animating principle within the body, but elsewhere it is hinted that one only becomes a *ba* after death, when it either dwells with the *ka* in the tomb or with Ra or Osiris in heaven. The *ba* is often referred to in connection with the spiritual soul (*khu*), which was regarded as imperishable and existed in the spiritual body (*sahu*). The *sahu* was originally considered to be a more material body, and may have formed part of an early and literal view of the resurrection, whereby the *sahu, ba, ka, khaibit* (shadow) and *ikhu* (vital force) all come together again after 3000 years, and the man was reanimated. Gradually the *sahu* came to be regarded as more spiritual in its composition, and the idea of physical resurrection lost its prominence. It was believed that this *sahu* was germinated from the physical body, provided that it was not corrupt, and that the priests had performed the appropriate ceremonies.

We are now in a better position to appreciate the Egyptian obsession with the preservation of the body, since this body must retain the capacity to germinate the *sahu*. This concern is most comprehensively expressed in Chapter 154 of the Book of the Dead:

> I would not perish and come to an end but would be even like unto my divine father Khepera, the divine type of him that never saw corruption … grant thou that I may enter into the land of everlastingness … I have never done anything which thou hatest, nay, I have cried out among those who love the *ka*. Let not my body become worms but deliver me as thou didst thyself. I pray thee, let me not fall into rottenness even as thou dost permit every god, and every goddess, and every animal, and every reptile to see corruption when the soul hath gone forth from them after their death. And when the soul departeth (or perisheth) a man seeth corruption and the bones of his body rot and become wholly stinkingness, the members decay piecemeal, the bones crumble into a helpless mass, and the flesh becometh fetid liquid, and he becometh brother unto the decay which cometh upon him, and he turneth into multitudes of worms, and he becometh altogether worms, and an end is made of him.

The pleading, fear and disgust could scarcely be more graphically expressed. Towards the end of the chapter, the positive hope and assurance of germination is expressed with the same note of urgency:

> Homage to thee, O my divine father Osiris, thou hast being with thy members. Thou didst not decay, thou didst not become worms, thou didst not diminish ... become corruption ... putrefy. I am the god Khepera and my members shall have an everlasting existence. I shall not decay, I shall not rot, I shall not putrefy, I shall not turn into worms, I shall not see corruption ... I shall have my being; I shall live; I shall germinate, I shall germinate, I shall germinate; I shall wake up in peace; I shall not putrefy; my intestines shall not perish; I shall not suffer injury; mine eye shall not decay; the form of my visage shall not disappear; mine ear shall not become deaf ... no baleful injury shall come upon me. My body shall be established, and it shall neither fall into ruin nor be destroyed on this earth.

The desperate tone of the passage speaks for itself.

Before the deceased can be admitted to life in the imperishable kingdom of Osiris, he must be judged. The judgement takes place soon after death, and is depicted in Chapter 125 of the Book of the Dead. It consists of two declarations of innocence, or negative confessions, which range from the broadly moral (I have not killed, poisoned, caused weeping, ill-treated animals) to the ritual (I have not captured the birds of the gods, extinguished a fire by force). The first declaration is made to Osiris, the second to forty-two assembled deities, and both are accompanied by repeated assurances of purity. There follows an enumeration of the deceased's good deeds and a ritual test of the names of the parts of the door through which the deceased hopes to pass. In Chapter 30 the deceased appeals to his heart (*ab*, which is more or less synonymous with conscience) not to bear witness against him when he is weighed in the scales of virtue. Brandon has some difficulty in reconciling the ritual of negative confession and self-justification with an impartial weighing of the *ab*, unless Chapter 30 is interpreted as a spell. However he does point out that the Egyptians were the first to conceive the idea of a post-mortem judgment, which determined the quality of the afterlife. Their idea of paradise corresponds closely with an idealised earthly existence. There is a passive conception in Chapter 68: 'I shall live upon cakes made of white grain, and my ale shall be made of red grain of Hapi. In a clean place shall I sit on the ground beneath the foliage of the date palm.' Chapter 110 depicts a rather more active existence: 'May I become a *khu* therein, may I eat therein, may I drink ... plough ... reap ... fight ... make love ... may my words be mighty therein, may I never be in a state of servitude therein, but may I be in authority therein'. Work and leisure as usual, but no subservience.

The Egyptians agree with the Primitives and the Tibetans in asserting a form of continued existence after physical death. Their notions are less psychologically consistent and subtle than those of the Tibetans, but much more complex and symbolically developed than those of the Primitives, whom they resemble only in the earliest stages of their civilisation. Their unique features centre round the overwhelming dread of physical corruption and the corresponding longing for the germination of the indestructible *sahu* in which the *khu* will exist 'for millions and millions of years'.

Ancient Greece

> Death is one of two things. Either it is annihilation, and the dead have no consciousness of anything; or, as we are told, it is really a change: a migration of the soul from this place to another.
>
> PLATO

> It has always been correct to praise Plato, but not to understand him'.
>
> RUSSELL

The Olympian gods made no claim to have created the world, only to have conquered it; nor did they pretend to attend to government, practise trades or promote agriculture: 'They find it easier to live on the revenues and blast with thunderbolts the people who don't pay ... they fight, and feast, and play, and made music; they drink deep and roar with laughter.' It was for such human indulgences that they were later so severely castigated by Plato. But the gods had important advantages over mortal man: they suffered neither from old age nor death and thus enjoyed unremitting strength and eternal beauty, for which they were held in awe. This corresponds to the Greeks praying for health as the first of blessings, expressing the wish 'May I dwell with you for the rest of my days, and may you be kind and stay with me.' We shall see that man's post-mortem existence is not nearly as vigorous as the life envisaged for the gods.

Homer regarded man as a composite being comprising three distinct entities, namely the body (*soma*), the *psyche*, and the *thumos*; this last term is untranslatable, but is always closely associated with the diaphragm/midriff (*phrenes*), which was considered to be the seat of the will and feeling, and perhaps even of the intellect. Brandon even contends that there are reasons for supposing that *phrenes* meant essentially mind or consciousness. At this stage (800-750 BC) the term *psyche* had not come to mean personal soul, but rather represented the impersonal life-principle dwelling in the body but unrelated to the intellect and emotions. A fourth component, the image (*eidolon*), might also be included in man's make-up; it was this which acted and appeared in dreams, where it was considered as a real figure.

Homer regarded the body as essential to the personality; thus 'when death comes the complete person is no longer in existence'. The composite unity has been destroyed, the life-principle escapes, the body itself becomes 'senseless earth' and falls to pieces. All that is left is the *eidolon*, which is helpless without a body; it has neither sensation, feeling, nor powers of thought, all of which are considered expressible only through the organic *phrenes*. However, like the Egyptian *ka*, this image preserves man's external form; it may wander around the scene of its death at first, and even appear in the dreams of the living, but, once the body has been cremated, the *eidolon* is banished for ever to Hades, and can thenceforth exercise no influence on the affairs of men. The rationale of cremation is interesting in this respect: originally the burial of the dead was probably connected with the cult of ancestors, but this practice provoked fear of the departed and possibly resentment at their inferred interference:

> Since the destruction of the body by fire is meant to result in the complete separation of the spirit from the land of the living, it must be assumed that this result is also *intended* by the survivors who employ the means in question; and consequently that the complete banishment of the psyche, once and for all into the other world, is the real purpose and original occasion of the practice of cremation.

Rohde seems to confuse the terms here: *eidolon* should be substituted for *psyche* and spirit, but the point holds good; unlike the primitive assumption, the dead have no further part to play in the affairs of the living, and should make their way to Hades with the minimum delay. No food offerings are presented for the journey, and a man's personal effects are not preserved, but are consumed with the body.

Commentators have exercised much verbal ingenuity in conjuring up visions of the Greek realm of the dead, which has been depicted as 'totally unrelieved gloom', a 'murky underworld', their condition being described as one of 'grim pathos'. With the exception of heroes such as Menelaus, all Greeks were thought to pass into this state of enfeebled vegetation; there was as yet no developed conception of bliss as a reward for a virtuous life, but, on the other hand, those who had in some way offended the gods were already paying the penalty. Their tribulations are portrayed in vivid and harrowing detail in Book XI of the *Odyssey* – the unquenched thirst of Tantalus and the exasperated frustration of Sisyphus:

> I witnessed the torture of Sisyphus, as he tackled his huge rock with both his hands. Leaning against it with his arms, and thrusting with his legs, he would contrive to send it toppling over the crest, its sheer weight turned it back, and the misbegotten rock came bounding down again to the level ground. So once more he had to wrestle with the thing and push it up, while the sweat poured from his limbs and the dust rose high above his head.

After reading Odysseus' account, one cannot but suspect that Camus was being a little sentimental in imagining Sisyphus happy.

After arriving at 'the frontiers of the world' where 'dreadful night has spread her mantle', Odysseus prepares libations on disembarking, then slaughters some sheep and pours the blood into a trench; by means of this blood the dead are able to recover temporarily the use of their faculties and are therefore able to communicate with the living. The prophet Teiresias whom Odysseus has come to visit explains this: 'Any ghost to whom you give access to the blood will hold rational speech with you, while those whom you reject will leave you and retire.' Thus Odysseus has complete control. He talks to his mother but finds that she slips through his eager embrace; this leaves him in despair, but she explains to him:

> You are only witnessing here the law of our mortal nature, when we come to die. We no longer have sinews keeping bones and flesh

together, but once the life-force has departed from our white bones, all is consumed by the fierce heat of the blazing fire, and the soul slips away like a dream and flutters on the air.

Agamemnon is literally a shadow of his former self 'for all the strength and vigour had gone from those once supple limbs'. Achilles is greeted as a mighty prince among the dead but asks Odysseus to spare him the praise of death and continues wistfully, 'I would rather be a serf in the house of some landless man, with little enough for himself to live on, than king of all these dead men who have done with life.' It is hard to imagine a more emphatic assertion of the value of physical life compared with this obviously undesirable and vapid post-mortem state. It recalls the after-death state envisaged in the epic of Gilgamesh, where the inhabitants are bereft of life, having dust as their food and clay as their sustenance.

In his poem *Works and Days*, Hesiod looks back to the Golden and Silver Ages many centuries ago, when men were not ineluctably claimed by Hades and his shadow world. The Homeric underworld, as we have just seen, promises a hopeless life devoid of activity, lacking even the compensation of rest: 'a restless purposeless fluttering to and fro, and existence, indeed, but without any of the content that might have made it worthy of the name of life.' The idea that a vigorous life was only possible in association with the physical body was followed up by some of the early philosophers, and is the cornerstone of the views advanced by the materialistic atomists Leucippus, Democritus, and Epicurus. Meanwhile, we must trace anther distinct current of thought, which had its roots in the so-called Eleusinian mysteries and finds its full expression in Plato.

It is curious that Odysseus reports sighting the wraith of Heracles in the underworld but mentions, at the same time, that 'he himself banquets at ease with the immortal gods and has for consort Hebe of the slim ankles'. Very few heroes were granted the privilege of enjoying the company of the gods, so that the gulf separating man and hero was scarcely less wide than that between man and gods. It is a far cry from the emaciated continuity of the *eidolon* to the desirable immortality of the individual soul; only divinity entailed immortality. It was impossible that the Homeric framework should give rise to the idea of an immortal soul without flatly contradicting its basic postulates; consequently any conception of the soul as divine and immortal must have had a quite different source.

One of the origins of this conception was the festival of the corn goddesses, Demeter and Persephone, held annually in Eleusis in September from around 700 BC onwards. Legend had it that Persephone, Demeter's daughter, was carried off to the underworld of Pluto. In her wrath, Demeter kept the seed-corn underground and vowed that it would never sprout again until she recovered her daughter. Mankind's starving to death was averted by a decree of Zeus, who commanded Pluto to relinquish his bride; it was ruled that she should spend half of the year in the upper world and half with her husband. Needless to say, the corn sprouted once more, and an annual rhythm of withdrawal and return was established. The society of the Eleusinian mystery festival was initially very exclusive, but gradually expanded to embrace anyone who claimed to be ritually pure (i.e. had not committed murder) on condition that he had attended a ceremony of ritual purification:

> with the calm assurance common to all close and confined religious associations, the Eleusinian society divided mankind into two classes: the 'Pure', that is those who had been initiated at Eleusis, and the innumerable multitude of the uninitiated'.

Although details of the festival itself are sparse, it is known that its popularity was largely due to the benefits, which were said to accrue to the initiate. He could hope for earthly prosperity and then a superior fate in the afterlife into the bargain: an irresistible package, even if the exact nature of this superior fate was nowhere specified.

Dionysus, or Bacchus, is best known as a personification of the vine 'and of the exhilaration produced by the juice of the grape'. And as well as being the god of trees in general and fruit trees in particular, he was a god of the corn; but these functions are a good deal less important than those associated with the vine. The legendary Dionysus was the son of Zeus and Persephone. He was said to have occupied the throne of his father for a short period but was then attacked by the dastardly Titans, whose assaults he initially evaded by changing himself into the various shapes of a lion, a horse, a serpent, and finally a bull. It was in this last form that he was overtaken by his enemies and met the Osirian doom of dismemberment; subsequently he was purported to have risen from the dead, although the Titans devoured his bodily remains. In his fury Zeus exterminated the Titans with a lightning flash. It was from their ashes that there sprang up the hybrid race of mankind, whose soul was divinely linked to Dionysus but whose body was composed of the unruly Titanic element. The significance of this legend lies in its account of the divine origin and nature of the soul, a conception that was to exercise such an influence on later Greek thought.

Dionysus' early followers in Thrace re-enacted his death and resurrection in a gruesome ceremony, where they tore a live bull to pieces with their teeth, and then roamed about the woods shouting frantically. Later rituals were hardly less barbaric and frenzied; all were calculated to induce a state of religious madness or mania. They took place at night to the accompaniment of loud music and cymbals, thus exciting the chorus of worshippers who soon joined in with shouts of their own. Dancing was so violent that no breath was left for singing, and eventually the worshippers induced through their excesses a state of such exaltation and rapture that it seemed to them that the ordinary limits of life had been transcended, that they were 'possessed', their soul having temporarily left the body. The soul was in a condition of *enthousiasmos*, (inside the god) and *ekstasis* (outside the body); liberated from the confines of the body it enjoyed communion with the god.

Rohde observes that wherever a cult aiming at the inducement of ecstatic experience has taken root, 'there we find, in close alliance with it, whether as cause or effect or both, a peculiarly vital belief in the life and power of the soul of man after its separation from the body'. In the Thracian case this correlation is due to the nature rather than the object of the cult, in other words to the actual experience. The idea of a second distinct self separable from the body had already been advanced to account for certain dreams and fainting fits; it was reinforced by the intoxication and delirium of the dances and ceremonial music leading to the experience of *ekstasis*, a foretaste of the bliss which the initiate might one day hope to enjoy for ever, and compared with which everyday existence must have seemed somewhat pallid and dreary. The next stage was that the distinction drawn between body and soul should harden into an actual opposition between the two. We have seen that such opposition would have been quite alien to Homer; it could only arise in association with the idea of the soul as a divine element residing in a perishable body. The emergence of this idea has important metaphysical and ethical consequences: the soul and body are set at odds, to the detriment of the body, and the purpose of human existence comes to be viewed in puritanical terms. Thus there germinated the seeds of mysticism which, even if they were choked by the luxuriant undergrowth of Thrace, were able to come to fruition elsewhere.

Although it was frowned upon by the orthodox, the cult of Dionysus soon overran both mainland and island Greece. Some of its success may have been due to 'a love of the primitive ... a hankering after a more instinctive and passionate way of life than that sanctioned by current morals'; and, in spite of the milder vegetation ceremonies, it is certain that the 'enthusiastic' cult pursued its tumultuous nocturnal revelries. In the event, the ecstatic element was so strong that the Apolline religion had to incorporate this novel feature; the tradition of inspired prophecy was one of the offshoots of the union. Another was the multiplication of purification ceremonies which, in conjunction with the conviction of the superior state of the soul in its free and separate state outside the cumbersome material body, led to the injunction that the soul should be purified in the lifetime of the body by 'the denial and inhibition of the body and its impulses'. This was the first step on the *via negativa*, a morality which later developed into Orphic and Pythagorean practices of abstinence and asceticism.

The relationship of the so-called Orphics to the Pythagoreans is obscure, to say the least. Dodds found himself saying of early Orphism that the more he read, the less he seemed to know, and concluded that there was no sure basis for distinguishing an 'Orphic' from a 'Pythagorean' psychology. At any rate the appearance of 'Orphism' in Greece during the sixth century BC did mark a further refinement of the conception of the divinity of the soul. Orpheus himself was reputed to have been dismembered during a frenzied bacchanal, and his followers continued to worship Dionysus, forming themselves into private cult-societies. It is fairly evident that they held certain doctrines, namely that the soul was of divine origin, but had to suffer imprisonment in the body on account of its sin; and that on leaving the body it entered into an intermediate state of rewards and punishments, the next form of life assumed depending on the degree of purity attained. The Orphics, therefore, went to considerable lengths to become 'pure' through a series of ceremonies and by abstaining from animal flesh and certain other foods such as eggs and beans. The ultimate goal was deliverance from the cycle of rebirths and a state, not of Nirvana, but of 'blissful consciousness in which the soul, unencumbered by the body, leads the life of a God in company with Gods'.

Radhakrishnan draws attention to the striking parallels between the philosophy of the Upanishads and that of the Orphics: 'The beliefs held in common are those of rebirth, the immortality and godlike character of the soul, the bondage of the soul in the body, and the possibility of release by purification.' In addition, he notes the common images of the Wheel of Necessity and the Cosmic Egg (of creation), commenting on the improbability of such a concordance arising from mere coincidence. Although he admits that it is historically impossible to corroborate any Indian influence, he does point out that the mystical tradition 'is definitely un-Greek in character', ant that the similarities between the two views are so close that they are certainly an expression of the same mystical and ascetic view of life. In contrast with *hubris*, the pride which violates the law of moderation, and which probably springs from intellectual blindness or infatuation, the Orphic notion lays stress on sins committed before birth; we must expiate these individually, and there can be no attempt to shift the responsibility elsewhere. This personal conception of sin, together with salvation through ascetic purity and initiation by sacrament, was to have a great influence on the development of Christianity. The nature and importance of the Orphics is summed up by Harrison:

> The great step that Orpheus took was that, while he kept the old Bacchic faith that man might become a god, he altered the conception of what a god was, and he sought to obtain that godhead by wholly different means. The grace he sought *was not physical intoxication but spiritual ecstasy, the means he adopted not drunkenness but abstinence and rites of purification* [my italics].

'Of the opinions of Pythagoras we know even less than of his life' and not a great deal is known about his life. He flourished in the latter part of the sixth century BC, and was described by Russell as a combination of Einstein and Mary Baker Eddy, of mathematical genius on the one hand and what Russell would regard as quackery on the other; this combination of qualities reflected the variety of roles that he played. Like the Orphics he taught that the intrinsic nature of the soul was divine, and that it had been cast down into a body as a punishment. Here it was condemned on the circle of necessity to seek new bodies after a period of purgation between lives; these bodies might be either animal or human; it is related that Pythagoras recognised an old friend of his in the body of a dog. One of the logical consequences of this doctrine of transmigration or *metempsychosis* was a feeling of kinship with animals, and even with certain plants in which the soul might reside. This led to the practice of abstinence from animal flesh and from the oft-quoted and derided beans. The object of such frugality was to obtain deliverance or salvation from the circle of necessity through purity. It also seems that the early followers of Pythagoras thought that knowledge could contribute towards salvation, although the mind boggles at the obscurity of their principle of the Limit and Unlimited. Pythagorean science, based as it was on mathematical and musical theory, later evolved a conception of the soul as 'a harmony of contrary elements united together in the body'. This formulation is more akin to the later materialist explanations of the soul which arose from speculations about the ultimate constitution of the world: if the soul is only a binding together of the elements of the body, it can hardly be expected to survive its disintegration.

It remains to consider, briefly, the figure of Empedocles (c.490-430 BC), whose life has attracted almost as much legendry accretion as that of Pythagoras. Scholars have been absolutely perplexed at the discrepancies between his cosmology and his religious ideas, expressed respectively in writings entitled *On Nature* and *Purifications*. Various theories have been advanced to account for the logical inconsistencies of the two works, including the suggestions that one work dates from his youth and the other from maturity, that he underwent a religious conversion, and that one work was for the thinkers while the other was for popular consumption. Another hypothesis, which the present writer finds more plausible, is put forward by Dodds:

> Empedocles represents not a new but a very old type of personality, the shaman who combines the still undifferentiated functions of magician and naturalist, poet and philosopher, preacher, healer, and public counsellor. After him these functions fell apart; philosophers henceforth were to be neither poets nor magicians; indeed, such a man was already an anachronism in the fifth century.

Modern interpreters tend to assume that all philosophers must have aimed at logical consistency, but it is clear that, for Empedocles, philosophy was only one branch of his activities. We shall deal here only with his religious ideas, reserving consideration of his cosmology for a later section. He sometimes went round proclaiming that he was a god, and was reputed to have been snatched bodily into the heavens. Another more cynical version of the tale relates that 'he leaped into the crater of Etna, that, the manner of his death being unknown, he might still continue to pass for a god – an expectation disappointed by an eruption which cast out one of his brazen sandals'. Elsewhere

Empedocles describes himself as condemned on account of sin 'to wander thrice ten thousand seasons from the abodes of the blessed, being born throughout the time in all manner of mortal forms, changing one toilsome path of life for another' and claims 'for I have been ere now a boy and a girl, a bush and a bird and a glittering fish in the sea'. These fragments are expressions of the Orphic/Pythagorean outlook, some of whose taboos also feature in the following pious injunctions: 'Fast from wickedness ... abstain wholly from laurel leaves ... wretches, utter wretches, keep your hands from beans ...'

Whitehead's contention that the whole of Western philosophy is a series of footnotes to Plato certainly holds good for the question of the nature and immortality of the soul and issues arising from his considerations. One of these is the distinction between mind and matter, which, Russell claims, has the religious origin of that between soul and body. We have already traced the origin of the idea of the soul as divine in the legend of Dionysus, and seen how the Orphics and Pythagoreans gradually refined this conception. In Plato we find a much fuller exposition of the essential features indicated by Radhakrishnan, but with a further development of morality beyond mere abstinence and ritual purity, and a much higher degree of abstraction than hitherto. Discussion of the *psyche* is frequent in dialogues written at all stages of Plato's life (*c.*427-347 BC). Pringle-Pattison observes that 'the belief in the divinity of the soul of man and its consequent immortality always appears in Plato as a primary religious conviction, independent of the particular and often unconvincing arguments by which he supports it.' No doubt Plato thought that this belief furnished the most coherent explanation of the phenomenon of life; at no time does he seem to have questioned the existence of the soul or the cardinal importance of its divinity.

It is clear that Plato attributed two distinct meanings to the word *psyche*: sometimes he speaks of it as the Homeric life-principle, but more often he takes it to represent the invisible and essential person in contrast with his visible body. In the *Phaedrus* he states:

> All soul is immortal; for that which is ever in motion is immortal ... this self-mover is the source and first principle of motion of all other things that are moved ... a first principle cannot come into being ... if it did, it would cease to be a first principle ... since it does not come into being it must be imperishable.

A similar passage occurs in the *Laws* when he comments on people's ignorance of the origin of the soul which, he says, 'is one of the first creations, born long before all physical things, and is the chief cause of all their alterations and transformations'. Plato begins with an axiom, in this case that all self-movers are immortal, from which he deduces that the soul, being a self-mover, is also immortal; then he adds that self-movers are first principles which have always existed by definition and that, having no origin, they must be imperishable, thus equating the two words imperishable and immortal. The argument is designed so that each part props up the other, but the whole edifice rests on an unprovable foundation; however, the issue here is not logic so much as establishing what Plato thought about the soul. In this context movement and life are associated in the broadest sense, even if this movement is confined to upward growth in plants.

In the *Timaeus* Plato distinguishes three parts of the soul, namely the reason, the motions, and the appetite. Only appetite is attributed to plants, then appetite and emotion to animals, while man alone possesses a rational soul in addition to the other two and it is this that was considered to be immortal and divine; the rational soul is located in the head, while the emotions are situated in the breast and the appetite in the belly. The neck is referred to as an isthmus or boundary, which serves to keep the head and breast apart, while the belly is strategically placed as far as possible from 'the seat of deliberation', so that it causes the least possible disturbance. Plato credits the creators of the human race with greater foresight than omnipotence when he remarks that 'they knew how ungovernable our appetite for drink and food would be, and how we should out of sheer greed consume more than a moderate or necessary amount'. Therefore they ensured that the belly could hold superfluous food and drink, and took the precaution of winding the bowels round in coils in order to prevent food going through the system too rapidly; without this measure, concludes Plato, the species would have been rendered 'incapable through gluttony of philosophy and culture, and unwilling to listen to the divinest element in us'.

Plato never had any illusions about the difficulty of reason's maintaining its supremacy over the other parts of the soul, as was required by aspiring philosopher-rulers. In the *Phaedrus* he compares the rational soul with the charioteer of two horses and describes the charioteer's task as 'difficult and troublesome'. In the *Timaeus* his account of the original uniting of the soul with the body elucidates the confusion with which the rational/divine part of the soul has to deal: to account for the composition and eventual decay of the body, Plato explains that the elements of Earth, Air, Fire, and Water are loans which must be repaid and whose bonding by invisible rivets is not dissoluble:

> And into this body, subject to growth and decay, they fastened the orbits of the immortal soul. Plunged into this strong stream, the orbits were unable to control it, nor were they controlled by it, and owing to the consequent violent conflict the motions of the whole creature were irregular, fortuitous and irrational.

We shall return to the question of control in dealing with transmigration. The soul originally dwelt in the rarefied atmosphere of true Being, accessible only to reason 'the soul's pilot'; this realm is the home and source of the 'Forms', which Plato considered to be real, in contrast to the phenomena of our world which are regarded as mere appearances – transient forms of becoming. In some obscure fashion the soul loses its vision of the whole of Being and, as a result of this loss together with the burden of forgetfulness and some unspecified wrongdoing, forfeits its wings and falls to earth to be incarnated. Under normal circumstances the soul is unable to regrow its wings and return home to the region of true Being in less than 10,000 years; however, the soul 'who had seen most of Being', that is to say the soul which retains the closest affinity with its divine origin, will become a philosopher – a seeker after wisdom and beauty. If, after each thousand-year interval between lives, the soul exceptionally chooses the life of a philosopher twice more, then it may return to true Being after not much more than 3,000 years. The other first incarnations of the soul are all as men, and vary in quality according to the vision of – and consequent affinity with – Being; thus, a king who abides by the law comes next in line after the philosopher, a man of business third and so on down to the tyrant in ninth place. After the first incarnation a judgment takes place and, according to how well the life has been lived, the soul passes the period between lives being chastised or 'living in a manner as is merited by their past life in the flesh'. The karmic logic apparent in this scheme is carried over the notion of the choice of the next earth life. In the *Timaeus* the man who failed to live well would be changed into a woman at second birth, and a persistent offender would become 'an animal suitable to his particular kind of wrongdoing'. The patriarchal element is not apparent in the more subtle treatment of the same theme in the myth of Er, where the sight of souls choosing lives moved Er to 'pity, laughter and wonder'. The soul is responsible for its own choice of life, but, at the same time, Er observes that 'for the most part they followed the habits of their former life'. The determinism is shifted from the outside to the inside. Although Plato states that it is possible for the soul of an animal which was once in a man to return to man again, it is not at all clear how this might happen; presumably the soul incarnated in a beast automatically loses its rational part, by which the appetites were subdued; but without this rational part there can be no control of the appetites, and hence no progress back to rationality and the human form.

During incarnation the soul is clearly associated with the body in some definite way. In the early dialogue Plato contends that man is the user of the body and that the user is the soul; he thus identifies the soul as the true man. This is strikingly echoed in a very late dialogue, the *Laws*: 'while I am alive I have nothing to thank for my individuality except my soul, whereas my body is just the likeness of myself which I carry round with me.' The Athenian continues: 'This means we are quite right when we say a corpse "looks like" the deceased. Our real self – our immortal soul as it is called – departs, as the ancestral law declares, to the gods to give an account of itself.' Thus the soul is the essential man and the body its form and medium of expression. Death is defined in the *Laws* as the departure of the soul, in the *Phaedo* as the 'release of the soul from the body', and in the *Gorgias* as the divorce of two entities, soul and body. On the grounds that pure knowledge is not possible in association with the body and that 'the soul can best reflect when it is free from all distractions such as hearing or sight or pain or pleasure of any kind – that is when it ignores the body' Plato recommends that the philosopher should free his soul from ties of the body; thus he may temporarily achieve what is only really possible for the soul in its discarnate state. The means employed is purification so that 'the true philosopher's occupation consists precisely in the freeing and separation of the soul from the body'. In active terms this means the pursuit of wisdom and beauty, of the knowledge of the Good, and avoidance of physical self-indulgence and petty selfishness. The model philosopher-ruler of the *Republic* 'must combine in his nature a good memory, readiness to learn, breadth of vision and grace, and be a friend of truth, justice, courage and self-control'. In other words the rational soul of the philosopher-ruler will hold sway over the emotions and appetites.

In the *Phaedo* Plato puts two further arguments for the immortality of the soul: on the assumption of a fixed number of souls, he claims that the dead come from the living and the living from the dead; and then that our knowledge of innate ideas and mathematics can only be derived from a pre-natal recollection. The argument (mentioned in connection with Pythagorean science) that the soul is an attunement or adjustment of tension in the body is dismissed. The first two arguments are not concerned with the nature and destiny of the soul, and so they need not detain us here.

The distance is considerable from the original frenzied bacchanals to the sober asceticism of the platonic philosopher with his vision of 'Being' and the 'form of the Good'. The conception of the soul has become rational and immaterial, the magical efficacy of initiations where 'remissions and absolution of sins may be had by sacrifices and pleasant trivialities' is summarily disposed of, and the individual's responsibility for his own spiritual progress becomes paramount. Socrates asserts that nothing can harm a good man, either in life or after death, and the moral argument for enlightened self-interest is summarised as follows:

> If the soul is immortal, it demands our care not only for that part of time that we call life, but for all time; and indeed it would seem now that it will be extremely dangerous to neglect it. If death were a release from everything, it would be a boon for the wicked because by dying they would be released not only from the body but also from their own wickedness together with the soul; but as it is, since the soul is clearly immortal, it can have no escape or security from evil except by becoming as good and wise as it can.

For all its moral vehemence and lasting influence, the Platonic conception of the soul and immortality is a religious rather than a scientific conviction, as we indicated at the outset of the inquiry. It remains to be seen to what extent it is consistent with the available empirical material. Few would, however, go as far as Bergson when he states that Plato's affirmation of the existence of the soul is sterile owing to its arbitrary nature, and that our knowledge of the soul has not been advanced by thinking along Plato's lines despite over 2,000 years of reflection; he maintains that the problem must be posed and answered in terms of experience. This is what the Atomists attempted to do, and it is to their formulations that we now turn.

The earliest Greek philosophers, known as the Milesian School, speculated about the nature of the fundamental substance of the world. Perhaps because he had been to Egypt where the Nile was crucial to the economy, Thales (flourished c.585 BC) thought that it was water. The next important figure, Anaximander (flourished c.560 BC), considered that everything was derived from the Infinite. He was followed by Anaximenes (c.500 BC) who asserted that the fundamental substance was air and that 'just as our soul, being air, holds us together, so do breath and air encompass the whole world'. Substances are differentiated by degrees of condensation and rarefaction, fire being the most rarefied- and stone the most condensed form. Anaximenes' reason for stressing the importance of air is not hard to imagine: in the human body, life and breath are closely correlated; when the breath leaves, the body disintegrates. Likewise, the earth is surrounded by air or wind so that it was assumed that, without the air, the earth too would disintegrate. Xenaphanes (flourished c.530 BC) is more famous for his caricature of anthropomorphic ideas of gods than for his comments on substance, but he does assert that 'all things are earth and water that come into being and grow'. However, he may have regarded this as mere conjecture:

> The certain truth there is no man that knows, nor ever shall be, about the gods and all things whereof I speak. Yea, even if a man should chance to say something right, still he himself knows it not – there is nowhere anything but guessing.

According to the cosmology of Heraclitus (flourished c.500 BC), the fundamental substance was fire, and the world was subject to a process of continual change and transformation. Thus he writes that 'Fire lives the death of earth, and air lives the death of fire; water lives the death of air, earth that of water.' Nor is the soul, a mixture of these elements, exempt from the flux; this leads some authorities to conclude that there is no room here for a permanent identity of the soul. Heraclitus states that a dry soul is the wisest and the best, that it is pleasure for souls to become moist, and that it is death to souls to become water. But then there are other fragments, which imply the transmigration of souls – another process of becoming. Fragment 78 states that 'the quick and the dead, the waking and the sleeping, the young and the old, are the same; the former are changed and become latter, and the latter in turn are changed into the former'; and Fragment 67 asserts that 'mortals are immortals and immortals, the one living the other's death and dying the other's life.' He also implies that a man may reappear as his own grandchild. However these metaphysical statements are less influential than his doctrine of universal flux, which was further developed by Empedocles.

Parmenides, who flourished in the second half of the fifth century BC, had a considerable influence on Plato with his contention that there is only one Being. He argued that if 'Being' came into being, then it cannot be the primordial substance; it cannot have an origin, it is indivisible and homogeneous. It is not 'scattered abroad through the universe nor does it come together'; it is finite, motionless and material. From this position it follows that Heraclitus' doctrine of flux is the result of deception by the senses: multiplicity, motion, space and time are illusory appearances. Parmenides considered that mind was of a similar nature to the body 'for that which thinks is the same, namely, the substance of the limbs'; this was something of a revolutionary departure, as was the fact that the primary substance was now considered to be a kind of 'thing in itself', uncreated and underlying all phenomenal appearances. The notion of the primary substance as a thing in itself reappears in the elements of Empedocles and the atoms of Leucippus and Democritus. For this reason, despite Plato's interpretation, Parmenides can be regarded as the father of materialism rather than of idealism.

We have already referred to the discrepancies between Empedocles' religious ideas and his cosmology. His starting point was the same as Parmenides in that he held that there existed an indestructible substratum of being 'for it cannot be that aught can arise from what in no way is, and it is impossible and unheard of that what is should perish. For it will always be, wherever one may keep putting it'. Unlike Parmenides, he does not consider change to be illusory, but accounts for it by 'mingling and separation of what has been mingled'. The elements may be mingled in the forms of men, animals, plants or birds; and death occurs when the elements are separated. Empedocles regarded death as the final victory of the principle of strife over that of love; love tries to unite the elements, while strife is constantly attempting to separate them. This cosmology treats matter, rather than the migrating soul, as the underlying constant; the elements are reabsorbed into new combinations, rather than the soul taking on a new form, as was hinted in the more Orphic sections of Empedocles' work.

Anaxagoras (c.500-432 BC) accepts the conclusions of Parmenides' and Empedocles' cosmology, and attempts to formulate his own solution to the problem of apparent change and underling substance. He claims that there is a portion of each element in everything, and that it is merely the preponderance of some elements over others, which confers upon a thing its characteristic appearance. However, things which live and move also contain Mind (*nous*), which is one, self-contained and present in varying degrees in all manifestations of life. But it is not actually mixed with the elements, for this would hinder the power which it is said to exercise over the bodily form: 'it is the thinnest of all things and the purest, and it has knowledge about everything and the greatest strength; and Nous has power over all things, both greater and smaller, that have life.' Anaxagoras reproves the Hellenes for their use of the expressions *coming into being* and *passing away*, 'for nothing comes into being or passes away, but mingling and separation takes place of things that are. So they would be right to call coming into being mingling, and passing away separation.' As regards death, he has been quoted as stating explicitly that death extinguishes the soul as well as remarking that sleep, and the time before we were born, provides us with two object lessons on death. In addition, it has been argued that since all animated being is derived from the single Mind, there can be no *independent* survival of souls after the dissolution of the body; this Mind is undifferentiated in its essence.

In the systems of Parmenides, Empedocles, and Anaxagoras the conception of one underlying primary substance tends to eradicate the notion of a distinctive rational human soul; human beings are but one manifestation and form among others in contrast with the Orphic/Pythagorean doctrine of the divine origin and immortality of the rational element in the human soul. In addition, the cycle of becoming is treated solely in terms of material transformations; the idea is not extended to cover rebirth of human beings in new bodily forms, but confined to recycling of the bodily elements. The founders of Atomism, Leucippus and Democritus, who in turn influenced Epicurus and through him Lucretius, further evolved these views on substance, movement and transformation.

Leucippus (flourished *c.*440 BC) held that the soul was the cause of life and sensation, and that it was evenly distributed in the body. He associated the atomic composition of the soul with that of fire. Both were thought to have similar 'rhythms' and to consist of spherical atoms; they could easily penetrate through everything and move objects in the same way as they moved themselves. As for the relation of life to death, Leucippus recognised the crucial importance of breathing.

He thought that the body was constantly exposed to 'blows' from the outside; These tended to squeeze out the soul-atoms, but respiration provided a fresh supply, thus maintaining the balance within the body. But eventually a sudden blow or gradual decay would upset the balance, respiration would fail, and life would pass from the body. Respiration was defined as the limit (*oros*) of life, so that no existence was conceivable after cessation of breathing.

Democritus (born *c.*460 BC) elaborated Leucippus' account, borrowing the notion that the soul consists of spherical atoms akin to those of fire: 'The soul consists of fine, smooth, round atoms like those of fire. These atoms are the most mobile and by their motion, which permeates the whole body, the phenomena of life are produced.' The following fragments echo some of the views of the earlier philosophers: 'Out of nothing arises nothing ... nothing that is can be destroyed. All change is only combination and separation of atoms. Nothing happens by chance, but everything through cause and necessity. Nothing exists but atoms and empty space.' The last two sentences are particularly interesting: chance is ditched in favour of determinism, which in turn is associated with mechanism, a connection which will be developed in treating Descartes and his followers. And the last statement posits only two categories within which the soul must be classified. If it were but empty space it could scarcely be said to exist – therefore it must consist of atoms. Democritus differentiates himself from Plato and Aristotle by saying that the soul and the mind are of the same atomic substance; he does not distinguish the rational from the other parts of man. His analysis of respiration and life is more carefully thought out than that of Leucippus: he equates inspiration (breathing in) with life, and expiration with death, maintaining that breathing prevents the soul from being squeezed out of the body. And he describes the process of death as follows: 'When the pressure of surrounding matter prevails and can no longer be checked by what comes in from without, as the creature cannot breathe, death results. For death is the departure of atoms of this shape from the body owing to the pressure of their surroundings.' The soul, or animating principle, perishes with the body. This is the view advanced by Simmias in the *Phaedo* when he maintains that the soul is an 'attunement' or 'adjustment' of the body and that 'being a temperament of physical constituents is the first thing to be destroyed by what we call death'.

Aristotle (c.384-322 BC) takes the deliberation of his predecessors into account, starting his book *De Anima* with a warning of the complexity of his task: 'Everywhere and in every way it is one of the most difficult things to get hold of anything reliable about it.' He defines the soul as 'the first principle of animal life', and contends that 'it is neither apart from the body nor the same as the body ... it is in a body ... a body of a definite kind.' He describes the soul as the 'form' of the body, by which he means that it confers unity on the body and holds it together – hence his reference to a body of a definite kind. Aristotle's formulation is not entirely unambiguous, as he says that the soul is not separable from the body, but immediately adds 'or certain parts of it' by way of qualification. The drift of his argument, however, is that the inseparability of the soul from the body indicates that the soul perishes with the death of the body.

In addition, Aristotle ridicules the Pythagorean/Platonic notion of the transmigration of souls, although he does distinguish between mind and soul. He defines mind as 'that whereby the soul thinks and understands', and follows Anaxagoras by contending that it is unthinkable that mind should be thought of as mixed with the physical object and hence with sensation. Its concerns are timeless: the understanding of the truths of mathematics and philosophy, rising to contemplation, which is considered unattainable by man. The *Nicomachean Ethics* sets out a tripartite division of the soul, reminiscent of Plato's *Timaeus*: the soul has a rational and an irrational element; the irrational is sub-divided into the vegetative and the appetitive, the former existing in all forms of life, and the latter only in animals. This rational part should not be interpreted as something personal but as a divine element in which we can all partake. To the extent that we partake of it we become similar and united, 'thus the immortality of mind or reason is not a personal immortality of separate men, but a share in God's immortality'. Only in so far as a man is rational can he participate in the divine and reach this mind of mental Nirvana, where the essence of the human being is fulfilled but the individual ceases to exist in his own right.

Epicurus (342-270 BC) continues the atomist tradition of the nature of the soul, which he defines as 'a body of fine particles ... most resembling breath with an admixture of heat'. The interdependence of soul and body is stressed by using the analogy of the vase which holds water; the body is thought to hold the soul together in a similar way: 'Neither can be itself without the other: the body without the soul could not live or grow or move: the soul without the protection of the body could not hold together or make the movements requisite for sensation.' The difference between a dead body and a live one is that the dead body has lost breath and heat, the two postulated components of the soul, which vanishes:

> If the whole structure is dissolved the soul is dispersed and no longer has the same powers nor performs its movements, so that it does not possess sensation either. For it is impossible to imagine it with sensation if it is not in this organism and cannot effect these movements.

This is the clearest and most unequivocal statement so far of the inseparability of the soul from the body, and of their consequent simultaneous disintegration.

Lucretius (99-55 BC) wrote a long eulogy of Epicurus, designed to convert the reader to the Epicurean viewpoint. In contrast to Plato he asserted that 'living things are begotten from senseless things', giving as an example the erroneous illustration that 'living works spring from dung': in other words that mind or soul is derived from matter, which antedates it. Book 3 of *On the Nature of Things* contains his views on the nature of the soul and death; he tries to demonstrate that death is not to be feared because it is the end of life and sensation. He asserts that unity of mind and soul, which he locates not in the head, but in the breast, because 'here throb fear and apprehension ... and soothing joys'. The rest of the soul 'disseminated through the whole body obeys and moves at the inclination of the mind', which retains the capacity to originate free action; thus Lucretius shies away from the determinism implied in his view that mind and soul are of a bodily nature because they are evidently so closely allied to the body; he points out that the mind suffers and feels in unison with the body (a truism in the light of any theory). He follows his predecessors in asserting that the mind is composed of extremely fine and minute bodies, which are capable of moving at great speed, reinforcing his argument by remarking that their smallness is proved by the fact that no body weight is lost at death.

He now advances a number of arguments to illustrate the closeness of the relation between mind/soul and body, all of which point to the conclusion that the soul, like the body, disintegrates at death: first, that the mind matures and ages with the growth and decay of the body; second, that wine and disease of the body can affect the mind, and that medicine heals mind as well as body – likewise the mind is disturbed when the body is stunned by an external blow; third, that because the eye and nose cannot feel and exist apart, nor can the mind (this argument assumes its own premise); fourth, if the mind were immortal it would not complain so much of dissolution at the time of bodily death; and fifth, if the soul is immortal, why does it have no memories of its previous existence? He adds that if there is transmigration, creatures should have 'interchangeable dispositions' owing to the different souls (Plato would answer that the choice of the form of animal conformed to the qualities of the soul, hence little variation would be expected). From all this he concludes that death 'concerns us not a jot, since the nature of the mind is proved to be mortal'. With the loss of air and heat from the body there can be no sensation; there can therefore be 'no other self to remain in life and lament to self that his own self has met death'. He pours scorn on those who lament the transience of life, and comments that 'no one feels the want of himself and life when mind and body together are sunk in sleep' so that death should be of no concern: 'No one wakes up, upon whom the chill sensation of life has once come.'

The atomist conclusion follows logically from the premise, indicated above, that anything which exists and is not empty space must be material; they cannot conceive of the soul as empty space since it produces movement – it must therefore be material. At death heat and air are expelled from the body, but there is no diminution of weight, therefore they assert that the soul must comprise very fine particles which they were unable to measure. If the soul is composed of very fine material it must be dispersed like the rest of the body's elements at death 'like smoke'. The facts of growth and decay, and the effects of wine and disease further indicate the bodily nature of the mind/soul, so that they conclude that no part of the body can feel and function apart from the whole. Therefore mind/soul dissolves with bodily death. We shall encounter many variations on this basic theme as philosophers and neurologists striving after a unified conception of man have refined it. All the debate centres on the issue of whether, as they contend, mind/soul is a function of the body, or whether the body is an instrument used by the mind/soul (conscious self), which is able to function separately.

Before turning to Christian formulations, we shall review the conceptions of three more philosophers – Cicero, the stoic emperor Marcus Aurelius, and Plotinus. The first borrows many elements from Plato, the second sees human life as a small episode in a vast universe, and the third fuses platonic thought with his own mystical experience.

Cicero (106-43 BC) respected the teaching of Pythagoras and Plato to such an extent that he almost felt justified in agreeing with their views merely on the grounds of their authority without examining the sources of their beliefs. He held the soul to be of divine origin, forced down into exile in the body; he also used the existence of prophetic dreams in sleep as evidence of the soul's divine powers. Other arguments for immortality include Plato's argument from recollection, the fact that the soul can only be conceived of as self-moving, and that its nature is not composite but indivisible and therefore imperishable. His conclusion recalls the hymn to man's achievements in Sophocles' *Antigone*: 'There is nothing beyond his power. His subtlety meets all chance, all danger conquereth. For every ill he hath found its remedy, save only death. Wonders are many on earth, and the greatest of these is man ...' Cicero does not speak of mastery, but introduces an argument frequently used by Christians as a corollary to divine justice: that a benevolent God could not have created man only to extinguish him at death.

> I have convinced myself and I hold – in view of the rapid movement of the soul, its vivid memory of the past, and its prophetic knowledge of the future, its many accomplishments, its vast range of knowledge, its numerous discoveries – that a nature embracing such varied gifts cannot be mortal.

This is an argument that we shall encounter in a slightly different form up to the present day; it is an appeal to the emotions and self-esteem rather than to rationality and facts – these remain of secondary importance.

The Emperor Marcus Aurelius (AD 121-180) was the last of the Stoic philosophers, who regarded virtue as the sole good and as an end in itself. One of his most constant themes was the transformation of phenomena through time: 'Motions and changes are continually renewing the world, just as the uninterrupted course of time is always renewing the infinite duration of ages.' This gives him an acute sense of transience, and hence of the insignificance of the individual life:

> How quickly all things disappear, in the universe the bodies themselves, but in time the remembrance of them; one man after burying another has been laid out dead, and another buries him; and all this in a short time. To conclude, always observe how ephemeral and worthless human things are, and what was yesterday a little mucus, tomorrow will be a mummy or ashes.

He naturally regards himself as part of the process: 'All things are changing: and thou thyself are in continuous mutation and in a manner in continuous destruction, and the universe too.'

He has two views on death: the first organic, the second which postulates the alternatives of extinction and change without coming to a conclusion either way:

> Death is such as generation is, a mystery of nature; a composition out of the same elements, and a decomposition into the same ... death is a cessation of the impressions through the senses, and the pulling of the strings which move the appetites, and of the discursive movements of the thoughts, and of the service to the flesh.

And in the second category:

> About death: whether it is a dispersion, or a resolution into atoms, or annihilation, it is either extinction or change ... he who fears death either fears the loss of sensation or a different kind of sensation. But if thou shalt have no sensation, neither wilt though feel any harm; and if thou shalt acquire another kind of sensation, thou wilt be a different kind of living being and thou wilt not cease to live.

Although Marcus Aurelius suspends judgement on the issue, he does agree with Cicero that it would be inappropriate divine planning for pious people to be extinguished at death; but he adds 'if this is so, be assured that if it ought to have been otherwise, the gods would have done it'. The important issue is not whether man survives death but how he conducts himself ethically while alive; nor does he accept the excuse of lack of talent:

> Show those qualities then which are altogether in thy power – sincerity, gravity, endurance of labour, aversion to pleasure, contentment with thy portion and with few things, benevolence, frankness, no love of superfluity, freedom from trifling magnanimity. Doest thou not see how many qualities thou art immediately able to exhibit, in which there is no excuse of natural incapacity or unfitness, and yet though still remainest voluntarily below the mark?

It is not the length of life but its quality that is paramount.

Plotinus (AD 204-270) taught that the soul was originally one 'concentrated all', and had some difficulty, like Plato, in explaining how it moved from that state. He divides Soul into two aspects, an inner and an outer: it is this outer which 'secedes' from the One and becomes a 'deserter from totality'; it descends from the state where it is immune from care and trouble to become partial and self-centred, severed from the One by differentiation: 'a partial thing, isolated, weakened, full of care, intent upon the fragment ... it nestles in one form of being.' This is described as the casting of the wings, the enchaining in the body, which is a claustrophobic experience when compared with limitless being in the One. The soul is defined as the authentic man, and it is argued against Lucretius that 'it is impossible that a collocation of material entities should produce life, or mindless entities mind'; the soul is the directing principle of matter, which could not even exist without the soul. The body is recognised as transient – 'dissolution is its very nature' – and in relation to it the soul is seen as 'the agent to this instrument' or as 'the Form to this Matter', giving it organic unity. He compares the soul with 'the workman in such operations as boring or weaving, the body with the tool employed: the body is passive and mental; the Soul is active, reading such impression as are made on the body or discerned by the body.' This formulation corresponds quite closely to the Interactionist theory of the mind/body relation, which we shall meet in later thinkers.

The outer part of the soul is thought to possess a longing for the original unity from which it emerged; the aim, then, is not limited personal immortality through the separate persistence of the individual soul, but recovery of its essence by immersion in the One, an immersion that seems to imply consciousness without a sense of separation. The experience of such ecstasy (*ekstasis*) seems to have been a regular occurrence with Plotinus:

> Many times it has happened: lifted out of the body into myself [i.e. soul]; becoming external to all other things and self-centred; beholding a marvellous beauty; then, more than ever, assured of community with the loftiest order, enacting the noblest life, acquiring identity with the divine; stationing within it by having attained that activity; poised above whatsoever in the Intellectual is less than the Supreme: yet there comes the moment of descent from intellection to reasoning, and after a sojourn in the divine, I ask myself how it happens that I can now be descending, and how did the Soul ever enter into my body,

the Soul which even within the body, is the high thing which it has shown itself to be.

This passage requires very careful reading as it is a very concentrated account of Plotinus' experiences, and shows that his speculations have a personal, empirical as well as a metaphysical basis. It explains why he sees the soul as simultaneously the one and the many: he realises himself as a separate bodily entity, but then experiences himself as at one with creation. Elsewhere he describes the absorption of the contemplator in his experience, and the consequent transcendence of personality:

There will not even be the memory of the personality; no thought that the contemplator is the self ... in this connexion it should be remembered that, in contemplative vision, especially when it is vivid, we are not at the time aware of our personality; we are in possession of ourselves but the activity is towards the object of vision in which the thinker becomes identified.

This is clearly an account of Plotinus' own experience, which reminds one metaphorically of Plato's cave simile. The transition indicated here has profound religious significance: it depicts not merely a state where there is some continuity of personality, but where the personality is transcended and fulfilled, where the limitations and contradictions of partial being are resolved into an all-embracing wholeness: the physical shades into the mystical.

3.

THE ORIGINS AND DEVELOPMENT OF CHRISTIAN VIEWS ON IMMORTALITY AND RESURRECTION

If men thought of God as much as they think of the world, who would not obtain liberation?

MAITRI UPANISHAD

Time is an image of eternity, but it is also a substitute for eternity.

SIMONE WEIL

We look upon the present as something to be put up with while it lasts, and serving only the way towards our goal. Hence most people, if they glance back when they come to the end of life, find that they have been living *ad interim*.

SCHOPENHAUER

I think of other ages that floated on the stream of life and love and death and are forgotten, and I feel the freedom of passing away.

TAGORE

The conflict between a collective ethnic faith and the individual's demand for significance is regarded by Brandon as the central point around which the development of the Hebrew conceptions of death, survival and judgement revolve. He points out that Yahwism 'was in origin and essence an ethnic religion, based on a special relation between one god and his chosen people'; one God and not a multiplicity of gods – out of this monotheism arises the idea of paternal providential care and, along with it, the attribute of omnipotence. Finally, Yahweh comes to be invested with the qualities of justice and righteousness. We shall see how the conceptions of post-mortem existence and retribution evolve within and in relation to this understanding of God.

We have already examined the Genesis myth of the origin of death, envisaged as a punishment inflicted on Adam and Eve for curiosity and disobedience. It takes only until Chapter 6 for Yahweh to regret his creation when he saw 'that man had done much evil on earth and that his thoughts and inclinations were always evil'. He is sorry that he ever created man and resolves to wipe him off the face of the earth; it seems that the rest of creation is to be eliminated along with mankind. But, providentially, Noah is spared, and the narrative continues. The idea behind the flood is sweeping retribution for man's evil deeds, for which he bears a collective responsibility; but the fact that Noah is spared indicates that Yahweh hopes that it will be possible for man to make a fresh start.

Despite Noah's exemption from the flood, the Hebrew conception of the afterlife draws no qualitative distinctions at this stage. All the dead are committed to Sheol where they survive as *rephaim* or shades. The terms that are used to denote spirit or soul are not exact counterparts: *nephesh* originally meant neck or throat, then vital breath or wind, and is also associated with blood, while the term *ruah* had the original meaning of wind, or air in motion. Some cabbalists state that the *nephesh* survives in Sheol, but the image/*rephaim* has much less vitality than the body. At any rate, in spite of the imprecise nature of the terminology, 'the Hebrews conceived of the human being as a psycho-physical organism, of which the parts were inextricably compounded to form a whole ... and that death is the shattering of this vital unity'.

58

The depictions of Sheol, whose etymology indicates a connection with digging and excavation, bear a striking resemblance to the Homeric Hades; it is based on the same line of thought which extrapolates the atrophy of strength in age and illness to a shadowy vitality only just substantial enough to persist as a separate identity. Job refers to Sheol as a 'land of deep darkness ... of gathering shadows, of deepening shadows, lit by no ray of light, dark upon dark'; it is a land cut off from Yahweh – 'It is not the dead who praise the Lord, not those who go down into silence.' Isaiah, who alludes to mankind as grass compared to the word of the Lord, pictures the dead foes of Israel being greeted by its dead leaders, who say 'So you too are as weak as we are, and have become one of us. Your pride and all the music of your lutes have been brought down to Sheol; maggots are the pallet beneath you, and worms your coverlet' – death is the great equaliser. Salmond gives a graphic description of the results of the transition: 'The living person becomes a dead person, retaining a negative existence, a weakened edition of his former self, his faculties dormant, without strength, memory, consciousness, knowledge, or the energy of any affection.'

By the mid-sixth century BC a series of disasters had befallen Israel, culminating in the exile in Babylon. The inevitable result was that people began to question either Yahweh's power or his justice: if He was omnipotent, why had Israel been delivered to her enemies? Surely this punishment was out of proportion to any sin that the Hebrews could have committed; hence their scepticism about the traditional explanation that the disasters were a just form of chastisement, that the sins of the fathers were visited collectively on the sons. Jeremiah and Ezekiel expressly reject this scepticism on Yahweh's behalf. Ezekiel explains that the man who is righteous and does what is right shall live, whereas the evil man will die; likewise the good man who turns to evil ways will die, and the evil man who repents shall live. So that it is concluded that it is not the Lord, but the Israelites who act without principle, and that, unless they throw off the load of their past misdeeds, 'their iniquity will be their downfall'. They will be caught up with in this life.

The book of Job develops the theme of the individual innocent sufferer considerably further. The orthodox position is stated in Chapter 4: Job is exhorted to have hope 'for what innocent man has ever perished? ... this I know, that those who plough mischief and sow trouble reap as they have sown; they perish at the blast of God and are shrivelled by the breath of his nostrils'. Paradoxically, Job looks upon the sinner's punishment as a possible welcome source of relief from his troubles. He has no illusions of another better existence, comparing man to a flower which blossoms and withers; a tree, he asserts, is better off than a man, for it may sprout again if it has been cut down. 'But a man dies, and he disappears ... he shall never be roused from his sleep.' At this stage there is as yet no post-mortem justice, and apparently precious little on earth.

The book of Ecclesiastes (c.300-275 BC) reaches a nadir of pessimism and scepticism about the meaning and worth of human life: 'In my empty existence I have seen it all, from a righteous man perishing in his righteousness to a wicked man growing old in his wickedness.' This clearly represents a practical repudiation of the scheme of justice championed by Ezekiel. The kernel of his objection is expressed as follows: 'This is what is wrong with all that is done here under the sun: that one and the same fate befalls every man.' There is hope for the man who is still alive from the mere fact that he is still alive and can enjoy some of the pleasures of existence – Ecclesiastes comments that a live dog is better than a dead lion; the living, it is true, know that they will die, but the dead know nothing. In Sheol, 'for which you are bound, there is neither doing nor thinking, neither understanding nor wisdom.' The writer does not even discern the hand of Providence on earth: 'Speed does not win the race nor strength the battle ... time and chance govern all ... no man knows when his hour will come.' Man is not different from animals:

> Man is a creature of chance and the beasts are creatures of chance, and one mischance awaits them all: death comes to both alike. They all draw the same breath. Men have no advantage over beasts; for everything is emptiness. All go to the same place; all come from dust and to dust all return.

The book of Ecclesiasticus (c.185 BC) is less blackly pessimistic than Ecclesiastes, who probably represented the views of a small cynical minority. Ecclesiasticus does not believe that the wicked man will go unscathed in this existence – 'Do not envy a bad man his success, you do not know what fate is in store for him' – a superstitious attitude at first sight, but elsewhere he states that the vengeful man will face the vengeance of the Lord, who keeps a strict account of his sins. Death is part of the natural cycle: 'The Lord created man from the earth and sent him back to it again.' In the grave he 'comes into an inheritance of maggots and vermin and worms'. Death is not to be feared, as it is universal and decreed by the Lord for all living men; there is no use arguing about this, and, regardless of the length of life, 'no questions will be asked in the grave'. So man is encouraged to give and receive, to indulge himself, because the body wears out like a garment and luxuries are not to be expected in the grave. This *carpe diem* philosophy, however, is not carried to extremes, and the rest of the book is full of practical wisdom and exhortations to do good, so that at least a man's name may be honourably remembered.

The theme of resurrection makes its first appearance in the vision related by Ezekiel, where he sees the bones of the dead being revivified, or rather recreated, symbolising the rebirth of the nation. Resurrection is mentioned more specifically in II Maccabees 12, when Judas Maccabeus collects money as a sin-offering in order to blot the sin out – this is described as a 'fit and proper act in which he took due account of the resurrection'. The contemporary Daniel (*c*.150 BC) speaks of resurrection and subsequent judgement, implying that any injustice and imbalances extant at the end of life on earth will be rectified afterwards:

> At that moment your people will be delivered, every one who is written in the book: many of those who sleep in the dust of the earth will wake, some to everlasting life, and some to the reproach of eternal abhorrence.

The book of Enoch, the oldest parts of which were composed in the second century BC, arrives at further subdivisions by partitioning Sheol. It describes the eternal torment of fallen angels, and divides the inhabitants of Sheol into four categories: those who are righteous, whether martyred or not; those sinners who lived prosperously and escaped punishment during their life on earth; those sinners who suffered during their lives; and a vague category of those 'who shall not be righteous but sinners'. The difference between the second and third categories is that those who escaped unscathed during life are suffering prior to the judgement and will continue to suffer after it, while those who paid some penalty during life are not so badly treated in the intermediary period. This moral distinction goes some way towards correcting the apparent injustices of life, which are only finally resolved at the assize. In later chapters the judgement of both righteous and wicked is depicted: their deeds are weighed in the balance, the righteous subsequently enjoy a state of bliss, while the wicked are 'cast into an abyss of fire and flaming, and full of pillars of fire' – the first reference to the flames of hell. There is no mention of any resurrection interrupting either torment or bliss.

The Wisdom of Solomon (first century BC) sounds a note of warning to the sceptic, but not without providing a succinct resumé of his philosophy:

> Our life is short and full of trouble, and when a man comes to his end there is no remedy; no man was ever known to return from the grave. By mere chance were we born, and afterwards we shall be as though we have never been, for the breath in our nostrils is but a wisp of smoke; our reason is a mere spark kept alive by the beating of our hearts, and when that goes out, our body will turn to ashes and the breath of our life disperse like empty air ... a passing shadow, such is our life, and there is no postponement of our end. Come let us enjoy the good things while we can, and make full use of the creation with all the eagerness of youth.

This attitude combines elements of the atomist formulation with the kind of sentiment which one associates with Omar Khayyam. These men went on to derive a might-is-right attitude towards life, indifferent to any sufferings that the poor might undergo at their expense. The writer describes such men, as cynical as the author of Ecclesiastes, as blinded by their own malevolence, contending that they failed to understand the hidden plan of God, which created man for immortality. The souls of the just are depicted at peace 'in God's hand'; after a little chastisement they will receive great blessings, which they have earned through passing God's test; they are likened to gold in a crucible, the evils of life being interpreted as a test of character rather than a punishment.

As a corollary to the idea of life as a test, God is treated as omniscient, 'a witness of the inmost being ... hence no man can utter injustice and not be found out ... no muttered syllable escapes that vigilant ear'; man is therefore exhorted to beware of 'futile grumbling', to avoid all bitter words, so that he does not stray from the path of life and court death; and death is not to be regarded as king, since justice is immortal. There will be 'great assize of souls' where all will be accounted for: kings will undergo a specially stern inquisition of their intentions, and should not be deluded into imagining that their exalted position on earth grants them any exemption from judgement: 'The powerful will be called powerfully to account.' Incidentally the writer's formulation of the relation of the soul to the body clearly owes something to Platonism in its reference to the divine element of the soul being obscured by immersion in matter: 'The reasoning of men is feeble, and our plans are fallible; because a perishable body weights down the soul, and its frame of clay burdens the mind so full of thoughts.' Despite this caveat, the author seems fairly sure of his own views.

In Philo (*c*.13 BC-AD 45) there is a meeting between the Hebrew and Greek (Platonic) views of man. The soul (*pneuma*) is considered to be pre-existent and divine, therefore immortal, while the perishable body is regarded as a prison or coffin – an idea already encountered in the Pythagorean/Orphic tradition. Philo makes the crucial distinction, later elaborated by Paul, between natural and spiritual death: 'The death threatened for eating the fruit was not natural, the separation of the soul from the body, but penal, the sinking of the soul into the body.' Originally the resulting death was considered to be natural, but it gradually acquired a more important religious significance in its association of being cut off from God. Indeed the phrase 'sinking of the soul into the body' implies that earth life itself is a kind of death, or at least an exile from the Divine; it seems to combine the Platonic idea of the descent with the Hebrew fall, a transition which marks the corruption of virtue and the assumption of vice. Philo asserts that ignorant men are mistaken if they regard natural death as the end of their punishments, whereas, in the light of divine judgement, these tribulations have scarcely begun. The righteous man is received into heaven while 'the reprobate man is dragged below, down to the very lowest place, to Tartarus itself and profound darkness'. Philo makes no mention of resurrection, and, perhaps surprisingly in the light of the Platonic connection, only vague references to rebirth.

It only remains to glance at the views of three of the sects prominent at the beginning of the Christian era: the Pharisees, the Sadducees, and the Essenes. The Pharisees attributed immortality to the soul, but maintained that only the souls of the good pass into another body and live again, while the souls of the evil undergo eternal torment commensurate with their deeds. The Sadducees rejected the idea of survival, and therefore of rewards and punishments after death, while the Essenes held that the soul, an emanation from the finest air, was immortal, although temporarily interlaced with a perishable body. At death the soul was freed; the virtuous travelled to a heaven beyond the ocean, whereas the evil were consigned to torment in the depths.

We have now traced how the manifest injustices of life, in conjunction with the idea of an omnipotent and just deity, forced the Hebrews to abandon the notion that the evil received their deserts during life on earth; this conflict between the idea of divine justice in theory and apparent injustice in practice also led the Hebrews to discard the undiscriminating shadowy existence in Sheol in favour of a conception which answered the claims of ultimate justice, whereby the just are rewarded and the unjust chastised. Hence the development of the notions of judgement, heaven and hell, and the resurrection, all of which were to play a major part in the Christian scheme of eschatology.

The Gospels

The Gospel parables of heaven, hell, and judgement imply the conscious survival of the soul, but Jesus's concern was less with survival *per se* than with the qualities, which the soul should seek to develop in order to be worthy of the Kingdom of Heaven. He tells his disciples that those who wish to follow him must leave self behind and not care for their own safety:

> Whoever cares for his own safety is lost; but if a man will let himself be lost for my sake, he will find his true self. What will a man gain by winning the whole world at the cost of his true self?

Salvation is to be attained through love, sacrifice, and service; and if God provides for the sparrows, he should be trusted to provide men with the necessities of life. The real danger is not so much destruction of the body as annihilation of the soul; hence the warning 'Do not fear those who kill the body, but cannot kill the soul. Fear him rather who is able to destroy both body and soul in hell.' This formulation seems to exhibit both Greek and Hebrew qualities in that the survival of the *psyche* is assumed, but it also contains the Hebrew notion that God is able to destroy the soul – an issue disputed by generations of theologians.

Matthew 25 relates the judgement and assignment of souls, which are divided according to their ethical performance on earth. The righteous inherit the kingdom, while the wicked do not appear to benefit from a second chance, and are consigned to eternal punishment. The tone is urgent and designed to impress: the sinner should therefore mend his ways forthwith while he still has the opportunity, or else he is damned; this message has been progressively watered down and ingeniously reinterpreted by liberal theologians who could not imagine that a loving God would reject any of his creatures, and who claim that social ills and crime stem from environmental influences. The passage in Matthew has the dual significance of setting out some of the fundamentals of Christian ethics as well as providing the starting point for speculations on the nature of the Second Coming and Last Judgement (or Grand Assize). It is interesting to note, in passing, that the imagined mechanics of the Second Coming – Christ's reappearance in clouds of glory to mankind – furnished an argument for the flat-earthers who argued that if the earth were not flat it would be impossible for all nations to catch a glimpse of Christ.

There are three recorded instances of Jesus's bringing the dead back to life. The first is the story of Jairus's daughter: when Jesus arrives at Jairus's house he is informed that the girl is dead, but remarks that she is only asleep. He then turns the others out and enters the room where the girl is lying, speaks to her, and she gets up. The Luke version adds that her 'spirit returned' on hearing Jesus's words; thus her body was literally reanimated. Jesus asks that no one should be told of the event, presumably because he did not want this kind of publicity. A second instance is recorded in Luke when Jesus is approaching the gates of Nain. Here he encounters a funeral procession where the dead man is the only son of a widowed mother and, thus, her only source of material support. Again the dead person is told to rise up, and does so. These two occurrences are not apparently treated as more extraordinary than his other miracles. But the same could not be said of the raising of Lazarus, related in the eleventh chapter of St John's Gospel. Jesus hears of Lazarus's illness but does not immediately rush to the invalid's bedside. Instead he says, 'This illness will not end in death; it has come for the glory of God, to bring glory to the son of God. He then explains that Lazarus has fallen asleep, and is misunderstood by his disciples who think that he is referring to natural sleep, from which he will awake; This misapprehension may be John's way of enabling Jesus to be absolutely unequivocal: he says that Lazarus is dead and that he will raise him, which will be for the good of their faith. Both Mary and Martha believe that their brother would not have died if Jesus had been there, and Martha seems to think that Jesus might even raise him now; but she is sceptical when Jesus asserts that this will indeed happen, and assumes that he is talking about the resurrection at the Last Day. Jesus replies 'I am the resurrection and I am life. If a man has faith in me, even though he die, he shall come to life; and no one who is alive and has faith shall ever die.' The utterance is somewhat cryptic, as it seems to refer both to physical death, from which Lazarus will be retrieved, and to spiritual death in terms of exile from God. The stone is finally rolled away, and the dead man emerges in his swathes; the miracle, which can be regarded in some ways as a prefiguration of Jesus's own resurrection, aims to show the strength and results of Martha's faith, as well as creating faith by demonstrating the power of God.

Before we come to Jesus's death and resurrection, there is one more highly significant event which must be mentioned: the transfiguration, in which Jesus's face is described as shining like the sun, with his clothes white like the light. It is impossible to say whether some kind of actual bodily transformation is implied, or whether the three disciples experienced a change in the level of consciousness and thus of vision, enabling them to perceive Jesus with some kind of inner eye in a body of light. In any event the transformation heralds resurrection from bodily death.

The Synoptic Gospels describe Jesus's death as being accompanied by a loud cry, before he says 'into thy hands I commit my spirit'. In John he says 'It is finished', before bowing his head and giving up his spirit. The death of Jesus signals the nadir of the disciples' fortunes. In Mark and Luke they are reported to be sceptical about initial rumours of the resurrection: 'The story appeared to them to be nonsense, and they would not believe them [the women].' In Mark, Jesus reproaches some disciples for their incredulity and dullness when he appears to them at table. As for the chief priests, they are perplexed and annoyed by the rumour, and pay the soldiers to say that the disciples came to steal the body during the night.

The main narratives of Jesus's post-mortem appearances are related in Luke and John. In the story of the road to Emmaus, Jesus is not recognised by the two followers, and expounds to them the significance of death and the resurrection; only when he breaks the bread do they recognise the familiar gesture – and then he vanishes instantly. In one sense he is physical in that he has been walking and talking with the two men, but then his sudden and complete disappearance exhibits the typical behaviour of an apparition body. Likewise he is able to materialise from nowhere in a room with his disciples. The first reaction is one of terror, but Jesus reassures them by saying that he has flesh and bones, and even eats a piece of fish. A similar bodily constitution emerges from the narrative in John, although it seems even stranger that Mark is told not to touch Jesus while Thomas is invited to feel his wounds. He manifests in the room like an apparition, and yet he appears to be materially solid.

Jesus's post-mortem appearances, then, contain paradoxical elements of bodily and 'spiritual' resurrection. On the one hand there is no body in the tomb, the disciples are able to touch Jesus's body, and he is apparently able to eat solid food; but then he has the ability suddenly to appear and vanish in a way which suggests that he has a body, which can pass through matter. As we shall see, this ambiguity turned out to be a bone of contention in the centuries that followed: are we to expect a fully bodily resurrection, or do we acquire a body of a different nature?

St Paul

'The Pauline eschatology is fundamentally and radically inseparable from his soteriological framework' is a jargon-ridden way of saying that Paul's views on the soul and immortality can only be fully appreciated in the light of his scheme of salvation, which is clearly set out in his Epistle to the Romans. Mankind is considered to be in a state of inescapable corruption and sinfulness in which he is deprived of 'divine splendour'. Because God wished to save man and 'reconcile him to Himself', He sent His only Son into the world to die for the wicked; this act, asserts Paul, is proof of God's love for man (a quite different version of this divine intervention can be found in Jung's *Answer to Job*; while the present writer has certain reservations about Jung's formulation, he finds it more congenial than the vicarious expiation postulated by Paul). Jesus was to be the 'means of expiating sin by his sacrificial death', so that the believer is 'justified' through faith and the grace of God; he is saved from the final retribution, and reconciled to God.

Just as death entered the world by one man, Adam, so the resurrection was also effected by one man. Paul is using death here in a largely figurative sense – the wages of sin – and Jesus is said to have died to sin by the manner of his death; so that the believer is invited to participate through Jesus in this death to sin, and in a new life achieved through his death. There is a superficially neat logic in Paul's scheme, but it rests on the ambiguous use of the word death. It is clear that Jesus did not abolish physical death from the world – indeed this would be impossible without changing the nature and basis of material transformation. What Paul is claiming is that Jesus healed the spiritual alienation of man from God, thus giving him the chance of a desirable eternal life. Adam, however, is supposed to be responsible for the advent of both physical and spiritual death. In fairness to Paul, one should add that his phrase 'justification by faith' did not mean mere intellectual assent to the efficacy of Jesus's sacrificial death, but involved an inner change of heart on the part of the believer.

Paul's most important statement on the soul and immortality is to be found in the fifteenth chapter of his first letter to the Corinthians. He starts by asserting that Christ died for the sins of man, was buried, and rose again on the third day. He then appeared to many people, and finally to Paul himself; one should bear in mind, however, that the appearance to Paul was of an overpowering kind in the form of a blazing light (not, therefore, a bodily appearance) reminiscent of the transfiguration. This was the nature of his own evidence for the resurrection, upon which the validity of his message depends: for if it did not occur, then all his preaching and faith is vain; and if Christ was not raised, then there is no hope for anyone else, either. We may as well indulge ourselves and not care a whit for the consequences.

If there is to be a resurrection, one of the most important considerations is the kind of body in which man will exist. Paul distinguishes between the forms and flesh of men, beasts, birds, and fishes, and then between heavenly and earthly bodies. He uses the analogy of sowing to illustrate his point:

> What is sown in the earth as a perishable thing is raised imperishable. Sown in humiliation, it is raised in glory; sown in weakness, it is raised in power; sown as an animal body, it is raised as a spiritual body.

The analogy is imperfect in so far as the new seed in nature is just as perishable as the parent; but the idea of re-creation and regeneration comes across clearly. Paul's formulation is also reminiscent of the late Egyptian belief that the spiritual body (*sabu*) germinates from the material body. Paul states the different qualities of the animal and physical bodies, and stresses that the animal body must come first, as the soul is created at birth; thus he rejects the Platonic conception of the pre-existent soul and reincarnation. The physical, represented by Adam, must precede the spiritual, signified by Christ; and the inheritance of the kingdom is the sole privilege of the spiritual body, as 'the perishable cannot possess immortality'. In order to accommodate this conception of the spiritual body to the scheme of the Last Judgement, Paul seems to assume that this spiritual body will only be put on at the last trumpet-call when 'we shall all be changed in a flash, in the twinkling of an eye' (a passage which one cannot read without thinking of Handel). Paul therefore rejects the idea of a straightforward bodily reconstitution in favour of the transfiguration of the animal body into a spiritual body. In doing so he remains within the Hebrew framework of the creation of the soul at the outset of a single earthly life, thus reject-ing, as we have seen, the Greek traditions of rebirth and pre-existence. However, the exact nature, and therefore needs, of the spiritual body are left open to interpretation, as we shall see when we come to con-sider the commentaries written on the passage by Luther and Calvin.

Some Early Fathers

Tertullian was born in Carthage around AD 160 and only became a Christian at thirty-five, after a period of indulgence. As was later the case with Augustine, his attitude is perhaps all the more uncompro-mising as a result of his early licentiousness. He reasons that the soul must have a body of some kind if it is to have a form and that this body cannot be 'a void and empty illusion, but such as would offer itself to be even grasped by the hand, soft and transparent and of an ethereal colour, and in form resembling that of a human being in every respect'. Even before resurrection and judgement, he argues, the soul must be of a corporeal nature 'for an incorporeal thing suffers nothing'; the rich man in the Lazarus narrative cannot be experiencing imaginary tor-ments. The Premise of Tertullian's thoughts on the resurrection itself is contained in the immortal sentence '*Credo quia absurdum est*': the resurrection itself is certain because it is impossible. He states unequiv-ocally that 'the flesh will rise again and indeed whole and indeed itself and indeed unimpaired', (a doctrine described by Edwards as 'disas-trously influential'). What is impossible to human reason, continues Tertullian, is possible through God's unfathomable omnipotence. After all, God created man out of nothing so 'He will be able to fashion flesh also out of nothing, flesh that is reduced to nothing'; if, on the other hand, He created man out of a different matter, 'He will be able to call forth from something else flesh by whatsoever absorbed.' Tertullian's crowning argument relates to the phoenix, the mythical bird that rose to new life out of its own ashes. He extends the Gospel argument that man is more valuable than many sparrows to say that, because man is clearly more valuable than many phoenixes, his resurrection is assured. In the final analysis it is contended that resurrection of the material body is required on two grounds: first that man may be judged as a whole, and second so that the damned are enabled to experience the pangs of hell in their most palpable form; nothing is said of the possible intensification of sensations of bliss in heaven. St Jerome adduces a similar argument: 'If the dead be not raised with flesh and bones, how can the dead after judgement gnash their teeth in hell?' Although Tertullian's conception of the soul has something in common with Paul's idea of the spiritual body, he insists on the corporeal nature of both the soul and the resurrection, thus ignoring the distinctions between the 'animal' and the 'spiritual'; in attempting to reach coherence, he abandons common sense in favour of faith in God's omnipotence to bring about the impossible.

Origen (185-254) is cited by Jung in his *Psychological Types* as the opposite character to Tertullian. His system is much closer to Plato, and he was later condemned as a heretic on a number of grounds, two of which concern us here: the doctrine of the pre-existence of souls, as we have seen in the Orphic/Pythagorean/Platonic stream of thought, and the contention that, at the resurrection, our bodies will be transformed into ethereal forms, and not reconstituted as flesh. Here Origen is in line with Paul, but out of phase with Tertullian. Furthermore he taught that all souls were of the same nature, and are imprisoned in material bodies for sins committed in the past; that the souls gradually ascend a kind of Jacob's ladder towards deliverance; and that all suffering is remedial and in exact proportion to the offence committed (a version of the eastern karma). Origen also rejected the Pauline idea that Christ suffered for mankind as a whole; so that while he rejected Paul's scheme of salvation, he did support his views on the nature of the resurrection body against the formulations of Tertullian.

St Augustine (354-430) is perhaps most famous for formulating the doctrine of predestination whereby, although all men are sinners and deserve eternal punishment, God has arbitrarily chosen some to be saved; it was a doctrine espoused by Calvin in seventeenth-century Geneva and by the Jansenists in France, but it was profoundly repugnant to the rationalist. Having spent periods as a Neo-Platonist and Manichean, Augustine was anxious to work out a coherent Christian system, which lacked the defects apparent to him in his earlier ways of thought. He states that man is made of soul and body; the body is compounded of the four elements, but the soul has an essence of its own, and is the means whereby man can perceive incorporeal things, which seem to include the notions of points, lines and widths. The soul is defined as 'a special substance, endowed with reason, adapted to rule the body'. There will be two resurrections, one of the soul at death, and another of the body at the time of the Last Judgement. Few details are volunteered of the soul's intermediary existence prior to the Last Judgement, but it is clear that Augustine believed that the physical body would be reconstituted at the second resurrection:

> Every man's body, howsoever dispersed here, shall be restored perfect in the resurrection. Every body shall be complete in quantity and quality. As many hairs as have been shaved off, or nails cut, shall not return in such enormous quantities to deform their original places; but neither shall they perish: they shall return into the body into that substance from which they grew.

The damned shall then burn eternally in hell without being consumed. Augustine reinforces the physical view of the resurrection advocated by Tertullian, and even elaborates on some of the details. We shall see that the debate continued in the Middle Ages.

The Middle Ages

Religion in the Middle Ages could scarcely be described as the people's opiate. A life of toil might be expected to find its continuation in hell. The whole outlook was dominated by fear: especially fear of God, Satan, death and hell. Unless the believer submitted to the guidance of the church during his lifetime, he was sure to find himself descending inexorably into one of the circles so graphically described in Dante's *Inferno*, from whence there would be no escape. There was much less emphasis on the positive side of faith – heaven and the mercy of Christ, while there was a good deal of score set by ordeals, witchcraft, and magic. Alger quotes one writer saying of the age:

> A gloomy mist of credulity enwrapped the cathedral and the hall of justice, the cottage and the throne. In the dark shadows of the universal ignorance a thousand superstitions, like foul animals of night, were propagated and nourished.

One area of credulity was in the efficacy of relics, which were the goal of many pilgrimages. No doubt faith was in some cases effective in healing through a mechanism of self-fulfilment, but it seems that the possession of relics was often a financial necessity for the religious institution. Draper cites the prizes obtained by a certain Abbot Martin for his monastery in Alsace:

> The following are the inestimable values:
> 1. A spot of the blood of our Saviour
> 2. A piece of the true cross
> 3. The arm of the Apostle James
> 4. Part of the skeleton of John the Baptist
> 5. – I hesitate to write such a blasphemy – a bottle of the milk of the Mother of God.

The sale of indulgences also reached epidemic proportions, and pilgrimages were encouraged by various means: the Pope offered free pardon for all sins committed since birth to anyone who entered the church of Assisi between the eve of the first and second of August each year – more than 60,000 pilgrims availed themselves of the privilege.

Works of art, and miracle plays, reinforced the message from the pulpit. The Last Judgement is featured in most medieval cathedrals, hell's mouth gapes wide open (volcanic eruptions interpreted as the uneasy belchings of inferno). The good are led away by angels, while the damned are cast headlong into the flames. Titles of some of the edifying mystery plays include 'The Extraction of the Souls from Hell'. In which the portals of hell fly open at the words 'Lift up your gates, ye princes, and be ye lifted up ye everlasting doors, and the King of Glory shall come in'. Expenses incurred for these plays include: 'Item: payd for kepying of fyer at hellmothe, four pence ... for a new hoke to hang Judas, six pence ... for mending and payntying hellmothe ... two pence ... God's coat of white leather, three shillings.'

In the midst of all the widespread ignorance and superstition arose the scholastic movement, culminating in the monumental achievement of St Thomas Aquinas (c.1225-1274), who systematised Catholic theology, and whose influence is still potent today. He argues that the soul cannot be corporeal, because nothing corporeal can be the first principle of life; he takes it as read that the body alone is not that first principle; likewise he contends that the mind or intellectual principle exists apart from the body, because it would not otherwise be able to know the body, being a part of it. So that if this principle is apart from the body, it must have some existence *per se*; and since only things which subsist can have an operation and existence of their own, it follows that the soul must have a substance. The nature of the soul is said to be that of incorporeal substance, a notion which the modern mind finds difficult to grasp as substance is equated with matter; here Aquinas is using it more in the sense implied in the creeds where it is asserted that Christ is of one substance (being) with the Father. Aquinas then asserts that this existence *per se* of the soul does not apply to brutes, so that their soul perishes with the body; from this it follows that there can be no transmigration of human souls into animal bodies; pre-existence is also rejected in favour of the soul being created at birth. It is contended that the human soul is indestructible, and that it retains all its faculties after death, with the exception of sensation, which requires the intermediary of the body. The soul, however, is not considered to be the man, as in Plato, because man is a composite being made of soul and body. Aquinas follows the Aristotelian view of the soul as the form of the material body. Because man is composite and not essentially soul, the resurrection has to take place if the whole man is to achieve the end of happiness which God had in view for him. Aquinas next addresses himself to the question of what body the soul will return to, rejecting the idea of reincarnation in another human body. He argues that 'since it behoves the end to be attained by the selfsame thing that was made for that end, lest it appear to be made without purpose, it is necessary for the selfsame man to rise again; and this is effected by the selfsame soul being united to the selfsame body.' Furthermore the very meaning of the word resurrection, which is second arising, requires this; anything else will entail the assumption of another body.

Thus the inexorable logic of Aquinas leads him to hold the inconceivable view of bodily resurrection. Alger quotes some of the topics discussed by other scholastic theologians:

> Will each one's hairs and nails be restored to him in the resurrection? ... When bodies are raised, will each soul spontaneously know its own and enter it? ... Will the deformities and scars of our present bodies be retained in the resurrection? ... Will all rise of the same age? ... Will all have one size and one sex?

Ludicrous perplexities arising from a preposterous premise. On one of these points, the age and form of the body at resurrection, Aquinas himself concluded that the substance that will rise will be that belonging to the individual at the time of his death: a grim prospect of many. When we consider the rise of the scientific outlook it will become clear how the rigorous logic of the scholastics, allied to the improbability of their premises, contributed to their downfall.

The Reformation

Luther does not depart from Aquinas's opinion that the nature of man is composite. In his *Table talk* he takes Plato to task: 'How can Plato speak about this matter?' he asks before stating his belief that the whole man was made by God from dust, as recorded in Genesis, and that the soul is created simultaneously with and from the body. It is corrupt by nature, he asserts, not through contact with the body. The idea that the soul can exist apart from the body is rejected and likened to tearing a part of the man off. The resurrection is to be awaited in belief.

Further light is shed on Luther's opinions in his commentary on the 15th chapter of *I Corinthians*; it runs to over 150 pages, and no stone is left unturned. Pagan and worldly-wise people are accused of not thinking beyond their swinish heads in connection with the resurrection of the body. They therefore proceed to reason foolishly.

> 'If man were to come alive, again, he would also have to eat and drink, keep house etc. Otherwise, how would he remain alive? If he were to meet again and live together under those circumstances, it would be an odd, nonsensical, and confused existence, so that we would all the more wish to remain dead. Therefore there can surely be nothing to it. For according to outward appearances, this does not make sense.' Indeed this does not make sense if we consult and ask reason how things will be in that life. Reason knows nothing and can know nothing about that.

He goes on to describe how the providence of God will accomplish all that is necessary in the new life. The corruptible 'grain' must acquire a new garb, which will no longer be subject to bodily wants and failings. According to this scheme, man will retain only his essence, and not what relates to his current transitory life, 'and yet it will be the same body and soul with all the members that man had here'. Further on he reaffirms the flesh and blood nature of his new body, which will not have any physical wants (and yet it will be the same physical body): 'When it is called the spiritual body this does not imply that it no longer has physical flesh and blood. No, then it could not be called a true body.' The state in which the risen will be living will apparently be so absorbing that man will never think of eating and drinking. In Luther, then, we are faced with the contradiction in terms: a physical body, which exhibits none of its known normal properties. We can either accept the possibility through faith in God's inscrutable power, or else reject the notion as inconceivable.

Calvin also wrote a commentary on *I Corinthians 15*. He fully admits that the tenet of resurrection is repugnant to the human reason – 'Does not our whole cast of mind reject it as incredible, even as absurd in the extreme?' We can certainly agree with him here. However Calvin ploughs straight in, and tries to overcome the question of the nature of the resurrected body by drawing a distinction between 'animation' and 'inspiration': the body is currently animated, which represents a frail kind of vitality requiring food, clothing, sleep, and drink; but the power of the Spirit will dispense with such needs by conferring a far superior kind of vitality. 'This', contends Calvin, 'is the straightforward natural meaning of the Apostle's words; and should prevent people from getting lost any longer in airy speculations. This is what happens to those who think that the substance of the body will be spiritual; when the fact is that no mention is made of its substance, and it will undergo no change.' Calvin's presentation is perhaps more ingenious than Luther's, but he tries to slip out of the question of the body's substance by saying that it must remain the same because no mention is made of any change, in spite of the fact that it has manifestly changed in every other respect. So we are no further forward than with Luther.

Later Protestant creeds stick to the positions outlined by Luther and Calvin: for instance the second Helvetic Confession of 1566 defines the body as the temple of the Holy Spirit which they truly believe will rise at the Last Day. The faithful, after death, go directly to Christ, and therefore do not stand in need of help or prayers from the living; while unbelievers are cast headlong into hell, where the living can be of no avail – hence any intercession is superfluous. Apparitions of spirits are counted among the delusions, crafts and deceits of the devil, who is labouring tooth and nail to overthrow the true faith, or else to call it into doubt. The Westminster Confession of 1646 takes a similar line:

> The bodies of men, after death, return to dust and see corruption; but their souls (which neither die nor sleep) having an immortal substance,

immediately return to God who gave them ... the souls of the righteous are received into the highest heaven and behold the face of God in light and glory, waiting for the full redemption of their bodies; and the souls of the wicked are cast into hell, where they remain in torments and utter darkness ... at the Last Day, such as are found alive shall not die, but be changed; and all the dead shall be raised up with the selfsame bodies and none other, although with different qualities, which shall be united again to their souls for ever.

Both creeds offer only the two stark alternatives of heaven or hell after death. Purgatory has been eliminated and the Helvetic Confession makes it quite clear that intercession is of no use. Ultimately the abolition of purgatory became an embarrassment to Protestantism, as there could be no half measures and second chances. In the Victorian era the notion of hell gradually became a stumbling block to belief, especially among the workers, and intellectuals began to feel increasingly uneasy about the Gospel teaching of eternal punishment in the light of their idea of a good and benevolent God; they tried to reinterpret the word eternal in order to alter the sense of Jesus's warning in Matthew. On the other hand the belief in hell was thought to be essential if morality were not to collapse. As one commentator put it: 'The fear of hell is a powerful deterrent to many educated as well as uneducated, and many a sin would be committed were it not for the wholesome dread of eternal misery before a sinner's eyes.' It is interesting to note, in passing, that the logic here is identical to that used in our day by proponents of capital punishment. Rowell points out that by 1880 the debate had shifted from the issue of whether or not eternal punishment was taught in the Gospels to that of the moral defensibility of the idea: whether it was consistent with contemporary ideas of progress and humanitarianism. In other words the question became one of marketing: the idea was rapidly becoming a sales liability – it might, therefore, be advisable to drop it quietly. The decline in the effectiveness of the idea of hell proved to be the precursor of other changes in attitude which have tended to remove from the individual the onus of responsibility for his own actions – these can now be accounted for ostensibly by some quirk in the person's upbringing. The pendulum has swung to the other extreme: we can claim the liberty to do what we like, but reserve the right to pass the consequences on elsewhere.

Alger gives a very succinct account of the articles of faith, which have gradually been eroded by the rationalists:

The plenary inspiration of the Scriptures as an ultimate authority in matters of belief; unconditional predestination; the satisfaction theory of the vicarious atonement; the visible second coming of Christ in person to burn up the world and hold a general judgement; the intermediate state of souls; the resurrection of the body; a local hell of material fire in the bowels of the earth; the eternal damnation of the wicked.

All this represents a complete reversal of general outlook, which we shall now consider from another angle by examining the genesis of the views of Descartes and his influence on his successors. We shall reserve for a later chapter the examination of the views of contemporary theologians, who achieve different compromises between the demands of faith and those of natural science.

4.

MIND AND MATTER IN THE SCIENTIFIC AND CARTESIAN FRAMEWORK

Even if the order of the world is created by our minds, our minds are a part of the universe.

RADHAKRISHNAN

Truth is a torch which gleams in the fog but does not dispel it.

HELVETIUS

Nous sommes composés d'esprit et de matière, nous ne pouvons connaître parfaitement les choses simples, spirituelles ou corporelles. [We are made up of spirit and matter and we cannot attain perfect knowledge of simple, spiritual or bodily things]

PASCAL

Men's categories changed; the things they took for granted changed.
Everything followed from that.

HULME

It is customary but misleading to begin any consideration of modern philosophical views with Descartes's *cogito*; one cannot suppose that Descartes lived *in vacuo*, uninfluenced by his antecedents and the prevailing climate of thought in his day. Descartes's influence still reverberates today, especially when considering the mind/body problem where his dualism is taken as the starting point of many contemporary discussions. Before tracing some of the more prominent of his precursors, we shall outline some of the major shifts in perspective which have occurred between the medieval and modern outlook; these need to be borne in mind when examining the development of scientific and philosophical thought.

1. The idea of the providential government of the universe through divine interference has gradually given way to explanations based on physical cause and effect; more recently, Russell and the French geneticist Monod have suggested the two principles of chance and necessity. Most evolutionists, except followers of Teilhard de Chardin, have dropped the Newtonian Clockmaker argument for the existence of God, and thus the concept of a God guiding the process of evolution. The intractable problems of evil and suffering have further eroded confidence in the plausibility of a benevolent deity, to the extent that some modern theologians like Bonhoeffer even base their view of the world on the absence of God.

2. Views on the relation between man and nature have undergone a parallel transformation, which is succinctly expressed by E.A. Burtt:

> Just as it was thoroughly natural for medieval thinkers to view nature as subservient to man's knowledge, purpose, and destiny, so now it has become natural to view her as existing and operating in her own self-contained independence, and so far as man's ultimate relation to her is clear at all, to consider his knowledge and purpose somehow produced by her, and his destiny wholly dependent on her.

The transformation has involved shifting man and the earth from the central point in the universe to a remote periphery, where he seems to himself, at least from a scientific angle, to be a chance by-product of nature. He has come to appreciate his physical insignificance with regard to vast vistas of space and time; the universe is inconceivably large in relation to man, and the process of evolution spans back into the unfathomable past. As Jung points out, a philosophy based on physical science turns man into a mass particle, a valueless exception to be considered only in the context of the whole, not in his own right.

3. We have already discussed the nineteenth-century decline in the belief in hell; this was, in turn, related to a change in the view of the innate nature of man. In the Middle Ages man was regarded as radically imperfect and tainted, perhaps irredeemably, by original sin: so that salvation was only available if the believer confessed himself to be a miserable sinner and cast himself on the mercy of God. Rousseau's idea of the noble savage corrupted by society was one of the most powerful influences in altering this conception, even if one disputes his claim that the savage was innocent – it is plausible to consider him amoral. Man and society were thought to be capable of attaining some kind of perfection on earth, albeit only in the very long term. The dogma of original sin was replaced by a new faith in the inherent potential of man towards good, even if guilt and evil remained only too apparent.

4. If the logical extension of the dogma of original sin and its contempt for the body was monastic asceticism and renunciation, then the decline of the dogma has led to a diminishing respect for the value of ascetic practices, except in special institutions. The individual is suspicious of the narrowness of the puritan outlook which condemns many of the activities that he enjoys; he is encouraged to work towards the more or less immediate gratification of his needs rather than postponing or even disposing of them; indeed the consumer economy depends for its very survival on the perpetuation of such an attitude. Camus's passionate espousal of this-worldly and humanistic values typifies twentieth-century suspicion and intolerance of any outlook which devalues the present world by subordinating it to another.

5. The social aspect of the above drift away from original sin appears in the transformation from quietism to activism: if the hopes of the individual are focused on post-mortem salvation, then his incentive to better the lot of his fellows on earth is bound to be curtailed, if not eliminated. Marx and Engels express the key point here by contending

that the job of the philosopher is not simply to interpret the world, but to change it; when combined with a materialistic philosophy which abolishes the possibility of personal immortality, the chief concern of the fervent atheist revolutionary is no longer his own post-mortem salvation, but the achievement of utopia on earth. Progress and evolution no longer operate in relation to the individual's eternal destiny, but in terms of society as a whole at some indeterminate time in the future.

6. The medieval outlook provided a framework of absolute moral values, with clearly defined notions of right and wrong and consequences for those who refused to toe the line. This was gradually eroded and qualified until the modern attitude of 'everything is relative' was reached. The behaviourist attributes crime to a deprived or faulty social environment, the individual is exonerated from the consequences of his actions (at any rate up to a point), and the idea of moral responsibility atrophies.

7. For our purposes, however, the most important development was the reaction against authority and religious tradition in favour of observation and experiment as the criteria of truth. The principal medieval authorities in the sphere of ideas were the Scriptures and Aristotle, both of which sources were drawn upon by Aquinas, as we have seen. In his discussion of the conflict between Galileo and the Inquisition, Russell points out that the essence of the dispute was between the spirit of deduction and that of induction: the deductive approach necessitates finding premises of knowledge somewhere, usually in a sacred book or in some ancient authority. Once these premises have been agreed on, they provide a ready-made yardstick with which to judge new issues. For instance the book of Genesis states that the world was created in seven days; and because the book represents the infallible word of God, any rival theory must be wrong and can be condemned as heretical; similarly it would be a Marxian heresy in our own day to doubt the truth of dialectical materialism. The inductive approach is by no means foolproof, but it is based on empirical observation, from which the inference of a general law can be drawn; and, even if the authority of certain 'laws' appears beyond question, further observation and experiment may result in modification of an existing hypothesis. The dispute between the two factions is rendered all the more acrimonious when the inductive approach questions the premises of the deductive since, by definition, no empirical justification can be offered

for an infallible authority; the deductive defender can only fall back on faith or force.

Whitehead devotes a revealing chapter in his *Science and the Modern World* to mathematics as an element in the history of thought. In the seventeenth century some of the most important scientific and philosophical thinkers were mathematicians of the first rank – Galileo, Spinoza, Newton, and Leibniz. Whitehead starts by pointing out that mathematics itself signals a level of abstraction which indicates a landmark in human intellectual advance: number was initially related only to groups of concrete objects such as oranges or fishes, or even days of the year. The advance consists of relating the notion of three oranges to three days, and subsequently to the ability to manipulate the numbers without reference to concrete particulars. Thus pure mathematics moves towards pure abstraction; absolute certainty and proof are obtainable within the limits of this self-contained world. But such absolute certainty cannot be extended to our relation with the external world of concrete objects.

Whitehead singles out the mathematical notions of functionality and periodicity as especially influential: functionality was developed through algebra and calculus, and stressed the relationship of various factors to each other; while periodicity (in abstract terms) arose partly from trigonometry with its deductions of the relations of angles of a right-angled triangle to ratios between the sides and hypotenuse of a triangle. In conjunction, these two factors were broadened out into the study of abstract periodic functions which were exemplified by the ratios of the triangle: *thus the notion moved into the realms of abstraction, from whence it would be re-applied to such commonsense periodicities or recurrences as seasons or lunar phases.* Whitehead comments that 'mathematics supplied the background of imaginative thought with which the men of science approached the observation of nature.' Common sense suffices to establish the existence of recurrences, but more detailed analysis is required if their exact nature is to be determined. Knowledge would be impossible without recurrence. Measurement leads in turn to classification, which Whitehead describes as the halfway house between the immediate concreteness of the individual thing and the complete abstraction of the mathematical notion.

Aristotle's logic is based on classification of syllogisms, but his science is only partly based on observation: for instance he asserted that men had more teeth than women without even looking inside his wife's mouth to verify the contention. Classification can be based on inductive or deductive principles: the deductive framework may classify actions as right or wrong in accordance with some pre-established canon, while the empirical observer classifies his specimens according to the criteria of the experiment – he may be examining colour or differentiation of some function. We shall see that classification acquires an empirical rather than an *a priori* basis as science proceeds, except in cases where scientists decide that it is their duty to defend a thesis, for instance materialism, as if it were an *a priori* truth. With this background we are now in a position to trace some of the precursors of Descartes.

With the decline of Hellenic civilisation, science was pursued by the Arabs, mainly in North Africa. Some of the scientists, however, found themselves up against ecclesiastical defenders of Moslem orthodoxy. The most contentious and influential of these men was Averroes, who was born in Cordova in 1126. He still held the teachings of Aristotle in great esteem, and like him posited the immortality of the intellect (*nous*) and not of the soul *per se*. His most significant distinction was between religious and philosophical truth: the dogmas of religion might be true in religious terms but false from the standpoint of reason and demonstration. This might enable Averroes to hold one opinion during the week and another on the Sabbath, but it was scarcely likely to satisfy either the pure theologian or the pure scientist, both of whom would regard their own approach as uniquely valid. Nevertheless his doctrine was widely influential in the thirteenth century and was taught in the universities of Southern Italy, Paris and Oxford.

Roger Bacon (*c*.1214-*c*.1294) was far more empirical in his approach than most of his contemporaries, even if he did write on and practise a form of alchemy. He has been described as encyclopaedic if unsystematic in his learning, but he did place great emphasis on experiment as a means of gaining knowledge. He was reputedly the originator of the experiment of putting a lighted lamp under a bell-jar and observing its extinction; it is interesting that he inferred that there was a kind of air which extinguishes flame, thus mistakenly attributing the cause of extinction to the presence rather than the absence of an element. Despite this error, Draper is impressed by the clarity of his views on gases 'for an age which mistook the gases for leather-eared ghosts'. His views on the causes of ignorance are of considerable interest: the example of frail authority, the influence of custom (both of these were levelled at Aristotle), the opinion of the unlearned crowed (those who disagree with him), and the concealment of one's ignorance behind a display of apparent wisdom. This last cause is said to be the most mis-leading and dangerous, as it not only obstructs the path of knowledge but also bolsters and defends the self-esteem. Bacon's impatience with humbug, unfounded authority and tradition, together with his com-mitment to experiment, mark him out as an important figure in the history of thought.

William of Occam, who lived in the first half of the thirteenth cen-tury, is best known for the so-called maxim of 'Occam's razor', which states that 'entities are not to be multiplied without necessity'. Russell contends that what he really said was 'It is vain to do with more what can be done with fewer', a substantially identical statement. Occam is not to be regarded as a forerunner of Descartes in so far as his main concern was to give the true interpretation of Aristotle in the face of the proliferation of abstractions which had sprung up in his name; Oc-cam was arguing that one should opt for the simplest explanation of a given phenomenon, and therefore shun 'unnecessary complications'. As we shall see, the principle of the non-multiplication of hypotheses has been raised to the level of a scientific incantation, so that it is ar-bitrarily invoked in order to dispose of inconvenient facts, which do not fall within the scope of an existing theory. It can, therefore, lead to over-simplification, and explanations which reduce complex events to a 'nothing-but' cause.

It is worth pointing out, at this stage, that the very development of logical and exact thought by the early medieval theologians carried the seeds of its own destruction, since the logical technique can be applied on the basis of different premises and to areas beyond theolo-gy; thus the very virtuosity of Aquinas can be turned against himself. The scholastic tradition also implanted into the minds of its practition-ers the idea of the uniformity and regularity of occurrences in terms of general principles underlying the phenomena; the same process as was evident in seventeenth-century mathematics. As Dampier puts it:

> As soon as they had thrown off the shackles of scholastic authority, the men of the Renaissance used the lessons which the Scholastic method had taught them. They began observing in the faith that nature was consistent and intelligible, and, when they had framed hypotheses by induction to explain their observations, they deduced, by logical reasoning, consequences which could be tested by experiment. Scholasticism had trained them to destroy itself.

It was during the life of Leonardo da Vinci (1452-1519) that some of the most important developments of the Renaissance occurred: the invention of the mariner's compass made extensive geographical exploration possible, leading to Columbus's discovery of America in 1492. Before setting sail he had been confuted by the Council of Salamanca on the authority of the Bible and the early fathers who argued that 'the rotundity of the earth would present a kind of mountain up which it was impossible for him to sail, even with the fairest wind' – a contention which displays a singular lack of imagination as the roundness of the earth could be regarded as a downhill slope from another angle. Thirty years later Magellan circumnavigated the globe, thus proving once and for all that the flat-earthers were mistaken: fact was beginning to gain ascendancy over authority. Another invention of the first importance was that of the printing press in the 1470s, which ultimately enabled the translated Bible to be read in languages other than Latin and Greek; men could see for themselves what was written and could form their own opinions instead of taking the words of the priest as canonical. Later development of biblical criticism went a long way towards undermining the authority of the church and stressing the validity of the individual opinion, which Descartes made the starting point of his philosophy.

Leonardo himself was the first important figure to work in almost complete emancipation from theological preconceptions; even Bacon had regarded theology as the highest form of knowledge. Leonardo wrote no systematic treatise on scientific method, so that what we know of his various researches has been gleaned from the extant notebooks. He maintained that the different branches of mathematics could provide certainty within their own realm, but that science itself began with observation not with *a priori* reasoning. In a similar vein to Bacon, he declared that 'those sciences are vain and full of errors which are not born from experiment, the mother of all certainty, and which do not end with one clear experiment'. He applied this method to various fields, including astronomy, where he rejected Aristotle's theory of incorruptible heavenly bodies in favour of the idea of a celestial machine operating in conformity with clear laws. He was the first to indicate the true nature of fossils as animal remains. He procured bodies for dissection, and made detailed drawings of various limbs; he studied aspects of physiology such as the valves and muscles in the heart; and, a hundred years before Harvey, understood the general principle of the circulation of the blood, which he compared with the circulation of water from hills to rivers to sea and back to hills again. So, as well as strengthening the case for systematic observation of nature, Leonardo applied this method to many different fields.

The Copernican hypothesis that the sun was at the centre of the planetary system was first advanced by Aristarchus in the third century BC, but was not taken seriously by many leading thinkers in the interim; the immediate evidence of the senses militated strongly against it. Copernicus himself, being an orthodox Catholic, did not allow his epoch-making work to be published until after his death in 1543. He had arrived at his hypothesis by a combination of mathematics and observation, and appealed to those to whom he disclosed his theory during his lifetime on the grounds of elegance and simplicity in his mathematical formulations; some aspects, such as the conjecture of the circular orbit of the planets, were later modified and corrected by Kepler. There was opposition to Copernicus's scheme on two counts: first from the theologians, who disputed his conclusions on the grounds that they conflicted with Holy Scripture. Luther's crushing rejoinder was that Joshua had told the sun, not the earth, to stand still. The empiricists of the day also raised objections which can only be understood when one remembers that Newton was not born until a hundred years after Copernicus's death: they argued that the part of his theory which held the earth rotating on its axis could not be true because a body thrown upward landed in exactly the same place, and loose objects on the earth did not fly away into space. The theory itself had to await empirical justification from Galileo.

Galileo Galilei (1565-1642) is regarded, along with Bruno, as one of the great martyrs in the cause of science, even if he did not share Bruno's fate at the stake. Perhaps his most important experiments were in the field of dynamics; in 1591 he dropped two unequal weights from the top of the leaning tower of Pisa: to the astonishment of the onlookers and the dismay of the Aristotelian professors, the two weights arrived at the ground simultaneously. Moreover, it was significant that the experiment was repeatable on a number of occasions. From the Copernican angle, Galileo's development of the telescope was more crucial, as it enabled him to discover innumerable stars until then invisible to the naked eye. Then in 1610 he discovered four of the moons of Jupiter, which, he thought, provided a miniature model of the solar system. The observation delighted the astronomers, but was greeted by the ecclesiastics as an optical illusion, a deliberate fraud or even as sheer blasphemy. The culmination of their absurd logic was the assertion that, since the pretended satellites were invisible to the naked eye, they must be useless and therefore non-existent. In 1632 Galileo published a defence of the Copernican system of astronomy, and once again drew the attention of the Inquisition who demanded that he should abjure the views expressed in the work. The propositions – that the sun was the centre of our universe and that the earth rotates and is not the centre of our universe – were condemned as 'absurd, philosophically false, and formally heretical'. But the action was a rearguard one: observation and experiment were now being established as criteria of truth.

One of the most immediate influences on Descartes was Harvey (1578-1657) who published his book on the heart and circulation of the blood in 1628, nine years before the appearance of Descartes's *Meditations*. He arrived at his theory at the end of a meticulous series of observations: 'I finally saw that the blood, forced by the action of the left ventricle into the arteries, was distributed to the body at large and its various parts.' Harvey was on intimate terms with Charles I, and followed the king in his first campaign; it is said that he did not take part in the Battle of Edgehill but wisely remained on the periphery of the action by sitting under a hedge and reading a book.

We have now sketched in enough background to be able to appreciate the contribution of Descartes (1596-1650), who showed how much unverified assumption underlay even the testimony of the senses and therefore of observation. The two most general principles, which he elaborated, were scepticism and individualism: he cast doubt on all phenomena (although he remained religiously orthodox) and sought to discover what he could not doubt. In the end he concluded that he could not doubt his own existence, at any rate when he was thinking about it. This, in turn, led to the individualism in his approach, as his starting point was not God but himself as a thinking being. Descartes was doing for philosophy what Copernicus and Galileo had done for astronomy: both God and the earth were removed from the centre of the stage, and were replaced by a conception of man the potential individual rather than man the fallen sinner.

Descartes's understanding of the body arose from his knowledge of anatomy, a study which he recommends to his readers as a preliminary to reading his views. He regards all living bodies as machines of varying degrees of complexity, within which organs operate according to design and disposition. The difference between a man-made machine and the human body is one of degree of perfection.

The body is regarded as a machine which, having been made by the hands of God, is incomparably better arranged, and possesses in itself movements which are much more admirable than any of those which can be invented by man.

The essence of all living bodies is said to be extension in space, in other words visible form. Descartes then proceeds to argue that if a machine was so designed as to resemble exactly the form of a monkey, there would be no way of distinguishing between the machine and the monkey. But the same would not hold for human beings. If a machine identical in appearance to our bodies were designed, it would still fail two crucial tests of humanity: it could never use speech constructively, and it could not act creatively from knowledge. This amounts to saying that the distinguishing trait of a man, even in an idiot, is some degree of reasoning power; if parrots are able to speak, they clearly have the necessary vocal equipment, but one can hardly then argue that they have any understanding of the exact nature of what they are saying.

We have seen that the Greek atomists thought that the soul was a compound of heat and light, and the cause of movement. This was inferred from the observation that dead bodies were cold and immobile. Descartes does not reach the same conclusion as the atomists but contends, instead, that the cause of death is the cessation of heat in the body together with the decay of some one of its principle parts. If Descartes were to attribute the essence of the human soul to some principle of vitality, he would find it hard to draw any distinction between man and the animals. But, as we have established, he asserts that the distinguishing characteristic of the human being is his reason. Thus, like Aristotle, he says that human beings have indestructible rational souls. In contrast with the world of extended matter, the essence of the human being is defined as follows:

I know that I exist, and at the same time I observe absolutely nothing else except the mere fact that I am a conscious being; and just from this I can validly infer that my essence consists simply in the fact that I am a conscious being. It is indeed possible (or rather, as I shall say later on, it is certain) that I have a body closely bound up with myself; but at the same time I have, on the one hand, a clear and distinct idea of myself taken simply as a conscious, not an extended, being; and, on the other hand, a distinct idea of a body, taken simply as an extended, not a conscious, being; so it is certain that I am really distinct from my body, and could exist without it.

On the grounds that he has two separate clear and distinct ideas, Descartes draws a sharp distinction between two kinds of being through the use of his reason. Although his kind of dualism has many antecedents, this is the first time that it is advanced in such a concise logical form, appealing to the knowledge and introspection of the reader, who may well disagree that the ability to conceive of the self apart from the body entails the possibility of its separate existence. We shall return to this point below.

Reverting now to his considerations on the differences between man and animals, Descartes argues that the rational soul could not possibly have been derived from matter, since conscious being is not extended like matter: it must therefore have been expressly created. He then warns (prophetically, as it happens) that 'feeble spirits' may be led from the path of virtue if they imagine that the souls of brutes are of the same nature as those of men 'and that in consequence after this life we have nothing to fear or hope for, any more than flies or ants'. The man who has investigated and appreciated the enormous differences between them (he continues) will conclude that the nature of the soul is entirely different from the body and therefore not liable to perish with it. Finally, Descartes states that since we can observe no other cause, which might destroy the soul, we must conclude that it is immortal. His arguments here hinge on his definition of the soul as unextended, and therefore its being unaffected by processes applying to matter; and it is interesting to note that he actually assumes that the burden of proof is on those who wish to demonstrate that the soul does *not* survive – a far cry from the twentieth-century view.

Descartes's argument for the immortality of the soul falls into two stages: reflection or self-awareness convinces him that conscious being can be thought of apart from the body; if it can be conceived of apart from the body, then it cannot share the body's attribute of material extension, and must be immaterial; and if it is immaterial, it cannot be subject to bodily decay and must necessarily survive the death of the body. Thus, with some logical elaboration, the basis of Descartes's argument is man's ability to conceive of himself as a distinct conscious entity, and the corresponding inability of this conscious entity to imagine itself as non-existent: man's self-awareness is defined as his soul. We shall see a similar formulation, dismissed as unsound, in Freud. A

materialist such as Lucretius might admit Descartes's distinction between thought and the body, but would counter his assertion of immortality by pointing out that after bodily death there can be neither
sensation nor self-awareness, therefore the 'soul' perishes with the
body. The assumption that consciousness could be derived from matter, because it is clearly seen in association with it, would complete the
consistency of this outlook and effectively destroy Descartes's *a priori*
approach. Any attack on materialism must be more empirical than this.

The most common criticism levelled at the Cartesian approach focuses on his conception of the interaction of soul and body. Although
he asserts that the soul is unextended, he does say that it is joined to
the whole of the body and exercises its functions more particularly
through the pineal gland; this is in accordance with his own theory
about the role of the brain in sensation, but has not stood up to any
advance in physiological research, which finds the seat of consciousness in the cerebral cortex. The self, Descartes argues, is not present in
the body like a pilot in a ship (this was Plato's view), but is much more
tightly bound to it: the pilot in the ship does not actually feel any damage sustained by the structure, while the self can have no sensations
apart from the body, and perceives all sensations running through it.
The problem of interaction is thrown into sharp relief by Popper: the
Cartesian view is that all bodies are machines moved by the physical
causality of mechanical push, with the sole exception of the human
body in voluntary movement; if the soul is immaterial, then how can
it affect the material body in any way? Many subsequent philosophers
as we shall see, regard the idea of the immaterial acting on the material as unintelligible; they therefore attempt to make out that the soul
is a function of the body (in which case the interaction is between two
sorts of material) or else they reformulate the idea of interaction.

In addition to the problem of psycho-physical interaction outlined
above, the influence of Descartes was felt in two other domains. First,
he completed the separation of the vital from the thinking principles:
the original Greek interpretation of *psyche* was as the principle of life
or vitality, but by the time of Aristotle this conception had been refined
to include the rational principle, in conjunction with the animal and
vegetative principles, the first being the distinguishing characteristic of
human beings; we have seen how Descartes follows this classification.
The vegetative principle is common to all forms of life and survived as
the vital force of vitalistic physiologists; it is used in a modified form by
Bergson. Second, by asserting the purely mechanical nature of animal

behaviour and bodies, Descartes laid the foundations for a mechanistic account of man himself, thus undermining his own original position. We shall find the fullest expression of this view in the behaviourist psychology of Watson: man is seen as a sophisticated kind of automaton.

Hobbes (1588-1679) was one of Descartes's first critics, and wrote a series of objections to various parts of the *Meditations*. After the plague and the fire of London, a committee appointed to look into the causes of such dire misfortunes found that they had been incurred as a result of divine displeasure, one of the chief sources of which was the materialistic outlook expressed by Hobbes; it was therefore decreed that no more of his works should be published in England. Hobbes restricted his definition of life to motion originated by some part within the body-machine (using Descartes formulation); this enabled him to make the glib claim that all machines have artificial life – 'for what is the heart but a spring, and the nerves, but so many strings; and the joints but so many wheels, giving motion to the whole body, such as was intended by the artificer?' Sensation, he argues, is caused by the impress of some external body or object on the appropriate sense-organ, and stuff (matter or atoms) is defined as the only substance existing in the universe. Hence Hobbes considers the idea of an incorporeal substance to be a contradiction in terms; he is equally scathing about the notion that essences such as Aristotle's *nous* can exist apart from the body. Man was created jointly as body and soul, so that his present form is the only conceivable one. Paradoxical as it might seem, this form of thoroughgoing materialism enables Hobbes to hold the doctrine of bodily resurrection which, like the theologians, he holds possible through the omnipotence of God: 'Cannot God, that raised inanimate dust and clay to a living creature by his word, as easily raise a dead carcass to life again, and continue him alive for ever?' This position is quite logical, if somewhat unconventional and no doubt embarrassing to the theologians, since mechanical man could hardly be held responsible for the fall and therefore the original sin. Hobbes's importance lies in his development of the mechanical side of Descartes's philosophy, even if the inspiration came less directly from Descartes himself than from Hobbes's own study of Galileo's mechanics and dynamics.

Spinoza (1632-77) held that God was the only substance, and that the Cartesian attributes of thought and extension were to be considered as God as Thinking Being and God as Extended Being, He focuses his criticism of Descartes on the contention that the soul functions through the pineal gland, a statement which he finds not only disappointing but frankly incredible. He further observes that Descartes had laid down that nothing is to be inferred except from self-evident truths, and yet he advances as an explanation of the interaction of soul and body a 'hypothesis more occult than the most occult quality' which renders the idea unintelligible. Spinoza's own answer is to assert that mind and body are the same thing, conceived of respectively as thought and extension of divine substance. He attributes a certain 'sagacity' to the body and points out that animals and sleepwalkers can accomplish complicated actions in the absence of reason, examples which indicate that Spinoza did not seem to appreciate the difference between reason and instinct. He completes his hypothesis by contending that 'the dictates of the mind are but another name for the appetites', that everyone shapes his actions according to his emotions, and that mental decision and bodily appetite are simultaneous in operation. This view is the first form of parallelism, which postulates that each mental impulse has a physical correlate and each physical a mental one. It is the precursor of the twentieth-century mind/brain identity hypothesis, which claims that mental and physical processes are two aspects of the same thing.

Both Spinoza and Leibniz (1646-1716) reacted against 'occasionalism', the earliest solution to the Cartesian interaction problem. This theory was developed by Malebranche (1638-1715) after an extensive study of Descartes. He came to the conclusion that the qualities of the body cannot have anything in common with those of the mind, so that there could be no question of direct mutual interaction. Malebranche then argued that both body and mind participate in God, 'who is the true cause of the mutual adaptation of their modifications'. From this he proceeds to postulate that God causes thoughts to arise in the mind on the occasion of bodily movements; similarly, when the mind wishes to move the body, God (who according to Descartes cannot be a deceiver) accomplishes the move. Thus physical causation is abolished as an explanation of the relations between mind and body, but only at the price of an apparently miraculous intervention by God. Leibniz remarks caustically that the difficulty of the interaction problem has been penetrated by showing us what cannot take place – it will not do to produce a *deus ex machina* as a solution to this intractable problem.

Leibniz then proceeds to develop his own form of parallelism which, in contrast to Spinoza, is based not on God as the only real substance, but contends that each individual or monad (from the Euclidian *monas*, meaning a point in space) has its reality independent of God. He takes

Descartes's starting point of matter as extension, but fills it with forces equated with mind-like substances able to act on matter (this is naturally a simplification of a theory which is developed at some length). The clearest illustration of Leibniz's own theory of soul and body is his analogy of the two clocks, which he supposes to be in perfect agreement. He postulates three possible explanations of this accord: first, that of natural influence whereby synchronisation takes place, as in an experiment in which two pendulums hung from the same piece of wood eventually adjust themselves; second, a skilled craftsman might make constant adjustments, which Leibniz terms the 'way of assistance' or the *deus ex machina* of the occasionalist theory; and the third possibility, proposed by himself, is that of pre-established harmony, whereby the two substances were created in such a way that, while each follows its own laws, each is in perfect harmony with the other *as if* mutual influence were taking place. It seems that Leibniz's theory gets no further than that of Malebranche; it solves the interaction problem by removing it altogether into the realms of unverifiable metaphysics. God is invoked on a new basis, but is still used to plug an incomprehensible gap; the *a priori* element in this theory will also make the empiricist feel uneasy.

Locke (1632-1704) followed the Cartesian scheme that there are two radically different kinds of substances – extended material substances and unextended mental substances. These ideas are derived from our experience as human beings, which Locke sees as complexes of these two substances, united by causal connections which run in both directions: mind influences and is influenced by matter. However he asserts that we are unable to perceive the nature of extension (matter) any more clearly than that of thought; all we have are the simple ideas derived from sensation and reflection, so that we are only directly aware of the ideas which objects cause in our minds, not of themselves. Locke states that we can infer the existence of the objects perceived precisely because they cause the perceptual sensations in our minds. God is defined as an infinite mental substance but plays no direct part in the interaction between the two substances. Locke retains an open mind on the question of God having superadded to matter another substance capable of thinking, so that he could not rule out the kind of mechanical materialism attributed to Newton. Newton himself reconciled himself officially to religion by means of the argument from design for the existence of God: the usual analogy used is that of a clock implying a maker; in a similar way the design of the earth was thought to bear the stamp of God. More recently it has been pointed out that this argument depends on the point of view of the observer and calls God to account for a good deal of suffering and misery. Newton's theory of gravity completed the work of Galileo and Kepler, and his science, ironically in the light of his religious views, became the basis of a mechanical view of nature, which was later extended to account for man as well. Thus Newton suffered the same fate as Descartes: although he himself was not an atheist, his arguments were employed to bolster the materialist position.

The Irish Bishop Berkeley (1685-1753) might be surprised to learn of his contemporary political significance in that his writings are proscribed in certain Eastern European countries as they contradict the basis of dialectical materialism. But in his own day he directed his fire against Locke, whose philosophy, he thought, contained the seeds of scepticism and atheism. The charge of scepticism rested on Berkeley's opinion that it is unintelligible that the mind should be able to know a substance radically different from itself: Locke attributed existence to extended non-mental objects, whether or not the mind was aware of them, and distinguished between the so-called primary and secondary qualities of an object. The primary characteristics were those of extension and solidity, existing independently of the perceived mind; while the secondary qualities were those such as colour or fragrance, which, it was contended, were added by the mind in perception. Berkeley argued that such a distinction between primary and secondary qualities was false, and that the existence of external objects was as ideas in the mind, of which we could be certain; We could not achieve the same degree of certainty if we did not consider the reality of objects as ideas rather than entities independent of the mind. Thus Berkeley abolished matter as a separate substance, and subsumed it under the category of the mental, which he took to be ultimate reality. Locke had argued that material objects were the cause of perception. For Berkeley this is inconceivable, since the material cannot be the cause of the mental; the passive and inert cannot move the active. It is at this point that God is invoked to account for perception and the continuing existence of objects in the material world. For Berkeley it is in God that 'we live and move and have our being'. Thus it is contended that objects exist in the mind of God and are known by Him, perception being the impressing of God on the mind of objects in nature, which already and continually exist in His mind. This doctrine may strike us as strange and far-fetched, but for Berkeley it seemed much more probable that

God, as a mental entity, should be able to impress mental contents on the mind than that a physical object should do so of itself. This scheme disposes of both scepticism and atheism: it is certain that material objects exist as ideas in the mind, and it is posited that the cause of these ideas is not in the objects themselves, but is God.

As for the mind itself, Berkeley's original idea was similar to Hume's formulation of a bundle of perceptions; in other words the mind is nothing beyond the aggregate of its states and perceptions, there being nothing underlying these. However, he came to think of ideas as passive and the mind as active, having been impressed by the unity and permanence of the mind's activity; he realised that it was something different from an idea and came to equate it with the will, which is itself certainly not an idea. Thus he states that:

> Besides all that endless variety of ideas or objects of knowledge, there is likewise something which knows or perceives them, and exercises divers operations, as willing, imagining, remembering about them. This perceiving active being is what I call *mind, spirit, soul* or *my self.*

The essence of the mind is perception and activity (Berkeley draws no distinction between this term and spirit/soul/self) but it is unknowable because it is not an idea as such; we are immediately aware of it. Nowhere does Berkeley elaborate on the immortality of the soul, but it is taken for granted in view of the traditional associations of immateriality and incorruptibility. He reinforces its plausibility with his remarks on the resurrection; he states that 'Eternity is only a train of innumerable ideas. Hence the immortality of ye soul I easily conceived', and argues that the behaviour of the disciples testifies to the resurrection, as they would have needed very strong evidence at the time; this last argument sounds rather like special pleading and an extension of Berkeley's own canons of evidence. However this is not the pivot of his influence, which lies in his championing of the primacy of the mental, treated as the only fundamental substance; he stands against both the materialism of Hobbes and the dualist interactionism of Descartes and Locke.

The main concern of Bishop Butler (1692-1752) was to counter the prevailing rationalist deism of his day whereby the attributes of a God of nature are discoverable by reason and whose laws are the embodiments of reason; the effect was to undermine the authority of his historical revelation. Besides the belief in God, the belief in a soul is the other primary article of natural religion. Butler followed a contemporary controversy between Clarke and Collins and sided with Clarke in asserting the unity and separate existence of the soul. He devoted the first chapter of his *Analogy of Religion* to discussing the question of a future life. Here he aimed to combat the materialist view that the idea of a future life is inherently improbable, and that the living powers will be destroyed at death. He starts by pointing out that our living powers have operated since birth in spite of considerable changes in bodily form. The arguments for the destruction of the living powers by death must rest, he asserts, on two grounds: the nature of death, or the analogy of nature. Of the nature of death itself nothing is known – we know only of its effects – and in addition we cannot be sure of the exact basis of the living powers, which are suspended, but not destroyed, in sleep. From the analogy of nature he argues that we can be none the wiser about the persistence of the living powers of animals than we are of our own. Butler's agnosticism, or appeal *ad ignorantiam*, must apply both to animals and humans if it is to remain consistent. He goes on to argue (like Berkeley) that consciousness is indivisible and that the body is no part of himself, so that he has no reason to believe that the destruction of the body entails the annihilation of himself. He attempts to reinforce this by contending that the loss of a limb does not affect our powers of perception or action, and that a mortal disease may leave our faculties unimpaired until the moment of death; this is clearly special pleading, as he selects instances which confirm his views while conveniently ignoring less favourable cases. Throughout his analysis Butler never asserts that he positively holds the opinions set forth, but simply that his proposed scheme is not unreasonable in the light of experience and probability. The weakness of his approach is pinpointed by Stephen who asserts that Butler 'by dwelling exclusively upon the absence of direct contradiction, and sinking the absence of confirmation, converts absolute ignorance into the likeness of some degree of positive knowledge'. He also sets himself up as a target for Hume.

Hume (1711-76) was one of the greatest philosophical iconoclasts: both the self and causality appear on his casualty list. His essay on the immortality of the soul was designed as a reply to Butler, and suggested that it was difficult to prove the soul's immortality by the mere light of reason; one therefore had to fall back on revelation. Hume deals with three kinds of argument, namely metaphysical, moral, and physical. Metaphysics treats the soul as immaterial, and assumes that thought

97

cannot arise from material substance. In agreement with Butler and Locke, Hume points out how confused the idea of substance is, and that matter and spirit are at bottom equally unknown. 'Abstract reasonings cannot decide any question of fact or existence,' he contends, a remark which some later philosophers would do well to note; we therefore fall back on experience, which cannot dictate whether or not thought is derivable from matter. Hume also rejects the introduction of the Supreme Cause (God) as an element of explanation, and concludes with two further observations on the soul: first that, logically, what is incorruptible must be ungenerable, so that our souls must have existed before birth – yet we are not concerned with what happened then, so why should we worry any more about what happens after death? Second, he asks why animals should not also have immaterial souls, since they function in a similar way to man. At this point the argument is structured from man to animals, whereas later versions argue from animals to men, thus tending to reduce man to the purely physical.

Hume now passes on to moral arguments, of which the chief is the necessity of an afterlife in order to redress the balance of right and wrong committed in this world; it is a vindication of divine justice, and made its first appearance among the Hebrews. Various considerations ('abstract reasonings') are advanced against this line: that God need not do what seems best for us; that our concern is centred naturally and apparently exclusively on this life, which implies 'barbarous deceit on the part of God' (one might equally well argue that this is due to the blindness of man); that heaven and hell suppose two distinct species of men, while the majority float between vice and virtue; that any idea of eternal punishment is out of all proportion to what Hume terms the frivolous indulgences of men (his own argument above of a different divine standard could be used to refute this); and finally the fact that so many die before achieving maturity tells against considering this existence as probationary.

Hume considers physical arguments to be the only philosophically admissible ones; he analyses the close correlation between the physical and the mental in a similar way to Lucretius:

> Where any two objects are so closely connected that all alterations that we have ever seen in the one are attended with proportionable alterations in the other; we ought to conclude, by all the rules of analogy, that, when there are still greater alterations produced in the former, and it is totally dissolved, there follows a total dissolution of the latter.

Sleep, a very small effect on the body, is attended with a temporary extinction, at least a great confusion in the soul. The weakness of the body and that of the mind in infancy are exactly proportioned; their vigour in manhood, their sympathetic disorder in sickness, their common gradual decay in old age. The step further seems unavoidable; their common dissolution at death.

Three further considerations are adduced in support of this argument: that forms of life when transferred out of the natural place cannot survive (a fish out of water); that the souls of animals are allowed to be mortal, so why should not the same apply to the souls of men; and that nature exhibits a constant state of flux, leading to the dissolution of existing forms. Against such contentions it might be argued that the dissolution of existing forms is only partial, for instance leaves on a tree, the life-principle never disappearing completely (the argument hinges on the nature of the connection between the new and old forms); and the analogy of a fish out of water could be countered by that of the caterpillar and the butterfly, where the new existence seems freer than the old.

Hume's analysis leaves unanswered some of the issues raised by Butler. Butler pointed out how the soul had survived birth and intervening transformation of matter in the body, so that it was not impossible that it should survive an even more traumatic change (one's answer to this question depends on one's views of the correlation between the mental and the physical, that is to say the analogy which one finds most congenial); the correlation in Hume of mind and body is oversimplified and takes no account of exceptions to the pattern; and lastly Hume ignores Butler's distinction between death and its effects – we know only of the latter. Hume does not always tackle Butler head on, but rather draws analogies, which suggest the probability of extinction in the same way as Butler's arguments tend towards the opposite conclusion. A decision one way or the other therefore becomes a question of temperament or psychology. Facts other than purely physical ones need to be adduced if a sound conclusion is to be reached.

We must now cross the Channel in order to find out what thoughts were prevalent in eighteenth-century France. The influence of Locke and Newton was exported principally by Voltaire (1694-1778), who spent some years in England and had been very favourably impressed by its spirit of tolerance and free enquiry (even if later in *Candide* he cites the summary execution of an admiral 'pour encourager les autres').

Newton was revered throughout the nation instead of being castigated as a heretic, religious tolerance was extended far more widely than in France, and inoculation was practised instead of quackery and magic. All this was reported in *Lettres philosophiques* (1734). Voltaire's views on the question of soul and body can be found in an article in his philosophical dictionary: they are broadly but inconclusively mechanistic; inconclusive because Voltaire's reaction to metaphysical speculation was usually one of exasperation. He was more concerned with morality and behaviour: 'God has given you understanding to conduct yourself well but not to penetrate the essence of what he has created.' He defines soul as the animating principle, but asserts that the limits of our intelligence mean that we can know no more than that; it is therefore a waste of time to speculate further or to try to locate the soul. Voltaire denies the separate existence of the vegetative principle, force, and instinct, and imagines a tulip reasoning that the vegetative principle was joined to its ego. Likewise he declares the ideas of a thinking atom and an immaterial being to be inconceivable, so that in the end the only criterion for the existence of the soul is faith.

A much more explicit declaration of materialism was made by La Mettrie in 1747, when he published a work entitled *L'Homme machine*, the thesis of which was described by J M Robertson as 'recklessly original'. Even though publication was originally anonymous, the author was obliged to leave Holland in a hurry; he was unable to return to France, as he had already been banned from there, so he took refuge at the court of Frederick the Great. The publisher was also called to account for his rash action, and as many copies as possible of the book were seized and destroyed. His thesis was basically that of Lucretius and Hume (which belies Robertson's remark) namely that the mental life is entirely dependent on bodily processes. But the form in which it is expressed makes it the first formulation of the so-called epiphenomenalist position, which holds that consciousness is a by-product of physical processes. Until now we have encountered theories of the causal interaction and the parallel functioning of the faculties of mind or soul and body, but La Mettrie goes further by declaring that the mind or soul derives its existence from the body, described as a very complicated machine. He states that the slaves of prejudice (probably those who disagree with him) can no more reach truth than frogs can fly, and that his approach will be based on experiment and observation. He then describes the correlations of mind and body with regard to illness, sleep, drugs (including coffee) and even climate. He compares the anatomy of man with that of animals, concluding that they are similar except that man has a larger brain, and therefore has more mind and less instinct than animals; the monkey, he claims is a small man in another form. The body as a whole can be compared to a clock, and, just as it is nonsense to talk of an immortal machine, so it is probably nonsense to speak of the immortality of man. He does, however, add a cautionary note of agnosticism by saying that our ignorance of the future is insuperable: we know more of our origins than of our destination. The explicit and detailed nature of La Mettrie's mechanical materialism would make him feel more at home in the twentieth century than in the eighteenth where his formulations were for the most part unacceptable. He is a striking forerunner of modern behaviourism.

Diderot, in his article in the *Encyclopaedia*, gives a survey of previous opinions on the soul and its relation to the body: experience leaves no room for doubting the close correlation between the two, he states, and cites at length a famous medical case involving the injury and recovery of a 2½- year-old child. He dismisses Descartes's location of the functions of the soul in the pineal glad as 'pure imagination', but advances no theory of his own to account for interaction of soul and body. He describes it as a 'fact which we cannot put in question but whose details are completely hidden from us'. His only comment on the supposed immortality of the soul is a psychological one: that the notion results from our pride. The ethos of eighteenth-century France was predominantly rationalist and optimistic about the possibilities of man and progress; although it had mechanistic leanings, following deductions from Newton, it was also deistic: it was frequently impatient of the dogmatic and doctrinaire aspects of religion, but retained its faith in God as the first cause and designer of the universe – arguments which were later disposed of by Kant.

In his *Critique of Pure Reason* Kant (1724-1804) takes up a position which he terms transcendental idealism. By this he means that objects which appear to the senses are to be considered as representations of the mind, and not as the things in themselves (a restatement of Berkeley's position); thus he is led to the conclusion that the things in themselves can never be known, our only knowledge being of our ideas of these things. He goes on to assert that space, time and causality are the categories through which we organise our experience, and in the same way as things in themselves have no existence independent of the mind. The net effect of this analysis is to unify awareness of self and objects: the self is that which experiences representations of the external world. In addition, this external world depends for its existence (at any rate from our viewpoint) on the thinking subject; however, unlike Berkeley but like Locke, Kant does argue that things in the external world can cause sensations, which make up part of the process of perception – the rest is supplied by the mind and its categories. Kant does not use the apparent independence of the thinking self as an argument for its possible continuance after death; all he does is claim that such expectations can neither be confirmed nor denied.

As for the problems of explaining the interaction of soul and body, Kant claims that the difficulties arise from regarding matter as something existing in itself rather than as a representation by the thinking self – 'the distinctive nature of those appearances of objects'. The question becomes that of linking 'the representation of inner sense with the modifications of outer sensibility', not the insoluble communion of the immaterial soul with the material world. In Kant's terms the real mystery is not the communion of soul with body, but how the thinking self attains any perception of space and things outside itself, a question which, he claims, is unanswerable. As is the case with thinking in this world, any dispute about the nature of thought before or after death must rest on the possible communion between thinking and extended being. Kant's conclusion is that the possibility cannot be either proved or disproved as it exceeds the scope of our knowledge: perception would certainly be in a different mode, by definition unknowable in the body (we shall later have reason to question this assumption, because there must be some continuity between states in and independent of the physical body if the identity is to be said to persist in any real sense). As he is unable to assert the immortality of the soul on empirical grounds, Kant claims to be able to do so on practical grounds. He argues that it is clear that the individual does not receive the just desserts of his conduct in this world, therefore, given the assumption of the justice of God (already challenged above by Hume), there must be another life which balances the accounts of this one. Kant dismisses all the traditional proofs of the existence of God, but asserts the necessity of his existence on the grounds of conscience. This argument is known as the moral argument; it assumes an anthropomorphic idea of justice, as already indicated, and can only be subject to empirical interpretation rather than verification. In addition to these speculations Kant did send his own investigator to check out the facts of one of Swedenborg's telepathic incidents, and professed himself mystified by the event; but he was extremely cautious about drawing any positive conclusions from it, and does not appear to have related it to his consideration on the nature of the soul.

Schopenhauer (1788-1860) elaborated some aspects of the Kantian exposition. He agreed that the antithesis of soul and body was false, that we perceive the appearance rather than the thing itself, and that we cannot know anything independently of our perception of it. He goes on to argue that all we can know of death is that a phenomenon has come to an end in time; at this point he becomes unverifiably metaphysical in contending that the thing itself cannot be affected by death, but exactly what is the nature of consciousness? Schopenhauer answers that it is a limited and animal kind, which is not to be regretted, since after death we return to our original primal state, which is more real than the world of appearance. In other words physical death spells the end of the individual; however, present individuality is not to be thought of as man's essential and ultimate being, but only as a limited aspect of it. Here the influence of eastern thought is clearly discernible: the present empirical self or atman is not to be confused with the unlimited Self or Atman – to escape from the confines of the empirical self is a liberation. The reader is therefore exhorted not to regret the passing of this limited form of consciousness, as he will subsequently feel like a cured cripple. It is not the producer of consciousness which is destroyed at death but the physical manifestation; we shall meet this theory again in Bergson, James and Schiller. Schopenhauer concludes:

> Whoever therefore regrets the impending loss of this cerebral consciousness, which is adapted to and capable of producing only phenomena, is to be compared with the converts of Greenland who refused to go to heaven when they learned that there would be no seals there.

From the western angle, Schopenhauer's originality consists in his assertion that the present self is a limitation of being, which will be transcended in death. This is not asserted in Christian but, rather, in philosophical terms. It is arguably the first trace of fresh oriental influence since the Pythagoreans.

As we outlined in the beginning of this chapter, the development of scientific and philosophical thought has eroded the closed world of medieval Christianity with its assertions of the divine origin of man, the omniscient providence of God and the framework of absolute moral values, which destined a person for heaven or hell. There emerged a new optimistic assessment of the nature of man and his capacity for social progress, for creating a kind of paradise on earth; but, at the same time, mechanical interpretations of his make-up became more frequent – he was looked upon, at any rate so far as his body was concerned, as a very complex machine. In the next chapter we shall see how, in the wake of Darwin, Marx, Freud, and the behaviourists and with the help of Occam's razor, many philosophers and scientists concluded that man could be explained on a purely physical basis. The influence of Descartes and Kant continues to be felt, but there is a good deal more research into the brain and its workings, while psychology and psychical research have become disciplines in their own right.

5.

MODERN THEORIES OF BODY, MIND, BRAIN AND DEATH

The rational man believes that the earth was given to man for his use. His most dreaded enemy is death, the thought that his life and activity are transient. He avoids thinking of death, and when the thought pursues him, he takes refuge in activity, he fights off death with redoubled striving: for possessions, for knowledge, for laws, for rational mastery of the world. His immortality is his belief in progress: he believes that as an active link in the endless chain of progress he will never entirely cease to be.

HESSE

At the bottom of the modern man there is always a great thirst for self-forgetfulness, self-distraction; he has a secret horror of all which makes him feel his own smallness. The eternal, the infinite, perfection therefore scare and terrify him.

AMIEL

There is nothing like a theory for blinding the eyes of a wise man.

SIR JAMES BAILLIE

We have more knowledge than our predecessors but no more understanding.

ARNOLD TOYNBEE

T wo of the most powerful and far-reaching influences on twentieth-century life and thought are Marx and Darwin. Of the two, Darwin has been more influential in our field of enquiry. When his book *The Descent of Man* appeared Marx saw in it the confirmation of his own materialism, although we do not know whether Darwin was reciprocally impressed. At any rate their views gave new momentum to advocates of various forms of materialism; the harvest of the seeds, which they sowed, will become apparent below.

Marx wrote that:

> thought and consciousness are products of the human brain ... and man himself is a product of nature, which has been developing in and along with its environment; whence it is evident that the products of the human brain, being in the last analysis also products of nature, do not contradict the rest of nature but are in correspondence with it.

On this basis, consciousness perishes with the physical body, and there can be no question of what Marx calls 'the tedious notion of personal immortality'. The determinism of Marx's theories of history, society, and economics stems from and corresponds with his physical view of man. In the early years of the century, Marx's views were echoed by Lenin, who wrote that 'materialism in full agreement with natural science takes matter as the prius, regarding consciousness, reason and sensation as derivative, because in a well-expressed form it is connected only with the higher forms of matter [organic matter].' Here one can discern the influence of Darwin's evolutionary theory as a court of appeal.

Darwin himself does not elaborate in any detail on the implications of his theory, but he was well aware that some of his contentions were bound to be controversial. The main conclusion of *The Descent of Man* is that 'man is descended from some less highly organised form', and, looking at nature as a whole, one 'cannot any longer believe that man is the work of a separate act of creation'. He sees the greatest difficulty of his view as 'the high standard of our intellectual powers and moral disposition', but argues that these, too, have evolved (although the present-day observer might think again about the evolution of our moral disposition). In the wake of his remarks on creation he goes on to say that although our minds refuse to accept life as the result of blind chance, it is impossible to maintain that the belief in God is innate or instinctive in man: 'The idea of a universal and beneficent creator does not seem to arise in the mind of man, until he has been elevated by long-continued culture.' This last point implies evolution in man's idea of God, a theme developed into a racy book by Grant Allen, and one that has been investigated by successive generations of anthropologists.

Darwin next considers the evolution of the belief in the immortality of the soul. He claims that the work of Sir John Lubbock shows that primitive people have no clear belief of this kind, but it is not evident whether he is saying that they have an unclear belief in some kind of persistence of the soul, or that they have no such belief at all; at any rate he does not set great value on this factor, and we have seen earlier how Lubbock's conclusions have been overtaken by the work of Frazer. His next point is cryptically expressed, and has turned out to be an ironic understatement:

Few persons feel any anxiety from the impossibility of determining at what precise period in the development of the individual, from the first trace of a minute germinal vesicle, man becomes an immortal being; and there is no greater cause for anxiety because the period cannot possibly be determined in the gradually ascending organic scale.

It may be true that there is no explicit debate about when a foetus acquires a soul, probably because the category is, on the whole, strange to the modern outlook, but the issue is crucial in relation to abortion. On the other hand, the question of the time-scale for the emergence of the soul has caused a good deal more anxiety than Darwin anticipated: if man is continuous with other forms of life, then there is no logical reason to attribute an immortal soul to man alone; either the rest of the animal world must be included, or else the soul is removed from man as well. This is usually the cue for the ground of argument to shift from physical to moral considerations in order to differentiate man. Darwin's formulation implies that he does believe in an immortal soul in man, but he makes no attempt to defend the view or relate it to animals. However, the combination of the prevalent mechanical physiological theory with Darwin's assertion that there is no physical line to be drawn between man and animals pointed towards the conclusion that man, too, was an automaton, albeit a complex and apparently self-conscious one. The other consistent view – that animals are also immortal beings – was discounted as a non-starter.

More ink has been spilled on the mind/body problem in the last hundred years than ever before; this makes a comprehensive account of all views and developments impossible within the scope of our study. We shall, therefore, have to confine ourselves to rather summary accounts of the most significant attitudes. We shall consider, first, various materialist theories of mind, of which the two most important are epiphenomenalism and the so-called identity or central state theory. Epiphenomenalism regards mind and consciousness as by-products of matter, on which they are completely dependent, so that when matter perishes, so does mind and consciousness; there is no possibility of consciousness persisting after the death of the body, nor can consciousness have any effect on matter. The identity theory regards mental processes and brain processes as different ways of talking about the same thing, so that states of mind correspond to physical states in the brain: one views from inside and the other from outside. It also considers consciousness to be dependent on the brain, thus perishing with it. We shall then consider theories which do not necessarily regard consciousness or mind as dependent on body or brain; thus, they posit some form of interaction between mind and brain, and leave open the possibility that the mind or conscious self may survive the dissolution of the body; not all so-called dualist thinkers cited state this explicitly. Finally we shall give an account of some contemporary religious views before summarising and commenting on the various attitudes.

The biologist T. H. Huxley disagreed with Descartes's view that animals were unconscious machines, asserting instead that they were conscious automata:

> The consciousness of brutes would appear to be related to the mechanism of their body simply as a collateral product of its working, and to be completely without any power of modifying that working as the steam whistle which accompanies the working of a locomotive engine is without influence upon its machinery. Their volition, if they

have any, is an emotion indicative of physical changes, not the causes of such changes.

Huxley goes on to claim that the hypothesis of animals as conscious automata is consistent with any view about whether or not they have souls, immortal or otherwise: if mortal, then the biblical assertion that the beast perisheth is borne out; and if they possess 'immaterial subjects of consciousness, or souls' then consciousness is an indirect, not a direct product of material changes. He is obviously not convinced by this second possibility, as his subsequent analogy shows: 'The soul stands related to the body as the bell of a clock to the works, and consciousness answers the sound the bell gives out when it is struck.' The fact that the bell depends on the works would seem to indicate that it perishes simultaneously with the works.

Huxley now reaches the most contentious aspect of his analysis in extending it to man. He offers 'a few remarks for the calm consideration of thoughtful persons, untrammelled by foregone conclusions, unpledged to shore up tottering dogmas, and anxious only to know the true bearings of the case'. 'To the best of his judgement', he continues, 'the argumentation which applies to brutes holds equally good of men; and therefore, that all states of consciousness in us, as in them, are immediately caused by molecular changes of the brain substance.' He further contends that there is no proof that any state of consciousness is the cause of change in the motion of the matter of the organism.' In other words that consciousness can only be an effect, not a cause, therefore free will is an illusion, and a voluntary act 'the symbol of that state of the brain which is the immediate cause of that act.'

He takes a rather cavalier view of the logical consequences of his position, which he fears will form the main line of attack against his theory. He rightly claims that it should be assessed for its truth or falsity rather than its value. He states that he is not a fatalist, as necessity has a logical rather than a physical foundation; not a materialist, as he cannot conceive of the existence of matter without mind to perceive it; and not an atheist, as the problem of the ultimate cause of existence 'seems to be hopelessly out of reach of my poor powers'. His first two contentions seem to be questionable: we have seen how his physical theory that mind cannot affect matter rules out free will or renders it illusory, so that this philosophical distinction between the logical and the physical is specious; and he is only not a materialist by his own definition, reminiscent of the idealism of Berkeley and Kant – he clearly conceives of mind as a by-product of matter and dependent on it. Huxley's contribution was to make explicit some of the assumptions of Darwinism, which he found annihilated the moral distinction between man and animals and led him to account for man in entirely physical terms.

T. H. Huxley's grandson, the biologist Sir Julian Huxley, took a slightly less radical view. He believed in the uniformity and the unity of nature, that mind and matter co-exist in the higher animals and in man, and in the unity of mind and matter in the one ultimate world substance, as two of its aspects: 'Mental and material are thus, to my belief, two aspects of one reality, two abstractions made by us from the concrete ground of experience; they cannot really be separated, and it is false philosophy to try to think them apart.' This view of man is a statement of the identity theory in a broad sense: the human being shows both mental and material characteristics, both of which are essential in a complete account. Huxley is agnostic concerning the existence of another world, but adds that he finds 'extreme difficulties, in the light of physiological and psychological knowledge in understanding how a soul could exist apart from a body; but difficulties are never disproof.' He examined the 'so-called evidence from spiritualism', and concluded that while there was a good *prima facie* case for clairvoyance and telepathy, as well as plenty of evidence for automatic writing, 'these have nothing to do with spiritualism in the sense of communicating with the spirits of the departed'. He asserted that the evidence in the 'messages' was for the most part trivial, and was obviously disgusted that some people accepted such phenomena so uncritically. He gave no account of evidence which he did not consider trivial, nor did he point out that the very triviality of detail is sometimes the best evidence. Huxley even admits that some of the messages remained mysterious, but prefers to dismiss this rather than try to formulate some explanatory hypothesis; this may not have the merit of being scientific, but it would at least be an attempt to account for the facts.

The geneticist J. B. S. Haldane rejected T. H. Huxley's assertion that the mind had no function, but he nonetheless maintained a materialistic standpoint, by which he meant:

1. Events occur which are not perceived by any mind.
2. There were unperceived events before there were any minds.
3. When a man dies he is dead.

The first two contentions stand together: matter precedes mind and must therefore be able to exist independently of mind. The third statement formulates the absolute dependence of mind on matter. Haldane admits to having found himself in a dilemma about the nature of the mind and its relation to the body and confesses, rather surprisingly for a scientist, that the books which 'solved my difficulties' were by Engels and Lenin. He backs up the view of these sages with his opinion on the state of scientific research:

> We are only on the very fringe of the necessary investigations, but it is becoming daily more plausible that our minds are physical realities acted upon by the rest of the world and reacting on it. Our minds are processes which occur in our brains.

It is curious that Haldane jumps from a statement of probability (plausible) to one of fact (are), thus revealing his own presuppositions. His explicit view on death is that it is a 'dissolution ... the end of a particular pattern of material and mental happenings which are bound up with each other'. He sees no room for the persistence of mind as an independent entity.

We will add, at this stage, the echoing views of two other biologists, H. S. Jennings and Sir Peter Chalmers Mitchell. Jennings argued that biological science gave no support to the doctrine that individuals continue to live in some form after death. He saw the continuation of life in the existence of successive individuals, rather than in the persistence of the same individuals after bodily death. He concluded that:

> If we are to found our outlook on the world on what we discover in the scientific study of life, we are compelled to break with the notion that personality, individual identity, continues after death. We are compelled to conclude that the individuals who have disappeared exist no more than they did before they began life, no more than they did before the species to which they belong had been produced in evolution.

Mitchell wasted few words in concluding:

> I am unaware of any facts or observations from which I can draw the inference that life is other than a function of the material bodies of human beings, other animals and plants, ceasing when these individual bodies decay, swiftly or slowly. I believe, therefore, that death is the end of every individual life.

It is abundantly clear that these two writers reached their conclusions exclusively on the data of biology, ignoring other areas which might have a bearing on the question.

F. H. Bradley (1846-1924) was one of the influential idealist philosophers in Oxford around the turn of the century. In his book *Appearance and Reality* he maintains that body and soul 'are mere appearance, distinctions set up and held apart in the Whole'; his idea is reminiscent of Julian Huxley but expressed in rather more abstruse terms. Body is defined as 'an intellectual construction out of material which is not self-subsistent'; nor is the soul considered to be self-subsistent; it is defined as a 'finite centre of existence, and again of a certain identity in character'. Having established these definitions as a starting point he goes on to dismiss T. H. Huxley's epiphenomenalism on logical grounds, and likewise the idea that the soul can exist in a bodiless state, since he argues that souls can only influence each other through bodies. Later on he reluctantly turns his attention to the question of a future life, defined as 'an existence after death, which is conscious of its identity with our life here and now'. His definition rightly assumes the necessary continuity of consciousness as well as its persistence. In this 'unknown field' he advances some considerations which, he says, are based on probability: that the probability of an unknown event is one half, but that judging by our actual experience and knowledge, such a life must be considered improbable. He does not specify what kind of experience he means, and there follows a good deal of abstract rambling and groping:

> When you add together the chances of a life after death – a life taken as bodiless, and again as diversely embodied – the amount is not great. The balance of probability seems so large that the fraction on the other side is not considerable.

After further meanderings Bradley concludes that 'a future life must be taken as decidedly improbable'. Altogether it is a strange and obfuscatory argument, which uses a vague sort of probability to shore up a prejudice: the analysis is conducted without naming the relevant factors so that the conclusion seems to struggle out from nowhere.

Elsewhere Bradley is more concrete, in an article entitled 'The Evidences of Spiritualism'. He is aiming to deny the theses that:

> Spiritualism, if true, demonstrates mind without brain, and intelligence disconnected with what is termed a material body ... it demonstrates

that the so-called dead are still alive; that our friends are still with us though unseen ... it thus furnishes that *proof* of a future life which so many crave.

Bradley castigates the spiritualists for jumping from the proposition that souls exist, which are not dependent on the matter connected with our souls, to the assertion that souls exist without anything that can be called matter at all. He then argues that we cannot be sure that there is not 'A kind of matter which we are unable to perceive, but which, if different ourselves, we should at once perceive'. This matter might interact with our matter under certain unknown conditions; furthermore the matter might be organised in such a way as to 'get' a soul which might communicate with us and produce all the facts ascribed wrongly to spirits. Bradley claims that his hypothesis accounts for the phenomena and is consistent with a thorough materialism. It is a response to the need for some kind of embodiment for the soul on the assumption that any shape and form which can interact with matter as we know it cannot be wholly discontinuous with it; it comes close to the theory advocated by many spiritualists that matter vibrates at a number of different frequencies of which we are able to perceive only a limited range. Bradley examines the question of the identity of the spirits and concludes that it is extremely difficult to be sure, adding that recognition would not necessarily imply that the spirit was immaterial and immortal (the old equation which goes back beyond Plato). If he himself were convinced that he had contacted one of his dead friends he still maintains that he 'cannot say what would stagger my reason and break down my intellect' – this revealing, once again, his intellectual resistance to the idea of immortality. The weakest point of the theory which Bradley outlines is the arbitrary fashion in which it is supposed that matter might organise itself and get a soul, so that the communications of this strange creation happen to resemble the personality associated with a certain dead English person. It is, perhaps, less far-fetched to contend that the embodiment of another kind of matter is the manifestation of a known dead person, or, at any rate, of a possible impersonator. This question, however, cannot be resolved in the absence of concrete examples.

When Bertrand Russell's grandmother first discovered his interest in metaphysics she told him that the whole subject could be resolved in the saying 'What is mind? no matter; what is matter? never mind'. Another of her grand-daughters protested that her barking dog was an angel, whereupon the formidable old lady exclaimed that this was nonsense, and asked her whether she thought that dogs had souls; she replied that she thought that they did, and was the target of her withering scorn for the remainder of the afternoon. At any rate his grandmother's strictures did not deter Russell from pursuing the study of metaphysics. In his article 'Mind and Matter' he uses as his starting point the new Einsteinian physics and states that 'a piece of matter is a group of events connected by causal laws, namely the laws of physics. A mind is a group of events connected by causal laws, namely the causal laws of psychology.' Ignoring the possibility that the 'laws' of physics and psychology may rest on a different basis, he goes on to explain that there are two kinds of space: one is the experienced visual field in which sensible objects are parts of minds, and another, which is the space of physics, existing independently of perception. The first space is a concession to Berkeley and Kant, while the second expresses the independence of matter from mind, the fact that it exists in its own right. Russell then submits a hypothesis 'which is simple and unifying although not demonstrable' to explain mind, matter, and their connection, namely that 'the events which make a living brain are actually identical with those that make the corresponding mind'. Had Russell substituted the word 'process' for 'events', this would have been an exact working of the identity theory. He means that the difference between mind and brain does not consist of their raw material, but rather the way in which this material is grouped; the difference is not one of quality but arrangement. He argues that if his theory is right, then there are certain inescapable connections:

> Corresponding to memory, for example, there must be some physical modifying of the brain, and mental life must be connected with physical properties of the brain tissue. In fact, if we had more knowledge, the physical and psychological statements would be seen to be merely different ways of saying the same thing. The ancient question of the dependence of mind on brain, or brain on mind, is thus reduced to a linguistic convenience.

This conclusion we shall see echoed by Ryle and others. Brain research reinforces Russell's physical connections but leaves unanswered, in the view of some researchers, the question of whether these connections are exclusively physical. We shall return to this theme below.

Russell also wrote two articles on the question of the survival of bodily death, the conclusions of which follow from his foregoing analysis.

He sides with Hume in considering that there is perhaps no such persistent entity as personality. In any event, such continuity as is apparent is a continuity of habit and memory, both of which would have to persist in any intelligible form of survival. But, he argues, memory and habit are bound up with the structure of the brain, and may be modified if the brain is damaged in certain ways; and, since the brain is dissolved at death, one would expect memory to be similarly dispersed. He asserts that it is not rational arguments, but emotions such as fear of death, and our wish to survive it, which compel belief; so his conclusion runs 'we have no right to expect the universe to adapt itself to our emotions, and I cannot think it right or wise to cherish beliefs for which there is no good evidence, merely on the ground that fairy tales are pleasant'. He deals what he regards as a crushing *reductio ad absurdum* blow to the argument advanced by Bishop Barnes – that God would not allow His wonderful creation man to perish – by impishly imagining a theologically-minded fly arguing for the immortality of flies on the grounds that they could do something beyond the capability of Lloyd George and Baldwin, namely walk upside down on the ceiling. Russell's rejoinder to Barnes's emotional argument makes a mockery of humanity and cancels itself out in its own clever absurdity. The basis of Russell's deductions on mind, matter and death is physics and biology; he makes no mention of phenomena which his theory cannot explain, so that his analysis seems cogent as far as it goes, following lines already mapped out by Lucretius and Hume.

Considerable support for the reductionist and materialistic view of man came from the psychologist J. B. Watson's *Behaviourism*, published in 1924. In a frantic attempt to make psychology into a quantifiable science, Watson abolished consciousness, introspection and free choice, replacing them with a view of man as a kind of robot, which responded mechanically to various external stimuli. Therefore, observation of behaviour assumes a crucial role: the more and closer observation, the greater the knowledge and, thus, the easier it will become to manipulate man's reactions. Much of the experimentation was on animals, and some of the responses observed in rats were then extrapolated to apply to man. The ecstatic review in the *New York Herald Tribune* can scarcely be accorded any real value on the basis of Watson's theory, as the stimulus of the book no doubt conditioned the response of the reviewer.

Freud counted immortality among the illusions of mankind, and his view of the role of the unconscious is largely deterministic. However, he makes some interesting observations in his article 'Thoughts for the Times on War and Death', written in 1915. He observes that in peacetime, although death is 'natural, undeniable and unavoidable ... we were accustomed to behave as if it were otherwise. We displayed an unmistakable tendency to "shelve" death, to eliminate it from life.' He goes on to say that people tend to stress the fortuitous causation of a death – accident, disease, infection, old age – thus modifying the necessity and inevitability of death into a chance happening, an attitude which we observed in primitive peoples. But war forces people to believe in death by dint of sheer accumulation. Freud makes one further notable observation, which he interprets as a wish-fulfilment:

> Our own death is indeed unimaginable, and whether we make an attempt to imagine it we can perceive that we really survive as spectators ... hence ... no one believes in his own death ... in the unconscious every one of us is convinced of his own immortality.

In Freud's view such wish-fulfilments are invariably deceptive illusions, but surely this phenomenon arises from the very nature of consciousness, which separates itself from the objects of perception and is, thus, unable to conceive of its own extinction or unrelatedness.

Wittgenstein does not seem to give a consistent account of the mind/brain problem. On the one hand, in *The Blue Book*, he describes a hypothetical subject-experimenter observing a correlation of two phenomena, the thought and workings of the brain. But then in a later work, *Zettel*, he makes the following remarks:

> No supposition seems to me more natural than that there is no process in the brain correlated with associating or with thinking; so that it would be impossible to read off thought processes from brain processes ... it is thus perfectly possible that certain psychological phenomena cannot be investigated physiologically, because physiologically nothing corresponds to them.

He then gives the example of recognising a man whom he has not seen for years, and asks why there must be a physiological cause or trace in his nervous system which triggers off the recognition (at this point one might have expected him to analyse the word re-cognition and its implications). He ends with the plea: 'Why should there not be a psychological regularity to which no physiological regularity corresponds?

If this upsets our concept of causality then it is high time it was upset.' These speculations seem to be designed to put a spanner in the concept of causality in mind/body relations within the Cartesian framework. Wittgenstein's approach is a speculative attack on the identity theory equation, but it does not refer to any brain research and takes the form of a plea 'why should such-and-such not be the case?' without really tackling the issue of why it *should* be so.

Wittgenstein's views on death are more unequivocal. He claims that:

> at death the world does not alter, but comes to an end ... Death is not an event in life: we do not live to experience death ... our life has no end in just the way that our visual field has no limits.

According to this interpretation, the visual field perishes at death, since death is not lived through. He puts the question of immortality in a wider perspective:

> Not only is there no guarantee of the temporal immortality of the human soul, that is to say of its eternal survival after death; but, in any case, this assumption completely fails to accomplish the purpose for which it has always been intended. Or is some riddle solved by surviving for ever? Is not this eternal life itself just as much a riddle as our present life? The solution of the riddle of life in space and time lies *outside* space and time.

Wittgenstein does not pose the question empirically, but in terms of the meaning and function of eternal survival; having done this he answers his own question by saying that the facts merely contribute to the setting of the problem, not to its solution. Eternal life may well be a riddle from our perspective, but, if it exists, it may become comprehensible and moreover provide a standpoint from which the present life become intelligible – in which case it would serve its intended purpose. But Wittgenstein 'solves' the problem another way: he asserts that if a question can be framed, then it is also possible to answer it, but conversely when the answer cannot be put into words, neither can the question, so that 'the riddle does not exist'. He goes on to contend that 'even when all *possible* scientific questions have been answered, the problems of life remain completely untouched. Of course there are no questions left, and this itself is the answer.' So he concludes that 'the solution of the problem of life is seen in the vanishing of the problem.'

We shall see that a similar judicious arrangement of terms enables both Ryle and Ayer to dismiss the mind/body problem as a kind of linguistic muddle. Wittgenstein himself defines all problems and answers as scientific, so that there are no real problems outside the realms of science, which necessarily operates within the space-time dimension. He does not mention any phenomena which transcend these boundaries and might thus provide him with some clues about 'the solution of the riddle of life'; although these lie beyond his idea of science, they cannot simply be spirited away into thin air.

Ayer argues that the distinction between mind and matter applies only to the logical constructions out of sense-contents, and not to the sense-contents themselves; here he follows the line which we have already seen in Russell. Therefore he infers that 'there is no philosophical problem concerning the relationship of mind and matter, other than the linguistic problems of defining certain symbols which denote sense contents'. He comments that the problems with which philosophers have vexed themselves in the past arise from the fictitious distinction between mind and matter as two substances, and concludes that there can now be no *a priori* reason why minds and material things may not be causally connected; thus he argues against the impossibility of interaction between the two, a theory propounded by those philosophers who hold that there can be no interaction between totally disparate categories: for Ayer there is no reason why mind should not act on body and vice-versa. As for the question of personal survival, he considers the notion intelligible but untrue:

> On purely logical grounds, I am inclined to think that personal identity depends on the identity of the body; and even when paranormal phenomena are taken into account, the weight of evidence is strongly in favour of the view that conscious processes are causally dependent on physical events.

In other words Ayer cannot envisage consciousness operating without the physical body. He comments that this leaves open the hypothesis of resurrection, which he cannot believe could be taken seriously by any rational man. Remarks like 'The weight of evidence is strongly in favour of ...' should always be handled circumspectly as, in many cases, they are a grander and more objective-sounding way of saying 'I think or feel'; Ayer does not specify which paranormal phenomena he has taken into account or on what grounds he feels that they do not alter the picture.

In *The Concept of Mind*, an enormously influential work, Ryle set out to demonstrate the absurdity of what he termed the 'Official Doctrine' or the dogma of the 'Ghost in the Machine'. He states the doctrine as follows:

> Every human being has both a body and a mind. Some would prefer to say that every human being is both a body and a mind. His body and his mind are ordinarily harnessed together, but after the death of the body his mind may continue to exist and function.

As we have seen in Descartes, minds are thought of as unextended in space, while bodies are extended and external; mechanical laws are advanced to account for the behaviour and interaction of bodies in space, while other laws must explain the workings of the mind. Ryle considers this explanation to be a dangerous philosophical aberration due to what he calls a category mistake, by which he means that the facts of mental life are represented as belonging to one category when they really belong to another. He illustrates what he means by a category mistake by envisaging a foreigner walking round Oxford or Cambridge for the first time and being shown a number of colleges, libraries, playing fields, museums, etc., and asking at the end of the tour where the university is. Ryle explains that such category mistakes are made by people who do not know how to wield the appropriate concepts; the puzzle arises from an inability to use certain items of English vocabulary. He argues that one cannot speak of mental states and processes enjoying one sort of existence, and bodily states and processes enjoying another, but rather that the word 'exist' is used in two senses: people are to be regarded as wholes, not as conjunctions of two processes. Novelists only talk of *people* doing and undergoing things, not of mind and body working in tandem. Ryle claims that the main consequence of his thesis will be:

> that the hallowed contrast between Mind and Matter will be dissipated, but dissipated not by either of the equally hallowed absorptions of Mind by Matter or of Matter by Mind, but in a quite different way. For the seeming contrast of the two will be shown to be illegitimate as would be the contrast of 'the came home in a flood of tears' and 'she came home in a sedan chair'. The belief that there is a polar opposition between Mind and Matter is the belief that they are terms of the same logical type.

Ryle's conclusions echo those of Russell, Ayer and Wittgenstein, but he has had the greatest influence in this field. He deliberately set out to demolish the traditional Cartesian dichotomy between mind and matter. While it is certainly true that we do refer to people as wholes, Ryle's 'solution' is purely philosophical. He does not refer his arguments to the paranormal or even to neurophysiological developments; this enables him to treat the issue in an abstract and speculative way.

We come now to three of the chief exponents of the identity theory, the starting point of which is the closely established correlation of brain processes and mental states. In his article 'Mind-Body, not a Pseudo-problem', Feigl argues against Ryle that the issue can be explained as a conceptual confusion. He takes the latest work of physiologists, and adopts the identity theory as a 'fruitful working hypothesis'. He admits that some still extremely problematic and controversial 'facts' may require emergentist explanations and adds that 'as an empiricist' he must at least go through the motions of an open mind. His deprecatory and sarcastic tone makes it clear that he does not really consider it necessary to keep an open mind on parapsychology. He states the identity theory as follows: 'Certain neuro-physiological terms denote (refer to) the very same events that are also denoted (referred to) by certain phenomenal terms' (i.e. states of mind). Feigl rejects the mysticism of Eddington because 'there is literally nothing that can responsibly be said in a phenomenal language about qualities that do not fall within the scope of acquaintance', in other words, whatever is inexpressible has no philosophical significance. This demonstrates a total ignorance of the nature of mystical experience and its relation to language. Feigl also dismisses the psycho-vitalism of Bergson because it involves dualistic interaction, which he is unable to countenance. His conclusion is that:

> for a synoptic, coherent account of the relevant facts of perception, introspection and psychosomatics, and the logic of theory construction in the physical sciences, I think that the identity view is preferable to any other proposed solution to the mind-body problem.

The key word here is 'relevant' – who defines its scope? While admitting that his conclusion is a matter of philosophical interpretation, he contends that a further merit of the identity theory is that it simplifies our conception of the world by positing a single reality represented in two explanatory conceptual systems. But simplicity itself is not a guarantee of truth – a simple theory may well be incomplete.

In *Sensations and Brain Processes* Smart relies heavily on Occam's razor, to which he seems to attribute inviolable status. Here it would, perhaps, be more accurate to speak of Occam's hatchet, as it is frequently used in a more or less arbitrary fashion as a reason for ignoring facts which, inconveniently, do not fit neatly into someone's conceptual scheme. At the beginning of his article Smart makes what he later admits is largely a confession of faith:

> It seems to me that science is increasingly giving us a viewpoint whereby organisms are able to be seen as physico-chemical mechanisms: it seems that even the behaviour of man himself will one day be explicable in mechanistic terms. There does seem to me, so far as science is concerned, nothing in the world but increasingly complex arrangements of physical constituents. All except in one place: in consciousness ... sensations, states of consciousness, do seem to be the one sort of thing left outside the physicalist picture, and for various reasons, I just cannot believe that this can be so. That everything should be explicable in terms of physics ... except the occurrence of sensations seems to me to be, frankly, unbelievable.

He remarks that sensations would be untidy 'danglers' in an otherwise unified theory of mind, and that the reason why he finds Wittgenstein so congenial is that he seems to deny the existence of sensations. Smart's analysis becomes a series of subjective value judgements – 'seems ... I just cannot believe ... frankly unbelievable' – which suggest that he has some emotional commitment to the identity theory and will search high and low for reasons to support his bias; and there is an element of pious hope in his anticipation that the behaviour of man will one day be explicable in mechanistic terms. Even if this were so, the explanation would be on only one level.

Man is described by Smart as 'a vast arrangement of physical particles', and his contention that sensations are brain processes is clarified by his explanation that 'In so far as "after-image" or "ache" is a report of a process, it is a report of a process which *happens to be* a brain process' (his italics). In another article he deals with the possibility of mind emerging separately out of matter (known as emergentism) and asks how a non-physical property or entity could possibly arise suddenly in the course of animal evolution; his scornful comment is that no enzyme could catalyse a spook – such a non-physical by-product would be inexplicable. Like Feigl,

Smart stresses the point (Occam's razor) that our cosmological out-look can be vastly simplified if we can defend a materialist theory of mind; he does not consider any inconvenient 'facts', nor does he make any mention of neuro-physiologists who maintain that mind and brain are distinguishable.

Armstrong argues likewise that one theory of mind 'is steadily gaining ground, so that it bids fair to become the established scientific doctrine. This is the view that we can give a complete account of man in *purely physico-chemical terms*' (his italics). He claims that such a view has gained considerable support from molecular biology and neuro-physiology, asserting that 'those scientists who still reject the physico-chemical account of man do so primarily for philosophical, or moral, or religious reasons, and only secondarily for reasons of scientific detail'. This may well be true in some cases, but Armstrong does not seem to consider that he may have some subjective bias himself. He then argues that such a consensus among scientists carries its own authority and obliges us to accept a materialist theory as the best clue we have to the nature of man; however, as Russell pithily remarked, 'Even when all the experts agree they may well be mistaken' – and then contrary authorities can always be found. Armstrong remarks that the behaviourist doctrine is bound to be attractive to any philosopher sympathetic to a materialist view of man, for:

> if there is no reason to draw a distinction between mental processes and their expressions in physical behaviour, but if instead the mental processes are identified with their so-called expressions, then the existence of mind stands in no conflict with the view that man is nothing but a physico-chemical mechanism.

This is a very clear statement of the way in which the identity theory can be tied up with Behaviourism and a reduction of man to a 'nothing-but' formula. According to Armstrong, a mental process is 'a state of the person apt for producing certain ranges of behaviour'; this, in turn, can be identified with the purely physical states of the central nervous system. It follows this that 'consciousness of our own mental state becomes simply the scanning of one part of our central nervous system by another. Consciousness is a self-scanning mechanism in the central nervous system.' Armstrong is confident that his theory will be vindicated by future scientific research but he does admit that parapsychology is 'the small black cloud on the horizon of a materialist theory of mind'; the cloud may turn out to be a good deal larger and more significant than he thinks.

Before concluding this section with Lamont's comprehensive account of the materialist position, it is worthwhile investigating the views of the historian and polymath Toynbee. He argues, like some philosophers already considered, that soul and body are verbal distinctions and that, therefore, the psychic part of man probably goes the same way as the body. Because the human mind has only a limited capacity for understanding the nature of the universe in which we find ourselves, we are bound to act on unverifiable assumptions. Having said this, he does not find any cogent evidence for immortality or rebirth, even if these hypotheses, if true, might answer some of the ultimate questions that we cannot evade. Nor does Toynbee find any cogent evidence for the ultimate spiritual reality in which he himself believes. All the foregoing analysis, however, refers to the time-dimension, in which it is certain that the soul ceases to exist at the moment of death. Toynbee now argues that death in the time-dimension 'does not rule out the possibility that a human soul may have an existence outside the time-dimension'. In terms of his belief in an ultimate spiritual reality he believes that personal human individuality is acquired at the price (which he considers high) of separation from this supra-personal reality, so that at death 'a human being's soul is re-absorbed into the supra-personal spiritual presence behind the universe'. This view reflects the Hindu adage of '*Tat Tvam Asi*' (that art thou) which means for Toynbee that:

> The root of an individual human being's soul is identified with and rooted in a spirit that is the ultimate reality behind the universe. If this is true; the root of a human soul may share in immortality, though the flowers and the fruit may be mortal.

Thus, like Schopenhauer, Toynbee advocates that the limited personality is mortal, but the essential human being partakes of immortality: scepticism is overcome by intuitive religious conviction, which has more of an Eastern than a Christian flavour. It is not surprising that Toynbee looks upon death as a release from the ego and the world. In his remarkable book *Experiences*, written in his late seventies, he writes:

> Death does eventually release each of us, in turn, from the burdens and injustices of this life. Death is, in fact, our eventual saviour from the tyranny of human society in this world – a tyranny which is

tolerable, if at all, only because it has an inexorable time-limit ... death limits life's liabilities.

Other passages are in a much less pessimistic vein, and it would be wrong to judge Toynbee's outlook on the above extract. He gives his last point a twist by saying that at last he will be delivered from the Inland Revenue.

One of the most extensive statements of the materialist position can be found in Lamont's *Illusion of Immortality*; the title speaks for itself. Lamont claims that at the outset of his investigations he was a believer in a future existence, but does not, unfortunately, give the grounds of the belief against which he reacted so strongly. He rightly contends that the fundamental issue is the relationship between the body and the personality, and explains that there are, broadly speaking, two positions: the monistic position, which asserts that the body and the personality constitute an indissoluble unity, and the dualistic position which maintains that the personality is a separable and independent entity able to exist without the body. Lamont is convinced that the facts of modern science offer decisive evidence for the monistic position, and 'thereby rule out the possibility of the individual human consciousness, with its memory and awareness of self-identify essentially intact, surviving the shock of death'. The scientific evidence adduced is the following:

1. Mind and personality grow along with the body; there is an intimate correlation between the physical organism and the self.

2. Our conscious experience depends upon our nervous system, and thinking on the cerebral cortex in the brain; memory patterns are to be found along the neuronic pathways of the cortex; these would be essential for the survival of the mind; but 'it is beyond all understanding how they could possibly outlast the dissolution of the living brain in which they originally moved and had their being'.

3. Destruction of brain tissue by disease or a severe blow to the head will impair normal mental activity; the functions of seeing, hearing and speech are correlated with the specialised sections of the cerebral cortex.

4. The physical exterior of man reflects his essential being; and personality is influenced by environment.

As for psychical research, Lamont contends that no findings have emerged in this field, which discredit the monistic psychology. He admits that a large number of supernormal phenomena have been accumulated, but implies that the vast majority are tainted by fraud (there is certainly some fraud, but not nearly on the scale insinuated); and he asserts that none of the evidence proves survival of death, as it is susceptible of many other interpretations. He predicts that psychical research may eventually be seen as a contribution to abnormal psychology and psychiatry. Lamont then turns his attention to religious arguments, pointing out that the Old Testament Hebrews did not believe in survival, and that the more sophisticated Protestants have felt obliged to discard the notion of a literal resurrection in favour of the idea of a spiritual body. Finally he gives short shrift to the ethical argument about the inherent value of human personality, commenting that such arguments are 'a rather pathetic process of turning human wishes into proofs'. He concludes by exhorting human beings not to be distracted by the thought of death, but to concentrate on building paradise on earth.

In summary, it emerges that the most powerful arguments for the materialist theory of mind are the correlation of mental processes with brain processes, and the effect of brain damage, drugs or simply age on personality; the inference drawn is that the correlation of mental and physical is so close that it is inconceivable that the mental should be capable of operating independently.

A good deal of energy of the founders of the Society for Psychical Research went into investigating *prima facie* evidence that the personality survived bodily death. The fact that the evidence remained open to differing interpretations and was of varying degrees of reliability accounted for differing assessments of its validity. Sidgwick, the first president of the Society, concluded that there was at least some *prima facie* evidence suggesting survival, but felt that the problems of interpretation were almost insuperable. Myers, author of *Human Personality and its Survival of Bodily Death* was not initially convinced but became certain in the course of his investigations, so that in a letter of 1890 he wrote: 'I do not feel the smallest doubt now that we survive death, and I am pretty sure that the whole scientific world will have accepted this before AD 2000'; this has not proved correct and still seems a long way off. Mrs Sidgwick, Principal of Newnham College, Cambridge (where Sidgwick was Professor of Moral Philosophy) and sister of the statesman Arthur Balfour, probably looked into more cases of apparent survival than anyone else, and over a period of fifty years. In 1932 she was made President of Honour of the SPR, and her brother read her presidential address. At the end he commented that conclusive proof of survival was notoriously difficult to obtain, but that the evidence may be such as to produce *belief*, even though it falls short of conclusive proof. On this basis Mrs Sidgwick was a firm believer both in survival and in the reality of communication between the living and the dead. We shall examine belief and attitude towards evidence more fully in the next chapter; meanwhile, as an example of the conclusions of one of the earlier researchers, we shall look at the views of the physicist Lodge, who lost a son, Raymond in the First World War.

Lodge was finally convinced of the reality of survival and of communication between the living and the dead, both through communications purporting to come from his son and from earlier associates such as Myers. There is an enormous accumulation of material supposedly emanating from Myers and transmitted through different mediums; the scripts contain a good deal of classical and literary material, some of which carries over into messages received by different mediums, so that a particular message is only fully comprehensible by referring to a passage received by another medium. This created what was known as a *cross-correspondence*, where the communicator claimed to transmit a message through the channel of different mediums in an attempt to prove his own continuing identity. Lodge called this process one of 'carefully constructed evidence of identity', and although it did not lead to any definite conclusion, it did suggest the possibility of communication as a coherent working hypothesis. Lodge's theories on the mind/body and mind/brain relationship were consistent with the evidence, which he accepted as indicative of survival, thus he argued in *Raymond* that in the event of brain damage it was incorrect to say that consciousness had been destroyed; one could only assert that it had been lost, that consciousness was no longer displayed. He drew a parallel with cases where the speech centres of the brain are affected, but not the arm, so that communication could still take place through writing. The body is regarded as a means of manifestation, which enables the person to operate in the space-time dimension, and to interact with others as a separate identity. He gives a careful definition of death:

The cessation of that controlling influence of matter over energy, so that thereafter the uncontrolled activity of physical and chemical forces supervenes ... It may be called a dissociation, a dissolution, a separation of a controlling entity from a physico-chemical organism ... the body weighs just as much as before, the only properties it loses at the moment of death are potential properties. So that all we can assert concerning the vital principle is that it no longer animates that material organism: we cannot safely make further assertion concerning it, or maintain its activity or inactivity without further information.

Like Toynbee, Lodge clearly states what we know explicitly about death, and warns people against assuming that the disappearance of the vital principle necessarily implies its extinction.

Lodge was aware that various explanations, such as telepathy from living people, were advanced to account for the phenomena of apparitions and mediumistic communications, but concluded that:

inasmuch as in my judgment there are phenomena which they cannot explain, and inasmuch as some form of spiritistic hypothesis, gives certain postulates, explains practically all, I have found myself driven back on what I may call the common sense explanation.

He claimed that the communications had taught him two things: the first was continuity – 'there is no such sudden break in the conditions of existence as may have been anticipated; and no break at all in the continuous and conscious identity of the genuine character and personality.' Secondly he learned that knowledge is not suddenly advanced, although powers and faculties may be enlarged, depending on the outlook of the individual. Readers who wish to follow up Lodge's extensive investigations are referred to his many books.

In 1891 there appeared a book entitled *Riddles of the Sphinx* by a 'Troglodyte' (cave-dweller). In the preface the author explains that the anti-metaphysical current is so strong that he would risk 'the barren honours of a useless martyrdom' if he were to reveal his name. He likens himself to the man who in Plato's *Republic* has glimpsed the 'truth', and returns to his fellow cave-dwellers only to find that they cannot take in his insights, and that they are rather intolerant of any innovation. The author turned out to be Schiller, an Oxford philosophy don. Whereas the prevalent tendency, expressed in Huxley, was to explain spirit in terms of matter, Schiller proposed to turn the formulation round by explaining matter in terms of spirit. On the basis of the relationship between an unlimited Deity and limited egos, he proposes that 'matter is an admirably calculated machinery for regulating, limiting and restraining the consciousness which it encases'. He argues that the simpler and coarser machinery of matter depresses the consciousness of 'lower beings' to a lower point, while the organisation of man is more complex, thus corresponding to a higher level of consciousness; his formulation comes close to the speculation of Teilhard de Chardin. Schiller's opinion of the normal consciousness of human beings is not very high, as he characterises it by the word 'somnambulism', rather like Gurdjieff, but he does add that we are able to leave the 'cave' and catch glimpses of another dimension. He infers that materialism has inverted the relationship between matter and consciousness: 'Matter is not what *produces* consciousness but what *limits* it and confirms its intensity within certain limits: material organisation does not construct consciousness out of arrangements of atoms, but contracts its manifestations within the sphere which it permits.' We shall meet this hypothesis of the mind/brain connection in James, Bergson, and Jung. James characterises the theory as 'transmissive' or 'permissive' rather than 'productive', since it is contended that the brain does not produce consciousness but transmits it from the mind. Schiller justifies the hypothesis as follows:

> This explanation does not involve the denial either of the facts or of the principle involved in Materialism, viz., the unity of life and the continuity of all existence. It admits the connection of Matter and Consciousness, but contends that the course of interpretation must proceed in the contrary direction. Thus it will fit the facts which Materialism rejected as 'supernatural'. It explains the lower by the higher, Matter by Spirit, instead of vice versa, and thereby attains to an explanation which is ultimately tenable instead of one which is ultimately absurd. And it is an explanation the possibility of which no evidence in favour of Materialism can possibly affect.

Like Lodge, he then argues that it is as good an explanation of a brain injury to say that the manifestation of consciousness has been prevented by the injury, rather than extinguished by it; and, with regard to memory, he proposes that it is forgetfulness, not memory, that should be accounted for: this would explain the total recall experienced under hypnosis, and 'the extraordinary memories of the drowning and dying generally'. In other words we never really forget anything but are prevented from recalling it by the limitations of the brain.

In the Introduction we have already seen how Schiller bemoaned the attitude of most people towards death, and that of science towards psychical research. In considering the event of death he warns against the 'spurious self-evidence of death' and asserts that our view of death is necessarily imperfect, and one-sided:

> For we contemplate it only from the point of view of the survivors, never from that of the dying. We have not the least idea of what death means to those who die. *To us* it is a catastrophic change, whereby a complex of phenomenal appearances, which we call the body of the dead, ceases to suggest to us the presence of the ulterior existence which we called spirit. But this does not prove, nor even tend to prove, that the spirit of the dead has ceased to exist. It merely shows that he has ceased to form part of our little world ... it is at least as probable that this ... is to be ascribed to his having been promoted or removed, as to his having been destroyed.

These considerations do not prove the existence of a future life, but merely make it plausible. Schiller goes on to put forward a theory of graded immortality in line with his earlier scheme of graded consciousness, but treatment of this falls outside the scope of our enquiry.

The French philosopher Henri Bergson advanced a similar view to Schiller, although it is not clear whether he had come across *Riddles of the Sphinx*. His answer to the apparent contradiction between the determinism of nature and human freedom was to formulate a theory of evolution whereby matter is crossed by a creative consciousness: the two factors interact, but are not identical. Starting from the assumption of the extra-cerebral location of the memory, he deduced that:

> the role of the brain was to *choose* at any moment, among memories, those which could illuminate the action begun, and to exclude the others ... the brain did not have thinking as its function but that of hindering the thought from becoming lost in dream; it was the organ of *attention to life* [his italics].

In other words the brain, defined as the point of insertion of spirit into matter, narrows the focus of attention by its choice; it necessarily excludes factors irrelevant to adaptation essential for biological survival.

Thus Bergson argues that mental life 'overflows' cerebral life: the brain canalises and limits the mind, so that we can concentrate on present action. Bergson supports his thesis of memory and mind by referring to near-death experiences where the entire life-memory appears before the subject; thus the memories are available but normally screened out for practical purposes – if this were not so, we could neither concentrate nor focus on particular memories. Hence the brain (matter) is both an instrument of focused consciousness *and* an obstacle to a wider consciousness. As for the mind/brain relationship, Bergson insists that observation, experience and consequently science allows us to confirm the existence of a certain *relation* between mind and brain; it does not follow, however, that the mind is therefore a function of the brain. His view on death extends the logic of his views on memory and consciousness: the only reason for supposing that consciousness is extinguished at death is that we see the disintegration of the physical body. He argues that if the brain is actually a limited obstacle to consciousness during physical life, freedom from the physical may well result in an extended and more intense awareness, which continues its path of creative evolution. These views echo the arguments of Schiller.

The thought of the American psychologist and philosopher William James exhibits some similarities to that of Schiller and Bergson, but his formulation of the theory of mind is different. In his massive *Principles of Psychology* he examines and rejects the so-called mind-stuff theory, whereby individual cells are endowed with mind, and falls back temporarily on the soul theory. Later in the same work, however, when analysing the correlation of brain and mind, he finds that he can give a satisfactory account without introducing the notion of a soul: it is 'a complete superfluity, so far as accounting for the actually verified facts of conscious experience goes'. He is inclined to view the mind as the stream of consciousness, so that in a later paper he denies that consciousness exists as an entity, while thoughts in the concrete are fully real; consciousness is just the relation to the outside world. James is not sure whether there is some kind of personality underlying the experience of the stream of thought; this might create difficulties in conceiving of survival of death, as there would be no real identity to survive. At the end of *The Varieties of Religious Experience*, having commented that for most men religion means immortality, he admits being impressed by the researches of Myers and others. The issue, he says, is a case for the facts to testify, and he leaves the matter of survival open. This seems to have been his final conclusion: 'I confess I have sometimes been tempted to believe that the creator has eternally intended this department of nature to remain baffling.'

In 1898 James gave the Ingersoll Lecture on human immortality. Here his analysis centres round the problem of the absolute dependence of our spiritual life on the brain. He argues that the crux of the issue relates to the exact *type* of functional dependence: it is normally thought of as productive, in the sense that steam is a function of the kettle; from this it follows that annihilation of consciousness and personality is inevitable at death. James advances two other possible kinds of functional dependence: the permissive, as is found in the trigger of a crossbow, and the transmissive, as in a lens or the keys of an organ. He then expounds the transmissive theory, using as a starting point Shelley's famous lines to the effect that life is a dome of many-coloured glass, which stains the white radiance of eternity. Substituting the brain for the glass, the white radiance comes through the dome with all sorts of staining and distortion imprinted on the glass – through the glass darkly, as St Paul put it. James follows the lines of thought set out by Schiller (whom he quotes) and points out that the experiences investigated by psychical researchers are 'quite paradoxical and meaningless on the production theory', while the transmission theory enables them to fall naturally into place, as well as being compatible with the possibility of a future existence.

The psychologist McDougall set out his views on the mind/body issue in a book *Body and Mind*, which is subtitled 'A History and Defence of Animism'. In it he takes James to task for his rejection of the soul-theory, and dismisses the stream of consciousness alternative as inadequate. He claims that James's rejection of the soul-theory was due to a combination of three factors: his physiological starting point, his acceptance of the prevailing tendency of 'psychology without a soul', and his neo-Humian formula of the stream of consciousness; all these grounds are regarded as flimsy by McDougall, who then advances his own conception of the soul as 'a system of capacities which are fully present as latent possibilities from the beginning of the individual's life; these potentialities are realised or brought into play only in proportion as the brain mechanisms become developed and specialised'. He is aiming at a conception, which allows development over the lifetime of the individual while retaining an underlying unity of personality.

Even if James and McDougall disagree about the nature of mind and consciousness, they do concur on the important bearing of psychical research on the psycho-physical relation. McDougall writes that psychical research has established the existence of telepathy, which is incompatible with the mechanistic assumption. He does not cite specific evidence, but refers to the phenomenon of cross-correspondences, saying that the evidence is 'of such a nature as to compel the assent of any competent person who studies it impartially'. McDougall himself does not feel the considerable mass of evidence accumulated by the SPR, pointing towards the survival of the personality, to be 'of such a nature that it can be stated in a form which should produce conviction in the mind of any impartial inquirer'. He still awaits the critical blow, and thinks that the evidential character of the observations has just fallen short of perfection. Nevertheless he points out that some first-hand inquirers have become convinced of survival, 'and among these persons so convinced are several who, in respect to their competence to form a sane and critical judgment on this difficult question, cannot be rated inferior to any other persons'. His conclusion is that while psychical research has not produced the verification of animism, the theory is the only solution of the psycho-physical problem that is compatible with any belief in the continuance of personality after death.

Rudolf Steiner, the founder of Anthroposophy, is one of the least widely known and most underrated of twentieth-century thinkers, probably because he was too far ahead of his time. He developed a 'supersensible cognition', which enabled him, so he claimed, to perceive the true nature of the physical world in relation to the spiritual; his approach resembles that of the scientist-mystic Swedenborg. He only imparted what he had repeatedly observed as supersensible facts, and did not encourage people to accept, unquestioningly, everything he said; they should think about it, and could, if they wished, acquire similar faculties and perceptions. His theories on the nature of man are both elegant and highly suggestive, even if we confine ourselves to essentials: Man has three bodies; the physical, the etheric and the astral. The first he shares with inorganic nature, the second (in which the principle of life is implicit) with plants, and the third (in which consciousness is implicit) with animals. Steiner explains that animals have no memory as such, despite appearances to the contrary, and that memory is proper to the Ego (*das Ich*), which distinguishes human beings. Just as the body is the means whereby knowledge and awareness are realised, so the soul is defined as what gives this knowledge permanence and duration. The sentient soul corresponds with the physical body, the intellectual soul with the etheric, and the spiritual soul with the astral. The Ego operates through these on different levels, and is itself a drop in the divine ocean: 'Man can find a Divine in himself, because his own and most essential being springs from the Divine.'

Steiner goes on to explain the nature and relationship of the bodies to each other. The etheric body is the 'architect' of the physical; it maintains its shape and form, preventing disintegration (except after death, as we shall see); it permeates and interflows with the physical body. The natural state of the etheric and physical bodies in the absence of the astral body (consciousness) is, logically enough, sleep – thus plants are in a perpetual state of 'sleep'. The astral body illuminates the other two in the waking state, while the Ego functions through all three. During sleep, the astral body and Ego (consciousness and will) withdraw from the etheric and physical. Complete withdrawal would correspond to a state of dreamless sleep; while in a partial withdrawal, where the astral body is completely detached from the etheric, there will be no memory, corresponding to the state of dreamless sleep; while if some connection subsists, there may be memory or visual impressions – such a hypothesis would explain, for instance, why not everyone who has a near-death experience has an apparently continuous memory of the events occurring during periods of physical unconsciousness; equally, given the Gurney-Myers theory that waking hallucinations are equivalent to dreaming, when the subject was ostensibly physically unconscious.

Whereas in sleep and out-of-the-body experiences the physical and etheric bodies remain united, this is not the case in death. At this point the connection between them is severed; the physical body ceases to be the instrument of the Ego. As the etheric body no longer holds it together, the physical body is, henceforth, subject to the processes and laws of the physical world; its dissolution is observable by the physical senses. Steiner explains that even during physical life the Ego and soul could only be observed by the senses in so far as they were manifested in physical processes; after death, however, no such expression is possible, so that physically-based science can say nothing of their fate. According to higher knowledge, the association of the physical and astral bodies elicits a tableau of memories of the life, accompanied by some degree of purgation, a process described by some of the subjects of near-death experiences. There then occurs a separation of the astral from the etheric body, which goes beyond the scope of this work. The cogency of Steiner's scheme can only become apparent in the light of the data treated in Part two.

We come now to the views of four distinguished neurophysiologists on the relation between mind and brain. They do not themselves infer the possible continued independent existence of mind from their theories, but it would not be illogical to do so. Sir Charles Sherrington, whose Gifford Lectures are entitled *Man on His Nature*, tries to establish the exact nature of the connection between mind and brain. For a start he cannot equate mind with life, as life is accessible to the senses whereas mind is not. Perhaps, then, mind arises from the nature of brain cells? This is impossible because 'a brain cell is not unalterably a brain cell ... cells, like those of the brain in microscopic appearance, in chemical character, and in provenance, are elsewhere concerned with acts totally devoid of mind, for instance a knee-jerk.' So he concludes that although cell-organisation may conceivably be the secret of the correlation with mind, the brain cannot derive its mind cumulatively and additively from a cumulative mental property of the individual cells composing it. A third line of enquiry is some kind of equivalence of energy and mind, but Sherrington finds no evidence of this, and even asserts that mind and energy are disparate categories, not mutually convertible, and untranslatable the one into the other; so that just as mind cannot be classified as matter, nor can it be classified as energy: life, matter and energy are granular in structure; mind is not.

Sherrington draws a radical distinction between life and mind when analysing the limits of scientific explanation. He argues that there is nothing in the phenomenon of life which does not fall within the scope of science, that is to say within the field of chemistry and physics; and he continues:

> But though living is analysable and describable by natural science, that associate of living, thought, escapes and remains refractory to science. In fact natural science repudiates it as something outside its ken ... life ... is an affair of chemistry and physics ... mind ... escapes chemistry and physics. And yet the occurrence of mind – recognisable finite mind – is confined to a certain particular field of chemistry and physics, namely, that of highly integrated animal lives.

What is significant here is the observation that natural science can ultimately only account for phenomena in terms of chemistry and physics, and that mind falls, according to Sherrington, by definition outside the scope of natural science: so that in so far as mind is recognised by science, the only strictly *scientific* explanation of it must reduce the nature of mind to the terms of physics and chemistry. This is exactly what we saw the identity theorists trying to do.

Given his view of the incommensurability of energy and mind, and in the light of the above considerations – that mental phenomena do not seem amenable to understanding in terms of physics and chemistry – Sherrington defines the brain as an organ of liaison between energy and mind, but not as a converter of energy into mind or of mind into energy; the brain might equally well be described as the organ of liaison between mind and the external perceived world. Action between energy and mind can take place in either direction, described as 'reversible interaction between the "I" and the body'; this contrasts with the T H Huxley view that the process of cause and effect can only run from the brain to the body and not vice versa, and is a point which will be amplified by Eccles below. Although he does not explicitly state his view on survival, Sherrington makes a series of observations about the 'I', which are reminiscent of those already encountered in Freud:

> The 'I', which thinks itself in the body, regarding the body as having in it 'life', identifies that 'life' with itself. It *is* the life. The actions of the body are *its* actions ... Although the body after a certain duration breaks up and as a body disappears, the 'I' proceeds to suppose that it the 'I' will still continue despite the dissolution of the body. It has supposed itself 'living'; then it proceeds to suppose that it will not 'die', that it is 'immortal'. The 'self-concept' becomes a 'soul-concept'.

Sherrington considers this Cartesian inference of the soul-concept from the self-concept to be illegitimate; and because what is described is a psychological process, it is not empirically relevant to the issue of survival, however interesting.

Wilder Penfield describes a fascinating experiment in which he stimulated parts of the cerebral cortex while the subject was still conscious. He sums up the results of the operation as follows:

> The patient's mind, which is considering the situation in such an aloof and critical manner, can only be something quite apart from the neuronal reflex action. It is noteworthy that two streams of consciousness are flowing, the one driven by the output from the environment, the other by an electrode delivering 60 pulses per second to the cortex. The fact that there should be no confusion in the conscious state suggests that, although the content of consciousness depends in large measure on neuronal activity, awareness does not.

The implications of this experiment are momentous: that a person can remain aware of two streams of consciousness at once without the stimulus to the cortex destroying other conscious processes. Penfield, therefore, 'after years of striving to explain the mind on the basis of brain-action alone' came to the conclusion that it is simpler to adopt the hypothesis that our being consists of two fundamental elements, likening the brain to a computer and the mind to the programmer – a view which we shall see shared by Eccles and Popper below.

Karl Pribram's starting point is to accept the mind-body problem as a biological fact. For him the fundamental question, given this state of affairs, is whether mind emerges in the course of the organism's interaction with the environment, or else whether mind actually reflects the basic organisation of the universe. On the one hand the brain constructs mental properties by organising the sensory input from the external world; on the other hand, these very mental properties are 'the pervasive organising principles of the universe, which includes the brain'. The starting point recalls Steiner and Bergson. Pribram's approach is based on holographic theory, developed by Gabor; the photographic hologram records the interference patterns of light in such a way that the original object is reproduced in three dimensions on a plate. Its most striking property is that the whole of the object is reproduced, albeit less distinctly, even when the pattern represents only part of the original object. Thus there is a sense in which the whole is contained in the parts. Pribram applies this insight to memory, claiming that memories were perhaps not localisable precisely because they were stored across the brain as a whole. The interception of light patterns on the hologram suggests to him that the brain, in its turn, interpreted and decoded frequencies, before re-encoding them in, for instance, language. He speculates that without the brain's neural interference patterns and its mathematical processes, reality might simply consist of events without space or time (the word 'event' is perhaps misleading here as it denotes time distinctions in the whole – for the same reason one could hardly even use the world 'flow'). The resulting theory is a neo-Kantian 'constructional realism', whereby reality is constructed by an interpretation of the frequency realm. Pribram suggests that a more direct access to this realm, bearing in mind the reflection of the whole in the part, might explain transcendental experiences: in such cases the brain is more attuned to the 'primary level of reality, a dimension of harmony and order'. Furthermore, if there is no time or space in the primary level, this may provide an explanatory framework for psychical phenomena which transcend these boundaries; logically it could be contended that man operates beyond space and time after physical death, 'nearer' the primary level of reality, but Pribram himself does not explicitly state as much. Space prevents a more elaborate discussion of the holographic theory, some of the applications of which are hotly disputed.

Although Sir John Eccles states that the aim of neurosciences is to formulate a theory that can, in principle, provide a complete explanation of all behaviour of animals and man in terms of monist materialism (reducing mind to matter as the ultimate and only underlying principle), he thinks that such a reductionist strategy will fail to account for the higher levels of conscious performance in the human brain: 'All varieties of identity theories', he argues 'imply that the mind's conscious experiences have a merely passive relationship as a spin-off from the operations of the neural machinery, which themselves are self sufficient.' In other words that the conscious self cannot initiate neural processes but only become aware of them. Eccles contends that a dualist-interactionist hypothesis will actually account comprehensively for all behaviour including these hither levels of conscious performance. The essentials of his hypothesis are these:

1. There is a unitary character of self-conscious mind.

2. The experiences of the self-conscious mind have a relationship with the liaison brain (defined as all those areas of the cerebral cortex that are potentially capable of being in direct liaison with the self-conscious mind); this relationship is one of interaction giving a degree of correspondence, not an identity.

3. There can be a temporal discrepancy between neural events and the experiences of the self-conscious mind.

4. There is a continual experience that the self-conscious mind can act on brain events; this is most apparent in voluntary action or in the attempt to recall a memory, word, or phrase.

Eccles proposes that the self-conscious mind exercises a superior interpretative and controlling role on neural events:

It is responsible for the act of attention, selecting from all the immense activity of our brain the neural bases of our experience from moment to moment ... not just receiving but ... actively engaged in modifying the brain.

The hypothesis is a good deal more radical than others we have encountered until now, as it actually suggests that the mind controls events in the cerebral cortex; it comes close to being a modern restatement of the Cartesian ghost in the machine theory, even if Eccles himself would be unhappy about this categorisation. He claims that his theory is not refuted by any existing knowledge and has the great advantage of explaining 'how a diversity of brain events comes to be synthesised so that there is a unified conscious experience of a global or gestalt character'. There is thus a self-underlying, controlling and unifying conscious experience; as in Schiller's formulation, the brain is the organ whereby consciousness is transmitted and conscious experience received.

In a discussion with Sir Karl Popper on Immortality Eccles almost sails into theological waters by saying that he cannot believe that this wonderful gift of a conscious existence (the word gift implies a giver) has no further future, no possibility of another existence under some imaginable conditions. This hope naturally has no scientific basis. But he thinks that it may be possible for self-conscious mind in its essential being to rise superior to the brain. 'Thus there may be some central core, the inmost self, that survives the death of the brain to achieve some other existence which is quite beyond that we can imagine.' This remains a speculative possibility, and in the end Eccles leaves the question open as to whether life is an episode of consciousness between two oblivions or whether beyond there exists some further transcendent experience. At any rate his theory of the mind/brain relation does not rule this out.

Popper shares most of the views of Eccles, but with some differences of emphasis. He divides the body-mind problem into two distinct issues: first, the relationship between physiological states and certain states of consciousness, and second the emergence of the self and its relation to the body. Like Eccles he is an interactionist as regards the correspondence of physical and mental states, but he is, perhaps, more interested in the second issue. He considers the self to have emerged in the course of evolution in which the most significant factors were the development of language and a sense of time, and then the growing ability to hand culture on from one generation to the next; we have seen how the child grows into a consciousness of its own selfhood. Popper insists that the self is not owned by the brain, which would imply passivity, but rather that the self 'owns' the brain and directs its activities:

> The active, psycho-physical self is the active programmer to the brain (which is the computer), it is the executant whose instrument is the brain. The mind is, as Plato said, the pilot. It is not, as David Hume and William James suggested, the sum total, or the bundle, or the stream of its experiences: this suggests passivity.

(It can be seen from Popper's terminology that self and mind are used in the same sense – elsewhere he uses the fuller and more explicit term 'self-conscious mind'.) Although Popper's theory of mind is compatible with the independent survival of the self-conscious mind, he himself is doubtful whether this happens. He finds the idea of an eternity of survival 'utterly frightening', and describes what is pictured by believers in psychical research as the most terrible of all prospects; here he envisages some kind of ghostly semi-existence on a particularly low intellectual level as the norm – an examination of the relevant literature reveals that this is by no means universal. He views death, in the sense of the limitation of life, as constituting life's value: it becomes for him an urgent task to achieve something for others. As a postscript he adds that if there is anything in the idea of survival, then he is inclined to take seriously those who maintain that it cannot just be in space and time – but that much is certain already.

We shall now make a temporary excursion to the east in order to examine the viewpoint of the Hindu philosopher Sir Sarvepalli Radhakrishnan, who was at one time Professor of Eastern Religions and Ethics at Oxford, and later President of India, having been Ambassador to Moscow: one of the few men who might approximate to being called a philosopher-king. He is fully conversant with the mind-stretching developments in modern physics, remarking that the solid atom has melted away and matter has become 'a structure of energy-units revolving with immense velocities in space-time'. In a passage reminiscent of Russell he writes that 'Nature is a complex of events, a structure of processes. Events are the stuff of concrete existence. They exist not in space separated by time, but in space-time ...' He describes the displacement of hard indivisible matter of electric influences as of the greatest importance from the philosophical point of view because 'the contrast between matter as inert and life as active, matter as reversible and life as irreversible, disappears. The difference between life and matter is not one of activity and passivity, but between two different kinds of activity.' The Cartesian theory of the incorporeal mind operating on matter of mechanical push has been overtaken by events. Radhakrishnan suggests that the mental has a higher degree of self-regulation and control than the body, and that it cannot be understood by the study of the living organism (a point already stressed in Sherrington) any more than sight can be understood merely by examining the eye.

Before advancing his views on rebirth, Radhakrishnan makes a brief reference to personal immortality; an idea which, he claims, is not properly understood. We could hardly desire endless youth or endless old age, the ardours of youth being incompatible with the insight of old age, and, in any event, we should be sick of any endless state. Within the reincarnation framework, bodily life is an episode in the larger career of the individual soul, and death is not a unique event in our progress. 'It is part of a continually recurring rhythm of nature, marking a crisis in the history of the individual.' It is the 'moment when the self assumes a new set of conditions'. He quotes the Chandogya Upanishad as stating: 'It is the body which dies when left by the self; the self does not die', and comments that the death of the physical body does not mean the dissipation of the self, the self being dependent on the body for its material only so long as it is connected with it. As for the vehicle of the self after the death of the physical body, the Hindus believe that it operates in a finer ethereal body, an idea which Radhakrishnan thinks is supported by some of the findings of western psychical research. Rebirth in another body is a continuation of the cycle and only a renewal of the instrument through which the self manifests itself and works. A discussion of the empirical 'evidence' for reincarnation is outside our present scope, but interested readers might like to consult Stevenson.

Our return to the West is not a complete break, as the psychologist C. G. Jung had a deep interest in Eastern philosophy and religion. He pointed out that since all scientific statements are merely probable, the possibility of survival can be discussed only in the light of knowledge which would cast light on the probability of such a hypothesis. 'The only scientific approach to the question of survival', he writes, 'is the recognition of the fact that the psyche [his composite term for the mind] is capable of extra-sensory perceptions, namely of telepathy and precognition, particularly the latter.' Hence Jung contends that space and time are not axiomatic truths of universal application, because the psyche is capable of transcending these categories; and the fact that such transcendence is comparatively rare suggests to Jung that forms of existence inside and outside time are sharply divided. But this does not exclude the possibility that there is an existence outside time, which runs parallel with existence in time, and that we may catch the occasional glimpse of this other dimension. Acceptance of telepathic phenomena as facts led Jung to postulate, like Schiller and Bergson, that the brain was the space-time limitation of the psyche. In telepathy the range of perception is extended beyond the limitations of the senses – the powers of the psyche are enhanced rather than curbed. This theory provided Jung with a coherent explanation of the out-of-body experience recorded by Geddes, who noticed that, while he was unconscious to the normal observer, his centre of consciousness was able to perceive his physical body on the bed and possessed other verifiable ESP attributes.

As a scientist, Jung realised that although there was 'no way to marshal valid proof of the continuance of the soul after death, there are experiences which make us thoughtful'; these he takes as 'hints', one of which is discussed more fully elsewhere. On the issue of so-called spirit communication Jung made the usual caveats about the difficulty of proving identity, and stressed the difference between subjective conviction and objective proof. But having said this, although he had to remain sceptical in individual cases, he admitted that, in the long run, the spirit hypothesis yielded better results in practice than any other hypothesis based on the qualities and peculiarities of the unconscious; this does not mean that the hypothesis is to be advanced to account for every likely looking case but simply that there are some cases where it is the most comprehensive. As for the possible location of another world, Jung advances some speculations that are interesting to compare with Price (treated below):

> If we assume that life continues 'there', we cannot conceive of any other form of existence except a psychic one [here used in Jung's sense]; for the life of the psyche requires no space and no time. Psychic existence, and above all the inner images with which we are here concerned, supply the material for all the mythic speculations about a life in the hereafter, and I imagine that life as a continuance in the world of images. Thus the psyche might be that existence in which the hereafter or the land of the dead is located.

The Psyche has its own space and time, which is clearly not physical.

In the light of the recent scandal about his statistics, it is ironic that two of the themes treated in Sir Cyril Burt's *ESP and Psychology* are fraud and self-deception. Nevertheless any reader of his book and articles on psychical research will testify that they are both well-informed and trenchant. Burt had little time for the grossly oversimplified cosmology of the behaviourists, accusing them of basing their doctrines less on the empirical study of consciousness and behaviour than on *a priori* considerations derived from the general principles of nineteenth-century physics and biology. As a cynical onlooker he described the progress of behaviouristic psychology in terms of having first bargained away its soul, then gone out of its mind, and, when finally faced with an untimely end, having lost all consciousness. His own view on the mind/brain relation follows the Schiller line, namely that:

> the brain is not an organ that generates consciousness, but rather an instrument evolved to transmit and limit the processes of consciousness and of conscious attention so as to restrict them to those aspects of the material environment which at any moment are crucial for the terrestrial survival of the individual. In that case such phenomena as telepathy and clairvoyance would be merely instances in which some of the limitations were removed.

Burt's formulation is very similar to Jung's. He also makes the same deductions as Penfield about electrical stimulation of the cerebral cortex during brain surgery: complex sensory experiences may be produced by the stimulation but the implication of this is that while it is clear that the brain can generate some of the contents of consciousness, it does not follow that the brain generates the actual awareness.

Like James and Lodge, Burt was very impressed by the evidence from the SPR cross-correspondences, which were designed to furnish proof of the identity of the spirit communicator. Some investigators have advanced a theory of so-called Super-ESP to account for the fact that a communicator who identifies himself as the same person speaking through two different mediums can leave half of a message with one and the rest with the other. As many messages consisted of classical allusions of which the mediums had no knowledge and could not therefore be expected to understand and transmit telepathically to each other, the odds of each selecting by chance an allusion appropriate to the other are to all intents and purposes nil. The full impact of these cross-correspondences can be appreciated only by detailed study of the cases, one of which is known as 'Alexander's Tomb'. Here the essential items were distributed among three automatists, Mrs Piper, Miss Verrall, and Mrs Holland:

> Mrs Piper: Moorhead, I gave her that for laurel.
> Mrs Verall: Alexander's Tomb. Laurel
> Mrs Holland: Alexander Moors Head.

The first two messages contain no discernible connection, and might have suggested some reference to Alexander the Great. The third message, written in complete ignorance of the other two, but by the same 'author', reveals the hidden connection between the first two: this turns out to be a reference to Allessandro de Medici. The laurel was the family emblem, especially of Lorenzo de Medici, with whom Allessandro was buried after his assassination in 1537. The third message was originally construed as a reference to the scientist Alexander Muirhead, but when connected with the first two messages takes on another more significant meaning: Alessandro was the son of Pope Clement VII and a mulatto slave – he therefore had a Negro-like appearance. This summary does scant justice to the details of the case but may give some indication of the structure of the cross-correspondences.

The spirit hypothesis explains this mind of correspondence much more directly than a Super-ESP theory which Burt considered 'involved assumptions which strain credulity to the very limit; it is one of those ingenious skeleton keys that open every lock and consequently provide a genuine fit to none'. The supporter of the hypothesis would maintain that the idea of survival is *a priori* so improbable that no other explanation, even if it pushes the notions of telepathy to hitherto unprecedented limits, can be as implausible as that of survival. Burt's own conclusion was that while science cannot provide any *positive* evidence against the possibility of survival, and the empirical evidence weights definitely but not conclusively in its favour, his own study of the available data led him to share Murphy's conclusion that the evidence cannot be by-passed, nor yet can conviction be achieved.

The philosopher C. J. Ducasse analyses the case for and against survival in his wide-ranging work *Nature, Mind, and Death*. He also sets out critiques of views advanced on both sides of the argument. The case against survival contains the usual physicalist assertions which we have encountered to date, such as the correlation of brain damage and the manifestation of consciousness, the one-side arguing that consciousness has been lost, while the other maintains that its complete manifestation has been impeded by damage to the transmitter. In considering the divergence of interpretation, Ducasse makes the interesting observation that the physicalists have an underlying assumption that only the material can affect the material because it is the only reality: he feels that such people underrate the reality of what lies inside themselves, which is equally real and without which there would be no conscious experience. In some cases, it is real in a different sense: one's dreams only become unreal on awakening.

Ducasse then reviews the empirical evidence for survival, especially apparitions and 'spirit communications'. He is aware of the possibility of the fraud explanation, but points out that the investigators of the SPR are very experienced at dealing with a good deal of this, and therefore try to take elaborate precautions or make extensive inquiries about some alleged incident. He also comments on the distinction between arguing in abstract and concrete terms about the nature of apparitions and communications.

> When, instead of stopping at summaries, one takes the trouble to study the detailed original reports, it then becomes evident that they cannot all be just laughed off; for to accept the hypothesis of fraud or malobservation would often require more credulity than to accept the facts reported.

The sceptic might dismiss this as a value judgment, but wrongly unless he himself has investigated the reports personally; if he has not, he lays himself open to the charge of what James called 'conceited ignorance'.

In his critique of the empirical evidence for survival, Ducasse refers to a well-known paper by E. R. Dodds, which suggests that the phenomena are by no means sufficiently uniform or clear-cut for some form of telepathy hypothesis to be totally excluded. And Ducasse himself concludes that while some evidence for survival is very impressive, there are nevertheless difficulties of interpretation, which are hard to dispose of:

> There is strong *prima facia* evidence that in some instances *something* survives, which appears to be some part or some set of capacities of the mind whose body has died. But the demonstrated realities of telepathy, clairvoyance, and retrocognition ... so complicate the facts

ordinarily adduced as empirical evidence of survival ... that nothing both definite and well-evidenced can yet be concluded concerning the actual, as distinguished from the theoretical, possibility of survival.

Theoretically, however, Ducasse speculates about the possibility of survival in a mind of dream world, as pictured also by Jung and H. H. Price. He suggests that this form of survival would account for some communication concerning mediumistic accounts of the afterlife such as scenery, houses and occupations, which seem like duplicates of earth life; and for the diversity of descriptions according to the individual concerned. In addition, some of the more bizarre occurrences reported, such as Lodge's son smoking cigars, might be real in the same way as we regard our dreams real during our experience of them.

Although Price (Ayer's predecessor as Wykeham Professor of Logic at Oxford) has no objections, in principle, to the behaviouristic method, which confines itself to investigating the publicly observable behaviour of human beings and animals, he does object to the behaviourist theory of mind on two counts: first, it seems to him indisputable that people actually are aware, that they do have states of consciousness; and second, he contends that there are some serious difficulties about the concept of 'publicly observable'. He illustrates these by asking the behaviourist what is happening when he observes a rat running about in a maze:

> Is it just receiving optical stimuli and responding to those by inscribing black marks on his notebook? If he has a colleague who is also observing the rat, he might perhaps try to maintain that this *is* all that is happening in his colleague. But can he possibly think that this is all that is happening in himself? On the contrary he is *being aware of*, being *visually conscious of*, the movements of the rat, and the black marks he inscribes in his notebook are a record of what he is being aware.

The behaviourist would be hard pressed to deny this. In addition, Price points out that the very meaning of the word public depends on the contrasting word private, so that if public becomes meaningless, then the same goes for private. He sums this up by saying that the error of the behaviourist is the philosophical error of denying the obvious, and not the scientific error of denying new and strange facts which fail to fit in with current scientific theories.

Price deals with this last issue elsewhere, pointing out that the materialist theory of human nature confines itself to the facts of normal experience, but that these are by no means the only relevant data available: supernormal phenomena must also be accounted for. If conclusive empirical evidence for the persistence of human minds after death were presented, then the materialist theory would finally be refuted. In Price's opinion, there is a good deal of empirical evidence to support the hypothesis of human survival, and even some mediumistic reports which are difficult to account for on any other hypothesis; but the extant evidence is not absolutely conclusive. While the man who denies the possibility is on dangerous ground, he still has half a leg to stand on.

Price now argues that the implications of telepathy are incompatible with the materialistic hypothesis, because any physical theory of telepathy would involve radiations detectable on sensitive physical instruments; and no such radiations have yet been detected. Moreover, the evidence for telepathy suggests that one mind is affected directly by another, and not indirectly through the normal channels of the senses. So Price feels bound to conclude that:

> there is no room for telepathy in a materialistic universe. Telepathy is something which ought not to happen, if the materialistic theory were true. But it does happen. So there must be something seriously wrong with the materialistic theory, however numerous and imposing the *normal* facts which support it may be.

In other words the physicalist theory, although adequate as an explanation of normal facts, is inadequate when it attempts to deal with supernormal facts, while an approach such as that of Eccles and Popper can deal theoretically with both sets of facts. Price also touches on the phenomena of precognition and clairvoyance, commenting with regard to the latter that perception seems to be direct in a similar way to telepathy. At the end of the article Price addresses himself to those who dismiss the queer facts of psychical research as mere curiosities and oddities of no particular importance:

> On the contrary [he argues] these queer facts are not at all trivial, and it is right to make the greatest possible fuss about them. Their very queerness is what makes them significant. We call them queer just because they will not fit in with orthodox scientific ideas about the universe and man's place in it. If they show, as I think they do, that the materialistic conception of human personality is untenable, and if they throw quite new light on the age-old conflict between the scientific

and the religious outlooks, we shall have to conclude that psychical research is one of the most important branches of investigation that the human mind has ever undertaken.

No punches are pulled about the importance of the psychical research and its implications, which may well turn out to be as important as Price makes out.

Price's concern in his lecture *Survival of the Idea of Another World* is not so much to prove survival (we have already seen that he considers the evidence inconclusive) but rather to make the idea of another world intelligible; for various reasons the hypothesis has been discarded as *a priori* unintelligible. What Price suggests is that the next world might be conceived as a sort of dream-world, a world of mental images in which the mental imagery plays the part currently assigned to sense perception. Although we are cut off from sensory stimuli, we still manage to have experiences while asleep, and these experiences, even if non-physical, are none the less real. The problem of survival of death is posed as that of whether experiences occur after death which are linked together in such a way as to preserve personal identity; and in considering such questions we are less concerned with physico-chemical processes than psychological ones, because in this sense 'being alive' means having experiences of various sorts: 'In this psychological sense of the word "life", it is perfectly intelligible to ask whether there is life after death, even though life in the physiological sense does *ex hypothesi* come to an end when someone dies'. Price then argues that the *images* of organic sensations of feeling alive could perfectly well provide the requisite criteria, thus rendering the notion intelligible. He then makes a number of observations which do not relate directly to the notion of intelligibility, but draw out some of the inferences of such a world: it would be subjective in that it would be mind-dependent, but might interact telepathically with other similar subjective worlds, thereby creating a common environment which would be the sum-total of the imagined desires (whether repressed or not) of its inhabitants; the fact that images and desires are linked, in conjunction with the fact that this world would exist in its own space, might suggest that travel would be simultaneous with the desire to be somewhere: the desire would immediately create or 'be at' the right place, in the way suggested in the *Bardo Thodol*; and the body could either be imagined or ethereal, a distinction which becomes almost irrelevant in an image-dependent world. Although Price is careful not to draw any such comparisons, the reader who consults the relevant literature purporting to describe the environment of the 'next world' (or rather worlds) will find many striking parallels to Price's speculations. His importance lies not just in his critique of materialist theories of mind, but also in being a philosopher of the first rank who appreciated the implications of psychical research for philosophy.

C. D. Broad has indicated the rarity of such an achievement and has, himself, made the most extensive and penetrating analysis of the possible connections between philosophy and psychical research:

> It has always seemed to me most strange and most deplorable that the vast majority of philosophers and psychologists should utterly ignore the strong prima facie case that exists for the occurrence of many supernormal phenomena which, if genuine, must profoundly affect our theories of the human mind, its cognitive powers, and its relation to the human body.

Broad, himself, was trained as a physicist but turned to philosophy, becoming Knightsbridge Professor of Moral Philosophy at Cambridge, the chair held by Sidgwick. His writings cover scientific thought and ethics, as well as the connections between philosophy and psychical research, where his principal works were *The Mind and Its Place in Nature; Religion, Philosophy, and Psychical Research*, and finally his *Lectures on Psychical Research*; this last work is an excellent introduction to the field, the *TLS* review of which commented on the book's 'admirable clarity of thought, its detailed precision of treatment, and its exact and impartial explanation of all that is meant, involved, and implied by psychical research'. Few readers could disagree with this assessment.

As indicated above, Broad did not consider it possible to deal adequately with the body/mind question without taking into account the phenomena of psychical research. Indeed he even maintains that apart from these phenomena there is nothing whatever to support the dualist view that a man's mind or personality can operate independently of the body, there being a good deal of *prima facie* evidence against such a hypothesis. He insisted that it was neither honest nor realistic to dismiss the authority and competence of SPR investigations:

> I have always found that those who deny it [the competence] have not carefully read the relevant literature, have conducted very few careful investigations for themselves, and are ignorant of the intellectual

calibre and scrupulous honesty of such men as Sidgwick, Gurney, and Podmore.

Pursuing his first point about conclusions derived solely on the basis of normal experience, Broad asserts that:

If, like most contemporary Western philosophers and scientists, I were completely ignorant of, or blandly indifferent to those [supernormal] phenomena, I should, like them, leave the matter there. But I do not share their ignorance, and I am not content to emulate the ostrich.

So he passes on to his own investigations.

Before considering the possibility of survival, Broad clarifies what he understands by a 'person'. He maintains that persons who exist are distinguished by three characteristics, namely a stream of experience (at present grounded in a living organism), an organised set of dispositions, and a body, which is described as 'perceptually central' – the point from which experience is perceived. He does not rule out other bodies co-existing with the physical body, but he cannot conceive of a stream of experience in a post-mortem state being entirely disembodied: even in dreams the perceptual centre seems to be associated with a body, a recognisable form. Like Price, Broad considers the phenomenon of dreams to be important in throwing light on the nature of identity and on the continuity of the stream of experience: they show that:

a human being has within him the mechanism and the materials for producing an extremely elaborate, and often fairly coherent and sustained, sequence of hallucinatory quasi-perceptions, as of an environment of things and persons in which he is living and acting and suffering, although at the time he is not having the externally initiated sensations which are the basis of normal waking perception.

Of the various characteristics of an existing person outlined above, Broad considers that the dispositional basis of the personality is the most important: if the whole or some considerable part of this did not survive, then the whole idea of identity would be undermined – we expect people we know to be reasonably consistent in their dress, tastes and habits. It is the commonplace assumption of the materialist, as we have abundantly seen, that the whole of this disposition resides in the structure and workings of the brain, and therefore perishes with it. If this is not the case, then the only view of human nature compatible with the possibility of a post-mortem existence is some variant of the Platonic-Cartesian dualist hypothesis. Because Broad cannot conceive of Descartes's 'res cogitans' as an unextended substance, he argues that what is required is some form of primitive animism. By this he means that in this life a human being is a compound of two factors, a soul and a physical body, the former 'animating' the latter; in addition, the soul is compounded of the mind and an 'astral' body to which it is intrinsically related. At death the soul ceases to animate the physical body, which disintegrates, but continues its conscious existence in the 'astral' body. Broad recognises that such a view is most unfashionable, but it is at least intelligible, and completes the cycle from the primitive conception to that of sophisticated modern philosophy.

Having formulated his version of the dualist hypothesis, Broad examines it in the light of psychical research. He claims that the existence of telepathy, clairvoyance, and precognition does not lend *direct* support to the hypothesis, although they do demonstrate that the materialist view requires radical revision (he is taking a weaker line than Price), and provides a basis not furnished by the materialistic standpoint for further theories which might explain paranormal phenomena. He feels that out-of-the-body experiences and mediumistic communications are favourably relevant data, the latter being the strongest support. He touches on pointers to reincarnation, but finds none of the evidence coercive, even if it is favourable. The most convincing of the cases of mediumistic communications are those where the medium speaks with the voice and behaves with mannerisms 'recognisably reminiscent of the alleged communicator', or produces script allegedly written 'under the control of the spirit of a certain deceased human being, and undoubtedly in his handwriting'. This kind of case is for Broad strong evidence of the post-mortem persistence of some entity which has similar dispositions to a known deceased person, and which is temporarily united with the organism of the entranced medium. Broad is very cautious in his deductions, and does not think that in most cases the personality survives. He argues that a 'psi-component' (a system of organised dispositions united before death with the physical body) is using the living physical body of a human being, and thus forming a compound temporary personality in conjunction with some of the medium's characteristics. Given known physiological considerations, he does not regard it warrantable in the majority of cases to assert that the psi-component can exist independently of some physical organism or other, whether it be its original living body or that of the medium; so his theory of the soul existing in an astral body is accorded less plausibility. The crux of the question is whether the so-called psi-component has experiences of some kind *between* the communications, which might equally well *limit* its effectiveness of communication: if the human brain acts as a filter in this life, it may likewise be an impediment to full communication in trance mediumship. We really only have the word of the communicator to go on, since we are not in a position to verify directly what is reported, in the same way as one cannot prove that a person had had a dream if he affirms it.

The above summary does scant justice to the range and subtlety of Broad's viewpoint, which the reader must peruse for himself if he is to fill out all the details. His carefully worded conclusion draws together the various strands of his argument, and comes to a cautious positive conclusion on survival:

> To conclude, the position as I see it is this. In the known relevant *normal and abnormal* facts there is nothing to suggest, and much to counter-suggest, the possibility of any kind of persistence of the psychical aspect of a human being after the death of his body. On the other hand, there are many quite well attested *paranormal* phenomena which strongly suggest such persistence, and a few which strongly suggest the full-blown survival of a human personality. Most people manage to turn a blind eye to one or the other of these two relevant sets of data, but it is part of the business of a professional philosopher to try to envisage steadily both of them together. The result is naturally a state of hesitation and scepticism (in the correct, as opposed to the popular) sense of that word. I think I may say that for my part I should be slightly more annoyed than surprised if I should find myself in some sense persisting immediately after the death of my present body. One can only wait and see, or alternatively (which is no less likely) wait and not see.

The zoologist Sir Alister Hardy, while remaining a convinced Darwinian, is unable to accept that the process of natural selection was brought about exclusively by chance. This theory of so-called random mutation goes hand in hand with a materialist assessment of human nature, which ignores the spiritual side of man. Nor does Hardy consider that the natural (biological) and spiritual sides of man are irreconcilable: while much natural selection is due to external environmental factors, he contends that 'conscious behaviour plays an increasing role in true Darwinian evolution as we come to the higher forms of life'. Superior mentality in terms of knowledge and technique can itself act as an indirect agent of evolution in creating and sustaining certain environmental factors which affect other forms of life, for instance in fertilisers and pollution. Hardy feels that the importance of consciousness has been badly underrated by modern physicalist biology and psychology, and rightly indicates that 'in the field of consciousness, as we experience it, lie all the feelings of purpose, love, joy, sorrow, the sense of the sacred, the sense of right and wrong, the appreciation of beauty, indeed all that really matters in life'. Because he felt the time had come for the scientific method to demonstrate whether or not it is reasonable to regard the spiritual side of a man as valid, Hardy set up the Religious Experience Research Unit in Oxford. Its purpose is to collect, analyse and classify records of experiences of a broadly religious or numinous nature; these have been published in several books and summed up in Hardy's own work *The Spiritual Nature of Man*.

Among the experiences reported to the RERU were some of a more psychic than mystical nature – psi-phenomena, as Hardy terms them. He considers these to be of profound significance for philosophy and religion, especially if they do not fit in with the materialist system: they would throw light upon the vexed mind/body problem and would undermine the supposed scientific grounds for materialism – an argument which we have already encountered in Price and Broad. With regard to survival, Hardy's opinion is that the evidence on the files of SPR (especially that from the cross-correspondences) would, if examined in a court of law, demonstrate one of two things: either the survival of some part of the human personality, or a degree of telepathy between living agents which is quite beyond that suggested by experimental methods. He points out that such a judgement would not constitute scientific proof, but it would at least suggest a direction for future research. In *The Divine Flame* he quotes Broad's conclusion cited above and adds that this is also his own 'except that I certainly should not be annoyed to find myself surviving'. He feels that much more needs to be known about the psychology of mediumship before any definite conclusions can be reached, but is nevertheless convinced that 'The phenomena of extra-sensory perception are sufficiently well attested to show that the present widely held materialistic-monistic conception of the universe must be false'.

We have now surveyed some of the major contributions to the interrelated problems of body, mind, brain, and death. Rather than follow the details of their reasonings as we have done until now, we shall quote the conclusions of a few other eminent psychical researchers.

In *The Enigma of Survival*, Hornell Hart examines all aspects of the case for and against an afterlife, with special emphasis on mediumistic and apparitional evidence. He considers the strength of every conceivable anti-survivalist argument, warning against an investigator allowing himself to be dominated either by the will to believe or to disbelieve – he will thus be prevented from arriving at the most *probable* truth on the questions in hand. In the light of the cumulative evidence, he favours the hypothesis that the brain is a transmitting instrument rather than the generator of personal consciousness and concludes: 'human personality *does* survive bodily death. That is the outcome which I find emerging when the strongest anti-survivalist arguments and the strongest rebuttals are considered thoroughly, with dispassionate open-mindedness.'

Robert Crookall was a geologist by profession, and in his retirement collected an unprecedented number of reports concerning out-of-the-body experiences, apparitions, mediumistic communications, etc. He classified these and wrote some twenty books in his attempt to correlate the reports and derive theories from them. His conclusion to one of these works is this: whereas some experiences are explicable in other ways,

> The whole of the available evidence is explicable only on the hypothesis of the survival of the human soul in a soul body. There is no longer a deadlock or a stalemate on the question of survival. On the contrary, survival is as well established as the Theory of Evolution.

G. N. M. Tyrrell was President of the SPR and author of a number of books, the best known of which is probably *Apparitions*. He was concerned with the background of thought, which prevented people from being able to understand the nature of psychical research. He regarded it as a matter of individual judgement as to whether psychical phenomena had given reasonable ground for a positive or negative conclusion on the survival issue, but added that

> psychical research has certainly not drawn a blank. It has, on the contrary, discovered something so big that people sheer away from it in a reaction of fear. They feel that they cannot cope with it, and are unwilling to make the drastic overhaul of their cherished convictions, which the subject demands.

Raynor Johnson was a physicist who has written a number of books on science, philosophy, psychical research and mysticism in which he analyses these different ways of interpreting experience. *The Imprisoned Splendour* draws upon the data of science, psychical research, and mysticism, respectively, in formulating a view of human personality, which he sums up as follows:

> We have enough trustworthy evidence to anticipate our survival of the change called death. If our conception of the Self as a hierarchy is true in broad outline – as I believe it is – we have enough to anticipate a great deal more. For myself, Birth and Death seem to be respectively the great Exile and the great Returning Home. I expect, when the immediate shock of change is over, to find myself with a body familiar to me (because it has always been a possession without my realising it), in a country from which come thronging back to me welcoming echoes of old familiarity. It will still be a world of Appearance; but since one veil at least will then have fallen from the face of Trust, I shall expect to find myself more responsive to her Eternal Beauty as I set out again – a pilgrim on endless way.

John Beloff was a psychologist at Edinburgh University and another past president of the SPR. He gives an assessment of the importance of the paranormal in his book *The Existence of Mind*:

> In the long run the case for dualism is likely to stand or fall with the success or failure of parapsychology. If parapsychology were to fizzle out there would be little reason to jib at a monistic or dual-aspect theory of the mind-body relationship, apart perhaps from certain metaphysical considerations, which would carry little weight in a scientific civilisation. Paranormal events are, in fact, the only *prima facia* empirical evidence we have for postulating a mind-matter interaction. If a point were reached where the occurrence of such events became too obvious to be ignored, two alternatives only would be open to us. Either we would have to expand our conception for what is physically possible, even if this meant sacrificing the theoretical simplicity of physics, or we would be forced to acknowledge that mind and matter obey fundamentally different laws and that, in special circumstances, mind can evince a certain measure of autonomy. But what is the position as it stands today? My own opinion is that, although the evidence for the paranormal is still, undoubtedly, highly

unsatisfactory on many counts, it is no longer reasonable to doubt that some paranormal events do sometimes occur.

Arthur Findlay was a senior partner of a Glasgow firm of stockbrokers, and started his investigation of mediums as a complete sceptic. He continued his research over twelve years before writing *On the Edge of Etheric*, the first of many books. He concluded that although his mind remained open to any further explanations submitted by science, there was only one explanation of mediumistic communications that fitted all the facts:

> That those we thought were dead are still alive; that they have bodies such as we have of a finer texture than our physical bodies; that they inhabit a world of finer matter than we do, and that certain individuals called mediums can supply them with a substance which, when mixed with ingredients of their own, enables them again, for a limited time, to assume physical conditions, and, with their memories, affections and character unimpaired, once more hold conversations with their friends still on earth.

Jacobson, a practising psychiatrist, wrote in his book *Life Without Death?* That no one set of the phenomena, which he describes, was enough by itself to prove survival. He investigated OBEs, lucid dreams, apparitions, communications through mediums, behaviour that indicates possession, alleged memories of a former life, paranormal taped voices, photography of the etheric body, and death-bed visions. He concluded that:

> The whole body of this material of human experiences and empirical evidence is consistent with the survival hypothesis, and part of the material is explained better by the survival hypothesis than by any other. Thus, instead of one single kind of experience indicating survival, there are several groups of experiences, very different from one another, all of which point in the same direction and all of which can be explained harmoniously by the survival hypothesis. In other words, the hypothesis does not depend on one single group of phenomena but rather is supported by several groups ... Even if the present material cannot, as has been emphasised, *prove* survival, it is nevertheless so rich and wide-ranging that it can indeed motivate a *rationally based belief* in survival. 'Science' has not proved that death

is the end of everything. Each of us must evaluate the material himself from his own viewpoints and judge the plausibility of survival, but no one can do this if he has tossed aside and dismissed the material as worthless before he begins. Even today we can take survival as a respectable, 'scientific' working hypothesis.

Following our survey of the history of Christian attitudes to mind, body, and death in Chapter 3, we now return to consider some twentieth-century developments. Russell Aldwinkle argues that the modern Christian has the difficult problem of finding appropriate symbols, myths or images to give at least some content to his understanding of what a future life might mean. Most Christians, he believes, 'have an uneasy feeling that the traditional symbols and images of the afterlife are no longer adequate. On the other hand they have not succeeded in replacing them. The result is a debilitating vagueness which has led to indifference to the whole question.' At the outset of a chapter ominously entitled 'Hell and Judgment', Aldwinkle states that although this neglect of the fact and meaning of life may to some extent be justified as a reaction to a one-sided other-worldliness, the whole gospel is mutilated if the reaction is carried as far as a radical and exclusive this-worldliness:

> The abandonment of the eternal hope, in the sense of survival of individuals after death into a worthwhile existence, is really the destruction of hope. However much men concentrate upon the transformation of this world, this hope of a better order here and now cannot be a satisfactory substitute for the confidence of the individual's preservation after death into the kingdom of God where death no longer reigns. To interpret eternal life as a new quality of existence here and now, however true and important, is only half the story. God, for Christians, does not care only for the quality of life in the abstract. He cares for individual persons, and their final destiny is his supreme concern.

Aldwinkle is arguing, here, against the existentialist and demythologising tendencies in theology which remove religion entirely from the metaphysical realm into the present, and redefine eternal life in terms of its here and now quality, without any reference to the future.

One of Aldwinkle's conclusions is that:

There will be a real existence of persons of an 'embodied' kind after death. This does not involve the view that man as such has an element in his nature which is intrinsically immortal. His continued existence after death depends on God's gracious concern and power to keep him in existence for a fellowship with Himself and his fellow men.

A number of points emerge from this statement as typical of the theological approach to immortality: first that the integrity and identity of the individual is preserved because it is cared for and loved by God; second, that the theologian makes no mention of the possibility that man might naturally be immortal; third, as a corollary of the above, that immortality is the gift of God; and fourth, it is implied that extinction at death would be incompatible with the love of God and with His final purpose of redeeming mankind – thus God's attribute of love and concern, combined with His omnipotence, demands the preservation and eventual salvation of the individual. These themes will recur in our treatment of other Christian thinkers.

In 'Survival and Immortality', W.R. Inge, then Dean of St Paul's, makes it clear that he regards the emergence of psychical research and spiritualism as a revival of superstition in reaction to the prevailing materialistic doctrines of science. He considers supernaturalism to be the refuge of the materialist who wishes to make room for ideal values without abandoning his materialism. Inge is contemptuous of the very idea of a natural or scientific approach to the question of survival, because for him eternal life is simply not commensurate with the material world:

The moment we are asked to accept scientific evidence for spiritual truth, the alleged spiritual truth becomes neither spiritual nor true. It is degraded into an event in the phenomenal world, and when so degraded, it cannot be substantiated. Psychical Research is trying to prove that eternal values are temporal facts, which they can never be.

This passage indicates Inge's misconception of the aim of psychical research: it does not necessarily have anything to say about eternal values and is far from attempting to prove that such values are temporal. What it *is* doing is investigating certain phenomena and states of consciousness reported by human beings to see whether they can shed any light on the survival of the personality. The *quality* of such survival is the matter which concerns the theologians, while psychical researches start from the *facts*, which indicate some form of survival.

In Inge's opinion 'Faith in human immortality stands or falls with the belief in *absolute values*', by which he means Truth, Beauty and Goodness. These values being supra-temporal by Inge's definition, it follows that 'in so far as we can identify ourselves in thought with the absolute values, we are sure of our immortality'. There seems to be some confusion here over the meaning of 'supra-temporal', as if values can be rendered imperishable by human thought and definition. Inge derives his logic from Plotinus, on the premise that 'values are eternal and indestructible' (if they were not, then they could not properly speaking be called values, or at any rate not *absolute* values). If the premise is accepted, then one can see how Inge can argue that one becomes immortal to the extent that one identifies oneself with these values; this is not the diffusion or dilution of the personality, but rather its consummation. However, this whole edifice rests on an unprovable value judgment. The kind of mystical identification suggested by Inge has little in common with Aldwinkle's approach except in so far as its idea of fellowship implies a similar transcendence of the personality.

Having asserted that he thought that if communication between the living and the dead were part of the nature of things, it would long since have been established beyond cavil, Inge concludes that a:

> Christian must feel that the absence of any clear revelation about a *future* state is an indication that we are not meant to make it a principal subject of our thoughts. On the other hand, the more we think about eternal values, the happier we shall be ... we are to live in the present but not for the present ... we must accustom ourselves to breathe the air of eternal values, if we desire to live for ever. And a strong faith is not curious about details.

It is evident that Inge draws a very sharp distinction between temporal attempts to investigate survival, and faith in eternal values as the only guarantee of eternal life. On this basis any conclusions drawn from temporal premises are thought to be deceptive, misleading, and liable to undermine faith, so that every effort to bridge this gap should be strongly discouraged. Psychical research is a 'detail' about which the Christian need not be curious.

W. R. Matthews, one of Inge's successors as Dean of St Paul's, takes a less censorious line on psychical research. He observes that the traditional attitude of the church towards it has been one of hostility, or at least of suspicion, on the grounds that all mediumistic phenomena emanated from the devil. Having indicated that the central question for theology is the reality of God, he says that the great enemy of theistic belief is materialism in a wider sense, where the higher is explained in terms of the lower. Any contribution towards refuting such materialism, while not equivalent to a demonstration of the reality of God, does strengthen the theologian's case for his belief. Like Inge, the theologian may have reservations about the status of survival as a spiritual belief, but Matthews argues that this is not a good reason for ignoring the evidence of psychical research. He feels that 'however persuaded a man might be on other grounds that the soul is immortal, he ought to welcome facts which tend to confirm beliefs that death is not final'. As for his view of the evidence of psychical research for what Matthews calls 'personal survival and continuity of the centre of consciousness', he states that when deceit, fraud, and illusion are discounted, 'There remains a residuum of established facts which, *prima facie*, suggest the hypothesis of survival.' Matthews is less paranoid and more constructive in his approach than Inge, and shows more sign of having sifted the evidence.

Karl Barth took an entirely theological view of death and eternal life:

> Death is the end of all present possibilities of life. Dying means exhausting the last of the possibilities given to us. However we wish to interpret dying physically and metaphysically, whatever may happen then, one thing is certain, that then there happens the last action that can happen in creaturely existence. Whatever may happen beyond death must at least be something different from the continuation of this life.

So far Barth has only succeeded in an exasperatingly long-winded statement of the obvious. He explains that he believes in the resurrection of the body, which means 'man' in the Bible,

> moreover man, under the sign of sin, man laid low. And to this man it is said, Thou shalt rise again. Resurrection means not the continuation of this life, but life's completion. To this man a 'Yes' is spoken which the shadow of death cannot touch.

As the reader can appreciate, Barth does not consider it necessary to go further than the Bible, whose message he wraps up in his own definition of resurrection and strange forms of theological circumlocution

like speaking a 'Yes' to man; it is tacitly assumed that everyone understands what this means, but it can conceal puffs of pious hot air.

Rudolf Bultmann was influenced by the philosopher Heidegger's view
of death, and Heidegger in turn owed a good deal to Tolstoy's novel
The Death of Ivan Ilyich. This story shows the devastating effect of impending death in middle age of a complacent and successful lawyer. His
illness leads to an urgent questioning and reassessment of his values:
'Maybe I did not live as I should', he thinks to himself, but immediately answers, 'But how could that be, when I have always done my duty?'
He had lived well and pleasantly, but now came to doubt the worth
of these enjoyments in the face of death. Heidegger was impressed by
Ilyich's predicament, and made awareness of death a key point in his
philosophy, accepting that the individual could only live responsibly if
he remained aware of death as a possibility, which might supervene at
any moment and put an end to his possibilities. As a theologian Bultmann thinks of death as an encounter with God, so that it is enough
for the believer to know that God is his future; 'The only certain thing
in man's future is that every man is faced with death. For the man who
is open to all future as the future of the coming God, death has lost all
its fear.' The believer's faith that nothing can separate him from the love
of God means that whatever the future brings must serve his ultimate
good. It seems that Bultmann is pretty confident of his own adequacy
to the situation; there is apparently no element of judgment present.

John Baillie makes the observation that no one wanted an endless
quantity of life until a new and quite particular and exceptional *quality* of life had been discovered. He shares St Paul's views on the nature
of the resurrection body, and asserts that Christianity has always giv-
en death a vitally important place in its scheme, regarding it as a most
solemn crisis and extremity:

> And yet it is not by this note of crisis and tragedy that the Christian
> spirit has ever allowed itself to be finally dominated but by the note,
> precisely, of joy and good cheer. To it the ultimate fact is not death but
> life, not the Cross but the Resurrection and the Crown. It is what it is only
> because it is persuaded that the sting of death has been drawn and the
> grave robbed of its victory; so that death has no more dominion over us.

Here Baillie is paraphrasing many well-known New Testament
statements about death and resurrection. He calls the Christian hope
a marvellous brightness of expectation, based on faith in God.

Leslie Weatherhead was a Methodist minister and psychologist; a succinct statement of his views can be found in a small publication *Life begins at Death*, where he starts by explaining that Christians believe in life after death for three principal reasons: first, that Christ assured the thief on the cross that they would both be in paradise that day (not an argument that many would set much store by); second, because they feel that another life is necessary to make sense of this one (the ethical argument already encountered in Kant and Barnes, among others); and third, that Christ himself rose from the death. This last reason is probably the most widespread basis of faith; here Weatherhead advances an interesting analogy to explain the disappearance of Christ's physical body and his subsequent use of what seemed to be an etheric body: the texture of a piece of wax is determined by heat; on a cold day it is hard, on a warm day malleable, and, if heated, it will become first of all liquid, and then gaseous. The physical process is that of heat increasing the speed of molecules, so that although the molecules remain the same, their texture is determined by their speed. Weatherhead speculates that it is not inconceivable that the spirit of Christ might have operated on the molecules in such a way as to alter their speed and make his body assume a gaseous form. There is no way of proving this assertion, naturally, but it is at least a coherent attempt to answer a particular intractable problem.

After wide reading of the literature of spiritualism and psychical research, Weatherhead reaches the conclusion that, despite a certain amount of quackery and deceit, the case for survival is proved:

> There are some situations which go to show that communion with the so-called dead is established, that any other hypothesis is less likely, less probable. I regard it as now proved that man lives after death, that his consciousness is not just the result of chemical changes in the brain and perishes with his brain but has an individual existence which, during his earth life, has used his brain.

His views on life after death are similar to those expressed by Radhakrishnan: the physical body wears out after a period and can no longer house the spirit; birth marks the beginning of a period when we inhabit the physical body, and death the end of that period. The spirit existed before the birth of the physical body and will exist afterwards, so that death and birth can be regarded as milestones. At death the essential personality needs another instrument through which to express itself, in the same way as a musician might take a new violin if his old one were worn out. Weatherhead calls this new instrument the etheric body, a duplicate of our physical body; it would be required in order for us to be able to express ourselves and to be recognised by others. It would evidently manifest in a different way from our present physical body, being perceptible to some, but not others, able to pass through closed doors and to travel great distances in a short time. In short, Weatherhead not only considers that man survives death, but that the instrument through which he will then express himself is not subject to many of the limitations of the physical body.

At the end of our survey of modern attitudes to body, mind, brain and death, we are left with two irreconcilable theories: on the one hand a theory which regards the mind and personality as entirely derived from and dependent on the brain, from which it is deduced that the mind and personality must necessarily perish at death with the brain; and on the other hand, the contention that the mind and personality, although at present intimately connected with the brain, cannot be wholly identified with it, and need not therefore perish at physical death. The former position is best supported by exclusive reference to the data of normal experience, while the latter seems to be rendered more plausible by supernormal phenomena, and can account for normal experience as well. Before investigating some of these supernormal phenomena and their apparent implications, we shall consider how people assess the evidence for such phenomena, and what kind of conviction might be derived from them.

6.

PSYCHOLOGY, LOGIC, EVIDENCE AND SHIFTING PARADIGMS

It is better to debate a question without settling it than to settle a question without debating it.

JOUBERT

Our desires attract supporting reasons as a magnet the iron filings.

DIXON

Men are so made that they can resist sound argument and yet yield to a glance.

BALZAC

My business is to teach my aspirations to conform themselves to fact, not to try to make facts harmonise with my aspirations. Sit down before fact like a little child, be prepared to give up every preconceived notion, follow humbly wherever Nature leads, or you will learn nothing.

T. H. HUXLEY

Thinking is called upon to solve the riddle presented to us by perception.

STEINER

Nature and Thought

Steiner's remark can be taken as a rejoinder to Huxley, whose tacit assumption is that the little child can apprehend a fact passively, without any participation on his part; even the etymology of the word 'fact' – something which is made – implies that this is impossible. The mechanistic worldview supposes that what is objectively given coincides with what is received through the senses, while common sense suggests that ideas are just as much objects of experience. Each complements the other. The relationship becomes clearer when one examines the etymology of the word reality. Bohm points out that it derives from the Latin *res* meaning thing, and that *res* is based in turn on the word *rere*, meaning to think. Since a thing is what is known, reality comes to mean what man can know. The reality that man can know, however, is defined and limited by his thoughts; and the very fact that thoughts are partial means that they abstract from the whole or from any underlying reality. The limits of thought are indicated by the paradox that the thought of the whole cannot grasp the whole, for two reasons: its idea of the whole is still partial, and this very idea is, by definition, part of the whole as well.

Intellect, the instrument of thought, is derived from the two Latin words *inter* and *legere*, meaning literally to choose or read between; its function is to divide, discriminate, distinguish and classify by means of ideas, concepts and theories. The words idea and theory originally had visual connotations: *idea* in Greek means, among other things, semblance and look, while theory is derived from the Greek verb *theorein*, meaning to look at or be present at, and the noun *theoria*, meaning contemplation, sight, speculation (another related notion). When asking someone whether he understands something we use the word 'see', and talk of insight. Ideas and theories, then, are ways of seeing things. The real meaning of the word 'concept' is also significant: it derives from *capere* meaning to seize, and *cum* (with). It is a tool with which we 'grasp' phenomena, a mediator between the senses and the intellect. Something that can be grasped as 'conceivable', its opposite 'inconceivable' or 'unintelligible'. Likewise we speak of 'comprehending': *prehendere* also means to seize.

Such considerations should clarify our understanding of the relationship of thought to the external world. Thought supplements and permeates sensation with concepts, so that phenomena become intelligible to us: 'This entire operation, which combines the multifariousness of perception into a conceptual unity, takes its course inside our consciousness.' The connection of cause and effect, for instance in the sound of a bell, is not actually given through the senses but is conceived by the mind. The individual percept, 'seized through' the senses, is made intelligible by the concept. On this view 'Truth' is not actually an agreement between the idea and the object, but rather the grasping and expression of a relationship or harmony between thought, theory or idea on the one hand, and external phenomena on the other. On this basis Steiner defines the scientific method as follows: 'that we show the concept of a single phenomenon in its connection with the rest of the world of ideas'. The single phenomenon has then been explained (literally 'unfolded') in its proper place in relation to the whole theory or vision.

The interaction between thought and object suggested by Steiner that investigations into epistemology should not start from the static concept of knowledge, but rather from the dynamic participation of *knowing*; the means rather than the end, thinking as an organ of perception. The sound of the bell triggers off memory associations and comparisons with sounds, which we think were similar. The recognition of its significance may be more or less immediate – a familiar clock – or else may require further thought. In either case the meaning is discerned, we understand the sound. The reasoning can be extended to observation, which has to be selective: 'it needs a chosen object, a definite task, an interest, a point of view, a problem. Observations are always interpretations of the facts observed.' Observation is systematic perception, but perception, nonetheless. Moreover, observation and theory are interdependent; the one entails the other: to observe is to perceive by means of a theory or concept. This being the case, theories and problems must have arisen simultaneously; the observation focused on a problem in the light of a theory.

Assumptions and Theories

(1) *The medieval outlook*

We have already discussed some of the contrasts of medieval and modern thought in relation to Descartes. As a whole they represent a *Weltanschauung*, which gives a unified picture of the world and of man's place in it – what Whitehead calls the Conceptual Order in terms of which the Observational Order is interpreted. Jung identifies as the fatal error of any *Weltanschauung* the tendency to regard its statements as objectively valid truth, rather than a partial (in both senses) interpretation. He claims, furthermore, that any radical change of attitude towards the status and relationship of mind and matter cannot have been brought about by reasoned reflection 'for no chain of reasoning can prove or disprove the existence of either mind or matter. Both these concepts ... are symbols that stand for something unknown and unexplored, and this something is postulated or denied according to the temperament of the individual or as the spirit of the age dictates.' The contrast between the church and the scientific rationalists is characterised as follows: 'Just as formerly the assumption that everything that exists originates in the creative will of a God who is a spirit, so the nineteenth century discovered the equally unquestionable truth that everything arises from material causes.' Theological reason interpreted reality in spiritual terms.

(2) *Cartesian science*

(a) *View of reality.* The dominant image was that of the machine or clock, with its constituent parts adding up to the whole. External observation, refined by ever more sophisticated instruments, revealed matter in terms of separate forms, fragmented by interacting with each other from the outside; the atom is conceived as a minute solid particle. Consequently, matter is basically solid and impenetrable. Space and time are real, so that reactions are strictly localised. A linear idea of time implies the unalterable sequence of cause and effect.

(b) *View of knowledge.* Observable phenomena are measured and classified, resulting in an accumulating body of definite knowledge;

from this, further calculations and predictions can be derived, enabling predictions of ever greater precision to be made. Although Hume showed that induction could never lead to certain knowledge and absolute proof, there has been a tendency for aspects of this *Weltanschauung* to be laid down dogmatically.

(3) *David Bohm's implicate order*

(a) *View of reality.* For Bohm the primary relativity is the 'implicate order', which he calls 'Undivided Wholeness in Flowing Movement', a 'holomovement' which is unbroken and all-encompassing. This implicate (or enfolded) order is the ground of what is manifest or explicate (unfolded): 'the flow is, in some sense, prior to that of the "things" that can be seen to form and dissolve in this flow.' Laws of nature are abstracted (withdrawn) from the unity of the flow, in the same way that ideas emerge from the stream of consciousness. The Cartesian reality of manifest three-dimensional matter is equated with the explicate order, whose whole function is to display things as separate; in Bohm's view Cartesian reality is partially valid, but it made the mistake of equating reality with what was measurable by its instruments. Quantum theory established that subatomic units of matter were abstract entities with a tendency to exist; sometimes they manifest as waves, sometimes as particles. Their movements cannot be predicted with any certainty; they are only expressible in terms of probability of interconnected events in which the observer himself plays a part. Space unites phenomena in the whole, rather than dividing them; reactions can no longer be said to be localised in the quantum field (they were in Einstein's original formulation). In accordance with the undivided flowing primary reality, Bohm comments that 'the line is the reality and the points are the abstractions'; as for time, 'the holomovement is reality and the movements are abstractions'.

Bohm considers that the function of matter is to provide the measure of space. It is the visible, three-dimensional part of the enfolded order, regarding as forming 'clouds in the holomovement', that is to say condensations or concentrations within the holomovement (or quantum field). In such terms the human body, as an open material system, is a *form of energy process* known by Prigogine as a 'dissipative structure'. The term denotes a dynamic structure or form, which maintains itself by a continuous dissipation or consumption of energy. The apparent wholeness and distinctness of its form conceals a flowing process within, a constant destruction and re-creation. Three-dimensional material substantiality results from electrons whirling round a nucleus at an enormously high velocity, which 'makes the atom appear as a rigid sphere, just as a fast rotating propeller appears as a disc'. Equivalent velocities would mean material objects in the same frequency range, which would interact *as if* matter were impenetrable. Solidity, therefore, is relative to frequency; the importance of this point will emerge when we consider explanations of apparitions in Chapter 8.

(b) *View of knowledge.* Science is not trying to prove, but to explain and understand. It aims to construct testable hypotheses in order to render a world more intelligible. There is no such thing as certain knowledge or absolute truth. Rather than a body of knowledge, science is a system of hypotheses or proposals which are the most plausible and comprehensive available at present. Their range of validity can only be known when they are superseded. Thus the range of validity of Newtonian physics can be defined as a limiting case of present hypotheses, which will be shown to be limited in their turn. In contrast to the previous two *Weltanschauungen*, this position actually realises that it is relative, and that it is not therefore entitled to make dogmatic pronouncements.

Apperception

We have already seen how intimately theory is linked with observation. A given theory forms a network of expectations, which can be tested, criticised and refined in the light of experiment or experience. Thinking can only be a response within already familiar theoretical frameworks and categories. When a new fact is encountered it can only be classified or understood in the light of present knowledge derived from past experience (i.e. memory); this will serve to fill the gap exposed by the new experience by extending or extrapolating the present classification or understanding. James points out that when we speak of our acquaintances being characterised by certain tendencies, we mean tendencies to association, in such a way that certain ideas are always followed by other ideas, which themselves trigger further images or associations. When certain mental networks or habits predominate, we can speak of someone having a definite attitude, a pattern which friends will recognise and find predictable. June defines an attitude in a technical sense as 'a particular arrangement of psychic contents oriented towards a goal or directed by some ruling principle'. Such an orientation means that an external stimulus will always be comprehended in a definite way; it implies an expectation which operates selectively, excluding factors that are considered irrelevant in order to focus entirely on what seems subjectively apposite.

The process by which we acquire new knowledge is known both by Jung and James as 'apperception'. New knowledge has to be associated with existing knowledge in order to be apprehended and understood. Existing conceptions are bound to condition and limit the way in which new knowledge is assimilated. This process of assimilation is influenced not only by this prior knowledge but also by the temperament or type (habitual attitude) of the individual. Jung devotes a chapter of his *Psychological Types* to a discussion of James's classification of philosophical temperaments into what he calls 'tough-minded' and 'tender-minded'. The latter quality should not, however, be equated with being 'soft in the head'. The tough-minded attitude corresponds to the empiricist who starts from what he regards as hard facts: his attention is directed outwards to objects, from which he may infer theories or 'laws'. He tends to be materialistic, deterministic, and sceptical. By contrast the tender-minded individual starts from an idea, which he finds within, and tends to see the connections between facts, rather than their isolation. Contrary to the empiricist he will be more idealistic (philosophically), free-willist and dogmatic. Clearly no one will exhibit all the traits of one attitude to the total exclusion of the other, but any temperamental bias in once direction will affect interpretation of new data in apperception. A more recent but similar classification can be found in LeShan's *Alternate Realities*, where the two main modes of viewing reality are termed the sensory and the clairvoyant. They correspond broadly with the contrasting views of the Cartesian framework and that of Bohm; also, respectively, with the left and right hemispheres of the brain. The left hemisphere is predominantly concerned with logical, analytical thinking and is associated with linear time and sequences of mathematics and language. The right hemisphere by contrast, relates phenomena into intuitive wholes; it is responsible for recognition of faces, artistic creativity and orientation in space.

James observes that, in the operation of apperception, a general law becomes apparent: the law of economy.

> In admitting a new body of experience, we instinctively seek to disturb as little as possible our pre-existing stock of ideas. We always try to

name a new experience in some way which will assimilate it to what we already know. We hate anything *absolutely* new, anything without any name, and for which a new name must be forged. So we take the nearest name, even though it be inappropriate.

Schopenhauer made a similar observation in differentiating between what he called natural and artificial education. Whereas the natural method consists in abstracting general ideas from particular observations,

> The ordinary method is to imprint ideas and opinions, in the strict sense of the word 'prejudices', on the mind of the child, before it has had any but a few very particular observations. It is thus that he comes to view the world and gather experience through the medium of those ready-made ideas ... experience will be a long time in correcting preconceived ideas, or perhaps never bring its task to an end; for, wherever a man finds that the aspect of things seems to contradict the general ideas he has formed, he will begin by rejecting the evidence it offers as partial and one-sided; nay, he will shut his eyes to it altogether and deny that it stands in any contradiction at all to his preconceived notions, in order that he may thus preserve them uninjured.

Here Schopenhauer is speaking only of the acquisition and persistence of conceptions without explicitly mentioning the role of temperament, although the exact effect of the corrective experience will depend on it. We shall be investigating resistance to evidence below. James calls this economical tendency to leave the old undisturbed 'old-fogyism', but adds a characteristic warning that young fogies can be found as well: he believes that, in the majority of cases, the process begins at twenty-five, and states that 'A new idea or fact which would entail extensive rearrangement of the previous system of beliefs is always ignored or extruded from the mind in case it cannot be sophistically reinterpreted so as to tally harmoniously with the system.'

The limitations of mental frameworks and patterns, combined with the simplifying wish to explain the unknown in terms of the known, are bound to lead to the kind of resistance referred to above. T.H. Huxley remarked that it was the customary fate of new truths to begin as heresies and end up as superstitions. Nor is this kind of resistance confined to the layman; the history of science is littered with examples. Beveridge makes observations similar to those of James and

Schopenhauer, namely that ideas are invariably judged in the light of prevailing beliefs, and that 'if the ideas are too revolutionary, that is to say, if they depart too far from the reigning theories and cannot be fitted into the current body of knowledge, they will not be acceptable'. And if the discovery is made before its time, it will almost certainly be ignored or ridiculed. Beveridge cites the genetic work of Mendel, ignored for thirty-five years after publication, and Röntgen's discovery of X-rays, which was greeted with almost universal ridicule and derision. The isolation of the innovator is reinforced by the herd-instinct of conformity and accompanying fear of ridicule and ostracism. Beveridge also points out that such resistance is not an entirely negative phenomenon, as science cannot afford to abandon the critical attitude in favour of credulity; a certain degree of caution must be exercised. But equally one should aim at freeing the mind as far as possible from preconceptions so as to arrive at as objective an assessment of the evidence as possible and to suspend judgment where evidence is insufficient or incomplete. Beveridge sums up the reception of an original contribution to knowledge as a division into three phases:

> During the first it is ridiculed as not true, impossible, or useless; during the second, people say that there may be something in it but it would never be of any practical use; and in the third and final phase, when the discovery has received general recognition, there are usually people who say that it is not original and has been anticipated by others.

There is a grain of truth in this humorous classification. In the first instance, the butt of the ridicule is an anomaly – what Kuhn defines as 'nature violating paradigm-induced expectations'. The anomaly is not regarded as counter-instance or falsification of the existing theory/paradigm; it is discretely ignored, swept under the carpet, or denounced. If it is then regarded as significant, the theory's defenders will devise 'numerous articulations and *ad hoc* modifications of their theory in order to eliminate any apparent conflict'. This is neatly illustrated by Rupert Sheldrake, and by the incredibly complex adaptations devised by rivals of Copernicus. When the new paradigm finally breaks through, knowledge and connections are reconstructed from new fundamental premises, as if one had picked up the other end of the stick. The range of the field is extended, the old theory is seen in its new context as a limiting model of the new, and the intersubjective consensus is reformulated.

The Basis of Judgement and Proof

Kant analyses the nature of judgment, reached by means of a man's stock of conceptions. Some judgements rest on a particular trait of the individual and only have private and subjective validity; while some can be communicated to others and their validity demonstrated to every rational man, despite their various characters. He distinguishes three degrees of subjective validity of a judgement in relation to conviction, namely Opinion, Belief, and Knowledge; they are differentiated as follows: 'Opinion is a consciously insufficient judgement, subjectively as well as objectively. Belief is subjectively sufficient, but is recognised as being objectively insufficient. Knowledge is both subjectively and objectively sufficient.' He defines subjective sufficiency as conviction (for myself) and objective sufficiency as certainty (for all). These distinctions may strike the modern reader as slightly crude, but they do pave the way for clarifying different degrees of validity and conviction in relation to judgement.

Kant wrote on the assumption that certain knowledge was both attainable and objective. This in turn implies that there is such a thing as conclusive proof, on which such certain knowledge might rest. It was Hume who indicated the pitfalls of this view in his work on induction, which provides the starting point for Popper's work on scientific method. Hume asserted that no number of previous instances of a conjunction of cause and subsequent given effect could make it certain that the same conjunction would in future necessarily result in the same effect: thus we know that the earth has been rotating and the sun rising for millions of years, but we cannot be *absolutely* certain that the earth will continue to rotate. Likewise we know that given proportions of chemicals produce certain compounds when combined, but we cannot state with absolute certainty that this will be the case in all future time. This means that a scientific theory is never conclusively verifiable, although it can receive continuing corroboration, which may increase the degree of certainty with which the theory is held, even if it is impossible to attain the desired absolute certainty. 'We do not know, we can only guess', says Popper. The scientific hypothesis must content itself with a tentative and provisional status. Sir Arthur Eddington writes that proof is the idol before whom the pure mathematician tortures himself, but that in physics one must be content to sacrifice before the lesser shrine of plausibility.

The limits of the strict scientific theory are the limits of repeatable testability. While it is both possible and desirable to repeat tests of physical and chemical hypothesis by experiment, this is impossible in dealing with legal or historical material: the event has occurred at a unique moment in the past and is not therefore repeatable. At best we can attempt to establish that the event really did occur as attested; and if we are trying to explain the circumstances or cause of the event, we can submit hypotheses, which can be judged only by their explanatory value in the light of the evidence adduced. We know that a certain murder has taken place, and that the man in the dock may or may not have committed the crime; there are two rival hypotheses which opposing counsels are doing their best to establish, and it is up to the jury to decide which of these is more plausible in the light of the evidence. Such evidence may consist of testimony, admissible hearsay, documents, things, or other evidentiary facts. All these bear on the 'facts at issue', that is to say those requiring proof. As in science, it is recognised that absolute certainty is unattainable in law; the degree of certainty demanded depends on whether the case is one of civil or criminal law. Before conviction on a criminal charge the degree of cogency 'need not reach certainty, but it must carry a high degree of probability. Proof beyond a reasonable doubt does not mean proof beyond a shadow of doubt', so that a remote possibility (where something is possible but not in the least probable) can be dismissed. In civil cases a reasonable degree of probability is demanded, but not so high as in a criminal case, the formula being 'we think it more probable than not'. It is hard to conceive of a case where there would be *absolutely* no doubts about the verdict, hence the necessity of judgment in the light of the available data. The preponderance or weight of the evidence cannot help being assessed subjectively, even if there is more or less universal agreement.

In the scientific and legal fields there is a constant attempt to arrive at some form of inter-subjective consensus or objectivity by interpretation of empirical data. But even in these disciplines the disposition or pattern of outlook determines, in some degree, assent to or dissent from a given hypothesis. This is *a fortiori* true for religious belief, in the sense of acceptance of dogma, tradition and religious authority. A belief may be of the kind derived from direct personal experience: there are many who have felt a presence or guiding principle at some stage in their lives, and may have called this God. Such a belief rests on a different foundation from that based on a wholly intellectual or emotional assent to a proposition asserting the existence of God. Some may believe in God because they were brought up to do so and have never questioned the teaching; others, of a more philosophical turn of mind, may find other reasons for belief. In the first instance authority has been accepted without thought or perhaps even reference to the individual's experience; and in the second case there may be a large measure of subjective interpretation – for instance acceptance of the argument from design depends on one's view of the nature of order in the world. As Kant indicated, the characteristic of belief (whether it involves the acceptance of dogma and tradition, the interpretation of experience or both) is subjective certainty or persuasion, which another person may fail to find logically compelling. So that the greater the proportion of subjective interpretation, the less likely one is to arrive at inter-subjective consensus on a scientific rather than on a subjective emotional basis.

Evidence in Psychical Research

We have now considered three possible approaches to the question of proof and certain knowledge, so that we can return to psychical research, the subject under investigation. Only laboratory controlled metal-bending and card-guessing type experiments are amenable to the rigorous scientific approach. This does not entail dismissing spontaneous cases as irrelevant, but simply that they are more suited to a different angle of approach, a variant of the legal and historical; there are, of course, those with a strong predisposition towards imposing a supernatural interpretation on all phenomena, but this is not a critical and discriminating method: it can hardly appeal to the rational person unless his rationality is exercised only within a particular religious framework. In endeavouring to assess and interpret spontaneous cases of apparitions, etc. there is one basic factor which differentiates them from legal cases, namely that it may be argued that the so-called paranormal event never occurred at all, that the whole report is a piece of delusive imagining or elaborate fraud. Accordingly, in discussing what philosophers euphemistically call 'antecedent probability', we must distinguish between the probability that an event did indeed occur, and the probability of the various competing explanations which assume that the event did happen.

Broad defined antecedent probability or improbability of an alleged event as follows: 'Its probability or improbability relative to all the rest of our present knowledge and well-founded belief *other than* the special evidence adduced in its favour.' From this it follows that the evidence for an antecedently improbable event must be stronger if it is to convince a reasonable person. So far, Broad has mentioned probability only in terms of relevant knowledge, and not the influence of disposition on interpretation. At one extreme, it is possible to argue that because the hypothesis of the occurrence of a paranormal event conflicts with some of the principles of our normal practical activities and scientific theories, the antecedent odds against its genuine occurrence are almost infinite; the report must, therefore, be due to careless observation, incompetence, or fraud – given the 'odds' this view must be more reasonable under any conditions. This standpoint is frequently accompanied by a brandishing of Occam's hatchet, and is perhaps best expressed by Burt's quotation from Hansel: 'In view of the *a priori* arguments against it we *know in advance* that telepathy etc. cannot occur.' Empiricism seems to be overtaken by dogmatism here, since nothing can be certainly known in advance except by those with closed minds.

In considering the readiness with which one might be prepared to assent to a conclusion, antecedent probability should not be regarded as the sole relevant factor. There is also the reliability of the evidence in question, and the extent to which it is open to alternative explanations. If, like Hansel, one rules out telepathy from the start, then any *prima facie* successful case must be the result of fraud or mal-observation. In this respect, Broad observes that a distinction should be drawn between a specific and a general scepticism; the latter attitude regards paranormal phenomena as *a priori* impossible, while the former advocates that individual cases should be carefully scrutinised without necessarily prejudging the issue in favour of a particular explanation – this is clearly more empirical and less biased. Frauds or careless observation may well account for some cases, but it is rash to rule out all other hypothesis in advance.

There is a point at which the will to believe seems to meet its sceptical counterpart, the will to disbelieve, at any rate in the opinion of those who do not regard the odds against the occurrence of a paranormal event to be infinite; credulity can operate in both directions. After an analysis of the work of J. B. Rhine and others Hans Eysenck gives the following assessment of the fraud hypothesis:

> Unless there is a gigantic conspiracy involving some thirty university departments all over the world, and several hundred highly respected scientists in various fields, many of them originally hostile to the claims

of psychical research, the only conclusion the unbiased observer can come to must be that there does exist a small number of people who obtain knowledge existing either in other people's minds, or in the outer world, by means as yet unknown to science.

He says that his conclusion should not be taken as indicating support for survival of death or philosophical idealism; his comments are directed at the results of experimental work. While it is possible to stick to the fraud or conspiracy hypothesis in the face of independent results all pointing in the same direction, the degree of doubt involved hardly remains reasonable.

In a fascinating paper of 1905, Charles Richet analyses his own resistance to paranormal phenomena. He starts by saying that most people are incredulous of the extraordinary, and unwilling to accept facts which do not seem to fit into the conventional framework. When he first encountered instances of *prima facie* clairvoyance, premonition, or telepathy, not only did he not possess the independence of mind to brave the ridicule of his colleagues, but he also shut his eyes to the phenomena, denying their existence altogether and putting them on one side. Later he conducted a series of investigations which convinced him of the occurrence of paranormal phenomena, which he paradoxically classified as facts observed but nevertheless absurd. At his point he noticed a remarkable psychological process in himself, by means of which he reverted to his usual ways of thinking: although he was convinced that he had at the time witnessed genuine phenomena, he felt disarmed when once more in the company of friends who laughed at his credulity, and in doing so began to sow the seeds of doubt in his mind; so that by a curious inversion of roles, it was the *negative conviction of those who had not even seen the event* which might weaken and even destroy the conviction of he who had actually witnessed it. From this Richet draws the significant conclusion that certainty does not follow on demonstration, but on habit; if the event concurs with everyday experience we can be certain that it occurred, but if it contravenes our normal ideas, then we may always doubt that it happened.

If we now turn to the investigation of spontaneous cases, as opposed to experimental work in the laboratory, it is plausible to some people that all ostensibly paranormal events can be explained normally or abnormally. Broad's assessment of the credibility of doing this in all cases is as follows:

Here I think that the utmost we can say is this. There is a considerable number of reports of sporadic cases which have been carefully investigated, and where the evidence that the phenomenon happened as described seems to be about as satisfactory as human testimony, direct or indirect, ever is. But it would always be possible, with regard to any particular sporadic case, however well attested and carefully investigated, to avoid the conclusion that a genuinely paranormal event happened. Provided that one is prepared to stretch the long arm of coincidence far enough, to postulate sufficient imbecility and dishonesty on the part of investigators who are known to be in other respects intelligent and truthful, and to suppose that the narrators have gone to considerable trouble in falsifying diaries and forging letters with no obvious motive, it is always possible to suggest a normal, or at worst an abnormal, explanation for any story of an ostensibly paranormal sporadic event. This procedure, which has a certain amount of plausibility when applied to each of even the most attested sporadic cases taken severally, becomes much less convincing when applied to the sum total of them taken collectively. For it then has to postulate imbecility and dishonesty on a very large scale in a large number of mutually independent reporters and investigators.

Broad's comments reinforce the observations of Eysenck, but this time with regard to sporadic rather than laboratory work. He concludes, soundly in the view of the present writer, that 'in order to cast doubt on the evidence for the best-attested sporadic cases, one needs to be so captious in one's criticisms that by these standards hardly any alleged historical event could be accepted with confidence, and hardly any criminal change could ever be ustained'.

The work of Warren Shibles is an example of the lengths to which dogmatic scepticism will go in its attempts to explain the data away in materialistic terms. He considers various arguments advanced by Ducasse and others in support of the possibility that the conscious self may survive death. On mind he comments:

Contemporary analyses show that mind is an unfounded and unintelligible concept; that we do not have minds. Mind was erroneously thought of as a metaphysical substance or container for ideas. This outdated view is now called the container theory of mind. Thus it makes no sense to say that the mind might survive the body. Mind cannot die because mind cannot live.

Shibles directs his fire against an outdated concept of mind, which has now been refined. In speaking of 'contemporary analyses' he can only be referring to the behaviourists and identity theorists, completely ignoring the views of Eccles and Penfield, which flatly contradict his fatuous thesis that mind does not exist. He then passes to death-bed apparitions, where the apparition of a person who may not be known to be ill appears to someone at a time closely corresponding to the death of the former. Shibles claims to be able to offer a 'better' explanation than some form of telepathic hallucination. He points out that if we know a person well, we know his personal habits and age, which may make it likely that he will die over a given period. He goes on:

> The 'apparition' seems as if it just came to the person but may rather be due to putting together a number of subliminal or small suggestive details without consciously or clearly being aware that one is doing so. In addition, the chances that a person will be ill or die are quite high generally. This allows correct prediction much of the time.

The most cursory glance at some of the examples of crisis apparitions given later in the book will reveal how preposterously glib and inadequate such explanations are in view of the data – and statements such as that alleging that the chances of a person dying 'are quite high generally' are arrant nonsense. The intricacies and subtleties of the cross-correspondence cases are dismissed on the grounds that 'any two fragments may be put together somehow to make an intelligible sentence'. In neither of the last two categories are cases refuted in any detail. Had Shibles measured his remarks against some specific instances of apparitions and cross-correspondence, his confident assertions would have looked much less impressive. He has simply ignored the detailed evidence, which does not fit into his materialistic framework, this exemplifying a process described by Bacon over 300 years ago:

> The human understanding, when any proposition has been once laid down (either from general admission and belief, or from the pleasure that it affords) forces everything else to add fresh support and confirmation; and although the most cogent and abundant instances may exist to the contrary, yet either does not observe or despises them, or gets rid of and rejects them by some distinction, with violent and injurious prejudice, rather than sacrificing the authority of its first conclusions.

In their investigations leading towards the compiling of *Phantasms of the Living* Gurney, Myers and Podmore tried to exclude reports of apparitions where there existed any possibility of error in the report due to mistaken identity, mistaken inference and narration, and faultiness of memory. They were also aware of the antecedent improbability of their hypothesis of telepathy as an explanation of the phenomena; but against this had to be weighed the sheer number of improbable hypotheses which have to be propounded if an explanation along the lines of telepathy is to be avoided. They argue that the charge of the general unreliability of human testimony would be legitimate if they are presenting a collection of unsifted second-and third-hand stories; but this is not the case, so that the evidence 'cannot be summarily dismissed; if it is to be got rid of, it must be explained away in detail. And it is the continued process of attempts to explain away which may, we think, produce on others the same cumulative effect as it has produced on ourselves.' The authors go on to sketch the kind of assumptions, which have to be made if the evidence contained in their collection of cases is to be explained away:

> The narratives are very various, and their force is derived from very various characteristics; the endeavour to account for them without resorting to telepathy must, therefore, be carried through a considerable number of groups, before it produces its legitimate effect on the mind. That effect arises from the number and variety of the improbable suppositions, now violent, now vague – contradictory of our experience of all sorts of acts and human relations – that have to be made at every turn. Not only do we have to assume such an extent of forgetfulness and inaccuracy, about simple and striking facts of the immediate past, as is totally unexampled in any other range of experience. Not only have we to assume that distressing or exciting news about another person produces a havoc in the memory which has never been noted in connection with distress or excitement in any other form. We must leave this merely general ground, and made supposition as detailed as the evidence itself. We must suppose that some people have a way of dating their letters in indifference to the calendar, or making entries in their diaries on the wrong page and never discovering their error; and that whole families have been struck by a collective hallucination that one of their members had made a particular remark, the substance of which had never entered that member's head; and that it is a recognised custom to write mournful letters about bereavements which have

never occurred; and that when A describes to a friend how he has distinctly heard the voice of B, it is not infrequently a slip of the tongue for C; and that when D says that he is not subject to hallucinations of vision, it is through momentary forgetfulness of the fact that he has a spectral illusion once a week; and that when a wife interrupts a husband's slumbers with words of distress or alarm, it is only her fun, or a sudden morbid craving for undeserved sympathy; and when people assert that they were in sound health, in good spirits and wide awake, at a particular time which they had occasion to note, it is a safe conclusion that they were having a nightmare, or were the prostrate victims of nervous hypochondria. Every one of these improbabilities is, perhaps, in itself a possibility; but as the narratives drive us from one desperate expedient to another, where time after time we are compelled to own that deliberate falsification is less unlikely than the assumptions we are making, and then again when we submit the theory of deliberate falsification to the cumulative test, and see what is involved in the supposition that hundreds of persons of established character, known to us for the most part and unknown to one another, have simultaneously formed a plot to deceive us – there comes a point where the reason rebels. Commonsense persists in recognising that when phenomena, which are united by a fundamental characteristic and have every appearance of forming a single natural group, are presented to be explained, an explanation which multiplies causes is improbable, and an explanation which multiplies improbable causers becomes, at a certain point, incredible.

The case cannot be put more fully or cogently than this.

Recently, the unreliability of human testimony has been the subject of psychological experiments in which a sequence of staged events suddenly takes place during a psychology lecture and the students are asked to write a description. In many cases this proves to be inaccurate in its details, sometimes wildly so. The result of this is then used to justify a wholesale rejection of the validity of human testimony. But we do not take human testimony at its face value. The law has an elaborate procedure of cross-questioning of witnesses, whose accounts are expected to square with other facts pertinent to the case, including that alleged perpetrators' own description. If the testimony reveals a discrepancy, then this is followed up in turn, so that either a more comprehensive account is arrived at, or some part of the evidence or testimony is rejected. In the end there are generally a number of facts and testimonies, which support a particular hypothesis as the most plausible account of the event, even if it is recognised that absolute certainty is ruled out. At this point it is worth mentioning a further *a priori* trick to avoid accepting evidence for the paranormal. A man might say that if Professor X conducted some experiments to test telepathy, then he would abide by the conclusions of the experiments, knowing Professor X as an honourable and intelligent man. The tacit assumption, however, is that a man of X's calibre is bound to come up with negative results. But in the event that he does not emerge with the desired negative outcome, the sceptic will be more ready to doubt X's competence than to accept a conclusion which he finds *a priori* so unpalatable. A variant of the same attitude is found among those who claim to have an open mind while adding that much more evidence is required if they are to be convinced of the genuineness of a paranormal phenomenon. The trick here is that it is arbitrary to fix a definite number of positive results, which would convince the person in question – should the figure be 5 or 500? And if 500, why not 499? As the reader will see in Part two, there is already ample evidence for the inquirer to reach a conclusion, and it is unlikely that new evidence would modify, substantially, the conclusion reached on currently available evidence. All too often, the demand for more evidence is an evasive smokescreen behind which the sceptic pretends to preserve an open mind.

As the authors of *Phantasms of the Living* point out, the plausibility of any hypothesis, advanced to account for certain sporadic and spontaneous events, depends on the concurrence of human testimony which is assumed not be wholly unreliable. They take the example of death-bed apparitions, and argue that the best analogy they can use is that of a traveller's description of an animal seen in a distant land; they ask whether it is likely that chance could explain the similarities of description:

> Have all our informants drawn an arbitrary line, and all drawn precisely the same arbitrary line, between the mistakes and exaggerations of which they *will* be guilty, and the mistakes and exaggerations of which they will *not*? We might imagine them as travellers, ignorant of zoology, each of whom reports that he has landed on a strange shore, and has encountered a strange animal. Some of the travellers have been nearer the animal, and have had a better view of him than others, and their accounts vary in clearness; but these accounts, though independently drawn up, all point to the same source; they all present a consistent

picture of the self-same animal, and what is more, the picture is one which zoology can find no positive cause to distrust. We find in it none of the familiar features of myth or of untrained fancy; the reports have not given wings to a quadruped, or horns or hoofs to a carnivore; they contradict nothing that is known. Can we fairly suppose that this complete agreement, alike in what they contain, is the accidental result of a hundred disconnected mistakes?

On this basis the authors argue that the reality of telepathy may not unreasonably be taken as proved, although they recognise that such proof is not absolute – they are therefore not dogmatic in asserting their conclusion. However the concurrence of similar testimonies in describing the phenomena associated with death-bed apparitions is thought to lend some weight to the so-called faggot theory, or what Price terms the 'coherence theory of truth'. Archbishop Whately has forcefully expressed the point:

> It is manifest that concurrent testimony, whether positive or negative, of several witnesses, when there can have been no concert, and especially when there is rivalry or hostility between them, carries with it a weight independent of that which may belong to each of them considered separately. For though, in such a case, each of the witnesses should even be considered as wholly undeserving of credit, still the chances might be incalculable against their all agreeing on the *same* falsehood.

In Part two the reader will find himself confronted with a number of separate cases which seem *prima facie* to be describing the same phenomenon, and might reasonably be explained in a similar way. In theory it can always be argued that the faggots are in fact leaky buckets and that no number of leaky buckets hold water; but we have already established that it is unreasonable to expect absolute certainty and objectivity even in science. The reader himself must judge, on the basis of 'beyond all reasonable doubt' whether the hypothesis, that the conscious self survives the dissolution of the physical body, is the most plausible explanation available to account for the various phenomena investigated.

Part Two:

Empirical

I didn't say it was possible.
I only said it was true.

CHARLES RICHET, Nobel Laureate

7.

SOUL, BODY AND TELEPATHY IN THE EXPERIENCES OF SWEDENBORG

Philosophy, which on account of its self-conceit exposes itself to all sorts of empty questions, finds itself often in an awkward embarrassment in view of certain stories, parts of which it cannot *doubt* without suffering for it, nor *believe* without being laughed at.

KANT

No choice is uninfluenced by the way in which the personality regards its destiny, and the body its death. In the last analysis, it is our conception of death, which decides our answers to all the questions that life puts to us. That is why it requires its proper place and time

– if need be with right of precedence. Hence, too, the necessity of preparing for it.

HAMMARSKJÖLD

Most educated people have heard something about Swedenborg, but one meets still with many who know little more than the name of that truly great man. It is vaguely identified in their minds with mysticism, with spiritualistic experiences, with dreams and visions, and much that is supposed to be included under the general term of 'occultism'.

These words were written in 1919, by one of Swedenborg's biographers, and are probably an accurate reflection of general opinion sixty years ago. Before describing Swedenborg's view of the soul and death, derived from his own experiences, it is essential to fill in some biographical details and to give some idea of the range of his abilities.

Swedenborg was born in Stockholm in 1688, and was the son of a Swedish bishop and professor of theology, Jesper Swedberg (the name was changed to Swedenborg when the family was ennobled in 1718). His grandfather had been associated for long years with the Royal Board of Mines, for which Swedenborg himself worked for many years. He was educated in the university of Uppsala, and in 1709 set off on a five-year tour of Europe, spending a considerable period in London and Oxford. There he met some of the leading mathematicians and astronomers of the day, and spent a good deal of time studying Newton. He worked on the problem of longitude calculation, and lodged wherever he had the opportunity of acquiring some new practical skill, for instance watchmaking and lens-grinding. At this stage he was also attempting to formulate a number of inventions, among which were an air pump, a flying machine, a quick-firing gun and 'a certain ship which with its men was to go under the surface of the sea and do great damage to the fleet of the enemy'; these inventions all seem to have had some military end in view.

On his return to Sweden in 1715 Swedenborg was appointed an extraordinary assessor of the Board of Mines, and worked closely with Christopher Polhem, the leading Swedish engineer of the day. Swedenborg started a scientific journal and began to write papers on geology, crystallography and algebra. In 1718 he refused the offer of the chair of astronomy in Uppsala University, and in 1724 turned down the chair of mathematics, both in favour of continuing his work at the Board of

Mines. In 1729 he was elected a member of the Swedish Royal Society of Sciences, and in 1734 became a corresponding member of the St Petersburg Imperial Academy of Sciences; in the same year he published his conclusions on physics and the origin of the universe in his *Principia*. In this work he anticipated much subsequent work on matter and the origin of the world; he formulated the nebular hypothesis 21 years before Kant and 62 years before Laplace, who generally receives credit for the formulation. However Swedenborg would certainly have disagreed with Laplace's remark to Napoleon that the hypothesis of God was now superfluous in relation to creation.

His subsequent interests moved in the directions of psychology and physiology, in a determined effort to ascertain the physical nature of the soul. He wrote two enormous volumes on the brain, which were only published 100 years after his death, and in 1740 published his anatomical findings in *The Economy of the Animal Kingdom*. He was unable to find a physical or chemical explanation of the soul, or life-principle, although he concluded that it must have something to do with the blood and the brain. Notebooks of the period contain extensive extracts from notable previous thinkers who had addressed themselves to the problem of the soul; starting with Plato's *Phaedo* and *Timaeus* he consults Aristotle and refers to other Greek philosophers such as Democritus and Empedocles; he also treats Augustine, and then the more contemporary thinkers Descartes, Leibniz, and Malebranche. Then around the middle of 1743 he started to have very vivid dreams and began keeping a dream journal, which gives an idea of the internal crisis that he was undergoing. In April 1744 he had a vision of Christ, who charged him to spend the rest of his life on the theological exposition of what Swedenborg referred to as the internal sense of the Bible. He did very little scientific work after this date, and left, unfinished, the book on which he was then working. He did not, however, become a recluse, or appear any less sane to his contemporaries. In 1761 the prime minister of Sweden, Count Hopken, considered that Swedenborg had one of the most solid and best written commentaries on the financial state of the country; in fact many of his theological works were published anonymously, so that his contemporaries could at first only speculate that he was the author.

A number of incidents are recorded which indicate that Swedenborg possessed what would now be regarded as psychic powers: some involve clairvoyance, one is a case of precognition, and three others were explained by Swedenborg himself by his ability to converse with spirits; modern researchers, depending on their presuppositions, might submit alternative explanations. The first clairvoyant incident took place in July 1759, when Swedenborg was one of fifteen guests at the house of a Gothenburg merchant, William Castel. At six in the evening Swedenborg suddenly became alarmed and explained that there was a fire burning in Stockholm, 300 miles away. He described where it was burning, where and when it had started, but was relieved when he informed the company that its progress had been halted not far from his own house. Swedenborg related the details to the governor on the following day, and only two days after the fire did messengers arrive with reports that corresponded in every detail with Swedenborg's description. The fame of this incident spread far enough to arouse the curiosity of Kant, who sent his own investigator to check up on the facts; this is one of the incidents referred to at the head of the chapter.

There was a similar occurrence in Gothenburg around 1770 at a dinner held in Swedenborg's honour. A manufacturer called Bollander was also present; he owned extensive cloth-mills, and suddenly found himself being abruptly addressed by Swedenborg who told him, apparently without any explanation, that he had better go to his mills. The manufacturer obeyed, and on arriving at his mills he discovered that a large piece of cloth had fallen down near the furnace and had started to burn. Any delay would have resulted in the complete razing of his property. On returning to the dinner he thanked Swedenborg and explained what had happened. Swedenborg replied that he had seen the danger and that there was no time to be lost – hence the abrupt tone. On another occasion he was attending a dinner (another public function) in Amsterdam just after the Russian Emperor Peter III had fallen from power and had been replaced by his wife Catherine. Swedenborg suddenly became unaware of his surroundings, and his expression changed radically; on recovering he was asked what had happened and at first refused to say anything; but he was then prevailed upon and described the gruesome death of Peter III, urging his fellow guests to note the date and his account. A few days later the newspapers featured the story, which corresponded to Swedenborg's description.

The next incident could either be classified as a case of precognition or, as Swedenborg himself would probably have said, an example of correct information given to him by the world of spirits. One evening in company he was put to the test: he was asked to state which of the assembled company would die first. After a few moments of silence he said that the first to die would be Olof Olofsohn – at 4.45 the next morning. One of Olofsohn's friends resolved to go to his house the next morning to see if the prediction was fulfilled. On the way he met one of Olofsohn's servants who informed him that his master had died, and that the clock in the apartment had apparently stopped at the moment of death, at 4.45.

In 1770 an Elberfeld merchant wanted to test Swedenborg himself: he related that he had an important discussion with a friend shortly before he had died, and asked Swedenborg to find out what the topic of conversation had been. Some days later he returned and informed the merchant that the subject was the restitution of all things. The merchant is said to have turned pale on hearing the correct reply and must have been even more surprised to learn that his friend was not yet in a state of bliss as he was still tormenting himself about this subject. Swedenborg explained that a man takes his favourite inclinations and opinions with him and advised the merchant that they were better laid aside before death. This story might equally be explained by Swedenborg's reading the mind of the merchant, although the detail about his friend's condition, if true, could not have been obtained in this way.

Queen Louisa Ulrica of Sweden had heard of Swedenborg's ostensible powers, and had serious doubts about his sanity. But she was reassured by Count Scheffer, who arranged for Swedenborg to come to court. The queen questioned him about his abilities and asked him to take a commission to her dead brother. Some time later Swedenborg was once again brought to court and had a private audience with the queen; no one ever found out what Swedenborg had told her, but she was so shocked that she had to retire – later she explained that she had been told something which no person living knew. An intrepid reporter made further attempts to find out what had been said, but he was dismissed with sovereign contempt – 'je ne suis pas facilement dupée' [I am not easily duped].

If the last two incidents can be explained by thought-reading, the same is not true of the following account. In 1761 the Countess de Marteville came to Swedenborg to explain that her husband, who had been ambassador to the Netherlands, had given her a valuable silver service before his death. The silversmith was now demanding an exorbitant payment, even though she was sure that her husband had paid for it already; but the receipt was nowhere to be found. The countess asked Swedenborg to contact her husband to ask about the receipt. Three days later he told her that he had spoken to her husband, who had informed him that the vital document was in a bureau upstairs. The woman replied that the bureau had already been searched, but Swedenborg insisted that she should remove a certain drawer and pull off its false back. The papers were duly found in the secret place, whose existence was only known to the dead count. The story is related by eleven different sources and vouched for by Swedenborg himself when he was later questioned about it. The only alternative hypothesis to a 'conversation' with the dead man in this instance is some form of so-called post-cognition, whereby Swedenborg had picked up the information from a sort of 'event bank', but this theory is extremely unspecific and is little more than a sophisticated and desperate question-begging device – as Burt pointed out.

Swedenborg himself did not regard these incidents as more than trifles, but they are perhaps helpful in that they relate him to more modern occurrences of a similar type. Throughout the rest of the chapter it should be borne in mind, as already mentioned, that Swedenborg went about his business in the world in a sane manner, and retained the empirical habits of mind which he had acquired as a scientist. At the beginning of his exegesis of Genesis he shows that he is well aware of what people will say about him:

> Many will say that no one can possibly speak with spirits and angels so long as he lives in the body; and many will say that it is all a phantasy, others that I relate such things in order to gain credence, and others will make other objections. But by all this I am not deterred, for I have seen, I have heard, I have felt.

Elsewhere, he refers to things which 'have been proved to me by the daily experience of many years'; and when talking of the fact that a man is essentially unchanged after death he asserts that this 'has been proved to me by manifold experience'. In other words Swedenborg retains the empirical approach and analyses these uncommon experiences in the same way as he would go about the examination of a crystal or a part of the anatomy. He never dramatises his writings, but relates the facts about the nature of the soul, its relation to the body and its persistence after the death of the body in a straightforward and down-to-earth manner.

Swedenborg gives a succinct definition of the soul and its relation to the body:

> As regards the soul of which it is said that it will live after death, it is nothing but the man himself who lives within the body, that is, the

interior man who in this world acts through the body, and gives live to the body. This man, when freed from the body, is called a spirit.

The terms spirit, soul, and internal man are used synonymously most of the time, although above spirit is used to denote the man freed from the body; occasionally soul is used to mean the spirit of a man while still in the body, a distinction which Swedenborg seems to have derived from Augustine (the use of the preposition *in* when referring to the relation of the soul to the body is significant and illustrates Swedenborg's idea of instrumentality). The other term, 'internal man', is peculiar to Swedenborg, who uses it in contrast with the external man who is manifest through his body. The use of these terms will become clearer in reference to the after-death state. One further synonym emerges, that of mind: 'The mind of man is his spirit and the spirit is the man because by mind are understood all the things of man's will and understanding.' These two faculties of will and understanding are said to act in harness: the understanding contains all that a man thinks of, while the will is all the things that affect a man (emotionally), thus the will operates through 'affections' and the understanding through thoughts. Swedenborg considers the explanation of the understating self-evident, but admits that the function of the will is harder to grasp. He compares the understanding to the sound of the voice, and the will to its tone: the meaning of the sentence is given in its structure, while the more subtle emotional message can be grasped in its tone. In practice these two operations are not separated; only in a reproduced synthesiser would the tone carry no significance. As the affection is related to the will, so it is related to love; not in the ordinary sense, but rather in terms of preoccupations and habits, which Swedenborg terms the ruling loves – the lines along which a man's thoughts usually run in opinions, tastes and inclinations. The qualities of the essential inner man are manifest in his thoughts and emotional tendencies.

Swedenborg expands on the nature of soul and body, and their respective functions in a very similar way to Plotinus:

> Whoever duly considers the subject can know that the body does not think, because it is material, but that the soul, which is spiritual, does. The soul of man, upon the immortality of which many have written, is his spirit ... this is also what thinks in the body, for it is spiritual ... all rational life that appears in the body belongs to the soul, and

nothing of it to the body; for the body, as said above, is material, and the material, which is the property of the body added to and, as it were, almost adjoined to the spirit, in order that the spirit of man may be able to live in the natural world, all things of which are material and in themselves devoid of life. And because the material does not live but only the spiritual, it can be established that whatever lives in man is his spirit, and that the body merely serves it, just as what is instrumental serves a moving living force. An instrument is said indeed to act, to move, or to strike; but to believe that these are acts of the instrument, and not of him who acts, or strikes by means of an instrument, is a fallacy.

This formulation turns on its head most of the twentieth century ways of thinking, and may require some mental acrobatics to appreciate: it is not the body which feels, but the *spirit which feels through the body*, a view which follows the line of Plato and which anticipates those of Schiller, James, and Bergson; the matter of the dead body has no sensation unless the spirit is operating within it, in the same way as a severed limb automatically loses sensation. More will be said below of the senses after death.

From the above conception, that the soul is the man within the body, it follows that death is the separation of the soul from the body:

Separation or death occurs when, from some sickness or accident, the body comes into such a condition that it is unable to act in unison with its spirit ... then man is said to die. This takes place when the respiration of the lungs and the beatings of the heart cease. But yet the man does not die; he is merely separated from the corporeal part that was of use to him in the world, for the man himself lives. It is said that the man himself lives, since man is not a man because of his body but because of his spirit, for it is the spirit in man that thinks, and thought with affection makes man.

In brief, for some reason or other the spirit and body are no longer able to act in conjunction, so that a separation takes place; because it is the spirit which lives in man, it continues to exist while the body decays.

Swedenborg explains that as soon as the heartbeat ceases the man is 'resuscitated', which means that the spirit is drawn out of the body. In order better to report the details, Swedenborg himself claims to have undergone the experience. He is brought into a state of bodily insensibility with his interior life and thought unimpaired so that he could better retain the memory of the experience. He describes that he first perceived celestial angels (he explains elsewhere that all angels have been men, and that heaven is divided into three broad categories, the highest of which is celestial, then spiritual, then natural – the highest angels come first); these celestial angels represent the highest and most spiritual forms of thought, corresponding to the Fundamental Clear Light of the *Bardo Thodol* – it will be remembered that those who can accept the light attain liberation. If the spirit is not of celestial quality, he will feel uncomfortable in the presence of celestial angels and will long to escape from them. Next come angels from the spiritual kingdom, corresponding to the secondary clear light; they will likewise withdraw if the spirit feels uneasy, and are then replaced by angels from the natural kingdom – 'But if he had lived such a life in the world as would prevent him enjoying the company of the good, he longs to get away from them, and this experience will be repeated until he comes into association with such as are in entire harmony with his life in the world; and with such he finds his own life, and what is surprising, he leads a life like that which he led in the world.' Thus a spiritual gravitation takes place, whereby the novitiate spirit finds the milieu which corresponds to his inner disposition. In a reincarnation framework, this would correspond to the choice of a new life, as in Plato's *Republic*.

Swedenborg describes sensations of bewilderment in the novitiate in similar terms to the *Bardo Thodol*

> I may state that much experience has shown me that when a man comes into the other life he is not aware that he is in that life, but supposes that he is still in the world, and even that he is still in the body. So much is this the case that when he is told that he is a spirit, wonder and amazement possess him, both because he finds himself exactly like a man, in his senses, desires and thoughts, and because during life in this world he had not believed in the existence of the spirit, or, as is the case with some, that the spirit could be what he now finds itself to be.

Swedenborg points out that no sight or hearing is possible in the absence of the appropriate organ, hence that the spirit as well as the body has to be in a form, a human form, which enjoys senses when separated from the body. The fact that the body is a duplicate of the physical body accounts for the confusion of the novitiate, who can only associate body with matter; thus when he sees that he is in a body he concludes that he must still be in a material body.

The senses, then, are manifest through another body which is substantial in the sense that it has form, but not in the sense that the form is material. This body cannot be seen with the eyes of the body but only with the eyes of the spirit, to which it seems like a man in the world. His senses are supposed to be far more exquisite 'for the things of the body, being comparatively gross, had rendered the sensations obtuse, and this the more because the man had immersed them in earthly and worldly things'. The thoughts are much clearer and more distinct – 'there are more things contained in a single idea of their thought than in a thousand of the ideas that they had possessed in this world.' The speech is said to be interior, thus communication is wordless and thoughts pass from one to the other without the medium of spoken language; nor can the thoughts be concealed, as their expression is immediate and spontaneous – an embarrassing prospect for those who, like Voltaire, reckon that our tongues are for concealing our thoughts. In conclusion, Swedenborg points out that 'life consists in the exercise of sensation, for without it there is no life, and such as the faculty of sensation is, such is the life' – a conception of life in terms of continued experience similar to the assumptions made by Price. After death, man is in a spiritual body, which has more refined senses than its physical counterpart.

Reactions to the burial of the physical body are mixed. Swedenborg explains that the scene can only be perceived by the spirit through his eyes (material) not through their own, and even then only because he is in the unique position of being in both the natural and spiritual worlds at once. One friend of his said at his funeral that they should throw his body away, because he himself was alive. The engineer Polhem, however, is reported by Swedenborg to have experienced a good deal of confusion owing to his previous views:

> Polhem died on Monday. He spoke with me on Thursday; and when I was invited to his funeral he saw his coffin, and those who were there, and the whole procession, and also when his body was laid in the grave; and in the meantime he spoke with me, asking why he was buried when he was still alive: and he heard, also, when the priest said that he would be resuscitated at the last judgment, and yet he had been resuscitated for some time; and he marvelled that such a belief should exist, as that man should be resuscitated at the last judgement,

when he was still alive; and that the body should rise again, when yet he himself was sensible of being in a body.

Polhem's witnessing of his own funeral should have enabled him to appreciate his true state. Swedenborg tells of acquaintances with whom he had conversed after their death, and who have:

> wondered exceedingly that during the bodily life no one knows or believes that he is to live when the bodily life is over ... they have desired me to tell their friends that they are alive, and to write and tell them what their condition is, even as I have related to themselves many things about that of their friends here. But I replied that were I to tell their friends such things, or to write to them about them, they would not believe, but would call them delusions, would scoff at them, and would ask for signs and miracles before they would believe; and I should merely expose myself to their derision.

Thus Swedenborg is extremely pessimistic about the possibility of convincing those still in the body of the continued existence of their friends. He gives three main reasons for scepticism about the immediate resuscitation of consciousness: that the spirit can have no existence apart from the body; that men will sleep until the day of judgement; and that the nature of the soul is to be unextended in space. The first two arguments are forms of materialism, in that neither can conceive of an existence apart from the physical body – the first a rationalist and the second a religious version. The third derives from the Cartesian assumption that while the body is substantial and extended in space, the soul or mind is unextended, and can therefore have no form. We shall look at each of these in turn.

Swedenborg comments that:

> when the sensuous and corporeal man thinks about the separation of the spirit from the body, it strikes him as an impossible thing, because he places life in the body, and confirms himself in this idea from the fact that brute animals also live, but do not live after death.

But, Swedenborg argues, he has forgotten his rational faculty, which distinguishes him from animals and which Swedenborg calls the 'inmost'; as we have seen, Aristotle and others made the same distinction.

The corporeal man also contended that the spirit cannot exist because it is invisible, to which Swedenborg replied that it was invisible only to the corporeal eyes, not to those of the spirit. Men who can only think in bodily categories, he concludes, find the existence of a separate spirit impossible to conceive.

We have already indicated the problems inherent in resuscitation at the last judgement with respect to Polhem's funeral. Swedenborg describes this theory of bodily resurrection as 'so universal that almost everyone holds it as a matter of doctrine'. But this opinion has prevailed 'because the natural man supposes that it is the body alone which lives; and that therefore unless he believed that the body would receive life again, he would deny the resurrection altogether'. In some cases, Swedenborg asserts, the last judgement has been awaited so long that it is believed that the soul will never rise again. He goes on to give his own view, which we have outlined above, of immediate resuscitation. And on one occasion he records having asked some spirits whether 'they wished to be clothed again in their earthly body, as they had thought before. On hearing this they fled far away at the very idea of such a conjunction, being filled with amazement that they had so thought from blind faith without understanding.'

The learned, it is remarked, have the idea that the spirit is abstract thought, and are unwilling to grant that it may have any extension. The thinking subject has extension in space (form), but the thought has none; and if the spirit has no extension, it can have no substance, and cannot be in any place. Swedenborg comments on this state of affairs (or rather confusion):

> But an abuse arises from the fact that philosophers abide in terms, and dispute concerning them without coming to an agreement, from which all idea of the thing itself perishes, and the comprehension of the man is rendered so limited that he ceases at length to know anything but terms. Accordingly, when such persons would master a subject by their terms they do nothing but heap them up, obscuring the whole matter, so that they can understand nothing of it.

A practical example of this is recorded: Swedenborg is conversing with one who in the world believed that the spirit has no extension, and asked him how he now thought of himself, seeing that he was a soul with all his senses and supposed himself to be exactly as if in the body. He replied that spirit was thought, whereupon Swedenborg pointed out that no senses could exist without the appropriate organs, and that the brain is required for the transmission of thought in the body; therefore the body in which he now found himself must be of some organic substance, even though not material, for without it there would be no sensation, and without sensation, no life (i.e. consciousness), 'whereupon he confessed his error, and wondered that he had been so foolish'.

The common thread running through the above three varieties of scepticism is the paradoxical situation which arises when the man still finds himself conscious and in a body after death. According to the materialists, they should have ceased to exist; but they are still conscious and alive in a sense, hence their first reaction, as we have seen, is to believe that they are not dead at all, but still alive in the physical body; only gradually, by conversing with other spirits, do they rid themselves of this illusion. The philosophers are less surprised to find themselves alive than to find themselves in a body, as they had equated the substantial with the material, thus concluding that anything which was not material could not be substantial or have extension. Their experience slowly convinces them of the real nature of their survival so that, in the end, all their *a priori* categories are dropped, and they experience themselves as they are. The empirical approach also has to be applied to an unfamiliar set of circumstances.

We shall now look briefly at Swedenborg's account of the development of man in the spiritual world; readers who wish to examine this in detail are referred to the original texts. The man arrives with everything except his earthly body: his disposition and memory are not changed in any respect. Swedenborg distinguishes two kinds of memory, the internal and the external: on the internal memory is inscribed everything that a man has thought, willed, spoken, done or even heard. Hence nothing whatsoever is lost and the man can be judged by the recreation of all his acts, thoughts, and intentions concerning any hidden crime or misdemeanour:

> Deceits and thefts ... were also enumerated in detail, many of which had been known to scarcely any in the world except themselves. These deeds they confessed, because they were plainly set forth, with every thought, intention, pleasure and fear which occupied their minds at the time.

The record is read as if in a book; and this book has been compiled by the man himself, so that his character has been built up by the thoughts and by the acts of his will.

The man, then, corresponds essentially to the 'ruling love' or primary disposition, in terms of which he thinks and acts, and which is responsible for his initial gravitation to a certain milieu or society. At first there may be some discrepancy between the 'internal' and the 'external', between what is thought and willed on the one hand, and what is spoken and done on the other. As the former internal man is the more essential, it gradually comes to predominate, thus eliminating the initial division; there is no longer an external restraint to be taken into account, so that man is able to act in accordance with his own nature. Corresponding to this, the face is transformed into an image of the ruling love, of which it is the outer form:

> All in the other life are brought into such a state as to speak as they think, and to manifest in their looks and gestures the inclinations of their will. And because of this the faces of all become forms and images of their affections.

When this is complete the man gravitates to his 'natural' abode in heaven or hell, a process which rounds off the gravitation expressed in the experience of dying described above.

Swedenborg makes two more important points: first that no one comes to heaven as a result of immediate mercy. In other words there is no justification by faith alone or last-minute repentance; mere knowledge without action is not manifested through the will, and is therefore not part of the essential man. In addition, because the man's ruling love is his life, destruction of an evil ruling love would involve annihilation of the man himself. The man whose bodily life has been the opposite of heaven cannot miraculously be transformed into the opposite of his nature. For a man to gain access (or rather gravitate) to heaven, his thoughts and affections must correspond to the heavenly.

Second, Swedenborg reassuringly maintains that it is not so difficult to lead a heavenly life as is believed. He warns against the hermit whose sorrowful life will continue to be sorrowful after death 'since life continues the same after death'. On the contrary, man is exhorted to live in the world and engage in duties and employments there. He must live an internal and external life at the same time, but must not content himself with practising virtues because of the restraints of the law, but rather because it accords with divine laws; thus he acts not out of fear but from love, with the result that there is no division between his internal and his external.

In terms of subject matter we have come a long way from the Board of Mines, but for Swedenborg this exploration was an extension of the empirical approach and of reason into the realms of the spiritual. He writes of experiences, which few have had, some of which are only now becoming more familiar in the light of parallel experiences in our own century. He predicted the day and time of his own death in March 1772, and paid his landlady exactly up to the end of the month. In the chapters which follow we shall see how Swedenborg's basis contention – that man is a spirit operating through the physical body and continuing to exist after death in another body – compares with other formulations and explanations.

8.

APPARITIONS

The present does not attain finality. Nor does the future, for it is only what will be present ... we want the future to be there without ceasing to be future. This is an absurdity of which eternity is the only cure.

SIMONE WEIL

Our birth is but a sleep and a forgetting.

WORDSWORTH

At the still point in the centre of the circle one can see the infinite in all things.

CHUANG TSU

If the doors of perception were cleansed, everything would appear as it is, infinite.

BLAKE

No doubt the reader has been asked more than once the tiresome question about whether they believe in ghosts, and have been expected to reply with a summary yes or no. Few people would dare to reply 'yes' unequivocally, for fear of being ridiculed or scoffed at as soft-headed or branded as a credulous crank. The man who replies 'no' usually adds that a person like him could scarcely be expected to believe in such nonsense. The question, however, is badly phrased, and falls into a similar category to 'Do you believe in God?', which some people think can be answered in terms of non-rational assent. But neither question can be answered in this way; the belief in God is frequently grounded in experience, while 'believe in' ghosts requires a much more complex and subtle reply than would be anticipated by the phrasing of the question. As Price points out, there is no doubt that people do experience apparitions, and that some of these apparitions are of people alive and well, others of people dying or who have just died, and still others of those who have been dead for some time. The question which remains though, is one of interpretation – whether the apparitions are simply imaginative constructs on the part of the percipient, whether there is any reason to suppose that there is an 'agent' or conscious personality willing the event, or whether an apparent connection just amounts to chance coincidence. In this chapter we shall confine ourselves principally to those phenomena which relate to death, although other examples may be adduced if they throw light on the main theme.

Despite more recent studies, the main source of case histories is still *Phantasms of the Living*, published in 1886 and written jointly by Edmund Gurney, Frederic Myers and Frank Podmore. The work required over four years to produce the book was prodigious: it contains over 700 documented cases together with analysis and commentary, making a total of over 1,300 pages; since that date, few works of comparable thoroughness and rigour have appeared on this subject. The object of the book was to set out and analyse reliable reports of telepathy and various kinds of hallucination, perhaps in the hope of burying scientific incredulity under a heap of facts. Reports, which reached the investigators, were scrutinised, then letters written to the percipient asking further questions and requesting corroboration by third parties of the experience and its aftermath. Two questions receive particular attention: the reliability of the testimony, and the role of chance.

A whole chapter of *Phantasms of the Living* is devoted to the discussion and criticism of evidence. In the first place testimony comes mainly from educated people who had no predisposition to believe in the reality of the phenomena: in many instances the experience was unique. Various possible sources of error are considered: in observation, narration, memory with regard to dates and times, etc; second-hand testimony is excluded from the main part of the work. The sort of questions asked includes: Was the account written down or related before the event was known to have occurred? Has the principal witness been corroborated? Was the percipient fully awake, and was he educated and of good character? Was the apparition recognised? Was the percipient anxious? Could relevant details have been read back into the narrative after the event? Given thorough investigation along these lines, Gurney concludes that the sweeping assertion about the unreliability of human testimony cannot be upheld, and that the evidence cannot be summarily dismissed.

The answer to the hypothesis of chance-coincidence as an explanation of the close *prima facie* connection between so-called crisis apparitions and death depends on the number of apparitions that coincide with a crisis event and those where no such connection is apparent. As we have already indicated, many of the cases were unique in the experience of the informants, and, as will be seen below, the correspondence of timing between the crisis event and the apparition is often extremely close. The typical pattern is that a very unusual or unique experience of an apparition happens to occur on a particular day at a particular time; the apparition indicates or suggests to the mind of the percipient that the person concerned is in danger or has died; the information is subsequently confirmed, and the timing of the apparition found to coincide with the event. It has been calculated that the odds against such an accurate precognition of death are, in some cases, astronomic; and yet they do occur – why?

The original investigators were all working within the framework of causality and probability; thus they conceived of two parties in an apparition: the agent and the percipient. The agent was supposed to influence the percipient telepathically, and thus 'cause' the apparition by means of 'psychic invasion'. In his essay on Synchronicity, subtitled 'An Acausal Connecting Principle', Jung distinguishes two realms of our experience: one in which we can make causal connections, rending these aspects predictable and reliable; the other realm is that of chance, which, as we have seen, the primitive mind subsumes under causality. Some coincidences can be dismissed as irrelevant or merely trivial, such as meeting strangers in different places on successive days;

but others, such as crisis-apparitions, are more significant and mean-ingful, at any rate *prima facie*, and may contain a time element which is absent from the more trivial instances. In *theory* they can still be conceived of as chance occurrences, but, as Jung points out:

> The more they multiply and the greater and more exact the correspondence is, the more their probability sinks and their unthinkability increases, until they can no longer be regarded as pure chance but, for lack of causal explanation, have to be thought of as meaningful arrangements

This is applied specifically to cases of our type: 'Psi-phenomena ... are contingencies beyond mere probability, meaningful coincidences due to a specific psychic condition namely ... an emotional objective situation like death ... or illness.' This hypothesis goes beyond the crude causality of agent and percipient, but may have to be supplemented in the light of the apparent connection between OBEs and apparitions.

Before citing specific cases, it may be helpful to outline some of the characteristics of apparitions. Celia Green states that the sense of sight, not surprisingly, is the most frequently affected – in 84 per cent of the cases in her survey; experiences of a mixed or purely auditory kind have been recorded, but we shall concentrate on the visual. G. N. M. Tyrrell's discussion of the characteristics includes (a) the fact that they can appear in various types of space – not just the common space, but also in crystals, visions and windows, or in dreams; (b) the fact that they are non-physical – they appear and disappear in locked rooms, vanish while being watched, or fade away in front of the percipient, pass through physical objects, are invisible to some people in the room but not others, and finally leave no physical trace behind them. The third characteristic is the more interesting: that they do not always strike the percipient as other than physically real and present. Green states that, of her sample, 46 per cent realised immediately that they were experiencing an apparition, 18 per cent before it ended, 6 per cent as it ended, and 31 per cent only after it had ended: this means that over half of the percipients did not *immediately* distinguish the apparition from ordinary waking sense perception, and that nearly a third were deceived throughout the experience. This fact speaks for the degree of realism in the image. Tyrrell suggests various reasons for this de-ception: that the apparition respects the arrangement of furniture in the room and is seen in normal relation to these items, that it usually occupies the centre of the visual field, and that, if the percipient shuts or screens his eyes, the apparition will disappear like a physical object, unless the experience is taking place in a dream. The apparition behaves in some respects like a non-physical entity for the reasons outlined above. Because it can be subsumed under neither of these two categories, its nature is extremely difficult to explain.

We shall look at the following types of phenomena in turn: first, visual experiences which indicate danger; second, dreams which coincide with deaths; third, apparitions which coincide with deaths; fourth, cases which suggest some relationship with OBEs or intentional 'projection'; fifth, the implications of some collective hallucinations and of apparitions seen some time after the death of the person appearing; and, finally, visions perceived by dying persons.

8A1 – told by Mrs Bettany, who, as a child, had many remarkable psychic experiences, which she looked upon at the time as quite normal. One afternoon she was walking along a lane reading a geometry book when:

> 'in a moment I saw a bedroom known as the White Room in my home, and upon the floor lay my mother, to all appearance dead. The vision must have remained some minutes, during which my real surroundings seemed to pale and die out; but as the vision faded, actual surroundings came back, at first dimly then clearly.'

Instead of going straight home, the child went to the doctor, who accompanied her home, where they found the mother prostrate and in the White Room as described. She would have died but for the timely arrival of the doctor. On further questioning, the following facts emerged: the child was in no anxiety about her mother at the time – she had been in perfect health; the White Room was out of use, so that it was unlikely that the mother should be there; and the father, who confirmed the child's statement, was in the house at the time but had no idea that his wife was ill.

8A2 – reported by a barrister, who had no other experience of a hallucination. One afternoon he was working at some papers in his chambers in the Temple when he suddenly became aware of a scene depicted in the bottom window pane: he saw the figure of the head and face of his wife, in a reclining position, with the eyes closed and the face quite bloodless and white, as if she were dead. He got up and looked out of the window, concluding that he must have dozed off; he then resumed his work. That evening his wife told him that she had taken one of her nieces to lunch with a friend, and that after lunch the child had cut her face and drawn blood; this had so alarmed the wife that she had fainted. The barrister ascertained that this must have occurred just after two o'clock, about the time when he had seen the image in the window. He added that, like his unique experience, this was the only time that his wife had had a fainting fit.

8A3 – is a record of a dream by Colonel V. On Sunday night 25 May 1884 he dreamed that his son, an officer in a regiment stationed at Gibraltar, was lying there very ill with fever and was calling: 'Father, father, come over and let me see you or my mother.' The following morning the Colonel went over to visit the Rev. G., who at that very moment was sitting down to write to the Colonel, and, before the Colonel had time to speak, asked him whether he believed in dream waves. The Colonel then related his dream, but thought nothing more of it as he had a cheerful letter from his son the same morning. On 29 May, however, he received a wire saying that his son was very ill with rock fever; it turned out that he had fallen ill on the 17th, and had become delirious on the 25th, so that a nurse had been put in charge of him. Colonel V. left for Gibraltar and arrived on 4 June to find his son still very weak. He saw the nurse and mentioned the dream; she explained that he had been delirious all through the night of the 25th, and had been calling out for his parents in the way perceived by V. in his dream. From the evidential point of view it is a pity that the nurse was told the dream before volunteering the information about the son's crying out; one can imagine her confirming the dream as a matter of tact; but, on the other hand, supposing what she asserted to be true, there is no reason why she should have mentioned the delirium as anything extraordinary, as such phenomena might have been common in her experience. However, the fact remains that the father perceived his son's illness as fever before he received any confirmation, that he had already told the dream to a third party, and that the timing of the dream coincided with the delirious stage of his son's fever.

The next four cases concern dreams coinciding with a death: 8B1 – the Rev W.B.B. informed Gurney that he had had an exceptionally vivid dream of the death of an acquaintance, whom he had no means of knowing was not in the best of health. The following morning he wrote to the son of the lady concerned, and mentioned the dream to his wife (independently confirmed by the wife). They heard of the death of the acquaintance a couple of days later; it had occurred on the night of the dream.

8B2 – The narrator also had a distinctly out of character experience when her husband turned out to be dying in Paris. On this occasion Mrs S. was staying in Düsseldorf with her daughter, who had been undergoing an operation in Bonn. Her mother-in-law was also in Bonn, and was in excellent spirits after her granddaughter's operation. A few days later Mrs S. dreamt that her mother-in-law had died; she was so stricken by the dream that she woke her daughter up and noticed that the time was between 3 and 4 am. The next morning she received a telegram asking her to meet her mother-in-law's sister at Cologne station, where she was informed of her mother-in-law's death; this had taken place after an operation the previous night for an ailment of which Mrs S. knew nothing.

8B3 is evidentially interesting, as the precognitive dream was recorded in writing before the event came to light. At 10.35 one morning a Dr Holbrook wrote to Hodgson informing him that five minutes previously Mr J.F. Morse had come into his room and announced that he had had a remarkable dream which indicated that his (Morse's) wife had died. He knew that his wife was ill, but not dangerously so, and had expressed some confidence about her immediate state in a letter two days before, stating that she had been taken on by a new doctor. In the event, he only learned of his wife's death, which had taken place on the night of the dream, on arriving at the hospital the next day. It also transpired that his brother-in-law had had a very vivid dream indicating his sister's death, but it was not known whether this occurred on the same evening as the husband's dream.

8B4 – related to Jung, who considers the incident to have been a message from the unconscious:

> I dreamed that my wife's bed was a deep pit with stone walls. It was a grave and somehow had a suggestion of classical antiquity about it (archetypal). Then I heard a deep sigh, as if someone were giving up the ghost. A figure that resembled my wife sat up in the pit and floated upwards. It wore a white gown into which curious black symbols were woven. I awoke, roused my wife, and checked the time. It was three o'clock in the morning. The dream was so curious that I thought it might signify a death. At seven o'clock came the news that a cousin of my wife had died at three a.m.

This case incorporated symbolic elements, but the timing of the dream is remarkable.

Arguing from the undoubted fact that the brain produces hallucinations in the form of dreaming during sleep, and on occasions when the subject undergoes the stress of starvation or takes certain drugs, Gurney analyses the relationship between apparitions and dreams: in both cases there is a repose or benumbing of the sense organs, so that the vividness of the impression depends on the subject not being preoccupied with other sense impressions; thus when we wish to picture a scene more vividly, we close our eyes, which is naturally the case when dreaming. Dreams are far more common than waking hallucinations, so that the alleged psychological identity between the two is apt to be overlooked. Gurney concluded 'We might call dreams the normal form of hallucination, or waking hallucinations the pathological form of dreaming; the normal dream fades on waking, and only occasionally does the apparition impose itself on the sensory world.' The following two narratives illustrate the possibility of this thesis, which also features in the Wilmot case.

8C1 – M. dreamed that his sister-in-law had been taken seriously ill. The next evening he went into the dining room to have a smoke before going to bed and saw his sister-in-law appear, walk around the room and out into the garden. M. opened the relevant door but there was nothing to be seen. Only three days later did he hear of the events which had befallen her. She had been visiting her parents and was apparently in good health. On the Friday evening of the dream she had gone to the theatre and at 1 a.m. had been stricken with violent internal pains, which continued all day. No danger was apprehended until 4.45 when she lost consciousness and died within half an hour. The coincidence of timing in this case is only approximate, but its content is no less remarkable on that account.

8C2 is recorded by a man who declared himself to be no believer in spirits and felt that the following experience, although factual, was the result of illness. He was once laid up with fever in the tropics and had a dream about an old lady friend of his; he suddenly woke up and thought he saw her at the end of the bed, and that she spoke to him. The next morning he related the incident to a friend, who, predictably, laughed at him and told him that he was ill. However he did write the date and hour of the occurrence; a few mails later he heard of the old lady's death at the same date and hour of his hallucination and dream. Although his illness might help to explain his susceptibility to the hallucination by lowering the activity of his senses, it cannot be advanced as an explanation for the actual occurrence and timing of the incident.

We come now to cases where an apparition alone coincides approximately with the time of death. We shall give six instances of this:

8D1 – submitted in 1882 by Captain G.F. Russell Colt. His elder brother of nineteen had been abroad fighting in Sebastopol. On the night of 8 September 1885 he awoke suddenly and saw what he took to be his brother kneeling by the window. He retreated under the bedclothes, not out of fear (having been brought up not to believe in ghosts and apparitions) but simply to collect his thoughts. When he re-emerged, his brother was still there, looking lovingly and imploringly at him. He tried to speak but found himself unable to, then leapt out of bed, ascertained that there was no moon, and found that it was raining hard outside. On turning round he found that 'poor Oliver' (note that he does not say Oliver's apparition) was still there. He closed his eyes and walked straight 'through' the apparition towards the door. Before leaving the room he turned round once more to see the apparition turn his head to the left, so that for the first time he noticed a wound on the right temple with a red stream on it and that the face was of a waxy tint. He left the room and told a friend of the incident. Then, the next morning, he told his father, who dismissed the description as nonsense. About a fortnight later news arrived of the brother's death on the night of the apparition. The colonel of the regiment and one or two officers who had seen the body confirmed that the death wound was on the right temple, just as the brother had described, but it was not known whether he had died instantly or not. Some months later a prayer book and a letter, taken from the tunic which Oliver had been wearing when killed, were returned home; the letter had been written by the younger brother asking him to appear in his room should anything happen to him. The most remarkable fact about this case, apart from the timing and the letter, is the fact that the wound on the apparition corresponded with that on the body.

8D2 was submitted by a lady through a Major Taylor. On one of the last days of July around 1860 at about 3 o'clock in the afternoon the lady in question was reading in the drawing room of the Rectory, when she looked up and saw distinctly a tall thin old gentleman enter the room and come up to one of the tables. He was wearing a peculiar old-fashioned cloak which she recognised as belonging to her great uncle. On examining the features of the face, carefully, she recognised the figure as her great uncle, whom she had not seen for some years. In his hand he was carrying a roll of paper, and appeared very agitated. The lady was not in the least alarmed as she firmly believed that it was her uncle and asked him if he wanted her father, who was not at home at the time. He then appeared even more agitated and distressed, said nothing, then left the room through a half-open door. The lady noticed at that point that despite the fact that it was a very wet day the uncle did not seem to be walking through the mud; he was not carrying an umbrella but a walking stick, which the lady recognised at a later date. The servants declared that no one had rung the bell and that they had seen no one enter.

A letter arrived in the next post with an urgent and sudden request that her father should go and see his uncle, who was dangerously ill. The father left at once, but on arrival was informed that the uncle had died at three p.m., the time of the apparition. He had apparently asked for the father several times in an agitated manner, and a roll of paper was found under his pillow. The lady surmised that the cause of the distress was that the uncle had wanted to alter his will in favour of the father at the last moment, but had been overtaken by events; the two had always been close, and the uncle had led the father to believe that he would receive a considerable legacy, which turned out not to be the case. The apparition was reported to the mother before the journey of the father and to the father only on his return from the fruitless journey to the uncle, so that it could not have influenced the reported statement that the uncle had been asking for the father just before his death. In addition, the niece did not immediately recognise that the figure was an apparition, perhaps partly because it respected the arrangement of the furniture – features indicated as typical by Tyrrell. And then the fact that the figure appeared even more distressed when informed that the father was not at home, together with the reported wish of the uncle to see the father, suggests a willed action and some degree of conscious presence in the room.

8D3 concerns a General Albert Fytche. One morning at Maulmain he was getting out of bed when an old friend, whom he had not seen for years, entered the room. The general greeted him warmly, told him to call for a cup of tea on the veranda, and said that he would see him shortly. He went out onto the veranda but there was no one to be seen; neither the sentry nor the servants had seen a strange gentleman, but the general remained adamant that he had seen his friend. A fortnight later he received the news that his friend had died 600 miles from where he was, at about the time when the general had seen the apparition. He stated that he had never had an experience of a similar kind, that he had not heard of his friend's illness, and, as is apparent from the narrative, that he had mistaken the apparition for the friend himself.

8D4 first appeared in the *Daily Telegraph* in October 1881 and was submitted by a newspaper correspondent. A friend of his named Gough had volunteered to serve in Natal, and had been obliged to ride over 80 miles in a day in order to join his regiment. On the way he suffered an attack of dysentery, and was ordered into the ambulances on arrival. Shortly afterwards he had to lead his men in an attack, but the exertion proved too much and was followed by total collapse. Some three weeks later the correspondent was sitting in the mess house writing a letter when he heard the last post being sounded outside; he walked to the door, where he was amazed to see Gough, who, he had been told, was dying. A few days later he was informed of his friend's death, and subsequently found a telegraph, which had been waiting in his pigeon-hole. It was from the civil surgeon asking him to come to Gough's bedside as soon as possible, as the patient had been asking for him all day. He then discovered that his friend had died at exactly the moment when he fancied that he had seen him outside the mess house. Although, in this case, the correspondent knew of the illness, the timing remains remarkable, as is also the fact that Gough had been asking for his friend as he lay dying – the correlation between thoughts and possible intentions to project an apparition will receive fuller treatment below.

8D5 – is reported in the SPR journal with details and corroboration. Mrs Jessie Finniecome had been on friendly terms with a Viennese family called Liebig, and knew the Baroness especially well. On the night of 29 April 1930 she went to bed early and awoke at about 11.15 with someone pressing a kiss on her forehead, and, on looking up, she saw the Baroness standing by the bed. Mrs Finniecome was unable to speak, but gazed at the apparition for a minute or two before it turned and vanished; its expression was sad and enquiring. She told her husband in the morning, but he said that she must have been dreaming. A few days later the death, but not its exact time, was announced in the papers; further enquiry revealed that the death had taken place at 11.20, which corresponded with Mrs Finniecome's vision. Mrs Finniecome had known that the Baroness was not well, but the latest reports suggested some degree of recovery, so that there was no reason for particular anxiety at that time. The timing and distance involved are the most striking aspects of this case.

8D6 was reported by Professor W.W. Grundy whose sister-in-law had been staying at his house. She had been reading downstairs when she suddenly had a vision of her aunt in the doorway. She looked at her watch, which marked 4.45. She had been worried by her aunt's illness, but the aunt had recovered many times before. That evening they received a telegram announcing the aunt's death, and on the following morning a letter saying that she had died at 4.45 on the Saturday, at exactly the time that the vision had occurred. Once again the percipient knew of the illness, but this does not really account for the synchronisation of timing.

8D7 – As a postscript to this section the following case is unusual as the percipient only identified the subject of the apparition some weeks later. The narrator, Father C., a well-known Catholic priest, was living with the Roman Catholic bishop of Southwark on 3 December 1908; as far as he knew, he was alone with the bishop in the house. At around 6.40 a.m. on this date Father C. got up and went downstairs to the bathroom. While on the landing of the second floor, he saw a strange elderly man standing at the foot of the stairs; he had gray hair and a very long straight upper lip. Father C. thought that he must have come on after dinner the evening before and was now looking for the bishop; he was just about to speak to him when the figure vanished completely. No trace of him could be found, and no one else had stayed overnight. At lunch the bishop told Father C. that he had received a telegram to say that a Father F. had died at Bromley at 6.30 that morning; this information meant nothing to C., who did not know Father F. About five weeks later C. was appointed to succeed F. in Bromley, and soon after his arrival he noticed a large framed photograph in the parlour: it was without doubt the man whom he had seen at the bottom of the stairs in the bishop's house on 3 December. On enquiry he learned that the photo was indeed of Father F. This case is remarkable in a number of respects: the subject of the apparition was unknown to the percipient at the time, when there can naturally have been no thought of Father C.'s being appointed to Bromley; the telegram stated the time of death as 6.30 a.m., the time of the apparition, and only subsequently was the figure recognised as Father F. It is also a difficult case to account for on the Gurney telepathic hallucination theory: F. may well have been thinking of the bishop and wished to transmit to him a message of his impending death, but it was a stranger, not the bishop, who perceived the apparition. Such a telepathic hypothesis would have to be supplemented with an unlikely case of precognition by F. of his successor, with whom he could have no rapport: an improbable explanation since the successor could not yet be appointed while he was still alive. The most straightforward account of the case is that some quasi-physical manifestation of F. was present in the bishop's house – not actually physical in terms of his behaviour, but quasi-physical as it was perceived in physical space.

There are cases on record which suggest some degree of overlap between apparitions and OBEs, the subject of the next chapter; they may throw light on the nature of perception both within and outside the body – sometimes there is an exact correspondence of the two perceptions, but in other cases the OBE percipient sees additional features in the room. Green cites two cases of corresponding perception: 8E1 – concerns a WAAF officer who was lying awake in her hotel one night when the kitchen door opened and a slightly unreal figure walked into the room and advanced towards the narrator, who was terrified. The next thing she knew she was on the ceiling looking down on her body on the bed. The figure was still there, apparently tucking her in, but it suddenly vanished. 8E2 is about a man who was living in the bush about 70 miles from Perth, Australia, and was head over heels in love with a 'certain young lady'. He was resting on his bunk when he saw the young lady approach, so he got up to greet her; as he did so he suddenly realised that his body was still lying on the bunk, upon which the apparition vanished and he found himself back inside his body. Unfortunately there is no information about whether the lady had a corresponding experience; and in the first of these two cases, the apparition remained unidentified. However it is significant that the apparitions were seen in identical terms from vantage points both inside and outside the body, implying a theory of perception whereby the physical body is an instrument rather than sole medium of perception.

One of the features of the Gough case (8D4) was a possible correlation between the thoughts of the dying person and the appearance of an apparition; the same applied to Case 8D2. We shall now examine other cases which exhibit similar features; their numbers are naturally limited by the fact that in the majority of cases occurring at or just after death, the 'agent' cannot by definition return to say that he/she imagined that she saw the percipient.

8F1 is collective and involves an OBE: the percipient, Anna, lived for some years with her aunt, then arrangements were made for her to live elsewhere. Anna slept in a bed with a girl named Lavinia, whose sister, Caroline, slept by herself in another bed in the same room. One New Year's morning Lavinia awoke Anna to tell her that her aunt was sleeping in Caroline's bed. Anna leapt out of bed and saw her aunt there lying slightly on her side, fast asleep, with her mouth a little open; soon the vision faded. Meanwhile the aunt had been unconscious for some time at home, but just before she died she awoke to say that she would die happy, as she had seen her favourite niece (presumably just before the niece had seen her aunt apparently asleep). The timing of the death and the apparition was subsequently confirmed; it was Anna's only hallucination.

8F2 was submitted by the Rev. J.A. Haydn LLD. On 16 October 1879 a close friend of his family, Mrs Phillips, had successfully given birth to a child; there had been some anxiety over the operation, but no difficulties had been encountered. On the following Wednesday Haydn went to bed around 10 in his bedroom downstairs; the rest of the family slept upstairs. As he was reading in bed he heard quick light footsteps approaching the passage leading to his study. He assumed that it was his wife, and asked what was wrong; the steps continued but there was no reply. He then saw and heard the door handle turn half way and then let go, as if the person entering had changed their mind. He looked round the house but could find nothing; no one had stirred, and no door was open that had previously been shut. A few minutes after returning to bed, the clock struck eleven. On Friday morning Haydn received the news that Mrs P. had died on Thursday morning, so he went off to comfort his friend, who recounted that his wife had been delirious on the Wednesday and that she had been 'raving about persons and places that had been familiar to her and evidently fancying herself present in those distant spots.' It turned out that Haydn was one of the people mentioned, and that she had imagined herself in his house and speaking to him; this was shortly before 11 pm. As to her speaking to the priest, there can be no evidence one way or the other, although the priest himself was only aware of the footsteps – but the timing of the footsteps did correspond with the time at which Mrs P. imagined herself to be in Haydn's house, and such footsteps certainly did not belong to a member of his family. Even if the explanation is unverifiable, it would account for Haydn's experience.

8F3 was recorded by a Mrs Windridge. Mr H., a friend of the family, lay dangerously ill; one night the Windridges were awoken by the loud sound of someone trying to open their bedroom door. Mr Windridge got out of bed to investigate, found nothing, but then heard a sound corresponding to a large dog entering and scratching on the floor with his feet. It was just 2 am. A couple of days later the Windridges heard of Mr H.'s death on the night of the disturbance. The widow said that Mr H; had died twice: they thought that he had already died, when he reopened his eyes, muttered something about Windridge, and then died 'again'; this took place around 2 am. In this case the allusion is more vague than in the previous case, but the sound of feet and the attempted opening of the door are similar – it seems that this may have been physically impossible in both cases. In the first case Mrs. Phillips imagined that she had spoken to the Rev. Haydn, which might mean that she 'saw' him 'through' the door; as an apparition she might have been expected to pass through it, although she herself would probably not be aware of this possibility: hence her trying unsuccessfully to open the door, the normal *physical* way of entering, which might be impossible to a non-physical agent.

8F4 is an occurrence related to Rev. Frederick Barker, and took place on 6 December 1873. He had gone to bed but was lying awake when he startled his wife with a deep groan. She was roused and asked him what had happened. He explained that he had just seen his aunt smiling beside him. At the time she was in Madeira for health reasons, but they had no special reason to suppose that she might die. A week later they heard the news that the aunt had died, at the time and on the day when the vision had occurred, and that she had been calling out for her nephew all the time she was dying. Here we have a case where the aunt does not state categorically that she has seen her nephew, but we do know that her thoughts were directed towards him at the time of her death.

We have seen how some of the formulations of Swedenborg were paralleled by those in the *Bardo Thodol*; in that text, the Bardo body was said to possess two properties: one of unimpeded motion – the ability to pass through solid masses – and the other of being able to arrive instantaneously at whatever place is desired. In other words this body is able to go wherever the thoughts (or consciousness) are directed. If this conception is taken as a hypothesis, it accounts satisfactorily for the cases above where the 'agent' imagined that he had been in some remote place, and was apparently perceived as an apparition by those who were imagined to have been seen. The physical body acts as a kind of anchor to the Bardo body and normally prevents any 'flights of the imagination', or thought. But when it is freed from the physical anchor, it seems that this body becomes the vehicle of the thoughts or imagination, and in some way travels instantly to the places thought of or imagined, where it is occasionally perceived by those present in the place concerned. At present this is only advanced as a tentative explanatory hypothesis; it will be considered in greater detail in the light of other phenomena.

We shall now examine two more cases where some degree of reciprocal knowledge seems to be involved, before moving on to cases where the apparition seems to have been produced deliberately.

8G1 – recorded by Mrs Bettany who says that one evening she was seized by an unaccountable anxiety about a neighbour whose name she knew, but with whom she was not on visiting terms. She did not sleep that night and constantly thought of this neighbour as dying. In the morning she discovered that the cook had had a dream to the same effect, in which she was told that this neighbour was dead. Enquiry revealed that the said neighbour had indeed died the night before, and had remarked to her daughter just before her death that Mrs Bettany knew of her impending death – thus implying that she knew that Mrs Bettany had somehow got the message, although the exact means remains obscure.

8G2 is a personal experience of Cromwell Varley, F.R.S. He and his wife had gone to visit his sister-in-law, who had heart disease. One night Varley had a nightmare and could not move a muscle. While in this state he saw his sister-in-law apparently by his bed, although he knew that she was confined to her room. She told him that if he did not move he would die, but he was unable to do so; she then suggested that he should submit himself to her instructions and that she would frighten him, which would enable him to move again. At first he objected, but finally consented, at which point his heart stopped beating. Her first efforts to arouse him were of no avail, but she suddenly exclaimed that she was dying; this frightened him exceedingly and awoke him at around 3.45am. The shouting arousing his wife, to whom Varley recounted the details of the experience with the caveat that she should say nothing of it to her sister, so that any allusion to the incident should be initiated by her. The following morning the sister-in-law said that she had spent a dreadful night, dreaming that she had been in their room, and that between 3.30 and 4am had noticed that Varley was in danger of dying. She had only succeeded in arousing him by exclaiming that she herself was dying. The timing and content of the two experiences tally exactly, so that there seems no doubt that there was some kind of conscious interaction between the two people. The sister-in-law was certainly out of her physical body at the time, and there is some evidence to suggest that Varley himself was as well, as his inability to move his physical body is a feature that appears in other OBEs and near-death experiences. The shock of the announcement seemed to have jolted him back into his physical body, which was then reanimated.

Experimentally produced cases of apparitions are few and far between, but it is significant that there are some well attested cases which illustrate the apparent connection between thought and transfer, the Bardo body, and the apparition. We shall look at three cases:

8H1 concerns a Mr Kirk who had tried to make himself visible to a Miss G. by an act of concentration. Miss G. knew nothing of this attempt and only complained of feeling uneasy and restless at the times when Kirk was trying out his experiment. However, one afternoon between 3.30 and 4pm he took a break from work and tried to 'project' himself to Miss G., although without any idea of her whereabouts. In a flash he found himself in her bedroom, where she was lightly sleeping in a chair. He mentioned nothing to Miss G. until she herself related her experiences of the same afternoon: she had been lying sleeping in an easy chair, and had woken to see Mr Kirk standing nearby, dressed in a dark brown coat. She described his various movements before he disappeared. The timing of the agent and percipient experiences correspond here, and it was significant that Kirk should have been 'seen' in his dark brown coat, which he did not normally wear, but which he had actually been wearing that afternoon.

8H2 recounts the experience of S.H. Beard. At 9.30pm on 1 December 1882 he went into a room alone and tried to fix his thoughts strongly on the interior of a certain house in Kew. He seemed to himself actually to be in the house, but then fell asleep and lost any recall of his actions there. Then at 10pm he went to bed, resolving that he would try to be in the front bedroom of the same house at midnight and for long enough to make his presence felt. This time he seems to have had no recall of having been in the house. The next day he called on the occupants and, in the course of conversation, it emerged that Beard had been seen twice on the previous evening: the first time around nine in the passage and then again around midnight, when he had come into Mrs L.'s bedroom, and stroked her hair while looking at her hand. Another similar and successful experiment took place in March 1884.

8H3 was inspired by the reading of Beard's experiences. On the night of 15 November 1886 the Rev. C. Godfrey resolved to try to appear to his friend Mrs H., who had no knowledge of the proposed experiment. He feel asleep after a period of intense concentration, then dreamt that he met Mrs H. the next day, asking her whether he had appeared to her, to which she replied that he had; he awoke at 3.40am. The following day Godfrey called on someone living in the same house as Mrs H. and was on the point of leaving when Mrs H. called to him from a window that she had something special to tell him. She came round later of her own accord and related that at around 3.30am she had suddenly woken up with the impression that someone was in the room. She went down for a drink, and on coming up again noticed Godfrey on the landing, dressed as she might expect. As she went upstairs the figure grew more and more shadowy before finally fading away; she ascertained the time around 3.45am. Godfrey made one more successful and one more unsuccessful attempt; in the successful attempt he resolved to touch Mrs H.'s head with his hand. As previously, he dreamt of meeting and questioning Mrs H., who said in confirmation that the apparition had been less distinct than on the first occasion. She came round spontaneously the following day and related the experiences of being touched by Godfrey on the head, and that her impression of the face had been less distinct; however she had no doubt that Godfrey had been visiting her.

The above three cases all seem to involve a conscious resolution on the part of the agent, but an unconscious fulfilment in that little or nothing is remembered by the agent himself; however his wishes were perceived being carried out by the person in mind. This suggests a distinction between these cases and the apparently deliberate appearances of dying people related in group 8F: that in this latter group the consciousness seems to have been present in some degree in the bodily apparition, while in the cases of 8H the agent himself does not remember the acts which he is said to have performed. This is similar to cases of so-called autophany, when people report seeing a double or apparition of themselves, while the conscious identity or self remains in the physical body.

Apparitions are occasionally not seen by all those present in a room, or they may appear only to two individuals; sometimes they are even seen in different places by different people, but at similar times. We shall give three more cases: one where an apparition appeared to three people separately, and two where only one person in the room saw it.

8I1 was contributed by Rev. Charles Tweedale. He awoke on the night of 10/11 January 1879 to find the moon shining in his room; gradually a face appeared on the panels of the wardrobe, and became clearer, so that he was able to recognise his grandmother and see that she was wearing an old-fashioned frill cap. The face faded away, and Tweedale concluded that he must have been deceived by the moonlight. The following morning at breakfast he recounted his experience to his parents, and it turned out that his father had also seen the figure of his mother, but that his wife had been asleep at the time; the two experiences had occurred at about 2am. Before noon a telegram arrived announcing that the grandmother had died at 12.15am. The next day, about 18 hours after the death, Rev. Tweedale's aunt also saw an apparition of her mother, but she had not been informed of her death at the time. The timing of this case is interesting in that both sets of apparitions took place after, rather than at, the moment of death; thus they would be classified not as phantasms of the living, but as phantasms of the dead, which will be discussed and illustrated below.

8I2 – Colonel V. and his family had been on close terms with Mr and Mrs B. His wife and daughter were in a bedroom one evening when the daughter suddenly exclaimed that B. was in the room, and pointed to him. The mother could see nothing, but the girl insisted that he was there and that he was waving goodbye, then the apparition disappeared. A thorough search of the house was undertaken, but nothing could be found. The girl was then closely questioned by her father but adhered to her story, and even gave details of what she had seen B. wearing. Two days later the papers carried the news of the suicide of B. at 8pm on the evening of the apparition.

8I3 was submitted by the Rev. Prebendary Carlile. On Sunday 14 February 1932 he attended communion in St Paul's Church, Woking, and was about to offer his assistance when he saw a second clergyman standing in the chancel, ready to assist. He looked closely at him to see what kind of robe he was wearing. Then, later, he saw him kneeling at the communion rail; when he looked again the figure had left, so that the narrator assumed that he must have retired to the vestry, unwell. After the service he went into the vestry to inquire how the other priest was, but was informed that there had been no other priest present. Subsequently Carlile discovered that an old priest friend of his, who used regularly to come to the communion service, had just died. He concluded that the apparition might have been of him, even though he had not recognised the priest, partly owing to the fact that the figure had its back turned to him. No one else in the church saw the apparition.

We come now to the cases of apparitions of people who have been dead for more than twelve hours. Hart indicates that these do not differ substantially from apparitions of those on the point of death, or indeed of those of people still alive. This raises the question of the purported agency of the dead person in producing the apparition: the materialist will have to insist that the whole hallucination is in the mind of the percipient, and has no kind of objective reality. The crux of the matter, then, is the question of conscious agency. Many hauntings have the character of 'psychic tape-recordings', where different people see a similar figure on different occasions performing the same action in a rather mechanical fashion. But some cases, usually unique sightings, are less easy to explain on this hypothesis. We shall give three examples, two of which are already very well known.

8K1 is the experience of Jung. One night he was lying awake thinking of the sudden death of a friend, whose funeral he had attended the day before. It seemed to Jung that his friend was standing at the end of the bed, beckoning him to accompany him. Jung was not at all sure whether his friend was a self-created visual image but, in the end, gave him the benefit of the doubt and credited him with reality. He then followed him in his imagination out of the house, into the garden, out to the road, and finally to his former house several hundred yards away. On arriving they went up to his study; his friend then climbed on to a stool and showed him the second of five books with red bindings, which stood on the second shelf from the top. At this point the vision broke off, but Jung was so curious that he went to visit his friend's widow the following morning and asked if he could look something up in his friend's library, which he did not know. He saw the stool and spotted the five books with red bindings: they were translations of Zola, and the second volume was entitled *The Legacy of the Dead*. Jung comments on the significance of the title in view of his experience, which he makes no attempt to explain. Two points are worth noting: first, that it is hard to make sense of the story without invoking some degree of agency on the part of the dead man; and second, it appears that Jung had an OBE, and was in some sense present in the library, as he was able to verify the details of the stool and the five red books, even if during the vision he had not caught a glimpse of the titles.

8K2 first appeared in Myers and is related by a Mr F.G. He had a sister who died of cholera in 1867. In 1876 he was travelling in the west of the United States. One morning he was occupied with drafting some orders for his firm, when he suddenly became aware of someone sitting on his left. He looked up and had a vivid impression of the form of his sister who 'appeared as if alive'; the apparition vanished instantly, but G. was so impressed by the experience that he took the next train home to tell his parents. His father was amused at first, but then amazed to learn that G. had seen a distinct scratch on the right-hand side of his sister's face. On hearing this the mother 'rose trembling to her feet and nearly fainted away'. When she had recovered her composure she explained that when her daughter had died she had been treating her face and had accidentally scratched her right cheek. She had touched it up as best she could with powder, and had told no one of the incident. The only explanation of this case which excludes some agency on the part of the daughter is some kind of unconscious visual telepathy from the mother; but the mind boggles at how a fact known only to one person can be unconsciously and telepathically impressed on an image of a second person while she is appearing to a third party.

8K3 is known as the Chaffin Will case. A North Carolina farmer, James L. Chaffin, who had four sons, made a duly attested will in 1905, leaving his farm to his third son Marshall, and nothing to his wife or to his other three sons. As it turned out, he made another will in 1919 after reading the story in Genesis 27 about Jacob defrauding Esau of his inheritance. In this second will he left his property equally to his four sons, enjoining them to take good care of their mother. This will was not attested, nor known of by anyone in Old Chaffin's lifetime; he placed it between two pages of an old family Bible at Genesis 27. Chaffin died in September 1921, and the first will took effect. Meanwhile nothing happened between that date and June 1925, when the second son James began having very vivid dreams as of his father appearing by his bedside but saying nothing. Some time later he appeared again, wearing and old black overcoat, which the son recognised. This time the dream figure pulled back its overcoat and said that its will could be found in the overcoat pocket. James found that his mother had given the coat to her eldest son John, so James went to his brother's home, where he duly found the coat. On examining it he discovered that the lining of the inside pocket had been sewn up; and on cutting the stitches he found a small roll of paper, tied with a string, which instructed him to read the 27th Chapter of Genesis in the old family Bible. At this point James called in a neighbour as a witness. They went over to the mother's house, and eventually found the Bible. Five people were present when the neighbour found the will, written in Old Chaffin's hand. Because they were quite convinced that Old Chaffin in fact wrote the will, the widow and son of Marshall Chaffin did not contest it in court. The story has been extensively corroborated, and was investigated by a North Carolina lawyer. If the materialist is going to avoid invoking the agency of the dead man in this case, he has to explain how the knowledge of the will came to be acquired by someone who did not know of its existence.

One more phenomenon remains to be considered in this chapter: deathbed visions. We have already seen how apparitions of the dying can be perceived by the living, usually those closely connected to them in some way. We shall now examine some reports of apparitions seen by the dying themselves. The earliest systematic work on the subject was done by Sir William Barrett whose book appeared in 1926. In it he gives details of hallucinations ostensibly perceived by the dying, and finds that they only perceive figures of those already dead. What is more significant are cases where a figure is seen who is not known to be dead, and news of the death arrives afterwards: for instance Adamino Lazaro saw a vision of her brother, who lived over 400 km away; news of his death arrived by telegram the next day. Perhaps more strikingly a dying lady claimed to see all four of her brothers, of whom she knew three were dead; unbeknown to her the fourth had died in India.

Two of the most interesting cases concern children, the first of which is more by way of a repeated apparition combined with precognition of death:

8L1 – Mr and Mrs H. had two sons aged 2½ and eight months. In August 1883 the baby died, and at the time the other child, Ray, was in perfect health. But every day after the death, and apparently at all hours of the day and night, Ray would tell his mother that the baby was calling him all the time, and that she must not cry when he went where baby was. He claimed to have seen the baby in his high chair, but the mother did not come quickly enough to catch sight of the apparition. Ray soon fell ill and died on 13 October, just over two months after the baby.

8L2 concerns the death of Daisy Dryden in October 1864 at the age of ten. She caught typhoid fever and appeared to be recovering, when enteritis set in; during the first twenty-four hours she suffered a great deal, but lingered on for another three days during which time she seemed to be existing simultaneously in a material and another dimension. She saw apparitions of her brother Allie, who had died seven months before at the age of six; she claimed that he was there whenever she thought of him and that they communicated directly by thought without the intermediary of speech – 'we just talk our think', as she expressed it. She said that her body was worn out, resembling an old dress of her mother's; that she would soon not wear her body any more but would have a new one like her brother, a body which she had even in the present. She told her father that Allie would come for her at 11.30, and then took leave of her sister. At 11.30 her last words before she died were, 'Come, Allie.' Daisy's matter-of-fact discussion of her other body is one of the most striking aspects of this case. She regarded death as something quite natural, and to be looked forward to as a release from her cramping body.

More recently Karlis Osis conducted a survey of 5,000 nurses and 500 doctors. He received only 640 replies, but this represented the witnessing of some 35,000 deaths; only 10 per cent of the patients were conscious in their last hours. Analysis of the reports showed that the predominant emotion just before death was not so much fear as exhilaration. There were 884 cases of non-human types of hallucination, of which most were concerned with religious imagery; but the most common deathbed experiences were hallucinations of people. Such apparitions were seen more often when the patient was fully conscious of his normal surroundings. As for the apparitions perceived, four out of five were of dead people, mainly close relatives and friends. In around 70 per cent of the cases the patient's remarks suggested that the relatives had come to meet them and, in a number of instances, death immediately followed the hallucination.

As indicated at the outset of this chapter, one of the most problematic aspects of apparitions is their quasi-physical behaviour. Hart points out in his conclusion that they are both semi-*substantial* and *semi*-substantial: on the one hand they may be perceived like solid objects and appear identical to them; they may appear to operate in normal space, be seen in normal perspective, and observed details may be verified at a later stage; but, on the other hand, they display erratic visibility, defy gravity and solidity, and communicate telepathically. Hart's answer to these problems is to formulate what he terms an etheric-object hypothesis, of which three points are especially relevant to our purposes: first that, given the supposition that every physical object has an etheric counterpart, such etheric counterparts exist in psychic rather than physical space, but these two kinds of space may have 'merging intersections' – in some cases it would seem that the one is almost perfectly superimposed on the other, so that there is no apparent distinction, like two circles of the same size; second, these etheric counterparts are regarded as having a time-dimension in addition to the normal three – this corresponds to the kind of instant travel postulated of the Bardo body and apparently functioning in some cases of deathbed apparitions; and third, that perception of the etheric counterpart is by means of the percipient's own etheric counterpart, which may or may not coincide with the physical body – the cases cited by Green of identical perception in and out of the body (8E1 and 2) would support this; further light will be shed on this question in the next chapter.

9.

EXPERIENCES OUT
OF THE BODY

Life is much more exultant and mysterious than our intellects can comprehend.

RADHAKRISHNAN

The birth and death of the leaves are the rapid whirls of the eddy whose wider circles move among stars.

TAGORE

To sleep! Perchance to dream: ay there's the rub:
For in that sleep of death what dreams may come,
When we have shuffled off this mortal coil,
Must give us pause.

SHAKESPEARE

Life might become altogether too bizarre and unpredictable if we could no longer assume that our centre of consciousness and identity was 'located' inside our heads: we would not know for certain exactly where we were or whether a companion was mentally present with us or was imagining himself to be somewhere else: communication would become rather sporadic. Despite this everyday assumption, however, people do evidently have experiences where the conscious self seems to be located outside the body and to be perceiving the world from another angle.

Various surveys have been carried out to assess the incidence of our belief in OBEs: Shiels published a cross-cultural survey of 54 cultures, and found a belief in OBEs in 51 of them; he also established that OBEs were most commonly expected to occur during sleep. However, he did stress that the belief in OBEs does not necessarily reflect their actual occurrence. Other surveys have been conducted in England, Iceland, the USA and Australia. They indicate an incidence of between 8 per cent in the case of adults from 30-70 years in Iceland to 44 per cent in marijuana users surveyed by Tart. It is interesting to note that in Palmer's 1975 survey the students were rated at 25 per cent incidence, while the townspeople were a more modest 14 per cent. The two most rigorous surveys showed results of 11 and 12 per cent; this last figure was reduced to 12 from 20 per cent after taking into account descriptions of the experience, which would not be classified as OBEs by a parapsychologist. And the respondents in the other survey were students who had heard lectures on the subject and therefore had a clear idea of what was meant by the term before answering the question.

Accounts of OBEs fall into three categories: there are books written by authors such as Fox, Muldoon and Whiteman who claim repeated personal experience; then there are recent laboratory reports on subjects such as Swann and Tanous; and finally collections of anecdotal material by Hart, Crookall, and Green. Hart's was the earliest study of this last type; he found 228 published cases of reported 'ESP projection', 99 of which contained evidence of veridical perception (i.e. correct perception of actions or objects located at an impossible distance for perception to have taken place in the physical body). Crookall collected over 800 cases, which are not all veridical, but many of which, nevertheless, have five characteristics in common with Hart's 99 cases: (a) the report of perceptions of distant places and persons via ESP; (b) an apparition might be seen by the percipient during the experience; (c) the subject saw his own physical body from a vantage point outside it; (d) the subject saw himself in an apparition body (etheric counterpart); and (e) this body defied gravity. Hart's additional points were that the subject was aware of being seen as an apparition, and that this body passed through solid matter as well as being able to move quickly through the air. The first point arises from the nature of Hart's selection and will be illustrated below, while the other points are extensions of the nature of the apparition body. Crookall's other observations were that the subject hovered over his physical body, that he often saw discarnate forms, and that the physical and apparitional bodies were connected by a cord. His first point relates to the emergence of one body from the other, a feature which may or may not be noticed – the subject may suddenly find himself outside the physical body without being aware of the transition. The perception of discarnate forms has already been referred to and discussed in the last chapter, where it was seen that this is more likely to occur when the percipient is dying. And the question of the cord is more vexed: it is by no means reported in a large number of cases. Other investigators find that there is practically no reference to such a cord in their surveys. The least that can be said, however, is that the physical body exercises some kind of pull on the separated conscious self, and eventually draws it back into itself.

Rogo suggests that not all OBEs describe exactly the same kind of experience. He observes that Hart's cases cover three possibly distinct types: travelling clairvoyance, where ESP of distant places occurs, but there is no sensation of being embodied; astral projection, where an apparition body is reported; and finally apparitions such as those experienced by Beard where the agent has no memory of the experience. These observations suggest the necessity of defining one's approach to the phenomena carefully if one is to avoid becoming entangled in a mass of apparent contradictions. Before doing this we shall discuss briefly the criticisms levelled at collections of anecdotal evidence, and the theoretical explanations currently advanced to account for the phenomenon.

Susan Blackmore puts forward three main arguments for dismissing the validity of Hart's and Crookall's studies in favour of laboratory experiments. First that the reports are liable to embellishment and errors of memory. However Murphy points out that convincingness and impressiveness are not necessarily equivalent: 'What is terribly impressive may owe its quality to the very elaborations which make it unconvincing to the careful critic.' In other words the addition of fantastic elements is liable to make the story incredible. And Prince comments that:

> The too general assumption is that a second-hand story, if it distorts any details, is bound to do so by their improvement, their exaggeration

in the direction of supernormality. But long experience in testing such matters shows that an authentic incident of this character is much more often than not improved after one has found the original percipient or a witness who was actually present. The second-hand narrator is very apt to have forgotten, or at least to have omitted, some of the chief evidential details.

This is backed up by illustrating that some well-known cases have improved their evidential content when more thoroughly investigated. The second objection is that details cannot be checked and that claims for veridicality cannot be confirmed; this has been partly dealt with by Prince above. In addition, however, Hart's selection of his 99 cases from the 228 published rests precisely on this criterion of veridicality and evidentiality: the cases eliminated were those where the psychic experience was not reported and confirmed before evidence of its veridicality was received; thus some contemporary confirmation existed. And it will hardly do to dismiss these cases simply because the witnesses or agents have since died – on this basis there could be no such thing as historical analysis. Crookall relies rather more heavily on the integrity and impartiality of his witnesses, which one cannot assess first hand, but of which one can form some kind of impression by reading his 800-plus accounts; these clearly display common features. Dismissing their validity amounts to accusing the reporters of a massive and impossible conspiracy on the scale suggested by Eysenck, and also ignoring the coincidence with Hart's findings. The third objection is that of uncontrolled or biased selection. We have already considered the incidence of OBEs, which in itself imposes a restriction on the source of one's cases. It is surely only sensible to select, from the mass of experiences, those which seem to be the best attested, as in Hart. Moreover, the bias is likely to be more pronounced in the interpretation than in the selection of the case material. We have already indicated the five common features noted independently by Crookall and Hart; on the basis of other studies one might well accuse Crookall of exaggerating the importance of, say, the connecting cord. But in the final analysis no investigator can go as far as denying that in the cases recorded both anecdotally and experimentally the conscious self appears to be located outside the space of the body. Needless to say, there is plenty of scope for differing interpretations of this: the limit of the statistical approach, which is a near obsession with some, is the actual incidence of the phenomena – it cannot explain them.

There are two principal theoretical approaches: the separationist and the psychological. The first is often referred to by proponents of the second as the classical theory, which implies a slightly naïve lack of sophistication not, of course, attributed to their own theory. The first variant of the separationist theory (which assumes that something leaves the body and is able to travel to a new location) is the physical one: that we have another material body able to travel round the physical world on its own. This is generally dismissed on the grounds that sensitive instruments have not detected such a secondary body, although recent research by Osis suggests that modifications to the electrical field have been recorded when the subject subsequently reported correctly on the nature of the target object. The problems of perception in relation to this second physical body are seemingly insurmountable; this drives people to the suggestion that something non-physical leaves the body. This theory is, in turn, dismissed as incoherent, because it is inconceivable in Cartesian terms that something non-physical should interact with the physical world, and because perception at the ostensible location is either poor or inaccurate.

These points will be taken up below, but we must first give an account of the psychological approaches, which attempt to overcome the apparent shortcomings of separationist theories. Blackmore suggests that perceptual distortions indicate an explanation along the lines of inhabiting an imaginary version of the place concerned, and proposes the concept of a 'cognitive map' as a coherent account of the OBE experience. The individual puts the cognitive map together from information acquired, stored and organised about a particular place. It has the characteristics of incompleteness and the addition of details when compared with perception of the real location; it can be used imaginatively to 'see through' walls, and to 'travel' from one place to another; and it exists in a kind of thought world in a space of its own. The cognitive map has to be combined with ESP if it is to explain maps of places where the subject has never been before. This theory accounts adequately for cases of so-called travelling clairvoyance, where the subject does not necessarily see his body, but is aware of a distant scene. It accounts less well for cases of conscious projection, where the subject feels himself to be at a distant location and is actually perceived by a person at that location. It also underestimates the veridical aspect of perception in cases where there is no apparent distortion by the imagination, in other words when the scene viewed from another point of space corresponds exactly with what one might expect to observe from that point; for instance a room seen from the vantage point of the ceiling. The question of perceptual distortion is related to the degree of interference by the imagination: the greater the imaginative element, the less veridical the perception of the place.

We must now examine the problems of space and perception outlined above, and formulate our own approach to the phenomena. The paradoxical nature of apparitions has already been indicated in the last chapter: they are substantial forms in space, and yet they exhibit the non-physical properties of defiance of gravity, the ability to pass through matter, and the propensity to appear and disappear quite suddenly. It is, therefore, rash to draw the line too sharply between the physical and the non-physical in this area. Nevertheless the problem of perception remains: the obvious starting point is that any perception from outside the physical body is, by definition, extra-sensory. Whiteman assumes that such extra-sensory perception cannot take place in the same space, and yet much of Green's evidence suggests that exactly the same space is being perceived: so that either it *is* the same place, or, as suggested by Hart, there are two spaces which may on occasion interpenetrate to such an extent as to be indistinguishable.

The problem is not, however, insoluble. We normally assume that the conscious self's perception and sense of identity depends on or even originates in the physical body: that without the eyes and ears, there can be no sense of sight or hearing. But, as the cases below will illustrate, the senses of sight and 'hearing' seem able to function at a distance from the physical body and, on occasion, even when the body is ostensibly unconscious; in many cases these senses are experienced as more acute than usual. This suggests that our normal notions need to be reversed, as proposed by Swedenborg: *that perception is essentially extra-sensory, despite the fact that it is normally associated closely with the physical body.* Thus the physical body is an instrument of perception, but not an indispensable instrument. The conscious self normally perceives the world through this body, but, in certain circumstances, it is able to perceive from a point outside the physical body without the use of the bodily senses. This notion will be unintelligible to anyone who assumes that no perception is possible apart form the senses, and who makes a rigid distinction between the physical and the non-physical, maintaining that neither can act on the other. Yet the above hypothesis seems to do justice to the known data and accounts for the reason why the conscious self is able to perceive 'normal' space from outside the physical body. All perception, then, is essentially non-physical, although in our everyday experience we perceive through the physical body.

There remains the question of errors and omissions noted by Blackmore. Green based her 1968 study on 400 reports of OBEs, backed up with two questionnaires, to which she received 326 and 251 replies respectively. The largest class, some 61 per cent, had only one experience, and a significant number – about 21 per cent – had more than six experiences; on this basis single cases are distinguished from the others; 84 per cent of all subjects reported their conscious self to be confined entirely to their new point of view; of the rest some had experiences of a dual consciousness, split between two locations, and, occasionally, people have been known to see their double from the point of view of the physical body. Of the 'single' subjects 81 per cent stated that they seemed to see their physical bodies from the outside, and many emphasised this point by declaring that they saw their bodies 'clearly ... distinctly ... vividly ... plain in every detail'. This is what Whiteman would call a full separation, where no consciousness is located in the body.

We have visual awareness of the physical body and, at the same time, we perceive that the form in which the consciousness is located is distinct and fully apart from that body (Whiteman does not identify a duplicate body as such – only 20 per cent of Green's single subjects *definitely* found themselves in another body, which, in such cases, was an exact replica of the physical). In addition to seeing their own physical bodies, Green states that 'subjects characteristically describe their field of perception in the ecsomatic (out-of-body) state as if it was an exact simulation of what they would normally perceive if they occupied the position in question. Of single subjects 89.3 per cent said that things looked normal from out of the body, and 82.3 per cent that colours were normal. Only one subject, who induced her experiences, maintained that colouring was quite different from normal. A case cited by Blackmore (from Green's book) of the man who saw an illusory chimney on the roof of his house is the exception rather than the rule. Green makes the important point that inaccuracies and perceptual distortions seem to be more commonly associated with subjects who induce their experiences voluntarily, rather than with single spontaneous cases; she comments that 'there is rarely any indication that the information about his environment which is conveyed to the subject by his perceptions in an ecsomatic state is in any way erroneous'. The correlation between voluntary inducement of OBEs and perception distortion is not surprising, but it makes laboratory work more difficult: many of the exercises used to induce an out-of-body state are exercises in imagination, such as visualising oneself floating, expanding, etc. These exercises might lead to impressions which are different from those experienced by single subjects, and the very use of the imagination in inducing the OBE surely makes imaginative omissions and accretions more likely. The induced experience is the only type amenable to laboratory testing, and the imaginary element is likely to be more significant here than in spontaneous cases; so that the experimenters risk only obtaining data which are necessarily fulfilments of their own psychological theory, and not actually explanations of the spontaneous cases. It would appear that there is a continuum with imagination at one end, and sensory realism at the other; it seems that spontaneous single cases are at or near the sensory realism end, while voluntary inducement and laboratory testing tend to push the subject along the continuum, so that his perceptions become a mixture of the imaginary and the real.

OBEs can occur in a variety of circumstances: Eastman groups most of them under five headings: dreaming and just before or after sleep; hypnosis; serious, often nearly mortal, illness; following shock; and drug states, including those induced by anaesthetics and hallucinogens. In this chapter we shall deal with examples of OBEs during dreams, under anaesthetic, and following shock, all in relation to perception by the conscious self while out of the body. In the next chapter, cases of illness and anaesthetics for serious operations will be treated in the context of the 'near-death experience'.

We have already referred to Gurney's contention that dreams and waking hallucinations are psychologically equivalent. Although a few ordinary dreams are found to correspond to OBEs, the lucid dream is even more closely correlated; recent studies suggest that those who often experience lucid dreams are more likely to have had an OBE. A lucid dream occurs when the dreamer is, or becomes aware that he is, dreaming; occasionally he may be able to exercise some control over the subsequent events and sensations in the dream by manipulating the imagination. Green points out that in both the dream and the OBE the subject is observing a complete and self-subsistent field of perception, and is aware that this state differs from normal waking consciousness. But there are differences as well: the lucid dream starts more often when the subject is asleep, and the dream world is less distinct and real than the OBE 'world', allowing less control and freedom of movement; in addition, the person who has an OBE starting from the waking state never actually thinks he is dreaming. Most lucid dreams involve only the subject, but there are cases on record of 'meetings' in lucid dreams.

9A – The most remarkable is recorded by Fox who had spent the evening with two friends, Slade and Elkington. Before parting, they decided to try to 'meet' on Southampton Common in their dreams that night. Fox dreamed that he met Elkington as arranged; they both knew they were dreaming, and commented on Slade's absence, whereupon the dream ended. The next day Fox met Elkington and at first said nothing; Elkington maintained that he had dreamt of meeting Fox on the common and of commenting on Slade's absence. Slade had not dreamt at all, as far as he knew. It is impossible to say in this case whether both men 'travelled' to the common, or whether they met in some kind of mutually imagined space, thus whether the dream was accompanied by an OBE or not.

The next class of dreams, although very vivid, is not necessarily lucid, but certainly entails travelling clairvoyance. The report does not enable one to assess whether the dreamers were actually present at the scene in some physical sense, although this hypothesis would offer one coherent explanation. The examples all come from *Phantasms of the Living*.

9B1 was submitted by Canon Warburton of Winchester, who states that his experience was the only one of its kind that he ever had. Around 1848 he had travelled up to London from Oxford in order to stay with his brother in Lincoln's Inn. On arriving he found a note to the effect that the brother had gone to a dance in the West End, and would be back soon after 1am. At exactly one, after dozing in a chair for some time, Warburton woke up exclaiming that his brother had fallen down; he had seen him come out of a drawing room on to a brightly lit landing, catch his foot on the edge of the top stair, and fall headlong down the stairs, just saving himself with his hands. He dozed off again and was woken half an hour later by his brother entering and explaining that he had narrowly escaped breaking his neck; he had come out of the ballroom, caught his foot, and tumbled full length down the stairs.

9B2 was investigated by Sidgwick. In August 1867 a Miss K. Gibson and her sister were spending a few days in the country with a friend. In accordance with an old custom, the guests agreed to tell their dreams to each other in the morning, as they had eaten some wedding cake the evening before. Miss Gibson awoke very early on the Thursday morning, then fell asleep again, whereupon she found herself in a bare, cheerless room with a bed in one corner, on which was lying a young man.

She recognised him as a friend of her brother's, although she had met him only twice, and had not heard his name mentioned since the last Christmas. At the time of their last meeting he had looked strong and healthy, but now he was 'a shadow of his former self, his face drawn and colourless, his eyes unnaturally large and bright'; his hand was thin and wasted and his hollow cough sounded incessantly around the room. She went up to him, and remarked how ill he looked. He replied that he was dying, having caught a cold a month ago and neglected it. It then settled on his chest, and his doctors had informed him that he was dying of rapid consumption.

The next morning Miss Gibson could not bear to tell her dream (which was not normally the case). She went home on the Saturday evening and did not see her brother until Sunday breakfast. He asked his sister whether she had heard that his friend had died on the Thursday morning: he had caught a cold a month before, had neglected it, it had settled on his chest, and he had died of rapid consumption. In his interview Sidgwick established that the salient details of the dream had corresponded exactly with the details given by the brother. Gurney found this case a tricky one to account for by telepathy, and postulated that the details were probably supplied by the dreamer – 'a clear case of something added by the dreamer's creative activity' – this explanation is rather procrustean, to say the least. In view of the timing and details it seems more likely that the dreamer projected into the friend's room, where she saw his condition, 'heard' his cough and ascertained details which could not conceivably have been either guessed or invented, since she had no knowledge of the friend's condition at the time.

9B3 contains an element of the bizarre, which the percipient herself attributed to chance. She dreamt that she was walking in a wood in her father's place in Kent, a spot she knew well, where there was some sand under fir trees. She stumbled over some objects, which proved to be the heads of ducks buried in the sand. This struck her as most peculiar, and she mentioned the dream at breakfast. Only an hour later the old bailiff came up unexpectedly for some instructions, and related that a strange thing had happened: there had been a robbery in the farmyard, and some stolen ducks had been found, with their heads protruding, at the very spot where the daughter had seen them in her dream. Gurney rightly comments that the case cannot be explained by telepathy, as there was no ostensible agent, so that clairvoyance is the least explanation of the experience, short of postulating that the subject actually travelled to the spot.

9B4 involves the distance from Newry to Australia. On the night of 10 January 1878 Mrs Green dreamed that she saw two respectably dressed females driving alone in a vehicle like a mineral-water cart. Their horse stopped at a water hole for a drink, but as there was no footing he lost his balance, and in trying to recover plunged right in. The two women stood up and shouted for help, their hats rising off their heads; as all were going down under water, the dreamer turned away, crying and asking if there was no one there to help them. At this point she woke up and told her husband of the dream, stating at the same time that she knew neither of the two women. Such a dream was unique in Mrs Green's experience and weighed heavily on her mind. In March she received a newspaper cutting from her brother in Australia, informing her that he had lost one of his daughters in a dreadful accident; Mrs Green had not met her niece. The time of the dream corresponded with the accident. The newspaper report stated that it appeared that the two women were driving along in a spring cart when they attempted to water their horse at a dam. They must have inadvertently driven into this deep hole. A station manager was the first on the scene; he found the cart and horse under water with two hats floating on the surface (an important detail). The bodies were recovered later. The accident is so unusual and the details correspond so closely that it seems as if Mrs Green was, as it were, a witness of the accident.

The next six cases are similar to the above group in that the subject has the impression of having travelled to a distant spot, but more evidential in that he was seen as an apparition at the place where he had the impression of being. Thus we seem to be dealing with cases of conscious OBEs from the angle of the agent, and conscious apparitions from the viewpoint of the percipient.

9C1 is the least specific as no definite confirmation of the sighting was received, but equally the report suggests strongly that the men in question saw the subject. Subject 'D' found himself in a street with overhead lamps along the middle of the road. He did not recognise it and decided to test the reality of the experience by going into a residential block. There was no one on the ground floor, but he saw two men talking on the second floor. He went through the motions of climbing the stairs, but could not feel them under his feet. He finally reached the men, who continued talking for a few seconds, then one of them looked in his direction: his eyes opened wide and he three up his hands. This last reaction is a fair indication of a sighting. Unfortunately the subject does not state whether he was able to see the two men in the normal way, or whether he went through the wall or door into the room; but this does not make the experience any less real.

9C2 was submitted by Miss Constance Bevan. On 10 June 1883 she dreamt that someone told her that Miss Elliot was dead, which made her, in her dream, rush instantly to Miss Elliot's room. She entered, went to the bedside, pulled the clothes off her face and found that she was quite cold, with her eyes staring at the ceiling. She was then so frightened that she dropped down at the foot of the bed, and the next thing she knew she was half out of her own bed and awake. Before leaving her room at 5am, Miss Bevan told the story to her sister, who confirmed this in writing. Miss Elliot stated that she had been lying awake with her eyes fixed on the ceiling when she seemed to hear the door open and someone come in. She knew that it was only Constance, who came up and bent over her; instead of kissing her she drew back and went to crouch at the end of the bed. Miss Elliot thought this very strange, so she opened and closed her eyes several times in order to ascertain that she was awake, and noticed that the door was closed. She was somewhat horrified and dared not look towards the crouching figure, who was gently moving the bedclothes from her feet.

She suddenly felt her foot being touched but was unable to call the occupant of the next room. The next thing she knew she was out of the bed searching for Constance, whom she assumed must still be in the room. But she was nowhere to be seen, and the doors of the room were both locked on the inside. She noticed that the time was shortly after 5am. Gurney investigated the possibility of sleepwalking, but ruled it out on discovering the details of the locks on the doors; the reasons are too complex to relate here but can be checked by the interested reader. The only ambiguity on the case is the alleged manipulation of the bedclothes (at this stage the consciousness of Miss Bevan was perhaps not fully present) but other details such as the timing, the staring at the ceiling, the sudden drawing back and the crouching at the end of the bed are all correct.

9C3 was the experience of the wife of T.W. Smith, a headmaster. For personal reasons he had asked his future wife to conceal the fact of their intended marriage from some of her colleagues; this could only be done by not writing to any of them. About six months after their marriage Smith was reading in bed with his wife sleeping at his side, when she suddenly woke up, saying that she had been back at her former place of employment. She was in a well-remembered room at the base of the building; there were two strange women there and two others she knew well – they were all talking and laughing. Just before retiring, she saw one of them turn off the gas; she followed them upstairs, went into a bedroom with two of them, saw 'Bessie' place some things in a book, undress, and get into bed; then she went to her, took her hand, and said 'Bessie, let's be friends'. The dream ended at that point. Three months later the wife went to visit her mother and found a letter awaiting her from one of her friends, urging her to write to say whether she was still alive. Smith went along to investigate the matter himself, but mentioned nothing of his wife's dream. The writer and her friend Bessie had gone to bed one Sunday night, when Bessie suddenly cried out saying that she had just seen the wife, who had touched her and said 'Let's be friends'. Other confirmatory details included the fact that the two women, whom the wife had seen, did indeed share the same room, and that two newcomers had arrived since the departure of the wife. The dream had produced an unusually vivid impression on the wife, and the apparition was associated with death by the percipient – hence the urgent letter written the following day.

9C4 - The Wilmot Case is one of the best known and most often cited. It features here so that its similarities to, and differences from, cases already treated can be appreciated; early investigators checked it extensively. Wilmot sailed from Liverpool on the ship *The City of Limerick* on 3 October 1863. The passage was very rough, so Wilmot did not get a good night's sleep until the night of 13/14 October, when he had the following dream. He dreamt that Mrs Wilmot, then in the USA, came to the door of his stateroom in her nightdress; she seemed to hesitate a little on entering. She advanced towards Wilmot, then stooped down and kissed him before withdrawing. The other occupant of the stateroom was a Mr Tait, a librarian. In the morning Wilmot was started when he was accused by Tait of having a woman come in and visit him in the middle of the night. After some pressing, Tait explained that he had witnessed a scene, which corresponded exactly with what Wilmot had dreamt. Wilmot cross-questioned Tait on three occasions before leaving the ship, but Tait would not alter his story.

The day after landing at New York, Wilmot travelled home and met his wife. Almost the first question, which she put to him when they were alone, was the startling one as to whether he had received a visit from her a week ago on Tuesday. Wilmot remonstrated with her and pointed out that this would have been physically impossible. However she stated that she had certainly had such an impression. Having heard reports of the wreck of the *Africa* (which had sailed from Liverpool just before *City of Limerick*) and known of the stormy weather in the Atlantic, she had been worried about his safety. On the night of 13 October she had lain awake thinking about him, and at around 4am it seemed to her that she had gone out in search of him. She seemed to cross a wide stormy sea, and finally came to a low black steamer; she somehow went up its side and located her husband's stateroom. She then seemed to see a man in the upper berth, looking straight at her, so that for a moment she hesitated to enter. But she did so, went up to her husband's berth, stooped down, kissed him, and went away. Subsequently she asked her husband whether they ever had a stateroom like the one which she seemed to see, where the upper berth extended further back than the lower one. This was in face the case, although Mrs Wilmot had never seen the interior of the ship.

Various ingenious and specious explanations, none of which do full justice to the facts, have been advanced to account for this story. The most straightforward explanation, in view of the timing, the details involved, and the separate but corresponding hallucination of Mr Tait, is the following: Mrs Wilmot had an OBE in which she travelled to the ship (drawn there by worry), was aware that she had been seen by Mr Tait, performed the actions perceived by Tait in his hallucination and Wilmot in his dream, and noticed the arrangement of the room as well as the fact that her husband was on the bottom berth; then she found herself back in her physical body.

The last four cases strongly suggest that the conscious self was operating in an 'apparition' body in a space merging with the physical: on the one hand the conscious self was present in the space which it imagined itself to be occupying; and, on the other hand, the apparition was perceived in the same place in which the conscious self imagined itself to be. Although her physical eyes were back in the USA, Mrs Wilmot quite clearly saw the other occupant staring at her and the arrangement of the stateroom. Before giving examples of OBEs under anaesthetic and after shocks, we shall cite two examples of waking OBEs, which correspond to the type of dream OBE just examined.

9D1 – Walter McBride was a bachelor farmer in Indiana. On 23 December 1935 he had been wondering about his father all day, and had the impression that he might be ill. He went to bed around 8pm, and, shortly afterwards, found himself floating in the room in a whitish light which cast no shadows; he stated that he was wide awake at the time. He seemed to find himself floating up through the top of the building. His apparition body then turned vertical, and he was able to see his physical body lying on the bed. Then he realised that he was moving through the air towards his old home in the north. He passed through the walls of his father's house and stood at the foot of the bed on which he saw his father reclining. The father's eyes were fixed on him, but he did not appear to hear when the son spoke. He found that his father was well, whereupon he seemed to travel back to his bedroom, where he once more saw his physical body on the bed. On re-entering the body he was immediately awake and alert. He then wrote down an account of his experience. Two days later he saw his father, who verified the experience by saying that he had seen his son at the end of his bed at a time (noted), which corresponded with the son's OBE.

In both this case and the last one, the subjects had been worrying about the percipients. Muldoon throws some light on this: from a lengthy study of his own projections he concluded that 'suppressed desire' was by far the most important single factor which induced unintentional projection. Thinking about someone but being unable to see them creates this condition, so that when the physical body is incapacitated or asleep, the so-called 'subconscious will' moves the 'thought-body', which is automatically drawn towards the subject of the thoughts and attention; thus there is no difficulty in locating the person because the thought of them immediately brings the traveller (in his Bardo/apparition body) into their presence.

9D2 provides a further illustration of this principle. At 10 o'clock one evening in 1887 a thirty-year-old engraver was feeling rather tired, so he stretched himself out on a chair; he immediately experienced a sensation of giddiness and vacuity, then found himself in another body in the middle of the room, and able to see his physical body. He found the experience acutely real, and had no impression that he was dreaming. He wondered whether he might be dead, and felt some regret at the things which he had not done. Soon, however, he became curious to find out what he could do in his present state, so he went to see if he could turn a light switch; he was able to feel it but could not actually turn it. He then penetrated the wall into his neighbour's room, which was dark, but which he was nevertheless able to see. It occurred to him to visit his neighbour's study; he found himself transported there in the moment of desire, and noticed that he was literally being carried around by his thoughts. He noted the titles of several books, and eventually returned to his body. The following day he went round to the neighbour's flat to check out some of the details of the flat and the books which he had seen, never having been physically in the flat before his experience. Everything was as he had supposed, and the neighbour was described as 'distressed' and no doubt not a little perplexed. The case fits the general pattern of behaviour of apparition bodies in its ability to penetrate the wall and to be carried around in accordance with the desire of the subject. It was not seen by a third party, but the details noticed and confirmed suggest that the conscious self was in the apparition-body and not in the physical.

We come now to OBEs induced by anaesthetic. The first three record experiences in the dentist's chair.

9E1 – The subject was given gas, and was lying practically on her back. Yet she seemed to be standing next to the chair, where she could observe the behaviour of the dentist, the nurse and the doctor; she could also hear their conversation. She checked the details with her husband afterwards.

9E2 – A man found himself standing in the far corner of the room looking at his body in the dentist's chair. He understood what the anaesthetist and doctor were saying to each other and counted the teeth as they were being pulled out. He knew that he was alive and thinking, though separated in space from his body. When he came round he was able to tell the two men what they had been saying while he had been under.

9E3 was reported by Dr Peter Leggett, Vice-Chancellor Surrey University, about one of his dentist friend's patients. After coming round the patient said that he had had the experience of looking down on himself from a point near the ceiling, while the tooth extraction had been going on. Leggett was sceptical, so his patient informed him that he had seen two pennies on top of a tall cupboard. Leggett did not know of this and only checked it up some months afterwards, as he was very busy. On climbing up he found the two pennies, as the patient had reported. In theory this could have been due to clairvoyance, but the fact that the patient described himself as looking down on the scene suggests that he really did see them owing to his position in space, unless one redefines the notion of clairvoyance to include 'localised viewing'.

9E4 concerns a man anaesthetised for an operation. He suddenly found himself standing outside his body in the operating theatre. He could see his body on the table, and there seemed to be some kind of panic on. The matron rushed out and came back with a glass ampule; she broke its top and jammed it against his arm. The next thing he knew he woke up in bed, and told the matron what he had seen; her reaction was that it was impossible for him to have seen anything, as he had been completely unconscious at the time. But the 'impossible' had occurred.

9E5 – similar scepticism was expressed in a case where a dysentery patient collapsed. He found himself lying three or four feet above the bed, face downwards. Below him he saw his body and witnessed a strange medical officer giving him an injection, then heard a conversation between the medical officer and two orderlies. The next thing he knew he was back in bed, and related the story to the two orderlies, who said that he could not possibly have heard the matter being discussed. They did confirm that a strange medical officer had been present.

9F is a further example of veridical OBE perception, but this time not under anaesthetic. The subject was in hospital after an operation for peritonitis and had subsequently contracted pneumonia. Her ward was L-shaped, so that it was impossible to see round the corner to the other part. One morning she felt herself floating upwards, and found herself looking down on the other patients. She also spotted her body propped up by pillows, looking very pale and ill. Then she saw the sister and nurse rush over to her bed with oxygen; the next thing she knew, she opened her eyes to see the sister bending over her. She told of her experience, but the initial response was sceptical. She then told the sister what she had seen: round the corner was a big woman sitting up in bed with her head in bandages; she had a very red face, and was knitting something in blue wool. This turned out to be absolutely correct. Yet the patient had not ostensibly left her bed, and could not possibly have ascertained this from her present location.

We pass now to cases of OBEs caused by some shocking and sudden event. Two incidents are connected with mountaineering, three with war, and three with motor accidents. They form a bridge with some of the experiences to be discussed in the next chapter.

9G1 – The mountaineer F.S. Smythe described his experience when he fell over a precipice. The rope held when he had fallen some twenty feet; he was half aware that he might be killed, and felt his whole being gripped by a curious rigidity which rendered him insensible to pain. He was also unaware of time. Then he experienced a feeling of complete indifference and detachment, seeming to stand aside from his body. He was not falling, because he was not in a dimension in which it was possible to fall. He himself (his conscious self) was apart from the physical body and not in the least concerned about its fate. It was as if the tenant had already departed in anticipation of disaster. He added that the experience convinced him that consciousness survived the grave.

9G2 – The Rev. L.J. Bertrand was climbing in the Alps with a guide and a group of students. He felt rather tired so he allowed the others to continue on condition that the guide took the students up the left-hand track, and that the strongest student should remain at the rear at the end of the rope. He sat down and, after a while, attempted to light a cigar, but found that he could not discard the match. He realised that he was freezing to death, but he was in an awkward situation; if he moved he might roll down into an abyss, but sitting still meant certain death. Gradually his limbs grew colder and colder, and Bertrand found his conscious self rising out of his body in a kind of captive balloon attached to his body by a sort of elastic string (the so-called cord). He continued to rise, thinking of himself as dead and his physical body, visible below, as 'the corpse in which I lived'. He never felt more alive than at that moment. Then he was able to see the rest of the group, and discovered that the guide had disobeyed his orders by taking the students up the right-hand path; in addition he spotted the guide surreptitiously drinking his (Bertrand's) wine and eating his chicken. He rose still higher, and saw his wife with four other persons in a carriage on their way to Lucerne; they stopped at a hotel in Lungren. Then he felt as if someone was hauling him down in the balloon towards his body. When he reached it he hoped that the balloon would be too large to reenter, but it did, and Bertrand reawoke in his physical body. The guide informed him that he had nearly frozen to death, whereupon Bertrand rejoined that he had been very much less dead than the guide. Subsequently the guide admitted having taken the students up by the right-hand path, and that he had eaten some of the chicken and drunk some of the wine; then his wife confirmed that there had been five of them in the carriage, and that they had stopped in a Lungren Hotel.

9G3 relates an officer's experience during the war. In August 1944 his car received a direct hit from an anti-tank gun, and he himself was thrown twenty feet. At this point he was aware of being two people – one lying on the ground and wildly waving his limbs around, and another as if hearing and seeing the incident from a point about twenty feet in the air. From this position he could see his physical body on the ground, as well as the hedge, the road and the burning car. Then he told himself that it was no use gibbering, and that he must roll over and put out the flames. His physical body on the ground did so, and he suddenly became one person again. Although this case exhibits a degree of dual consciousness, the will, or rational directing principle and the centre of perception are both outside the physical body.

9G4 – S. Bourne was on duty at the Eastbourne fire station on 4 February 1943, when there was a raid and a direct hit on the station. He heard a roar and, after a momentary blackout, found himself about five feet above his physical body. He felt free as air, his mind was quite clear, he had a form, and could feel no pain. He was conscious of every detail in the room, and saw his physical body lying under a ceiling joist and a pile of debris. He then noticed two other things: that the window frame had been blown in on the hearth and was alight; and that a colleague, who had been sitting by the window knitting, was trapped under a pile of bricks and glass with a gash on her face. He describes how he got back into his body with a kind of thunderclap sensation, and was somehow able to emerge from under the joist to help his colleagues.

9G5 – Dr X., a retired consultant, narrated the following experience to his friend Professor Stratton, who in turn submitted it to the SPR. In 1916, C. had been medical officer in the second brigade of the RFC, with HQ at Clair Marais aerodrome. On 21 April he was summoned to Abeele aerodrome in order to attend to a patient, and the commanding officer, Major Malcolm, decided to fly X. there himself. Unfortunately Malcolm was not the most competent of pilots, and Clair Marais was badly sited. Malcolm did a steep turn too early, and the plane crashed with X. on board. X. remembers knowing that the crash was inevitable, but nothing of the actual impact. The pilot escaped unhurt, but X. was thrown well clear of the wreckage, landed on his back, and sustained injuries which later proved to cause extensive paralysis. His body lay inert, showing no signs of consciousness.

The layout of the aerodrome meant that the hangers could not be seen from the location of the wreckage. The details of what X, ostensibly remembered are only verifiable in outline, as the detailed corroboration and statement were lost when Major Malcolm was killed in an accident some weeks later. This does not invalidate X.'s general account, because from the position where he was lying much of what he did see, and which did take place, would have been invisible. The standard rescue procedure was put into operation when the sentry near the hangar saw that a crash was going to occur: the Crossley tender, fitted with an ambulance but without a self-starter, should immediately move to the scene with medical aid.

X.'s ostensible experience was as follows. He seemed to be looking straight down on his physical body from a height of about 200 feet. He saw the Brigadier, the Lieutenant-Colonel and the pilot running towards his body, and wondered why they were so interested in it. Then he saw the Crossley start out of the hangar; it stalled almost immediately, so the driver had to get out in order to restart it before jumping back in and driving towards the scene of the crash. Meanwhile X.'s medical orderly had rushed out of the medical hut and jumped into the back of the Crossley, which then stopped again in order to allow the orderly to go back to the hut to fetch something. When he returned, the Crossley resumed the journey. None of this sequence of events would have been visible from the point where X.'s physical body was lying.

He then had an experience of travelling in his secondary apparition-body. After a while it seemed to lose speed, and then felt himself being pulled back until he was once more hovering over his physical body. Then he suddenly regained consciousness and became aware that the medical orderly was pouring sal volatile down his throat. He realised that he was paralysed and ordered that he should be left undisturbed until the arrival of qualified medical help. Dr Abrahams, the doctor who eventually arrived on the scene, was able to give the SPR details of the accident and of the treatment of Dr X. Later the commanding officer took down a report of what X. had ostensibly seen. Later he repeated the story to the head of the RFC as well as to a number of eminent psychical researchers. X. adds that the experience removed from him all fear of death. In this case the conscious self is so clearly dissociate from the physical body as to be indifferent to its fate.

9G6 – E.C. Colley had been travelling along at 80mph on a motor cycle with a friend when they came to a bridge over a canal. For some reason the front of the bike went down, and he was thrown against the railing of the bridge and then catapulted over into the water. He claims that he saw these events as if he had been a bystander about thirty feet behind the scene. He saw his physical body trying to grasp the rail and being thrown into the water. He re-entered his body with the shock of impact on the water.

9G7 – Green cites a case where a man became completely separated from his body and machine. His other self stood in the middle of the road, and, like Dr X. and Bertrand, felt no pain or concern. He watched the motorcycle fall over and his physical body tumble towards him, then saw the driver of the car which he had hit scramble out, and another car at a standstill immediately behind the bike. The other driver got out, stopped the engine, and lifted the bike in order to free the physical body, while the first driver put his hand on the injured body's shoulder and lifted the body up. At this point the subject regained consciousness in the physical body.

9G8 is an example of an accident given by Moody. A young man was driving back home in a car with a friend when they came to an intersection. The driver looked to see if there was anything coming, but noticed nothing, and therefore pulled out. His friend yelled and the driver saw the blinding lights of a car bearing down on them. There was a terrific crash followed by a blackout. Then the driver seemed to be floating about five feet above the street and about five yards from the car. He saw people running up to the wreckage and his friend climbing out in a state of shock. He could see his own body with people trying to disentangle it; his legs were all twisted, and there was blood everywhere. The report does not indicate the point at which the subject rejoined his physical body.

We mentioned, earlier, that 84 per cent of Green's subjects claimed that their conscious self was confined entirely to their new point of view, and that the vast majority felt that their perception of the environment was no different from what would be expected. In the light of some of our cases it is interesting to look at some of the features of OBEs noted by Green in her survey. Subjects do not normally report feelings of mental confusion, but, if anything, they feel more alert and alive than usual – 56.3 per cent of the single cases reported that they felt more awake and keenly observant than usual. There was also no doubt about the identity which they felt with their normal selves: 'the part of me that was out of the body was the real me, as I knew it, the part that thinks, sees, and feels emotionally', as one respondent put it. This is borne out by our examples. In fact the conscious self's awareness of its detachment from the body is the *sine qua non* of any report at all. This detachment seems not only to manifest itself physically but also emotionally. X, in particular, was unconcerned about his body, and wondered why such a fuss was being made over it. Words used by Green's respondents to describe this feeling are calm, relaxed, indifferent, unconcerned and uninterested. The body is thought of as remote and separate from the self; the subjects are interested observers of the physical events. Movement is associated with the sense of lightness and freedom experienced in the new state. One subject described all movement as instantaneous, so that to think is to have acted; what the *Bardo Thodol* called the power of miraculous actions extending the visual field infinitely, so to speak, as one would be present at the place at the moment of thought. The thinking of someone is a direction of the attention towards them, so that without the encumbrance of the physical body, thought and travel are both instantaneous and simultaneous.

The data considered in this chapter constitute a *prima facie* case for the ability of the conscious self to perceive and operate outside and independently of the physical body. We have seen how individuals are apparently able to observe their bodies from the outside, and perceive events going on in the vicinity, or even locations at some distance from the physical body, where they are occasionally perceived as apparitions by a third party. Green cites a minority of respondents who report travelling to scenes, which could not be part of everyday experience, and some subjects who apparently met deceased relatives. These reports indicate access to another level of dimension or consciousness altogether: one which cannot be confused with the real word, but which is, nevertheless, experienced as more real than normal. The subjects of the near-death experience, which we shall investigate in the next chapter, report encounters with the physical world out of the body, and with these other more transcendental levels of experience; we shall concentrate mainly on their observation of the physical world.

10.

NEAR-DEATH EXPERIENCES

Know that when the eye looks into space it is the Spirit of man that sees: the eye is only the organ of sight. When one says 'I am hearing', it is the Spirit that hears: the ear is the organ of hearing.

CHANDOGYA UPANISHAD

Now. When I have overcome my fears – of others, of myself, of the underlying darkness:

At the frontier of the unheard-of

Here ends the known. But, from a source beyond it, something fills my being with its possibilities.

HAMMARSKJÖLD

We must all become familiar with the thought of death if we want to grow into really good people ... only familiarity with the thought of death creates true inward freedom.

SCHWEITZER

The near-death experience has been defined as the 'experiential counterpart of the physiological transition to biological death': it is the record of conscious experience from the inside rather than the outside, from the point of view of the subject rather than the spectator. Plato describes the earliest recorded 'resuscitation'. Er was killed in battle, and, when the dead were taken up on the tenth day, his body was still intact, while those all around were decaying. He was taken home to be buried on the twelfth day and came to life on the funeral pyre – just in time. He related how his soul had left his body, in company with many other soldiers, and how he went to a strange place. There he saw, among other things, the souls choosing their next lives and then drinking from the forgetful river in order to obliterate memories of the strange place and of their former lives. Er was not allowed to drink, hence the rationale for his remembering the vital metaphysical information, although he had no idea of how he returned to his body.

Before turning to more contemporary material, we shall look at two older cases:

10/1 – Dr A.S. Wiltse nearly died of typhoid fever in 1889. Gurney and Myers investigated his case, and sworn testimony was obtained of all the events, which occurred during the coma, which lasted about four hours, and during which Wiltse's body was without pulse or perceptible heartbeat. He recalls being about to emerge from the body, then watching the process of separation of soul and body. He no longer identified himself with the physical body and at this stage appeared to himself like a jellyfish in colour and form; then he had the sensation of floating up and down laterally like a soup bubble attached to the end of a pipe until:

> I at last broke free from the body ... and fell lightly on the floor, where I slowly rose and expanded into the full stature of a man [by this stage his ball-like form seems to have been transformed into the shape of a body]. I seemed to be translucent, of a bluish cast, and perfectly naked. As I turned, my elbow came into contact with the arm of one of two gentlemen who were standing in the door. To my surprise his arm passed right through mine without apparent resistance [body passing through matter], the severed parts closing again without pain, as air reunites. I looked quickly up at his face to see whether he had noticed the contact but he gave me no sign ... I directed my gaze in the direction of his and saw my own dead body. It was lying just as I had taken so much pains to place it, partially on the right side, the feet close

together, and the hands clasped across the breast ... I was surprised
at the paleness of the face ... and saw a number of persons sitting and
standing about the body ... and ... attempting to gain the attention of the
people with the object of comforting them as well as reassuring them
of my own immortality ... I passed among them, but found they gave
me no heed. Then the situation struck me as humorous and I laughed
outright ... I concluded that they 'are watching what they think is I, but
they are mistaken'. That is not I. This is I [the conscious self] and I am
as much alive as ever. How well I feel, I thought. Only a few minutes
ago I was horribly sick and distressed. Then came the change called
death which I have so much dreaded. This has passed, now, and here
I am still a man, alive and thinking, yes thinking as clearly as ever,
and how well I feel; I shall never be sick again, I have no more to die.

There follows a description of his experiences in another dimension, culminating in his having to decide whether his task on earth
is finished. He finally decides that it is not, loses his awareness, then:

without previous thought and without apparent effort on my part,
my eyes opened. I looked at my hands and then at the little white cot
upon which I was lying and, realising that I was in the body, and in
astonishment and disappointment, I exclaimed 'What in the world
has happened to me? Must I die again?'

He then related his experience. One of the remarkable features of
this case is the subject's continuous awareness when leaving the physical body; in many cases there is a period of blackout at this point.

10/2 dates from 1937, and was recorded by Lord Geddes, a Professor of Anatomy and Cabinet Minister. It forms part of an address giv-
en to the Royal Medical Society of Edinburgh; at the end the audience
was assured that the experience was not fake, or else it would not have
been brought to their notice. At the time, Geddes claimed that the experience was that of a friend, but later admitted that it was his own.
Presumably he did not wish to be branded as crazy by his colleagues.

On Saturday 9th November, a few minutes after midnight, I began to
feel very ill ... and was definitely suffering from acute gastroenteritis ...
by ten o'clock I have developed all the symptoms of acute poisoning ...
pulse and respirations became quite impossible to count, I wanted to
ring for assistance, but found I could not and so I quite placidly gave up

the attempt. I realised that I was very ill and very quickly reviewed my whole financial position. Thereafter at no time did my consciousness appear to me in any way dimmed, but I suddenly realised that *my* consciousness was separating from another consciousness, which was also me.

These he calls A- and B-consciousnesses and states that the ego attached itself to the A-consciousness. He saw the B-consciousness begin to disintegrate while:

The A-consciousness [the conscious self], which was now me, seemed to be altogether outside my body, which it could see. Gradually I realised that I could see, not only my body and the bed in which it was, but everything in the whole house and garden, and then realised that I was seeing, not only 'things' at home but in London and Scotland, in fact wherever my attention was directed [thought-travel and clairvoyance]; and the explanation which I received, from what source I do not know, but which I found myself calling my 'mentor', was in some way equivalent to 'here' in the ordinary three-dimensional space of everyday life.

This is a succinct statement of the space-time characteristics which we have already noted in connection with apparitions and OBEs: it can be conceived either as the abolition of space or as the abolition of time. The narrator then says that his further experiences can only be described metaphorically since, although he seemed to have a two-eyed vision, he 'appreciated' rather than saw things:

I was conscious of a sort of psychic stream flowing with life through time, and this gave me the impression of being visible ... Around each brain, as I saw it, there seemed to be a condensation of the psychic stream which formed in each case as though it were a cloud ... Then I realised that I myself was a condensation, as it were, in the psychic stream, a sort of cloud that was not a cloud. The visual impression I had of myself was blue. Gradually I began to recognise people and I saw the psychic condensation attached to many of them [he then describes various people as having different coloured condensations – blue, pink, grey-brown, etc] ... I saw B. enter my bedroom; I realised that she got a terrible shock and I saw her hurry to the telephone. I saw my doctor leave his patients and come very quickly, and heard him say or saw him think 'he is nearly gone'. I heard him quite clearly speaking to me on the bed, but I was not in touch with my body and could not answer him. I was really cross when he took a syringe and rapidly injected my body with something, which I afterwards learned was camphor. As the heart began to beat more strongly, I was drawn back, and I was intensely annoyed [like Wiltse] because I was so interested and just beginning to understand where I was and what I was 'seeing'. I came back into the body really angry at being pulled back, and once I was back, all the clarity of vision of anything and everything disappeared and I was possessed of a glimmer of consciousness, which was suffused with pain.

This case is particularly fascinating with respect to perception. In the last chapter we saw that the majority of OBE subjects seemed to find themselves in the same apparent space as the physical bodies. One of Green's respondents reported a more comprehensive field of vision, and the ability to see objects and see through them at the same time. Correspondingly, as we have seen, Wiltse was able to pass through physical bodies which are solid to us. The capacity to see through objects is associated with the state which, in Geddes's words, makes now equivalent to here. Others describe a similar sensation: 'this spiritual sense had no limitations ... it seemed as if I could look anywhere and everywhere'. And again:

> Whenever I would look at a person to wonder what they were thinking, it was like a zoom-up, exactly like through a zoom lens, and I was there. But it seemed that part of me – I'll call it my mind – was still where I had been, several yards away from my body. When I wanted to see someone at a distance, it seemed that part of me, kind of like a tracer, would go to that person. And it seemed that if something happened any place in the world I could just be there.

Clearly the same kind of instant travelling clairvoyance is being described. Geddes's record of his perception goes further than this, though; he relates that he has to use metaphorical terms, suggested that he had moved into a dimension, or was operating at a level of consciousness which could no longer be adequately expressed in physical terms. His sight seems to have become 'interior' in that he was no longer perceiving the bodies themselves but the condensations around them; this refined perception identifies people through their qualities rather than their bodily form. Geddes speaks in terms of two levels of visual perception: one which is an extended replica of physical space, and another, at any rate applying to people if not to objects, which has a more interior quality. The same goes for the sense of hearing. At one level he seems to hear physical sounds, when the doctor is speaking to him on the bed; one can only assume that this is through the awareness of his A-consciousness, since his consciousness on return to the body is but a glimmer. On the other hand the previous sentence expresses an alternative to hearing 'or saw him think'. One of Greene's subjects reports an acute sense of hearing outside the body when listening to the breathing of another patient. In the other mode, as it were, a number of Moody's subjects report picking up the thoughts of those around them rather than hearing physical voices: 'I could see people all around, and could understand what they were saying. I didn't hear them audibly, like I'm hearing you. It was more like knowing what they were thinking, but only in my mind, not in their actual vocabulary' (although the actual words are in fact frequently reported). This is quite a logical statement in the clairvoyant/clairaudient state. After all, speech is only materialised thought; we think what we are going to say just before speaking or writing it. And some thoughts, which we grasp, may take many words to express.

Data on the near-death experience are growing all the time. Moody published the first and most well known findings on the subject in 1975 in his book, *Life after Life*. Since then there have been studies by cardiologists Rawlings and Sabom and a statistical study by Ring who has also started a journal devoted to the phenomenon. The above writers document well over 400 cases.

Of Ring's subjects, 95 per cent of those asked stated that the experience was not like a dream (the same result appears in Sabom): they stressed that it was too real, being more vivid and more realistic; however some aspects were hard to express, as the experience did not resemble anything that had happened to them before. The essential part of the self, 'the sole conscious identity', was reported to be separate from the body, which was regarded as an 'empty shell'; in most cases there was no remembered awareness of bodily form outside the body. The mental processes were typically described as clear, sharp and rational: respondents reported that they could think very clearly and were extremely alert – one person said that it was as if his whole body had eyes and ears. In movement there was a feeling of weightlessness and the ability to project themselves wherever they wanted, as indicated above; space ceased to exist as a limitation. One further interesting finding in both Ring and Sabom was that religiousness, religious affiliation, and prior knowledge or ignorance of the phenomenon of the NDE had no effect on the experience.

Ring's estimate of the frequency of occurrence of some kind of experience is slightly lower than that of Rawlings and Sabom – around 15 per cent – which means that the majority of people with near-death encounters either had no conscious experience during the period, or else the memory of it evaporated on awakening. Rawlings suspects that this may indicate suppression of unpleasant experiences – an unverifiable hypothesis by definition. Gold suggests that a lack of rigorous yogic training may be responsible – only the development of a deep level of self-awareness would enable a person not to lose consciousness during the process of death – no correlation of this kind has yet been studied. Steiner's theory, discussed in Chapter 6, would at least provide an intelligible framework for this 15 per cent figure. Those who remember nothing had their astral body (illumination) and conscious self withdrawn from the physical and etheric bodies, and were thus in a state corresponding to deep sleep; while the conscious self and astral body of those who remember something, whether of a transcendental nature or not, remained in contact with the etheric and physical. Thus, in the latter case only, could the experience be mediated into the physical world. In any event we do have a substantial number of reports of conscious experience to go on; they exhibit a sufficient number of recognisably similar traits for some inferences to be drawn. Moody, Rawlings and Ring have all constructed a 'composite' NDE: the experiences vary, but point to a common underlying pattern or description of the Gurney-type strange island animal.

Moody's description is as follows:

A man is dying and, as he reaches the point of greatest physical distress, he hears himself pronounced dead by his doctor. He begins to hear an uncomfortable noise, a loud ringing or buzzing, and at the same time feels himself moving very rapidly through a long dark tunnel. After this, he suddenly finds himself outside of his own physical body, but still in the immediate physical environment, and he sees his own body from a distance, as though he is a spectator. He watches the resuscitation attempt from his unusual vantage point and is in a state of emotional upheaval.

After a while, he collects himself and becomes more accustomed to his odd condition. He notices that he still has a 'body', but one of a very different nature and with very different powers from the physical body he has left behind. Soon other things begin to happen. Others come to meet and help him. He glimpses the spirits of relatives and friends who have already died, and a loving, warm spirit of a kind he never encountered before – a being of light – appears before him. This being asks him a question, nonverbally, to make him evaluate his life and helps him by showing him a panoramic, instantaneous playback of the major events of his life. At some point he finds himself approaching some sort of barrier or border, apparently representing the limit between earthly life and the next life. Yet, he finds that he must go back to earth, that the time for his death has not yet come. At this point he resists, for by now he is taken up with his experiences in the afterlife and does not want to return. He is overwhelmed by intense feelings of joy, love, and peace. Despite his attitude, though, he somehow reunites with his physical body and lives.

Later he tries to tell others, but he has trouble doing so. In the first place, he can find no human words adequate to describe these unearthly episodes. He also finds that others scoff, so he stops telling other people. Still, the experience affects his life profoundly, especially his views about death and its relationship to life.

Rawlings's aggregate example runs:

A dying person simply faints or painlessly loses consciousness as death occurs, and yet he is still able to hear himself pronounced dead by his doctor. He then discovers that he is out of his own body, but still in the same room, looking on as a bystander and observing the procedures. He watches himself being resuscitated, and frequently is compelled to walk around other people who might be obstructing his view. Or he may look down upon the scene from a floating position near the ceiling in which he sometimes finds himself. Often he is standing or floating behind the doctor or nurse, looking down on the back of their heads as they work to revive his body. He notices who is in the room and knows what they are saying. He has difficulty believing he is dead, that the lifeless body used to be his. He feels fine! The body has been vacated as if it were a strange object.

After he becomes more accustomed to this odd condition he notices that he has a new body which seems real and endowed with superior senses. He is not a ghost. He can see and feel and think and talk just as before. But now fringe benefits have been added. He notices his body as infinite capabilities of transportation and thought-reading, and is capable of doing almost anything. He may then hear a peculiar noise after which he finds himself moving through a long dark passage with walls. His speed may be fast or slow but he doesn't touch the walls and is not afraid of falling. As he emerges from the tunnel he may see a brilliantly lighted environment of exquisite beauty where he meets and talks with friends and relatives who have previously died. A being of light or a being of darkness may then interview him. This environment may be inexpressibly wonderful, frequently a rolling meadow or a beautiful city; or it may be inexpressibly horrible, frequently a dungeon or a huge cave. His whole life may be played back as an instant review of all the major events of his life, as if anticipating a judgment.

As he walks along with his friends or relatives (frequently his parents in a good experience), a barrier is usually encountered beyond which he cannot go and still return. He usually is turned back at this point and suddenly finds himself back in his body where he may feel the shock of an applied electric current or chest pains from someone pushing upon his chest.

And Ring's account:

The experience begins with a feeling of easeful peace and a sense of well-being, which soon culminates in a sense of overwhelming joy and happiness. This ecstatic tone, although fluctuating in intensity from case to case, tends to persist as a constant emotional ground as other features of the experience begin to unfold. At this point the person is aware that he feels no pain nor does he have any other bodily sensations. Everything is quiet. These cues may suggest to him that he is either in the process of dying or has already 'died'.

He may then be aware of a transitory buzzing or wind like sound, but, in any event, he finds himself looking down on his physical body, as though he were viewing it from some external vantage point. At this time, he finds that he can see and hear perfectly; indeed, his vision and hearing tend to be more acute than usual. He is aware of the actions and conversations taking place in the physical environment, in relation to which he finds himself in the role of a passive, detached spectator. All this seems very real – even quite natural – to him; it does not seem at all like a dream or an hallucination. His mental state is one of clarity and alertness.

At some point, he may find himself in a state of *dual awareness*. While he continues to be able to perceive the physical scene around him, he may also become aware of 'another reality' and feel himself being drawn into it. He drifts into a dark void or tunnel and feels as though he is floating through it. Although he may feel lonely for a time, the experience here is predominantly peaceful and serene. All is extremely quiet and the individual is aware only of his mind and of the feeling of floating.

All at once, he becomes sensitive to, but does not see, a presence. The presence, who may be heard or speak or who may instead 'merely' induce thoughts into the individual's mind, stimulates him to review his life and asks him to decide whether he wants to live or die. This stocktaking may be facilitated by a rapid and vivid visual playback of episodes from the person's life. At this stage, he has no awareness of time or space, and the concepts themselves are meaningless. Nor is he any longer identified with his body. Only the mind is present and it is weighing – logically and rationally – the alternatives that confront him at this threshold separating life from death: to go further into this experience or to return to earthly life. Usually the individual decides to return on the basis, not of his own preference, but on the perceived needs of his loved ones, whom his death would necessarily leave behind. Once the decision is made, the experience tends to be abruptly terminated.

Sometimes, however, the decisional crisis occurs later or is altogether absent, and the individual undergoes further experiences. He may, for example, continue to float through the dark void toward a magnetic and brilliant golden light, from which emanated feelings of love, warmth, and total acceptance. Or he may enter into a 'world of light' and preternatural beauty, to be (temporarily) reunited with deceased loved ones before being told, in effect, that it is not yet his time and that he has to return to life.

In any event, whether the individual chooses or is commanded to return to his earthly body and worldly commitments, he does return.

Typically, however, he has no recollection *how* he has effected his 're-entry', for at this point he tends to lose all awareness. Very occasionally, however, the individual may remember 'returning to his body' with a jolt or an agonising wrenching sensation. He may even suspect that he re-enters 'through the head'.

Afterward, when he is able to recount his experience, he finds that there are simply no words adequate to convey the feelings and quality of awareness he remembers. He may also be, or become, reluctant to discuss it with others, either because he feels no one will really be able to understand it or because he fears he will be disbelieved or ridiculed.

The common features of these three descriptions is quite apparent – the separation, the tunnel, the perception of the immediate physical surroundings, the encounter with relatives and friends and perhaps with a spiritual being, the review of the life, the decision to return, and the abrupt reawakening. Moody is mentioned by Rawlings in his bibliography, but there is no direct comparison between his own and Moody's aggregate example. Ring, however, does comment on their striking similarity which he claims does not stem from any desire to mimic Moody but rather from the (apparent) 'Extraordinary similarity between his findings and mine'; this is doubly significant, since Ring's book is deliberately more statistically rigorous. One of the most significant differences is that only Rawlings reports some unpleasant experiences. He contends that other investigators, not being cardiologists, are not present at the moment of resuscitation, and that unpleasant experiences have been forgotten through repression by the time later interviews take place. The latest work is actually by another cardiologist, Sabom, who does not record any such experiences; and against Rawlings Ring argues that he has been over-selective in his data in order to back up his undoubted Christian evangelical leanings, which are reassured by the presence of the traditional heaven and hell. While agreeing with Ring that some pleasant experiences may also have been forgotten, it can hardly be argued that Rawlings's reports of unpleasant encounters are the result of evangelical wishful thinking. Their proportion may have been slightly exaggerated, but there seems no good reason for rejecting the unpleasant and retaining the pleasant data.

In the following cases we shall concentrate on the so-called autoscopic elements – where the subject is able to see his own body and perceive what is going on in its vicinity. The reader will then be able to get the flavour of the experiences.

10/3 Miss Blakeley became seriously ill, and fell one evening into a deep sleep; she awoke to find the room in darkness:

> This awakening was not like the usual drowsy awakening from the sleeping state. The consciousness was strangely calm and clear. I was no longer in pain ... Gradually the consciousness, which normally suffuses the whole body, became condensed in the head. I became all head, and only head. Then it seemed that 'I' had become condensed into one tiny speck of consciousness, situated somewhere near the centre of my head ... Then I became aware that I was beginning to travel further upwards. There came a momentary blackout and then 'I' was free; I had left my body. I had projected in space somewhere above the bed on which still lay my inert body. And I knew this – this is what the world calls the state of death ... Contrary to general belief, there was no loss of consciousness.

There followed an experience of panoramic review and judgment, and an encounter with a being of light before returning to the body. Miss Blakeley regarded the event as a revelation and its memory remained vividly with her.

10/4 Mr Cole needed to have some teeth extracted, and was warned in a dream that he might have heart trouble. However he took no notice of this and had a general anaesthetic. He found himself outside his own body behind the bed, and felt indescribably elated. He was between the doctor and the dentist who were talking about a house sale. He then found that other people were present as well, among them the '(deceased) Italian lady of whom I had a sketch by the clairvoyant Ronald Bailey and a full description by Mrs Hester Dowden'. The lady said that he had been warned about this and that there was some heart trouble. Cole noticed that the doctor was concerned and that his physical body had stopped breathing; he managed to make his lungs start breathing and observed the rest of the operation before re-entering the body. When out of the body he had noticed that the walls were transparent and that he could see into the passage, even though the doors were closed. The case is unusual with the 'conversation' with the Italian lady, but otherwise exhibits no special features.

10/5 Mrs Adler went to bed one night in a state of total exhaustion. She suddenly felt as if she were completely paralysed, then had a sensation of falling. She knew she was awake not dreaming, but then blacked out and found herself hovering up near the ceiling; she thought she was dead. The room was in half-light and she was able to see her husband and baby below; she then looked up and noticed that the roof was no longer there – her vision was both expanded and sharpened. Suddenly she was travelling at tremendous speed with a sense of freedom and exhilaration rather than fear; then equally suddenly her thoughts were directed back to her baby on earth and she felt herself falling back, blacking out, and landing on the bed 'with a tremendous repercussion'. She instantly felt heavy and clumsy in comparison with her previous state; her experience removed all fear of death.

10/6 Two doctors recorded this case of one of their patients who suffered a cardiac arrest. He blacked out then found himself looking at his own body: 'Almost immediately I saw myself leave my body, coming out through my head and shoulders. The "body" leaving me was not exactly in vapour form, yet it seemed to expand slightly [cf. Wiltse] once it was clear of me.' It occurred to him that this is what happens when one dies. He then found himself travelling at great speed, with similar feelings of exhilaration to Mrs Adler. Suddenly he was aware of sledgehammer blows to his left side and he reopened his eyes. The nurse described his experience as 'a bad turn'.

10/7 is quite a detailed report quoted verbatim by Rawlings:

I turned over to answer the phone and began to have another very severe pain in my chest. I pushed the button to summon the nurse and they came in and started working on me. They put medicine in the bottle hanging up on a stand beside the bed and running into my arm. I was miserable lying there. It felt like an elephant's foot standing in the middle of my chest. I was sweating and about to vomit when I noticed that I was losing consciousness. Everything was turning black. My heart stopped beating! I heard the nurses shouting 'Code 99, Code 99!' One of them dialled the phone to the hospital loudspeaker.

As they were doing this I could feel myself leaving my body from the headward position, detaching and floating in the air without any sensation of falling. Then I was lightly standing on my feet watching the nurses push down my chest. Two more nurses came in and one orderly and then I noticed that they had gotten my doctor back from his visits in the hospital. He had seen me earlier. When he came into the room, I wondered why he was here. I felt fine!

Then my doctor took off his coat to relieve the nurse pushing on my chest. I noticed he had on a blue-striped tie. The room started getting dark and I had the sensation of moving rapidly down a dark corridor. All of a sudden I felt this horrible shocking in my chest. My body moved, my back arched and I felt this terrific burning in my chest like somebody had hit me. Then I woke up finding myself back in my bed. Only two nurses and an orderly were left. The others had gone.

All the above events and numbers of people involved were subsequently verified, as was the fact that the patient was without heartbeat or consciousness during the entire sequence.

10/8 is quite similar to the above. The patient experienced severe chest pains and remembers hearing someone shout that he had had a cardiac arrest:

> everything was black, and then I remember seeing them working on me and it seemed so strange because I felt perfectly fine [no pain when not in the physical body]. I had to move to one side to see my face to make sure it was my body ... the next thing I remember I was feeling this thud on my chest; somebody was pounding on me and pushing on me. I thought my ribs were breaking ... I didn't want to come back.

Coming back meant sacrificing the feelings of floating and exhilaration for his cramping bodily condition.

10/9 is a further cardiac case, from Moody. The narrator is a woman.

> About a year ago, I was admitted to hospital with heart trouble, and the next morning, lying in the hospital bed, I began to have a very severe pain in my chest. I pushed the button beside the bed to call for the nurses, and they came in and started working on me. I was quite uncomfortable lying on my back so I turned over, and as I did I quit breathing and my heart stopped beating. Just then, I heard the nurses shout 'Code pink! Code pink!' As they were saying this, I could feel myself moving out of my body and sliding down between the mattress and the rail on the side of the bed – actually it seemed as if I went *through* the rail – on down to the floor. Then I started rising upward, slowly. On the way up, I saw more nurses come running into the room – there must have been a dozen of them. My doctor happened to be making his rounds in the hospital so they called him and I saw him come in, too. I thought, 'I wonder what he's doing here.' I drifted on

up past the light fixture – I saw it from the side and very distinctly – and then I stopped, floating right below the ceiling, looking down. I felt almost as though I were a piece of paper that someone had blown up to the ceiling.

I watched them reviving me from up there! My body was lying down there stretched out on the bed, in plain view, and they were all standing around it. I heard one nurse say, 'Oh, my God! She's gone!', while another leaned down to give me mouth-to-mouth resuscitation. I was looking at the *back* of her head while she did this ... Just then I saw them roll this machine in there, and they put shocks on my chest. When they did, I saw my whole body just jump right off the bed, and I heard every bone in my body crack and pop. It was the most awful thing! ... I thought 'Why are they going to so much trouble? I'm just fine now.'

The return is not recorded here, but the same detachment from the body and pain is expressed.

10/10 is the first part of an experience recorded by an architect, Stevan von Jankovich, who was thrown out of his car on 16 September 1964. He was lying unconscious on the road with eighteen broken ribs:

I hovered over the site of the accident and saw my lifeless, badly injured body lying there, exactly in the position which I later found described in the police report. I also saw clearly our car and the onlookers. Then I noticed a man who was attempting to bring me back to life. I was able to hear what the people were saying. The doctor was kneeling on the right hand side, giving me an injection. Two others were holding me from the other side and were pulling off my clothes. I saw how the doctor forced my mouth open with a spatula and tried artificial respiration, and I heard him say: 'I can't give him cardiac massage, his ribs are broken.' Then he stood up and said – in funny Bernese German – 'There's nothing to be done. He's dead.' People wanted to move my body away from the side of the road and asked the soldiers where there was a blanket to cover my body. I wanted to laugh, and to say to them, 'Don't make such a scene, folks; I'm not quite dead yet.' I found the whole thing rather funny, but it didn't worry me at all. I actually found it amusing to be able to look on at people's efforts. Then I saw someone in bathing trunks approaching, with a little bag in his hand. He talked to the doctor in standard German. He exchanged a few little words with him, then knelt down beside me and did something to me. I was perfectly well able to fix the man's face in my mind. And in fact a man came into my hospital ward a few weeks later ... I got a shock, for I knew at once that I had already seen him somewhere at some time or other. He said that he was the doctor who had given me the life-saving cardiac injection – I myself would say the 'devilish' injection, because it was with the injection that my sufferings began. I recognised him immediately and was even able to remember his voice quite well. We immediately became friends.

It was interesting to see this terrible scene, a man dying 'down there' after a car accident. What was especially interesting was that the man was myself and that I was able to observe myself exactly, from above, as an onlooker, without any emotion, quite calmly, in a heavenly, felicitous state, in 'divine harmony'. It was very seldom that a person sees himself dying. But it is more interesting still that this should happen without excitement and with the contented feeling: at last I'm dying. This was my first four-dimensional experience. I hovered about ten feet above the site of my accident. My sensory organs functioned; my memory was able to register everything. I wasn't conscious of any hindrance.

The case describes the experience, the reactions, and the surprise that the experience was so different from what the narrator had anticipated: once again the feeling of detachment from the body, the lack of pain, and the complete perceptual awareness of someone supposed to be totally unconscious.

10/11 Jeff Barker is a TV engineer in his mid-fifties. He had a blood ailment and required regular transfusions; and in February 1977 lost consciousness and was rushed to hospital. Only his family knew of the crisis. He found himself out of the body at his place of work, where his apparition was seen by Sheila Nolan, a technical director; Barker, however, did not himself see Nolan, who realised that she was seeing an apparition of Barker and noticed that he was wearing a green gown with purple dots on it in one area. A few weeks later, back at work, Nolan described the experience, which Barker at first discounted until she described his hospital gown with blood spots on it. It is surprising that Barker did not perceive Nolan, but equally clear that she saw his apparition.

The general effects of undergoing an NDE are of two kinds: philosophical and ethical. The main philosophical changes are in attitudes

towards death and the afterlife. Sabom's figures are extremely interesting in this respect: he asked those who had and those who had not
had an NDE when unconscious whether there was any change in their
views of death and the afterlife. Of the 45 who had *not* had any conscious
experience, 39 were just as afraid of death as before, 5 more afraid and
1 less afraid; while of the 61 with an NDE none were more afraid, 11
just as afraid and 50 less afraid. The patterns were similar concerning
belief in an afterlife: of the non-experiencers, none had any change of
attitude; while of the experiencers, 14 found their attitude unchanged
and 47 stated that their belief in the afterlife had increased. Ring found
a correlation between loss of fear of death and what he called the core
experience, broadly that with a positive transcendental element in it.
Typical phrasings of these reactions are:

'The experience was very pleasant. If that is how one feels after death,
I have no fear of dying.'

'This experience convinced me of a future life.'

'The facts convinced me that man has an Astral Body capable of
existing independently of the physical body.'

'I was always afraid to die, but not now.'

'To me there is nothing truer than "There is no death".'

'The sensation when I lost connection with material things was
delightful. I can only say that it made me look forward to the moment
of death with a pleasant sense of anticipation.'

'Here was absolute proof that our Spiritual Self can and does function
not only as well, but better than, when it is confined to our physical
body. Therefore, for us, life after death became an established fact,
because of complete independence of the Spiritual from the physical
body.'

Moody comments that there is a remarkable agreement about the
'lessons' brought back from NDEs: 'Almost everyone has stressed the
importance in this life of trying to cultivate love for others, a love of a
unique and profound kind.' And he adds that a second characteristic

is a realisation of the importance of seeking knowledge, of not confining one's horizon to the material. The following comments are typical:

> All I knew was that I felt like I had aged overnight after this had happened, because it opened up a whole new world for me that I never knew could possibly exist. I kept thinking 'There's so much I've got to find out.' In other words there's more to life than Friday night movies and the football game. And there's more to me that I don't even know about. And then I started thinking about 'What is the limit of the human and of the mind?' It just opened up to me a whole new world.

> But since I died, all of a sudden, right after my experience, I started wondering whether I had been doing the things I had done because they were good, or because they were good for *me*. Before, I just reacted off the impulse, and now I run things through my mind first, nice and slow.

> I always thought about social status and wealth symbols as the most important things in life until life was suddenly taken from me. Now I know that none of these are important. Only the love you show others will endure or be remembered. The material things won't count. Our present life is nothing compared to what you'll see later. Now I'm not afraid to die again. Those that are afraid of dying must have a reason, or else they don't know what it's like.

A number of reductionist physiological explanations have been advanced to account for NDEs; one doctor refers to 'the giddy heights of uncritical thought' involved, and thinks that the experiences will take some hard knocks against reality. Sabom refutes such explanations in detail. We shall mention the two most common, namely cerebral anoxia and 'depersonalisation'. Cerebral anoxia accounts for the experience by saying that it is a hallucination due to an oxygen shortage in the brain. We have seen that such 'hallucinations' frequently turn out to correspond to the physical events actually occurring – can this be labelled a hallucination? perhaps – but certainly not a delusion. And Ring and Moody both point out that patterns of experiences are no different when there is clearly no shortage of oxygen. Noyes starts by pointing out that none of the subjects can really have been dead if they were resuscitated, so that their reported experiences cannot be taken as 'proof' of survival of consciousness. Moody never actually states this,

but confines himself to asserting that the experiences have a suggestive value; even if, for the subjects themselves, the experience *is* proof.
Noyes explains that the experience is an adaptive pattern of the nervous system, with the following characteristics:

> An altered perception of time, an increased speed of thoughts, a sense
> of detachment, a feeling of unreality, a lack of emotion, a revival of
> memories, a sense of harmony or unity with the universe, and sharper
> vision or hearing.

The reader will recognise the traits of the experiences that we have
been describing, except, perhaps, the feeling of unreality, which seems
to be an unwarranted inference from the sense of detachment: the subjects describe the experience as, if anything, more real than normal.
Noyes tries to account for the experiences along lines of wish-fulfilment: first that the unconscious, as postulated by Freud, cannot envisage its own death; but this psychological comment is totally inadequate
when it comes to explaining the veridical reports of the subject during
the OBE. Second, the state of mystical awareness experienced by many
'may bring a culmination and fulfilment of his most cherished beliefs';
but it has already been established, both by Ring and Sabom, that religious belief is not a determining factor of the kind of NDE experienced.

The common factor underlying all the physiological explanations
of the NDE is the attempt to avoid the *prima facie* interpretation of
the experience as an OBE. Sabom concludes that this hypothesis is the
best fit with the data, while Ring concludes that:

> there is abundant empirical evidence pointing to the reality of out-of-
> body experiences; that such experiences conform to the descriptions
> given by our near-death experiencers; and that there is highly suggestive
> evidence that death involves the separation of a second body – a double
> – from the physical body.

If perceptions were not so clear and accurate there might be a stronger case for some kind of delusive physical explanation. But the subjects
describe their surroundings in detail from a vantage point outside
their physical body; the conscious self is detached from the physical
body and its pain and is located at this new point in full possession
of its mental and perceptual faculties; if anything these faculties are
sharpened and widened when, in view of the unconscious state of the

physical body, one might anticipate the opposite. These observations provide further backing for the conclusions of the last chapter and indicate that the conscious self can think and perceive even when the physical body is in a comatose state.

One of the more celebrated earlier cases of resuscitation concerns George Ritchie, who 'died' on 20 December 1943. He had an extensive experience which, it was thought, he might be able to 'relive' through hypnosis. Accordingly he was hypnotised by another psychiatrist at the University of Virginia Medical School, and taken back to the time of his experience. This proved to be rather dangerous, as all the physical symptoms of his congestive heart failure reappeared: his veins bulged, his face flushed, and his blood pressure went up considerably. This is an instance of so-called hypnotic regression, where the subject is taken back in time so that he is not able merely to visualise an earlier experience, but actually to relive it. Iverson states that 'it is difficult for the layman to grasp that, as an ordinary feature of hypnosis, an adult can relive the days of his childhood, recalling long-forgotten events, and becoming to all intents and purposes a young child once again.' In such cases it is not suggested that the individual is fantasising about the experiences: they actually happened to him. But what of 'experiences' before birth and possibly in previous existences? The above regressions show that it is possible to remember details of one's past in this life, but does this entitle one to make the metaphysical leap beyond birth?

The sceptic may wish to accept the validity of relived experiences which, clearly fall in the present life, and dismiss the rest as elaborate fantasies woven by the dramatic powers of the imagination. No doubt this is correct in a number of instances, some of which involve narratives reconstructed out of material read in a historical novel. Acceptance of reported experiences of the period between conception and birth clearly assumes the existence of some kind of sustained reasoning power, which is hardly associated with embryos. Wambach's subjects speak of their decision to be born, their relationship to the foetus, their experiences of birth, and early OBEs when the conscious self reasons as an adult and finds the baby's physical brain very cramping. Acceptance at face value of the material relating to previous lives implies a framework of reincarnation, and the possibility of storing detailed information about these lives in the mind; the term *mind* is used advisedly, since presumably only experiences of this lifetime can be stored in the brain. Hypnotic regression in this lifetime and the experience of the panoramic review in the NDE show intricate recall of long-forgotten incidents in the past; logically, alleged memories of former incarnations are extensions prior to birth of this kind of memory in (or 'on') the mind. If these memories are of real events experienced by the conscious self in association with another body, this suggests that similar detailed memories of this life are registered simultaneously on the brain, as shown by Penfield and on the mind independently of the physical brain. The assumption of a conscious self and memory operating independently of the physical brain becomes more or less vital if one is to accept (a) any early experiences of the embryo; (b) any alleged reports of the death of the physical body; and (c) any ostensible memories of 'previous incarnations', if taken at face value.

For present purposes we shall assume that descriptions, which the regressed subjects give of deaths, are *bona fide*, in order to compare them with the data of the NDE. This is not a commitment to accepting a face value every report which claims to describe some incident in a previous life. But if we are to attach any credibility to the following descriptions, we should expect them to conform broadly to the patterns of experiences already encountered.

Fiore devotes a chapter to her subjects' accounts of death – numbering over 1,000, enough for some patterns to emerge. She reports that consciousness seems to continue without a break, and that all her subjects describe a release from physical and/or emotional pain at the moment of death or just before. Typically they describe themselves as feeling peaceful ... free ... relieved ... no pain, sensations which are equally typical of the NDE. Immediate bodily impressions are those of floating, rising into the air and viewing the scene below – the autoscopic aspect present in nearly all of the OBE and NDE experiences cited. At first the subjects seem to be alone but they soon feel the presence of 'spiritual guides', which may be experienced as a bright light or else they may be met by deceased relatives. A few cases are given below.

10/12 – Roger died during a jousting match in France. He describes a warmth going through his whole body: '...and I saw a white light, and floated away.' Asked to expand on this he explains:

I was lying face down, then I floated face down ... floated up and ... at first for about three feet ... and then I floated upright ... just floated away ... it means I died ... I feel relief ... I see the whole area. I can see everything.

10/13 – A woman patient describes a death in the jungle. Cannibals are pursuing her, it is very dark, she trips and falls into some quicksand:

> I'm struggling in this quicksand ... and I can't get out and I keep struggling and struggling ... it's in my throat ... it's just coming up to my nose ... I'm just going ... it's going into my nose. It's horrid ... smell and putrid ... the weight is so heavy on me ... I can't move ... I finally give up and just sink ... this gritty sand kind of burns and ... it's fading away, and I'm overcome with peace ... then I die. It seems if I'm momentarily watching myself sink and then I see the warriors come and I ... it looks as if my spirit is laughing, like I finally beat them out ... they didn't catch me ... then I float away.

10/14 – A woman describes a death from falling when she had been a primitive young oriental living with his grandmother. One day there was no food, so the young Wong-to had to try to steal some from a neighbouring village. But he is seen and pursued back as far as a precarious bridge overhanging a 10,000-foot ravine. His pursuers do not chase him over but start shaking the bridge instead. First he lets go of the stolen chicken then he slips

> and I'm hanging there from the rope on one side, on the left side of the bridge ... and I'm beginning to scream for help ... I can see way down. It's all rocks, way down, so far down rocks and water ... I'm falling ... seems like I'm falling for ever ... I can see my body falling, but I'm not afraid any more. It's as though I were floating ... the body falls onto the rocks ... my face is down on the rocks ... but I don't feel anything ... I don't know where I am ... I'm just floating around. The body was falling but I stopped falling.

This case recalls the mountaineer Smythe who described himself in a dimension in which he could no longer fall.

10/15 is a more peaceful experience, supposedly of a fifteenth-century abbot: 'It's peace ... just aware of floating ... It's like I'm in the universe ... my body ... it's just like floating ... and there's no pain, just floating.'

Despite the traumatic nature of many of the deaths reported in Fiore's work, the general reaction to re-living the experience was, as in the NDE, to dispel the fear of death; it also reinforced or created the conviction that the conscious self survives bodily death – regarded not so much as the end as the beginning.

Wambach's data reveal the same positive attitudes towards death and the death experience. She bases her observations on over 100 cases. An average of 49 per cent reported feelings of deep calm and peace, accepting their death without difficulty, while a further 30 per cent experienced feelings of positive joy and release; less than 10 per cent experiences fear, or sorrow at leaving people behind. Many subjects, who had a considerable fear of death before the regression, had lost this fear after going through death in a 'previous life'. Wambach gives the typical response as:

> Dying was like being released, like going home again. It was as though a great burden lifted when I left my body and floated up toward the light. I felt affection for the body I had lived in, in that lifetime, but it was so good to be free.

The tone of relief and the sensation of floating have already been encountered above. We shall cite three instances from Wambach:

10/16 – A death in old age: the subject describes herself as willing to go. Her family is gathered round her crying. She continues:

> as soon as I get out of the body, I want to tell them that I'm fine, but I can't reach them. Then it seems as though I'm going somewhere. It's almost like being pulled somewhere. The feeling is like a subway, I'm going through a tunnel, and there's a lot of white light, hazy white light at the end of the tunnel. Then when I get through the tunnel on the other side there are friends who meet me. It's really nice.

The experience of the tunnel and a white light feature in all three composite NDE experiences, and the meeting by friends or relatives in Barrett's and Osis's reports of death-bed visions.

10/17 – Another death in old age, apparently at Arles in France:

> I was in the hut, lying on straw. I seemed to be dying of old age ... it was a very gentle and easy death, and when I floated out of my body, I thought I had done well in that lifetime. I don't know why I had that feeling. Death was the best part of the trip for me. After I saw my body, I was soaring higher and higher into the sky and I left my body with no regrets.

The conscious self floats away from its outer casing.

10/18 – A possible violent death:

> When you started to take me to my death experience, I seemed to be in my 50's. But just as I started to experience the cause of death, I found myself back on the cloud ... I saw my body lying on a bed of straw. It looked as though there had been some damage to the head. I really don't know what caused my death. But leaving the body was very pleasant.

A few detached impressions from the same material may help to build a fuller picture:

> Release, looked down at the form wrapped up in blankets [the body]. Buried under an avalanche – I pulled out of my body ... very blue colours everywhere. Flowing ... rippling outward. Rocks crumbled under my hands, and I slid down feet first, facing mountain ... the transition to death was imperceptible ... while still sliding ... no longer in my body ... just lifted away from mountain. Peaceful light, rising sensation. Freedom ... spirit floated free ... dark but calm and excited at the same time. Calmness ... sorry to leave family. Didn't want to leave my body [smallpox aged 10], reluctant to die ... felt sorry for my grieving mother.

The descriptions are not of what most people associate with death – pain, distress and dissolution of consciousness with the physical body, but they do show some remarkable similarities to the OBE and NDE experiences already cited: feelings of release, joy and peace. In all cases the essence of the experience is the separation of the conscious self from the physical body, which was the instrument through which it had operated; it now detached itself and floated away. In the next chapter we shall examine reports of the 'transition' as reported through mediums; this will enable further comparisons to be made and conclusions to be drawn about similarities and differences of experience.

II.

POST-MORTEM DESCRIPTIONS OF BODILY DEATH

Who knows if to be alive is not really to die, and if dying does not count in the nether world as being alive? Who knows if this experience that we call dying is not really living, and if living is not really dying?

EURIPIDES

For what is it to die but to stand naked in the wind and melt into the sun? And what is it to cease breathing but to free the breath from its restless tides, that it may expand and seek God unencumbered?

KAHLIL GIBRAN

The thread of life does not end with death; it is simply transferred to another spool.

'LISZT'

Being divine, you will be at one with the Tao
Being at one with the Tao is eternal
And though the body dies, the Tao will never pass away.

LAO TSU

At this very point some readers may have the uneasy impression that the writer is asking them to take a header into uncharted waters, to commit themselves to the possibility of survival before they have had a chance to assess it. In relation to the death experience we have so far examined reports of those who have been resuscitated and have experiences to report, and then of those who claim to have relived the death of another lifetime; and we have summarised similarities of experiences of the conscious self leaving the physical body and yet maintaining its identity and awareness. We must now examine some examples of 'communications' to see whether any degree of overlap is found in this further source of data.

Beard discusses the problems associated with the sources of communicated material. The intentions of the 'communicator' must be assessed, then the integrity of the medium, and, more importantly, the amount that they themselves may contribute (perhaps unconsciously) to the scripts which are allegedly communicated telepathically. In theory the hypothesis of multiple unconscious personality, which may well account for some of the material, can be extended to cover all cases of so-called telepathic script. However there are circumstances where the hypothesis becomes vastly improbable; for instance in the case of Mirabelli, quoted by Greber:

> To the present Mirabelli has written in 28 different languages while in a trance, setting down his words at a rate of speed which no penman in a normal state can equal. Thus in 15 minutes he wrote out 5 pages of Polish on: 'The resurrection of Poland'; in 20 minutes he wrote 9 pages of Czechish on: 'The Independence of Czechoslavakia'; in 12 minutes, 4 pages of Hebrew on: 'Slander'; in 20 minutes a German composition on: 'Greater Germany, Its Downfall and Restoration'; in 40 minutes, 24 pages of Persian on: 'The Instability of Great Empires'; in 15 minutes 4 pages of Latin on: 'Famous Translations'; in 12 minutes, 5 pages of Japanese on: 'The Russian-Japanese War'; in 22 minutes, 15 pages of Syrian on: 'Allah and his Prophets'; in 15 minutes 8 pages of Chinese on: 'An Apology for Buddha'; in 15 minutes, 8 pages of Syrio-Egyptian

on: 'The Fundamentals of Legislation', and in 32 minutes, 3 pages of hieroglyphics which have not yet been deciphered.

Over 550 professional people observed Mirabelli; his writing was done under the supervision of scholars who took elaborate precautions against fraud.

Further evidence of personal identity and continuity of character in cases where different people are alleged to communicate can be found in the regularity of handwriting, if the means of transcription is automatic writing (where the hand is 'controlled' by a 'discarnate entity'). Some people are convinced of the persistence of the conscious self when details of the alleged communicator's earthly life and connections are given – in some cases these include facts unknown to any person alive; but others explain this on some kind of unfalsifiable (thus metaphysical) Super-ESP hypothesis. In still other cases, where communication is by direct voice trance medium, friends of the alleged communicator may attest that the voice, mannerisms and phrases used are those associated with him during his life; this is necessarily a subjective value judgement, whose conviction cannot be passed on to a third party. Thus the individual himself must assess the exact status of any given script or communication. Beard concludes by saying that:

> the quality of the text is a far better criterion than its mode of production. Seriousness of purpose, watchfulness, wariness, self-discipline and strenuous effort to reach and maintain the right level of consciousness are the hallmarks of the best scriptwriters.

As in the case of the hypnosis material, we would expect to find a broad measure of agreement about the events described in the scripts if they are not to be discounted; we would also expect a good deal of individual variation, but not beyond the stage where the experience (or island animal) seems to be of a different nature altogether. Some find the event incomprehensible and, like Swedenborg's friend Polhem, believe themselves still alive on earth; and there is some suggestion of a slightly different pattern of experience between those who die naturally and those who died suddenly, perhaps in an accident or war. These will be commented on at the appropriate point.

11/1 Dr Karl Novotny died in Vienna in April 1965. Grete Schröder, a former patient and great friend of his had dreamed of a figure appearing to her two days before Novotny's death, and announcing that he was dying. Although she had no previous contact with spiritualism, she was persuaded after Novotny's death to visit a medium; Dr Novotny announced his presence on the first visit. Ultimately the medium agreed to transcribe a series of scripts, which were apparently in Novotny's handwriting. He describes his death as follows:

It was a lovely evening in Spring and I was spending Easter in my country home. I had not been really well for some time, but was not confined to bed. So I agreed to go for a walk with some friends. As we started out, I felt very tired and thought perhaps I ought not to accompany them. However, I forced myself to go. Then I felt completely free and well. I went ahead and drew deep breaths of the fresh evening air, and was happier than I had been for a long time. How was it, I wondered, that I suddenly had no more difficulties, and was neither tired nor out of breath.

I turned back to my companies and found myself looking down at my own body on the ground. My friends were in despair, calling for a doctor and trying to get a car to take me home. But I was well and felt no pains! I couldn't understand what had happened. I bent down and felt the heart of the body lying on the ground. Yes – it had ceased to beat – I was dead. But I was still alive! I spoke to my friends, but they neither saw me nor answered me. I was most annoyed and left them. However, I kept on returning. To say the least it was upsetting to see my friends in tears and yet paying no attention to what I was saying. It was very upsetting, too, to look down at my dead body lying in front of me, while I felt in perfect health.

And there was my dog, who kept whining pitifully, unable to decide to which of me he should go, for he saw me in two places at once, standing up and lying on the ground.

When all the formalities were concluded and my body had been put in a coffin, I realised that I must be dead. But I wouldn't acknowledge the fact; for, like my teacher, Alfred Adler, I did not believe in an afterlife. I visited my university colleagues: but they neither saw me nor returned my greeting. I felt most insulted. What should I do? I went up the hill to where Grete lives. She was sitting alone and appeared very unhappy. But she did not seem to hear me either.

It was no use, I had to recognise the truth. When finally I did so, I saw my dear mother coming to meet me with open arms, telling me that I had passed into the next world – not in words of course, since these only belong to the earth. Even so, I couldn't credit her statement and thought I must be dreaming. This belief continued for a long time. I fought against the truth and was most unhappy.

He adds that the transition would have been much simpler had he believed in the continuance of life after death while still in the body. The following points from the narrative are significant:

    (a) Death made him feel completely free and well; he was neither tired nor out of breath any more.

    (b) He was frustrated at not being able to make contact with his friends or colleagues: they simply did not see him.

    (c) He was able to look down on his own body.

    (d) He could not or would not acknowledge the fact that he was dead.

    (e) When he finally admitted his state he was met by his mother; they communicated telepathically.

11/2 – Bertrand Russell. In view of his opinions on mind, body and death while alive, it is ironic that Russell should ostensibly communicate through Rosemary Brown; any genuine communication constitutes a refutation of his former attitude. But he seems to have been open-minded enough to accept the change:

If revelations come which present a challenge to some of our present ideas, we must accept them and designate their position in the scheme of things. All the formulations in the world will not arrest the tide of advanced thinking from sweeping away false conceptions and false gods.

A few other extracts from 'Russell' will give the reader some flavour of the trenchant writer: 'Is happiness an impossible ideal for all mankind?' he asks.

Perhaps it is, but that should not deter us from cultivating it as widely as we can ... There can be no universal panacea for happiness, which is obvious to anyone who had studied, as I have, the root causes of happiness and its opposite [perhaps a reference to *The Conquest of Happiness?*]. Happiness is a state which is created within us by a very large and very varied number of factors. One man is happy with nothing less than a luxurious mansion and estate and a fleet of fast cars; another man is happy in a monk's cell with the minimum requirements for life. It would seem, therefore, that it is not what we actually possess which provides us with happiness, but our reactions to what we possess.

The essay continues for a further two pages and stresses the importance of zest and interest in life; it contains illustrations which the Russell reader might find characteristic: in distinguishing between things which are meant to bring pleasure rather than pure happiness he remarks 'An alcoholic drink, for instance, can bring pleasure to the palate, but does not necessarily convey any joy to the brain or ease the body.' And in an appendix there is a three-page essay on world politics, which concludes:

> The world needs men of vision and courage, men who will not court popularity at the expense of wise and long-sighted policies, which may not meet with the approval of the impatient who clamour for immediate results. Yet if they do not draw some measure of popularity, they will not be elected in the first place; or, if already elected, they will not remain in power longer than the populace will tolerate. A cool head, a steady hand, and a warm heart: these are the attributes which are perhaps the most essential to the present-day successful politician. Men of such stature are rare: if we find any amongst us, we would be wise to head them.

The theme and the style are by no means alien to Russell's lifetime preoccupations.

As one would expect, 'Russell' is very aware that we may not take him to be the real Russell:

> You may not believe that it is I, Bertrand Arthur William Russell, who am saying these things, and perhaps there is no conclusive proof that I can offer through this somewhat restricted medium. Those with an ear to hear may catch the echo of my voice in my phrases [one of which was 'credulous cretin'], the tenor of my tongue in my tautology; those who do not wish to hear will no doubt conjure up a whole table of tricks to disprove my retrospective rhetoric.

No doubt he would not have believed it himself had he been on earth. In talking of himself he says 'I am far less of a cynic than I was, although I remain to be convinced of many things. I am, however, still very cynical as regards human nature, the more so, perhaps, because I can now see its pettiness in sharper detail.' 'Do I believe in God now?' he asks – 'Many people will want to know my answer. Yes, I now believe without equivocation, with a positive intellectual comprehension which was and is the sole acceptable proposition so far as I am concerned' (no softening discernible here). He says that he has not seen God but has seen Jesus. He was awed by his purity and compassion to such an extent that he felt that he was in the presence of God – 'It is a disconcerting feeling to one who measures things by the intellect,' he adds.

We come now to Russell's description of his own death:

After breathing my last breath in my mortal body, I found myself in some sort of extension of existence that held no parallel, as far as I could estimate, in the material dimension I had recently experienced. I observed that I was occupying a body predominantly bearing similarities to the physical one I had vacated for ever; but this new body in which I now resided seemed virtually weightless and very volatile, and able to move in any direction with the minimum amount of effort. I began to think I was dreaming and would awaken all too soon in that old world, of which I had become somewhat weary, to find myself imprisoned once more in that ageing form which encased a brain that had waxed weary also and did not always want to think when *I* wanted to think.

Several times in my life, I had thought I was about to die; several times I had resigned myself with the best will I could muster to ceasing to be. The idea of B.R. no longer inhabiting the world did not trouble me unduly. I felt the world had had enough of me, and certainly I had had enough of the world. Befitting, I thought, to give the chap (myself) a decent burial. Now here I was, still the same I, with capacities to think and observe sharpened to an incredible degree. I felt earth-life suddenly seemed very unreal almost as though it had never happened. It took me quite a long time to understand this feeling until I realised at last that matter is certainly illusory although it does exist in actuality; the material world seemed now nothing more than a seething, changing, restless sea of indeterminable density and volume. How could I have thought that that was reality, the last word of Creation to Mankind?

Yet it is completely understandable that the state in which a man exists, however temporary, constitutes the passing reality, which is no longer reality when it has passed.

The following points are significant in this case:
(a) B.R. clearly found himself immediately removed from the physical dimension, hence no report of seeing his body.
(b) He notes that he is occupying a second body similar to the physical one (thought of as a prison), but that it has certain new qualities such as weightlessness and freedom of movement.
(c) He perceives that his identity remains, that he is the same conscious self as before, but that his mental and sensory powers have sharpened considerably.
(d) The feeling of the reality of surroundings is relative; matter is seen in its sub-atomic identity. What is real is the environment in which the conscious self currently finds itself.

11/3 – George Hopkins. This is one of 500 cases in Randall's book, all of which are based on tape recordings through a medium called Leslie Flint. The theory is that a discarnate entity is able to use the vocal cords and brain of the medium in order to communicate. This method is explicable on an interactionist hypothesis: normally our conscious self and mind operates through our own physical brain, producing reproductions of thought in the sound waves of speech; in this case it is another mind who is operating in the same way and using someone else's physical equipment – which he no longer has. Unless one accepts some variant of this hypothesis, one has to fall back on the multiple unconscious personality hypothesis. The book contains testimonials by, *inter alia*, a QC who attests that one of the taped voices was that of Lord Birkenhead. The best kind of test would be to invite people who might recognise the taped voices, but without giving them any hints in advance. It could then be ascertained whether the alleged identity corresponded by inviting the participants to identify any of the voices. However, we do know that some sensible, rational people were convinced of the identity of some well-known communicators; the majority, though, as one would expect, are ordinary people like George Hopkins:

I just had a stroke, or seizure, or heart attack. Or something of that sort. As a matter of fact I was harvesting. I felt a bit peculiar, thought it was the sun and went down in the 'edge'. I felt a bit drowsy, a bit peculiar, and must have dozed off. But dear, oh dear, I had such a shock.

I woke up, as I thought. The sun had gone down. And there was me, or what appeared to be me. I couldn't make it out at all, I was that puzzled. I tried to shake myself to wake myself up. I thought, well this is funny. I must be dreaming. I couldn't make head nor tail of it. It never struck me at all that I was dead.

Anyway I found myself walking along the road to the doctor's. I thought well, perhaps he can help me. I knocked on the door but no one answered. I thought well, I shouldn't have thought he would have been out because people were going in the surgery door.

I saw one or two of my old cronies. They all sort of seemed to walk through me. No one seemed to make any comment about me. I thought this a how-de-do.

I stood there for a bit trying to work it out. Then I saw someone hurrying down the road like mad to the doctor's. He rushed in, pushed past me and everybody, and next moment I heard them talking about me. I thought what the hell's wrong? I'm here! I heard them say I was dead!

The doctor went in his car up the road and I thought I don't know about being dead. I can't be dead. I'm here, how the hell can I be dead?

Then I thought to myself 'that's funny, I saw myself lying down. But when you're dead you're done for. You're in heaven or hell. I'm certainly not in heaven and not in hell. I'm 'ere, listenin' to what they're talkin' about.' Gradually it dawned on me that I must be dead.

The next thing I saw was them picking up my body and bringing it back. They put me in the Chapel. 'Oh dear' I thought 'this is the last straw. I must be dead. I've heard about people dying and I've had it now. I suppose the best thing to do is to go and see the parson. He's sure to know something.'

So I went up to the vicarage and waited. I saw him come in and sit at his desk. I noticed that nothing was solid. If I sat in the chair – in a sense I sat and yet I didn't – I didn't feel any weight under me.

I saw the old parson. He came in, walked right past me, went to his desk, started to write letters and doing things. I started talking to him. And he didn't take any notice!

I thought 'He's like the rest of them. I should have thought he would know something.' So I tapped him on the shoulder. Once he turned round as if he thought there was something there, and I thought, 'I'm getting on a bit there', so I tapped him again. He didn't take any notice. Then he got up and sort of shook himself and then I think he was shivering. It was quite a decent sort of morning. I could see no reason why he should have felt cold. Anyway, he didn't seem to realise I was there at all. I thought 'I'm not getting anywhere here.'

Several days later:

They were carrying my body down the old churchyard in the box, and they put me there with the old lady. It suddenly dawned on me about Poll, my wife. I thought 'That's funny. If it's as how I am dead, I should be with her. Where is she?'

I was standing there watching them put this body of mine in the grave. After the ceremony I was walking behind them down the path. There, right in front of me coming up towards me, was my wife!

But not my wife as I had known her, in the last few years of her life. But as I first knew her when she was a young girl. She looked beautiful, really beautiful. And with her I could see one of my brothers who died when he was about seventeen or eighteen. A nice looking boy who was fair-haired. They were laughing and joking and coming up to me. I thought well here I am and there they are, so I'm all right. They're sure to know what to do now.

My wife and brother made a proper fuss of me, saying how sorry they were that they were late. They said 'We knew you hadn't been too well, but we had no idea you were coming as sudden as you were. We got the message but we're sorry we couldn't get here quicker.'

I thought that's odd. How the hell do they get about? I knew I'd got about, but as far as I was concerned I seemed to be walking about, same as I did before, except that everything was much lighter. I didn't seem to have any heaviness of the body, and no more aches and pains like I used to have. They started to try to explain things but they wouldn't say too much. They said I'd got to get sort of adjusted and settled.

The following points emerge:

(a) He was not conscious at the time of death, but 'came to' later in the day.

(b) He was aware of looking down on his body.

(c) He was quite perplexed about his state, which seemed to involve the contradiction of being simultaneously alive and dead.

(d) Except marginally in the case of the vicar, he is unable (like Novotny) to make contact with anyone in the physical world, in spite of the fact that he can see and hear them. He notices that matter is not solid, that his cronies seem to walk through him, and that his body is weightless when he sits down in a chair.

(e) He observes his own burial, suddenly thinking that his wife, also dead, should be with him. Soon after this thought, he notices his wife coming towards him.

(f) He has no more of his former aches and pains.

11/4 – Monsignor Robert Hugh Benson who was a priest and son of an Archbishop of Canterbury, in his lifetime had had certain psychic experiences, which he attributed, in the orthodox way, to some diabolical agency. In the scripts he is apparently concerned to remove some of the preconceptions from those who share his earthly view of the subject. He describes his death as follows:

I suddenly felt a great urge to rise up. I had no *physical* feeling whatever, very much in the same way that physical feeling is absent during a dream, but I was mentally alert, however much my body seemed to contradict such a condition. Immediately I had this distinct prompting to rise, I found that I was actually doing so. I then discovered that those around my bed did not seem to perceive what I was doing, since they made no effort to come to my assistance, nor did they try in any way to hinder me. Turning, I then beheld what had taken place. I saw my physical body lying lifeless on the bed, but here was I, the *real I*, alive and well ... I could see the room quite clearly around me, but there was a certain mistiness about it as though it were filled with smoke very evenly distributed. I looked down at myself wondering what I was wearing in the way of clothes ... I was extremely surprised to find that I had on my usual attire ...

Such knowledge of the spirit world as I had been able to glean from my own experiences instantly came to my aid. I *knew* at once of the alteration that had taken place in my condition; I knew, in other words, that I had 'died'. I knew, too, that I was alive, that I had shaken off my last illness sufficiently to be able to stand upright and look about me. At no time was I in any mental distress, but I was full of wonder at what was to happen next, for here I was, in full possession of my faculties, and, indeed, feeling 'physically' as I had never felt before ... I found myself joined by a former colleague – a priest – who had passed to this life some years before. We greeted each other warmly, and I noticed that he was attired like myself ... I had yet to accustom myself to the newness of things. For you must remember that I had just relinquished a bed of final sickness, and that in casting off the physical body I had also cast off the sickness with it, and the new sensation of comfort and freedom from bodily ills was one so glorious that the realisation of it took a little while to comprehend fully.

The following points are significant here:
(a) He feels himself rising up (cp. floating).
(b) He sees those around his bed, and his own physical body.
(c) He realises that they do not perceive that he is rising out of his bed.
(d) He realises that his conscious self is outside the body, and that he is feeling well, mentally alert; he experiences a feeling of relief from the bodily ills which he had been undergoing.
(e) He does realise that he has died, through his prior 'knowledge' of death. Therefore he does not experience confusion, like Hopkins.
(f) He is met by a former colleague and close friend.

We come, now, to some cases of death as a result of an accident or in war. Crookall, who studied an enormous amount of material, remarks that the person whose death is abrupt is apt to be a good deal more confused than someone who has been ill in bed for some time, and who can therefore reasonably expect to die within a limited period. The risk of war is of a different kind, since death is likely to be sudden, even if expected. Crookall's other significant finding is that, while the natural death of average men is typically followed by a period of sleep, this is rarely the case with sudden death. We noticed how Hopkins seems to have slept a little – an exception for Crookall; the fact that Russell did not see his physical body, but 'immediately' found himself in an unfamiliar body suggests that he too may have slept. This observation may also have a bearing on the NDE: if the majority of people experience a period of sleep (unconsciousness) immediately after death, this might explain why they have nothing to report.

11/5 concerns a Polish pilot shot down in the Second World War:

> Yes, I am shot down and out. I have survived many fights, but not this one, I am wounded, I cannot control the aircraft, it was my leg, you feel the pain, I could not move the controls and I fall, I cannot leave the aircraft, I fall quite consciously. I get up without any pain, I see the observer and gunner, he is hurt too but not so much. The Germans come to find us, they do not see me, I run and hide, but they do not look for me, my friend they take away; I wander about, I feel well and cannot think how I came to crash my aircraft. My leg is healed. I wander about, I go to the French peasants and ask for help, but they do not see me, and I begin to wonder, I am neither hungry nor thirsty nor particularly tired. I begin to see things changing, I see first colours everywhere, it is sunset, or sunrise, and it looks as if the colours take form, it was like a cinema when one picture fades out and another takes its place. I was astounded, I do not know where I am. I ask, I pray, I forget that I have no faith in religion, I pray for help and it comes to me. Someone looking very strange and yet quite like ourselves comes to me, he tells me not to mind the change it is best for all and that I shall be happy in this land. I am very confused, I think I am taken prisoner, then he explains that there are no prisons or prisoners and I feel free again. He took me away and told me to sleep, he touched my eyes and I sleep at once. When I wake he is there still and I am on earth again in the occupied territory with Germans all round. I have come back to my body. I find it difficult to leave it.

The significant points are here:

(a) When he had been wounded he felt the pain, but after death he got up without any; he feels well, is neither hungry nor thirsty and not very tired.

(b) He is not seen by the Germans, but sees them.

(c) His prayer is answered by the arrival of a helper.

(d) It takes him a long time to realise that he is dead; he also finds it hard to leave his body, which he can see.

11/6 – Private Dowding, who tried to help two friends carry his own body down the trench labyrinth to the dressing station:

> When I found that my pals could carry my body without any help, I dropped behind. I just followed in a curiously humble way ... My body went first to the dressing station, and after examination was taken to the mortuary. I stayed near it all night, watching, but without thoughts. It was as if my being, feeling, and thinking had become 'suspended' by some Power outside myself. This sensation came over me gradually as the night advanced. I still expected to wake up in my body again – that is, so far as I expected anything. Then I lost consciousness and slept soundly ... When I awoke my body had disappeared! How I hunted and hunted! It began to dawn on me that something strange had happened, although I still felt I was in a dream and would soon awake. My body had been buried or burned, I never knew which. Soon I ceased hunting for it. Then the shock came! It came without any warning, suddenly. I had been killed by a German shell! I was dead! I was no longer alive! I had been killed, killed, killed. Curious that I felt no shock when I was first driven out of the body. Now the shock came, and it was very real ... How does it feel to be 'dead'? One can't explain because there is nothing in it! I simply felt free and light. My being seemed to have expanded.

Significant points:
- (a) He observes the post-mortem state of his body.
- (b) He is concerned to find his body, and seems to expect to wake up in it.
- (c) It takes him a long time to realise that he has been killed; at first he can only interpret the experience as a dream – the nearest corresponding feeling.
- (d) He felt free and light compared with his physical state.

11/7 – Alf Pritchett. The name given by the communicator was found on the military records. He gave the name of a friend, Billy Smart, who had been killed a few months earlier; this was also checked out. Pritchett was killed near Ypres in 1918:

> I was running forward. Some of the Germans were coming towards me. They rushed straight past me as if they didn't see me! I thought, 'God, this is it.'

But instead of them attacking me or in any way taking any interest in me, they were rushing past me!

I thought, 'Well, Good lord, I can't make this out at all.'

I went on. I can remember running and running and I thought, 'Well, if they're not going to see me I'm certainly not going to bother about them. I'm going to get into a little cubby hole somewhere and get out of it.'

I remember getting into a hole in the ground, created by a bomb, I expect, at some time. I got into this hole, and just crouched down, and thought, 'Well, I'll wait until this shindy's over, and hope for the best, I might get taken prisoner. Who knows?'

I was lying there thinking to myself, 'Well it's damned odd they didn't see me. They *must* have seen me. Yet they went straight past.' And I started to think about it. And I thought, 'Well, I don't know.'

Pritchett then fell asleep, and, on waking up, saw a bright light in front of him; the whole place was illuminated. Then a figure, that of Billy Smart, emerged. He then felt himself getting up and thought he must have been lying in the hole all night and day: 'I ought to be feeling stiff and uncomfortable. But I didn't. I felt as light as a feather. I thought, "Well, something's gone to my head. Perhaps I've got a crack or something."' He was drawn towards his friend and could see that he (the friend) was 'full of vitality, full of life'. Then it dawned on him that his friend was dead: 'When I first saw him, I didn't think of him being dead, although I must have remembered and realised in a way that he had been killed some months before.' His friend stretched out a hand; Pritchett could not make it out when he was assured that he was all right: 'This is damn daft this one. There's something wrong somewhere'; he thinks he may be dreaming. Having got hold of his friend's hand, Pritchett experienced a floating sensation:

There was a sort of floating – I can't say I was doing anything else but floating just with my feet off the ground – going gradually higher and higher as if everything was getting further and further away. And I could see in the distance down below the battlefields, the guns and the lights and the explosions. The war was obviously still going on. And I thought, 'Well, this is a most peculiar dream this is.'

He finds himself in another environment and scoffs at his friend's suggestion that he is dead:

> Don't be silly,' I says, 'How can I be dead? I'm here. I can see all that's going on around me. I can see you. But I know you died some months ago. You got a packet. But how is that ... I don't know. You may be dead, but I'm dreaming.'

Smart explains that he, too, got a 'packet' in a charge, and Pritchett eventually accepts his present state.

Significant points:

(a) He is not aware of having been killed, and interprets the experience as a dream.
(b) The Germans neither see him nor do they take any interest in him.
(c) He sees a bright light out of which emerges the figure of a dead friend.
(d) He experiences a feeling of weightlessness, and has a floating sensation.
(e) He sees the battlefield below.

11/8 – Rupert Brooke. No specific details are given of the location and events leading up to death, but he does describe his immediate reactions:

> I came over in the First World War. It was all very sudden. It seemed as if I was in a body, which no longer seemed, at first, to be the same, and yet in appearance it was the same. I just couldn't understand it. I just didn't realise that I had died.

> Everything seemed in a sense quite natural, and yet the body I was using seemed quite foreign to me. I didn't feel it had any weight. There was a terrible lightness about myself.

> I pinched myself and was startled to find that I did not feel anything. That worried me terribly. Then I had one or two shocks when I realised people didn't see me ... I thought if I can't feel myself when I pinch myself, why should a person see me who was still on earth in the old body? I thought it must be that I am on some vibrational rate, which is not common to Earth, and therefore people can't see me. I could see other people but they couldn't see me. It all seemed so strange.

I remember vividly sitting beside a river and looking at myself, and not seeing myself. I could see no reflection. I thought 'that seems most extraordinary. I have a body and yet it has no reflection'. I couldn't adjust myself at all. I was going round to various people that I had known, trying to tell them that I was alive and well, and they just didn't realise that I was there.

I realised that the reason they couldn't see me was because if my body didn't have a reflection, it couldn't be solid to them. It just couldn't be on the same vibration: it couldn't be the same sort of matter. I had to adjust myself to the fact that I had a body, which was to all outward appearances the same, and yet obviously was not a real body from the point of view of Earth. Therefore I was in what I suppose one would term a spiritual body, and yet I was not particularly spiritual, I was puzzled and bewildered.

The communicator is clearly of an analytical turn of mind: he notices the incongruities of his condition and immediately sets about trying to understand them, even if the result is confusion. The significant points are here:

    (a) He finds himself in a spiritual body with the same appearance as his physical body but apparently with quite different qualities.

    (b) He experiences a feeling of lightness.

    (c) People did not see him, although he could see them.

11/9 – Ted Butler killed by a lorry:

I was crossing the road, and before you could say Jack Robinson, something hit me. It was some lorry that I think had got out of control down the slope. It got me pinned against a wall and I was out. No memory of pain ... It all happened so sudden ... I saw a crowd of people all standing looking down at something. I'ad a look with the crowd and saw someone who looked exactly like me!

At first I didn't realise it was me. I thought 'That's a coincidence. That fellow looks the same as I do. It might be a twin brother.' I didn't cotton on. Then I realised that my wife was there crying her eyes out. She didn't seem to realise that I was standing beside her.

They put my body in an ambulance, and the wife got in, and some nurse. I got in and sat with my wife, and she didn't seem to realise that I was sitting there at all. Then gradually it came on me that that was me lying down there.

I went to the hospital. Of course they put me in the mortuary. I didn't like that at all. So I got out quick and went home. There was the wife, Mrs Mitchen next door, trying to comfort her. I think that was the worst time of the lot.

Then there was the funeral. Of course I went to that. I thought to myself, 'All this fuss and expense for nothing, because here I was.' I thought it's all very touching, but at the same time it all seemed so damn silly, because there I was. Nobody took any notice.

The old parson was standing there reciting away. I thought, 'He should know if anyone knows.' So I went and stood beside him, and kept nudging him with me elbow in the side. He didn't take any notice at all. He just went on with the ritual.

So far as the first part of the narrative is concerned, there are some striking similarities to the OBE experiences of accidents in 9/G7 and 9/G8; only on this occasion there was no return. The other significant points are:
(a) He had no sensation of pain.
(b) He sees a crowd looking at his body.
(c) His wife does not see him.
(d) He does not immediately realise that he is dead and finds the funeral bizarre; he is unable to analyse the implications of his experience.

11/10 Roger Greaves, husband of the medium Helen Greaves, was hit on the head by a snapped cable, and ostensibly never recovered consciousness. His case recalls many of the features of the NDE, and yet it is narrated by someone who actually died:

It was the queerest feeling. I was there, and I wasn't there, if you understand what I mean. I didn't seem to be on the bed at all. I wasn't even inside my body. I could see my body on the bed. I was lying up above it ... A sort of hovering helicopter. I couldn't move. I couldn't go away from that body, and I couldn't get back into it. The oddest sensation. I puzzled about it. Worried, too, because

I thought I'd lost the secret of getting back. I'd done this sort of thing before in dreams. Only I'd always hopped back into the body when I woke up. Now I couldn't seem to wake up. But worse than that I could still hear and see, though not, somehow with my eyes. And I couldn't speak.

There followed a description of the intern and a report of the conversation between him and Greaves's son, Mike, who later confirmed the accuracy of what his father had seen and heard while out of the body. In the NDE the patient returns to tell the story; here this was impossible, and yet the events were confirmed as veridical. Unless the mother was reading the son's mind, the description must have come from Greaves himself. Later she was told of the number of a combination lock known only to her dead husband, which reinforces somewhat the hypothesis that the dead man was communicating.

Correspondences between a large number of Spirits can be studied in Crookall's *The Supreme Adventure*; a huge variety of 'communications' are analysed into what Crookall considers to be the component parts of the death experience, such as the review, the shedding of the body, the sleep, the awakening and the judgement. Our approach of quoting a number of narratives at some length should enable the reader to build up his own picture of typical sequences of events and variations; not all accounts of the review and judgement have been included, as they will form part of a separate study. The implications of this stage of the experience are more moral than perceptual, which is the main focus of the present work. We shall now give some extracts from scripts which form a commentary on, rather than a personal experience of, death.

1. W. Stainton Moses was one of the most famous of the early spiritualist mediums, and his book *Spirit Teachings* was very influential; he was also an Anglican parson and an active member of the SPR.

The spirit-body is the real man; the earth body being only its temporary clothing. The dead body of earth thrown aside leaves the real man with all his individuality untouched ... Immediately on its release from the body, the spirit gathers a new body from its new surroundings, and is clothed with a refined substance like to the flesh it has cast off. The spirit is always encased in a body of matter, as you would say; but matter impalpable to your senses though as perceptible to us as is the grossest material substance to yours.

The statement is consistent with the experience of Rupert Brooke cited above.

2. 'White Eagle', the 'control' of Grace Cook, gives the following description of death:

> Lastly the moment comes when man has to 'die', as you call it. But of course man never dies; the spirit and the soul which clothes it is gently withdrawn, and passes upward through the head. The physical body is left like an empty shell ... the passing out from the physical state is the same as birth into this physical life.

The separation of the conscious self is described, and the body regarded as a husk.

3. 'Zodiac', the 'control' of Winifred Moyes; his teachings are extensively used in Christian Spiritualist churches. Death is described as:

> that point when the real Self slips from that which, to you, seems so vital to your being; and in many cases the sensation is this: though the body may have had its stress, the Spirit has made full preparation and those who are free minister on either side; so, with something like a sigh of relief, that which at one time meant so much is left behind, and gladness and a sense of lightness and freedom tells you that a difficult stage is over ... Whether the consciousness is retained and the spirit passes from the body depends on the individual.

The departure of the 'Self' from the body, and the feeling of lightness, will now be familiar.

4. Two of Jane Sherwood's communicators, E.K. and 'Scott' (who later identified himself as T.E. Lawrence and whose story is told in *Post-Mortem Journal*) discuss death and its relation to life in some detail. *The Country Beyond* is one of the most obvious refutations of the half-baked charge that nothing other than inconsequential nonsense comes from Mediumistic sources.

They start by pointing out that science assumes the indestructibility of matter; their assumption is put in a slightly different relativistic way: that energy is indestructible –

Two systems are interlocked in the organism as you know it. They work together and modify each other and the whole story of the organism is the story of their gradual disentangling. They finally draw away from each other at death. The inorganic body is returned into the downward trend towards entropy and the invisible body of life is set free into the upward trend towards development. Of necessity it goes on to develop higher phases of activity for you must think of this body which is only invisible to you, as being perfectly material on its own plane. Get rid of the notion of the ephemeral stuff of which phantoms are made. Life is simply matter which has been pushed upward into a higher phase of activity and has thus gained the power to exist and continue in another degree of being ... All living energy systems tend towards greater complexity and the consequent creation of higher forms of activity; all dead systems of activity tend towards greater simplicity and end in stagnation. The organism represents the interaction of both these processes and at its death they draw apart.

The normal experience is described by E.K as follows:

As old age comes on the two forms of being represented in the body begin to draw apart. Failing health and failing senses are the symptoms of this withdrawal. The brain tissues often seem to sever connections first before the other organs of the body are ready. This is the meaning of a senile decay. When the final breath is drawn the process of severance is practically complete and rounded off by unconsciousness ... death is a kind of birth and it should proceed with a quiet inevitableness and not be accompanied by pain or distress. Much of the apparent suffering of a death-bed [as we have seen elsewhere] is not consciously felt by the sufferer. His real life is already half retired from the mortal body and neither experiences nor records its pangs. Shakespeare is very near to the literal facts when he speaks of 'shuffling off this mortal coil'.

E.K. then gives an account of his own experiences:

I found myself awake in the transition state of which we have spoken. I thought myself still weak and ill, but I arose from my rest feeling marvellously refreshed and happy and I wandered for a while in the something-nothing surroundings of this queer world and was unable to make any sense of it. The brooding silence drugged me into unconsciousness for a long time, because when I next woke my body felt quite different, no longer frail and weak as I had supposed, but vigorous and ready for anything as though I had suddenly stepped back into youth.

He then describes the review of his life, where his successes and failures became apparent, and comments that his whole religious outlook had to be rethought in the light of the unexpected experience.

'Scott' thinks that the experience of death must vary considerably, since it is governed by the state of mind in which the individual passes over. In his own case he reckoned that he had the maximum difficulties due to 'an attitude of blank unbelief in any future life, a repressed and powerful state, and the shock of a violent death'. In answer to a question about what leaves the body at death, he states:

> What leaves the body is a facsimile of the familiar earth body, built up atom by atom on that body, but functioning in a different world of movement; at a more rapid rate, if you like, or in another dimension of being. What death does is to set this body free from its dependence on physical atoms, molecules and cells so that it can lift into an invisible form of activity.

He goes on to explain that the body, although exactly similar at first, is strikingly different in its powers and make-up (as Brooke discovered); it was being built up during earth life during which it interpenetrated the earth body, and its qualities are the external manifestation of the conscious self that 'felt, desired, reasoned and thought'. And, as the body is based on the physical, it is modified in association with it. On this hypothesis it is this body which is perceived in apparitions on earth, a point which will be further discussed in the concluding chapter.

5. Sir Donald Tovey, the musician, claimed to be one of Rosemary Brown's communicators. He comments that 'considerable uncertainty and no little apprehension arises in the human mind concerning the experience of death and transition to another life' and adds that countless numbers of people have no idea at all of the process by which a soul leaves the physical body. Before describing the experience of the

review of life and the surroundings which the average person finds himself in, he depicts the transitional process:

> I could not myself believe that I had passed through death's door upon my arrival here: the entire experience is so natural, so automatic, so serene, and so imperceptible from the soul aspect. Those who fear some strange and unnerving passing might await, may dismiss their apprehension as totally groundless. At the moment of death, or prior to that instant, consciousness is suspended, and the soul, released from the corpse, floats freely to its new abode ... they come ... their new bodies which are provided for their souls upon cessation of their physical existence. In actual fact, those new bodies already existed although merged with the physical bodies and linked to them by the silver cord, as it is known. At Death, this cord is dissolved or severed, and can be compared with the umbilical cord which is also dispensed with after birth. Death, after all, is like another birth into another world, excepting that one's new body is a counterpart of the lately vacated physical body. When you are born on earth, you enter a body provided by your parents; when you are born into the World of Spirit, you emerge in the counterpart of that body at whatever stage it has reached, excepting that it is without defect: for defects are characteristic of the world of matter and not of the world of spirit.

The descriptions of death, the counterpart body and the transition are very similar, as can be seen, to those of Sherwood's communicators.

6. *The Spirits Book* of Allan Kardec came out as early as 1857, and is remarkable for the range of metaphysical issues which are considered through the medium. In this work, death is defined as the separation of the soul from the body; the soul never loses its individuality. The separation is not painful as the soul is usually unconscious of what is happening to the physical body. This separation takes place when the bonds, which retain the soul to the body, are gradually broken. The spirit finds itself in company with those whom he knew on earth more or less promptly according to the degree of mutual affection, and may go to visit those still incarnated. For a time the spirit may be in a state of confusion whose degree and length varies according to its dependence on bodily things.

7. Seth, the 'control' of Jane Roberts, has an original angle of approach. He points out that there is no separate, indivisible, specific point of

death, that life is a state of becoming, and that death is a part of this process of becoming: the body's elements are constantly dying and renewing themselves. Death is when the conscious self is no longer focused on physical reality, when it has withdrawn from the body, not temporarily as in experiences out of the body, but permanently; the connection between consciousness and the body is severed. After leaving the physical body:

> You will immediately find yourself in another. This is the same kind of form in which you travel in out-of-body projections ... this form will seem physical. It will not be seen by those still in the physical body however, generally speaking. It can do anything that you do now in your dreams. Therefore it flies, goes through solid objects, and is moved directly by your will, taking you, say, from one location to another as you may think of these locations.

As we saw, for instance, with Geddes and in the *Bardo Thodol*, desire creates motion; in Seth's words, 'After death it does not take time to go through space ... space does not exist in terms of distance. This is illusion.' He adds that experiences out of the body can help the conscious self appreciate the true nature of space and time.

Although there are many variations of detail in the foregoing narratives, there are nevertheless a number of strands running through all the accounts: death is the irrevocable separation of the conscious self from the physical body. This conscious self survives intact. It finds itself released from any pain; it experiences feelings of freedom and lightness; and it expresses itself through a body identical in form to the physical body but not subject to its limitations of space and time. Those who do not immediately realise that they are dead but think of themselves still in a physical body are perplexed and confused when they find themselves unheeded by people whom they can see and hear; they may see the physical body, but the conscious self is no longer identified with it. They may then be met by friends or relatives who help them to adjust to their new state and explain what has happened – any paradoxical confusion is resolved.

12.

CONCLUSIONS, IMPLICATIONS AND CHALLENGES

Human reason was not given strong enough wings to part clouds so high above us, clouds which withhold from our eyes the secrets of the other world.

KANT

The body is always in time, the spirit is always timeless and the psyche is an amphibious creature compelled by the laws of man's being to associate itself to some extent with its body, but capable, if it so desires, of experiencing and being identified with its spirit and, through its spirit, with the divine Ground.

ALDOUS HUXLEY

There is only one problem on which all my existence, my peace and my happiness depend: to discover myself in discovering God. If I find Him, I will find myself; and if I find my true self, I will find Him.

MERTON

The person who lives in the light of God is conscious neither of time past nor of time to come, but only of one eternity.

ECKHART

If you merge your life in the Ocean of Life, you will find your life in the Supreme Land of Bliss. When love renounces all limits, it reaches truth.

KABIR

Considered from the external viewpoint of the survivor, the death of the physical body might be taken to signify not simply the absence of the conscious self but its permanent extinction. Thus McQuarrie argues that a person who undergoes death is by that very fact robbed of any possibility of understanding and analysing it. Because the death of others is a loss sustained by those who remain, it is supposed, by analogy, that the deceased himself has sustained a loss of being which cannot by definition be communicated. The basis of such an analogy is the loss of a limb, extended to suggest that loss of the body is loss of being; this results in a state of complete experience-lessness. Within such a framework it is naturally 'ludicrously absurd' to pose the question of how Hume's death appears to him, for 'Hume cannot be both dead and attend to his deadness: if he is dead, then he can do no attending of any kind; if he can attend to anything, he is not dead and hence cannot attend to his deadness.' This elegant logic assumes that conscious experience is only possible through the physical body, hence the nonsense of Hume describing his death. The real nonsense, however, is the limitation of the framework within which the question is posed. On a different basis it can be posed and legitimately answered.

We will now summarise the findings of Part II:

(1) Some people have perceived apparitions of a semi-substantial nature; as an image they resemble the physical body; they sometimes respect physical arrangements in space, but have been known to pass through 'solid' matter; they may be perceived successively from points inside and outside the percipient's physical body; they may on occasion correspond to an ostensible OBE on the part of the agent; apparitions of the dead have been perceived by those dying – usually when the percipient is fully conscious.

(2) People have experienced visual perception from a point ostensibly located outside their physical bodies; they may perceive their own physical body and its immediate surroundings apparently in everyday space; some perceive locations at a distance from their physical body, where they may be perceived by the person whom they ostensibly see in the place where they ostensibly are; in such cases the limits of the body, space and time are transcended – the subject has the impression of being able to travel instantly with his thoughts.

(3) Near-death experiences are an extension of OBEs: the same features are noted, but in this case the ostensible conscious experience is all the more remarkable as the patient is seen by the doctors and nurses to have been physically unconscious during the time when conscious experience is reported; such experience frequently proves to be veridical, that is to say it corresponds with what the doctors and nurses claim occurred while the patient was unconscious; typical feelings associated with the NDE are those of joy, peace, lightness and freedom from pain; the conscious self does not identify itself with the physical body, but feels separated from and indifferent to it; patients are often distressed or disappointed to return to the physical body.

(4) Reports of the death experience include the features noted under NDEs, but this time there is no return to the physical body; existence continues and is manifest through another body (or other bodies); the conscious self feels essentially unchanged, death indicating its permanent separation from the physical body operating in the three-dimensional physical world; the conscious self is now focused on another level of reality/consciousness, probably more real than the physical world left behind.

If we now revert to the appearance of physical death portrayed at the beginning of the chapter we find that, in terms of conscious experience, the data outlined above contradict it completely: the lifeless body gives the impression that no more conscious experience is possible; while, if we accept the general validity and application of our deductions above, there is the probability of a continued and perhaps more real and intense conscious experience after the death of the physical body. In this case the experience of the spectator does not seem to correspond with the experience undergone by the subject. Materialists from Lucretius to Feigl have assumed that the body or brain actually produced consciousness, that perception was confirmed to the view-point of the body by means of the physical senses; and that, consequent-ly, conscious experience and/or the conscious self cannot survive the death and dissolution of the body and brain. No one would disagree that there is an intimate connection between sensation and conscious-ness on the one hand and the brain on the other, but the crucial issue, as James indicated, was the *type* of functional dependence: whether this was productive, as the materialist maintains, thereby implying the cessation of consciousness at death; or whether the dependence is permissive and transmissive, thereby enabling consciousness to oper-ate through the brain during physical life, but not precluding the pos-sibility of conscious experience outside the physical body or even after its death. The hypothesis that the brain produces consciousness and is the only medium of conscious experience fails to account for our four deductions. At this point we might, on logical grounds, dismiss the evidence which does not fit, but we argued earlier that this would be ostrich-like behaviour; equally we would invoke the fraud hypothesis and conjure up an incredibly elaborate conspiracy – this might be an indication of intellectual paranoia; third, we could argue that all the cases are special and do not warrant generalisation – but *the cases are concrete* and therefore must be explained on the basis of some theoret-ical model. Last, we can accept the data as genuine and valid and then attempt to formulate some form of explanatory hypothesis which can account, not only for the supernormal phenomena considered above, but also for the range of normal conscious experience and perception.

It is already clear that the range of materialistic hypotheses is in-adequate. What about the Christian idea of resurrection? Modern apologists argue that such resurrection is superior to the only other postulated alternative of disembodied survival (survival in another sort of body is frequently omitted from this game); first, the notion of disembodied survival is held to be either unintelligible or irrele-vant because the person does not survive in his integral form; and second, the doctrine is held to be consistent with the modern idea which cannot define a person without a form of physical body, and since this physical body will be resurrected, the person will be rec-reated intact. Underlying both arguments is the idea that a person's identity is inseparable from the physical body which, together with the mind, forms a psycho-physical unity. There is, perhaps, an overflow from psychology and medicine here: it has become popular to think of therapy and treatment for illness as directed towards the whole person, and not to regard him simply as a manifestation of a certain set of symptoms, thus treating his body alone. This is admirable and valuable in its field, but should not be allowed to cloud the judgment on the mind/body issue. From our data it appears that the conscious self does not lapse into a long sleep after death, only to be awakened by the last trump; moreover it would appear that judgment of a kind takes place almost immediately and the conscious self is embodied in a much more flexible form. Resurrection cannot logically be ruled out at some later date, but in the light of our data on conscious experience and our knowledge of matter and its transformation, the hypothesis is frankly incredible.

If materialism and resurrection fail to provide adequate explanations of our data, we must look at some form of interactionism, which would be theoretically compatible with two possible metaphysical outlooks: (a) the linear, one-life view postulating survival of consciousness; (b) the cyclical, reincarnationist view indicated at the end of Chapter 10 and held by Plato and Indian philosophers, whereby the soul lives in successive material bodies. It is outside the scope of the present work to discuss the relative merit of these two outlooks; our concern is more directly with the present relationship between the conscious self and the material body. We see interactionism in its earliest form in the primitive outlook, which regarded man as a compound of a material body and a material-like soul capable of leaving the body temporarily in sleep and trance, and finally abandoning it at death – the separation of the soul from the body. This formulation was refined by the Pythagoreans, Orphics and Platonists who considered that the immaterial and rational soul was the immortal essence of man operating through a perishable body – common images were those of the pilot and charioteer. Descartes and his followers developed the contrast between mind as unextended substance interacting with the extended and manifest body. Such a view was based on a now superseded conception of matter, and was regarded as unintelligible by many modern philosophers. Finally, a more sophisticated version of interactionism was advanced by James, Bergson, Schiller and Steiner, whereby the brain was regarded as a transmitter or telephone exchange – it was both the organ of perception and selection and also filter which inhibited an indiscriminate influx of irrelevant sensory data. The physiologists Sherrington, Eccles, Penfield and Pribram have further refined the idea. It is along these lines that we shall attempt to construct a theory which makes the findings of Part II intelligible.

Having outlined the scheme, each point will be elaborated in turn:

(1) We normally perceive through the physical body, with which we identify, and which is limited in space-time.

(2) We can also perceive the world from a point outside the physical body; such perception collapses space-time boundaries; the conscious self may be embodied in an etheric form, perceptible to third parties.

(3) The conscious self operates through a physical body, an etheric body and an astral body; the etheric and astral bodies are mirrors of the physical; separately or interpenetrated they may be manifest as an apparition.

(4) The brain filters, interprets and limits reality.

(5) At physical death the conscious self, etheric body and astral body are severed from the physical body; the unanimated form is subject to organic decay and dispersal, while the conscious self is focused in another dimension of reality.

1. Normal perception

In waking consciousness we perceive and interact with a three-dimensional physical world. We experience our physical body as 'perceptually central', especially with respect to sight and hearing. Our concepts structure and organise the sensory data of which we are aware; our range of perception is very narrow: for instance we can see light wavelengths only between 400 and 700 billionths of a metre. Philosophers advocating a theory of Direct Realism are misled by the impression that external stimuli 'cause' a brain process which is experienced as a perception. This approach ignores the element of interpretation and construction. It is also inclined to make the physical body the fundamental criterion of identity; mental and emotional characteristics are considered secondary to this, if not actually derivative.

2. Perception out of the body

This is, strictly speaking, unthinkable for the materialist, since the conscious self is no longer experiencing the physical body as perceptually central, and indeed claims to observe the physical body from a point of space outside that which it is occupying. If this perception is veridical, which on occasion is indeed the case, then it follows that the physical senses are not essential for conscious experience and perception; this, in turn, suggests that normal perception by the conscious self is *via* rather than because of the physical senses, although the latter must impose physical characteristics and limitations on any perception which is channelled through them. The conscious self finds itself in a dimension where thought and desire collapse space-time; so that to think of a person or place is immediately to be present with the person or at the place. This suggests a possible solution to the discrepancy that not all OBE subjects find themselves in a body: perhaps the same power of imagination which enables instant travel might materialise, that is to say make manifest, the etheric body. When the etheric body is perceived in an apparition (presumably through the etheric 'senses' of the percipient) it is an exact replica of the physical body of the person concerned, and may even be wearing thought-replicas of his clothes. The focus of the conscious self is in another dimension of reality, at least as real as the physical, which permits a greater range of conscious experience.

3. Man as conscious self, physical body, etheric body and astral body

For the materialist, the physical body is the only certain given factor – even the self can be abolished, or exist simply as an epiphenomenon of the brain, with which it perishes at death. We found, above, that the conscious self can have experiences outside the physical body, sometimes in another body which is an exact counterpart of the physical; also that the physical body was not the only instrument of perception. At this point it is well to remind ourselves of the nature of the physical body – a condensed form of energy process in the physical field or 'holomovement'. Its solidity is only apparent.

We saw in Chapter 5 how Steiner explained the relationship of these bodies and their functions. The physical body is the instrument whereby the conscious self manifests and acts in the physical world; its real nature is only apparent when it decays after physical death. During physical life its constituents are constantly being exchanged, and the matter, which it 'contains' at physical death, is dispersed and transformed. The etheric body, an exact likeness of the physical with its own instruments of perception, normally interpenetrates, permeates and flows through the physical, preventing it from decaying irreversibly during physical life; in common with organic nature, the etheric maintains only a vegetable state of life, a sort of sleep. The astral body is the principle of consciousness, and interpenetrates the etheric and physical bodies during waking life. Through the astral, the conscious self may use organs of perception of either of these bodies.

We can now apply this model to our data on apparitions, OBEs and NDEs. In normal waking experience the conscious self operates through the physical body, which is interpenetrated by the etheric and astral bodies. The very fact that these bodies can interpenetrate the physical body suggests that the condensation, which constitutes their form, is in a higher frequency range than tangible matter. Given this interpenetration, it is quite logical that apparitions (the etheric body with or without he astral) should be observed to walk through doors and furniture: *'walking through' is simply interpenetration.*

We now need to draw a further distinction, corresponding, as Steiner suggested, to the difference between dream sleep and deep sleep. In dreams the conscious self is scarcely, if at all, linked with the physical body, but the astral body illuminates the etheric with images. The conscious self is able to 'participate' in dreams created – there is a sense of identity. Bearing in mind that some dreams were found to be out-of-the-body experiences, some close connection might be expected between the two. If we assume that the conscious self is operating through the interpenetrating astral and etheric bodies, we can account for (a) conscious OBEs, (b) cases where there is a reciprocal apparition and OBE, and (c) NDEs (whether transcendental or not). In such cases self-identity no longer coincides with the body, the subject being conscious outside the physical body and sometimes able to observe it and its surroundings. In deep sleep, however, the conscious self and astral body are withdrawn from the etheric and physical bodies. There is no contact with the physical world; if the focus of consciousness is 'elsewhere', there is no way of verifying this physically, as the subject remembers nothing when woken up. This would apply to deep trance mediumship, to those who remember when resuscitated from a cardiac arrest, and to the 8H group of cases where a projection of the etheric body was known to have occurred, but the projector knew nothing beyond having willed the experience before going to sleep. The comparison with dreams suggests one further possibility for resuscitated patients who remember nothing. If one is woken up during rapid-eye-movement sleep, one will have a dream to tell, but not if one is awoken from a deep sleep. Given the fact that we all dream every night, but that we certainly do not remember all our dreams, it is logically possible that any conscious experience during the crisis may have been rendered irretrievable by the intervening deep sleep.

4. The brain filters, interprets and limits reality

This proposition is of the essence of the approaches of Bergson, Schiller and others, including Aldous Huxley and Ornstein, whom we have not mentioned by name. Bergson's telephone exchange image has developed into that of a computer or frequency analyser. In Chapter 6 we examined the selective and reconstructive nature of perception and observation, so that data not relevant to the situation in hand are excluded; selection is reinforced by the associative nature of memory and thought responses. Jung has suggested that the brain is the space-time limitation of the psyche, a proposition which can be interpreted on two levels: it is literally true, as the brain is composed of matter (condensed energy-form) existing in physical space; second, in perceptual terms it limits and adapts reality/normal experience to three-dimensional expression. The body itself is an essential precondition for individual existence. The very word 'individual' signifies something that cannot be seen as two; there is no form or shape without limit, separation and distinction. Even if this is obvious at the physical level, we shall see how further implications unfold from this in terms of the conscious self's widened experience outside the body.

5. Death as severance from the physical body of the conscious self, the etheric body, and the astral body

We saw, above, how the conscious self was able to make temporary excursions from the physical body, and, in the last chapter, how 'communicators' described the separation from this physical envelope. The transition of death, representing the permanent separation of the conscious self from the physical body, is its refocusing in another, wider dimension of reality which is not subject to space-time limitations. The apparent end of consciousness is, in fact, a new beginning.

In Chapter I we saw how the child's sense of identity gradually emerges from a prior unconscious unity with the world. Boundaries are drawn, the separate self is defined; but the definition gives rise to a sense of isolation. The ego realises that it is perceptually the centre of its own universe; in addition, its self-centredness is encouraged by the biological need to survive. Sooner or later, however, the ego realises that the separation and isolation cannot be overcome by attempting to organise the universe round itself – it simply does not have the capacity. James sums up two of the characteristics of religious life as (a) 'the belief that the visible world is part of a more spiritual universe from which it draws its chief significance', and (b) 'that union or harmonious relation with that higher universe is our true end'.

If thought remains at the separative ego level there is little chance of attaining any harmony or peace. Moreover, as Huxley among others has stressed, the harmony requires a change of being, as the insight or knowledge is not simply intellectual apprehension, it is a comprehension through love. Tagore explains the distinction as follows:

> Knowledge is partial, because our intellect is an instrument, it is only part of us, it can give us information about things which can be divided and analysed, and whose properties can be classified, part by part. But Brahma is perfect, and knowledge which is partial can never be a knowledge of him.

> But he can be known by joy, by love. For joy is knowledge in its completeness, it is knowing by our whole being. Intellect sets us apart from the things to be known, but love knows its object through fusion. Such knowledge is immediate and admits no doubt. It is the same as knowing our own selves, only more so.

The knower and the known are one, as Eckhart put it. Unity and harmony are attained and expressed through love; the boundaries of the conscious self are melted and dissolved insofar as love fills and flows through the human being.

Jung, at the age of eighty, spoke of the *magnum opus*: 'to escape in time from the narrowness of its embrace and to liberate our mind to the vision of the immensity of the world, of which we form an infinitesimal part.' These remarks make more sense if we relate them to his experiences following a heart attack in 1944.

He had a series of visions in which he seemed to be floating in space, as it were safe in the womb of the universe – without any sense of separation. He was filled with the highest possible feeling of happiness, sense of eternal bliss. He describes the contrast of these experiences with the drabness of the everyday world:

> It is impossible to convey the beauty and intensity of emotion during those visions. They were the most tremendous things I have ever experienced. And what a contrast the day was: I was tormented and on edge; everything irritated me; everything was too material, too crude and clumsy, terribly limited both spatially and spiritually. It was all an imprisonment, for reasons impossible to divine, and yet it had a kind of hypnotic power, a cogency, as if it were reality itself, for all that I had clearly perceived its emptiness. Although my belief in the world returned to me, I have never since entirely freed myself of the impression that this life is a segment of existence which is enacted in a three-dimensional boxlike universe especially set up for it.

The following passage from Plotinus, on the casting of the wings or the enchainment in the body, makes an interesting comparison with Jung:

> There comes a stage when they descend from the universal to become partial and self-centred; in a weary desire of standing apart they find their way, each to a place of its very own. This state long maintained, the Soul is a deserter from the totality; its differentiation has severed it; its vision is no longer set in the Intellectual; it is a partial thing, isolated, weakened, full of care, intent upon the fragment; severed from the whole, it nestles in one form of being; for this it abandons all else, entering into and caring for only the one, for a thing buffeted about by a world full of things: thus it has drifted away from the universal and, by an actual presence, it administers the particular.

Both passages complain of the limitations and imprisonment of separate existence, compared with a transcendent sense of bliss or unity where the separate self is absorbed. Like Plato, Plotinus thought that the task of man was to regain the primordial sense of unity which the soul had deserted. His efforts are related elsewhere, and typify the implications of mysticism outlined by Underhill:

The abolition of individuality; of that hard separateness, that 'I, Me, Mine' which makes of man a finite isolated thing. It is essentially a movement of the heart, seeking to transcend the limitations of the individual standpoint and to surrender itself to the Ultimate Reality; for no personal gain, to satisfy no transcendental curiosity, but purely from an instinct of love.

Laski divides statements describing experiences of 'ecstasy' into feelings of loss and gain. She found feelings of loss of difference, time, place, limitation, worldliness, desire, sorrow, sin, words and/or images, and sense. And the feelings of gain were: 'unity and/or everything, timelessness, and ideal place (heaven), release, a new life, another world, satisfaction, joy, salvation, perfection, glory, contact, mystical knowledge, new knowledge, and knowledge of identification.' Other more discursive analyses of these qualities can be found in James and Happold. Two of Laski's respondents express their feelings of release from boundaries and limitations as follows:

A) In a curious way, a sort of merging into experience – the hard lines round one's individuality are gone, one flows over them – essentially a *moment* of complete peace – the ultimate trademark is a feeling that this does touch reality – allied to this thing of completeness, wholeness, other forms of so called reality are not wholly real, only particles of reality.

B) A complete absence of a sense of specific time and place, complete involvement of one's whole being, at the same time a loss of the sense of being yourself.

The dissolution of the boundaries of the self is accompanied by a heightened sense of reality, making the experience absolutely convincing and self-authenticating for the individual; but this very dissolution of boundaries, of separate selfhood, of space and time, makes it impossible for the experience to be conveyed in words: the meaning overflows the words, which stand revealed as inadequate abstractions and representations; they try to encapsulate the experience, but only succeed in making it static and depriving it of its immediate reality.

Sometimes, as with Bucke's experience of 'cosmic consciousness', the intuitive knowledge includes the perception that the universe is not composed of dead matter but is a living presence. He goes on:

I became conscious in myself of eternal life. It was not a conviction that I would have eternal life, but a consciousness that I possessed eternal life then; I saw that all men are immortal ... that the foundation principle of the world is what we call love.

If Bucke draws the philosophical conclusion from his experience, Schweitzer reminds us that an intellectual mysticism is not enough: the tree must be known by its fruits in ethical mysticism. The universe is not interpreted as a living presence, but Schweitzer contends that 'all Being is life, and ... in loving self-devotion to other life we realise our spiritual union with infinite Being'. Thus the union is achieved both in contemplation and action, although each day is a renewed attempt to approximate to this ideal while we exist in a world of time and flux: even our experience of the timeless is transient.

After our brief excursus into mysticism, we have arrived at the point of judgment. The writer can take the reader no further. As already indicated, the data surveyed are not in themselves coercive or conclusive proof that the conscious self survives bodily death; they are, nevertheless, concrete pointers which demand a coherent and comprehensive explanation. If reports of apparitions, OBEs, NDEs and death experiences are accepted as valid evidence, then materialistic theories of mind have only a very limited application – to normal processes in the explicate order of appearances. The materialistic analysis of the phenomenon of death is highly misleading: apparent loss of consciousness is interpreted from the outside as extinction, while from the inside conscious experience may well be continuing in an enhanced state, released from the cramping confines of space-time, the physical body, and perhaps even the separate ego. In this context, Hume's experiencing of his own death is no longer such a 'ludicrously absurd' question. We may reasonably expect life and light at the end of the tunnel.

BIBLIOGRAPHY

Adam, James, *The Religious Teachers of Greece*, Edinburgh, T. and T. Clark, 1908.

Aldwinkle, Russell, *Death in the Secular City*, London, Allen & Unwin, 1972.

Alger, W. R., *A Critical History of the Doctrine of a Future Life*, New York, Middleton, 1871.

Aurelius, Marcus, *Meditations*, London, Collins.

Ayer, Sir A. J., *Language, Truth and Logic*, London, Gollancz, 1946.

Ayer, Sir A. J., *Probability and Evidence*, London, Macmillan, 1972.

Bacon, Francis, *Novum Organum*, London, Longmans, 1870.

Badham, Paul, *Christian Beliefs about Life after Death*, London, SPCK, 1978.

Badham, Paul and Badham, Linda, *Immortality or Extinction*, London, Macmillan, 1982.

Bailey, L. R., *The Biblical Perspective on Death*, New York, Fortress Press, 1979.

Baillie, John, *And the Life Everlasting*, London, Oxford University Press, 1934.

Baird, A. T., *A Casebook for Survival*, London, Psychic Press.

Barrett, Sir William, *Death-Bed Visions*, London, Psychic Press, 1926.

Barth, Karl, *Dogmatics in Outline*, London, SCM Press, 1966.

Bartlett, Sir Frederic, *Thinking*, London, Allen & Unwin, 1958.

Beard, Paul, *Survival of Death,* London, Psychic Press, 1966.

Beard, Paul, *Living On,* London, Allen & Unwin, 1980.

Beloff, John, *The Existence of Mind,* London, MacGibbon & Kee, 1962.

Berdyaev, Nicolas, *The Destiny of Man,* London, Bles, 1937.

Bergson, Henri, *Les deux sources de la morale et de la religion,* Paris, Presses Universitaires de France, 1932.

Bergson, Henri, *Matiere et memoire,* Paris, Presses Universitaires de France, 1939.

Bergson, Henri, *The Creative Mind,* New York, Citadel Press, 1946.

Beveridge, W. I. B., *The Art of Scientific Investigation,* London, Science Book Club, 1955.

Blackmore, Susan, *Parapsychology and Out-of-the-Body Experiences,* London, Transpersonal Books, 1978.

Bohm, David, *Wholeness and the Implicate Order,* London, Routledge & Kegan Paul, 1980.

Borgia, Anthony, *Life in the World Unseen,* London, Psychic Press, 1974.

Borst, C. V. (ed.), *The Mind/Brain Identity Theory,* London, Macmillan, 1970.

Bowra, Sir Maurice, *The Greek Experience,* London, Sphere, 1973.

Bradley, F. H., *Appearance and Reality,* London, Oxford University Press, 1893.

Brandon, S. G. F., *Man and his Destiny in the Great World Religions,* Manchester University Press, 1962.

Brandon, S. G. F., *The Judgment of the Dead,* London, Weidenfeld & Nicolson, 1967.

Breasted, J. H., *The Development of Religion and Thought in Ancient Egypt,* London, Hodder & Stoughton, 1912.

Broad, C. D., *The Mind and its Place in Nature,* London, Kegan, Paul, Trench & Trübner, 1925.

Broad, C. D., *Religion, Philosophy and Psychical Research,* London, Routledge & Kegan Paul, 1953.

Broad, C. D., *Lectures on Psychical Research*, London, Routledge & Kegan Paul, 1962.

Brown, Rosemary, *Immortals at my Elbow*, London, Bachman & Turner, 1974.

Burnet, John, *Early Greek Philosophy*, Edinburgh, A. & C. Black, 1892.

Burt, Sir Cyril, *Psychology and Psychical Research*, London, Society for Psychical Research, 1968.

Burt, Sir Cyril, *ESP and Psychology* (ed. Anita Gregory), London, Weidenfeld & Nicolson, 1975.

Burtt, E.A., *The Metaphysical Basis of Modern Science*, London, Routledge & Kegan Paul, 1924.

Butterfield, Herbert, *The Origins of Modem Science*, London, Bell, 1949.

Calvin, John, *Commentary on I Corinthians*, Edinburgh, Oliver & Boyd, 1960.

Capra, Fritjof, *The Tao of Physics*, London, Fontana, 1976.

Charles, R. H., *The Doctrine of a Future Life*, London, A. and C. Black, 1899.

Charles, R. H. (ed.), *The Book of Enoch*, London, Macmillan, 1903.

Cicero, Marcus Tullius, *Two Essays on Old Age*, London, Macmillan, 1903.

Crawshay-Williams, Rupert, *The Comforts of Unreason*, London, Kegan, Paul, Trench & Trübner, 1947.

Crawley, A. E., *The Idea of the Soul*, London, A. and C. Black, 1909.

Crookall, Robert, *The Study and Practice of Astral Projection*, London, Aquarian Press, 1960.

Crookall, Robert, The Supreme Adventure: Analyses of Psychic Communications, *Cambridge, James Clarke, 1961.*

Crookall, Robert, *More Astral Projections*, London, Aquarian Press, 1964.

Crookall, Robert, *Intimations of Immortality*, Cambridge, James Clarke, 1965.

Crookall, Robert, *What Happens When You Die*, Gerrards Cross, Colin Smythe, 1978.

Cross, Sir Rupert, *On Evidence*, London, Butterworth, 1967.

D'Arcy, M. C., *The Nature of Belief*, London, Sheed & Ward, 1934.

Dampier-Whetham, Sir W. C. D., *A History of Science*, Cambridge University Press, 1950.

Darwin, Charles, *The Descent of Man*, London, John Murray, 1901.

De Brath, Stanley, *Psychical Research and Religion*, London, Methuen, 1925.

Descartes, Rene, *Philosophical Writings*, London, Nelson edn, 1954.

Donnelly, John (ed.), *Language, Metaphysics and Death*, New York, Fordham, 1978.

Dobzhansky, Theodosius, *The Biology of Ultimate Concern*, London, Fontana, 1971.

Dodds, E. R., *The Greeks and the Irrational*, Berkeley, University of California Press, 1949.

Dowding, Air Chief Marshal Lord, *Many Mansions*, London, Rider, 1976.

Draper, J.W., *History of the Conflict between Religion and Science*, New York, King, 1875.

Draper, J. W., History of the Intellectual Development of Europe *(2 vols)*, *London, Bell, 1914.*

Ducasse, C. J., *Nature, Mind and Death*, Illinois, Open Court, 1951.

Ebon, Martin, *The Evidence for Life After Death*, New York, Signet, 1977.

Eccles, Sir John, *Facing Reality*, Heidelberg, Springer, 1970.

Eccles, Sir John and Popper, Sir Karl, *The Self and its Brain*, Heidelberg, Springer International, 1977; London, Routledge & Kegan Paul, 1984.

Eddington, Sir Arthur, *The Nature of the Physical World*, Cambridge University Press, 1928.

Edwards, David L., *The Last Things Now*, London, SCM Press, 1969.

Eliade, Mircea, *No Souvenirs*, London, Routledge & Kegan Paul, 1978.

Evans-Wentz, W. Y., *The Tibetan Book of the Dead*, London, Oxford University Press, 1960.

Ey, Henri, *Consciousness*, Indiana University Press, 1978.

Evans-Pritchard, Sir E. E., *Theories of Primitive Religion*, London, Oxford University Press, 1965.

Eysenck, H. J., *Sense and Nonsense in Psychology*, London, Penguin, 1970.

Feifel, Hermann, *The Meaning of Death*, New York, McGraw-Hill, 1959.

Ferguson, Marilyn, *The Aquarian Conspiracy*, London, Routledge & Kegan Paul, 1981.

Findlay, Arthur, *On the Edge of the Etheric*, London, Psychic Press, 1931.

Fiore, Edith, *You Have Been Here Before*, London, Sphere, 1980.

Fiore, Charles and Landsburg, Alan, *Death Encounters*, New York, Bantam, 1979.

Firth, Raymond, *Tikopia, Ritual and Belief*, London, Allen & Unwin, 1957.

Flew, Antony, *A New Approach to Psychical Research*, London, Watts, 1953.

Flew, Antony (ed.), *Body, Mind and Death*, London, Macmillan, 1964.

Flew, Antony, *An Introduction to Western Philosophy*, London, Thames & Hudson, 1971.

Frazer, Sir J. G., *The Belief in Immortality*, vol. 1, London, Macmillan, 1913.

Frazer, Sir J.G., *The Golden Bough* (12 vols), London, Macmillan, 1937.

Freud, Sigmund, *Collected Papers*, vol. IV, London, Hogarth, 1925.

Gauld, Alan, *The Founders of Psychical Research*, London, Routledge & Kegan Paul, 1968.

Gooch, Stan, *The Paranormal*, London, Wildwood House, 1978.

Greaves, Helen, *The Dissolving Veil*, London, Neville Spearman, 1967.

Greber, Johannes, *Communication with the Spirit World of God*, New York, Greber Foundation, 1932.

Green, Celia, *Lucid Dreams*, London, Hamish Hamilton, 1968.

Green, Celia, *Out-of-the-Body Experiences*, Oxford, Institute of Psychophysical Research, 1968.

Green, Celia and McCreery, Charles, *Apparitions*, London, Hamish Hamilton, 1975.

Grof, Stanislas and Halifax, Joan, *The Human Encounter with Death*, London, Souvenir Press, 1978.

Gurney, Edmund, Myers, F. W. H., and Podmore, Frank, *Phantasms of the Living* (2 vols), London, Trübner, 1886.

Haldane, J. B. S., *Science and Life*, London, Pemberton, 1968.

Hampe, J. C., *To Die is Gain*, London, Darton, Longman & Todd, 1979.

Happold, F. C., *Mysticism*, London, Penguin, 1963.

Hardy, Sir Alister, *The Divine Flame*, London, Collins, 1966.

Hardy, Sir Alister, *The Biology of God*, London, Cape, 1975.

Hardy, Sir Alister, *The Spiritual Nature of Man*, Oxford, Clarendon Press, 1979.

Harrison, Jane, *Prolegomena to the Study of Greek Religion*, Cambridge University Press, 1903.

Hart, Hornell, Six Theories about Apparitions, *London*, Proceedings of the Society for Psychical Research, *vol. 50, Part 185, May 1956*.

Hart, Hornell, *The Enigma of Survival*, London, Rider, 1959.

Hastings, James (ed.), *Encyclopaedia of Religion and Ethics* (12 vols), Edinburgh, T. and T. Clark, 1913.

Haufing, O. (ed.), *Fundamental Problems in Philosophy*, Oxford, Blackwell, 1972.

Hick, John, *Death and Eternal Life*, London, Collins, 1976.

Hinton, John, *Dying*, London, Penguin, 1967.

Homer, *Odyssey*, London, Sidgwick & Jackson edn, 1980.

Hook, Sidney (ed.), *Dimensions of Mind*, New York, Collier, 1961.

Hume, David, *Essays*, London, Grant Richards, 1903.

Hussey, E., *The Presocratics*, London, Duckworth, 1972.

Huxley, Aldous, *The Doors of Perception*, London, Chatto & Windus, 1954.

Huxley, Sir Julian, *Religion without Revelation*, London, Watts, 1931.

Inge, W. R., *Outspoken Essays*, London, Longmans, 1933.

Jacobson, Nils, *Life Without Death?*, London, Turnstone, 1974.

Jackson Knight, W. F., *Elysion*, Rider, 1970.

James, William, *Principles of Psychology* (2 vols), New York, Macmillan, 1890.

James, William, *Human Immortality*, London, Constable, 1899.

James, William, *Talks to Teachers*, London, Longmans, 1899.

James, William, *The Varieties of Religious Experience*, London, Longmans, 1903.

James, William, *Papers on Philosophy*, London, Dent, 1917.

James, William, *Letters* (ed. Elizabeth Hardwick), New York, Farrar, Straus & Cudahy, 1960.

Jeans, Sir James, *The Mysterious Universe*, Cambridge University Press, 1930.

Jeans, Sir James, *The New Background of Modern Science*, Cambridge University Press, 1933.

Johnson, Raynor C., *The Imprisoned Splendour*, London, Hodder & Stoughton, 1953.

Johnson, Raynor C., *Nurslings of Immortality*, London, Hodder & Stoughton, 1957.

Journal of the Society for Psychical Research.

Journal of the American Society for Psychical Research.

Journal of the Churches' Fellowship for Psychic and Spiritual Studies.

Jung, C. G., *Memories, Dreams, Reflections* (ed. Aniela Jaffé), London, Routledge & Kegan Paul, 1963.

Jung, C. G., *Collected Works*, vol. 8 (*The Structure and Dynamics of the Psyche*), London, Routledge & Kegan Paul, 1969.

Jung, C. G., *Collected Works*, vol. 10 (*Civilisation in Transition*), London, Routledge & Kegan Paul, 1970.

Jung, C. G., *Collected Works*, vol. 11 (*Psychology and Religion. East and West*), London, Routledge & Kegan Paul, 1970.

Jung, C. G., *Letters*, vol. I (1906-1950), vol. II (1950-1961), London, Routledge & Kegan Paul, 1973 and 1976.

Kant, Immanuel, *Dreams of a Spirit-Seer*, New York, Sonnenschein, 1900.

Kant Immanuel *Critique of Pure Reason* (tr. Meiklejohn), London, Bell, 1917.

Kardec, Allan, *The Spirits Book,* Lake, Sao Paulo, Brazil.

Kenny, Anthony, *Wittgenstein,* London, Penguin, 1973.

Kirk, G. S. and Raven, J. E., *The Presocratic Philosophers,* Cambridge University Press, 1957.

Kübler-Ross, Elisabeth, *On Death and Dying,* London, Tavistock, 1970.

Kuhn, Thomas J., *The Structure of Scientific Revolutions,* Chicago University Press, 1970.

La Mettrie, Jean de, *L'Homme machine* (tr. A. Vartanian), Princeton University Press, 1960.

Lange, F., *History of Materialism* (tr. T. C. Thomas), London, Trübner, 1877.

Lamont, Corliss, *The Illusion of Immortality,* London, Watts, 1952.

Laski, Marganita, *Ecstasy,* London, Cressett Press, 1961.

Leith, John H. (ed.), *Creeds of the Churches,* Oxford, Blackwell, 1973.

LeShan, Lawrence, *The Medium, the Mystic, and the Physicist,* London, Turnstone, 1966.

LeShan, Lawrence, *Alternate Realities,* London, Sheldon, 1976.

Lewis, H. D., *The Elusive Mind,* London, Macmillan, 1970.

Lewis, H. D., *The Self and Immortality,* London, Macmillan, 1973.

Lewis, H. D., *Persons and Life after Death,* London, Macmillan, 1978.

Locke, John, *An Essay on Human Understanding,* London, Routledge & Kegan Paul, 1923.

Lodge, Sir Oliver, *The Survival of Man,* London, Methuen, 1909.

Lodge, Sir Oliver, *Raymond,* London, Methuen, 1916.

Levi-Strauss, Claude, *The Savage Mind,* London, Weidenfeld & Nicolson, 1974.

Levy-Bruhl, Lucien, *Primitive Mentality,* London, 1923.

Lucretius, *On the Nature of Things,* London, Bell edn, 1933.

Luther, Martin, *Table Talk* (ed. Tippert), New York, Fortress Press edn, 1967.

Luther, Martin, *Commentary on I Corinthians, (Works,* vol. 28), St Louis, Concordia, 1973.

McDougall, William, *Body and Mind,* London, Methuen, 1911.

Malinowski, B., 'The Role of Magic and Religion', in Lessa, W. H. and Vogt, E. Z., *A Reader in Comparative Religion,* New York, Harper & Row, 1965.

Marchant, Sir James (ed.), *Immortality,* London, Putnam, 1924.

Maslow, Abraham, *Motivation and Personality,* New York, Harper & Row, 1954.

Matthews, W. R., Psychical Research and Theology, London, Proceedings of the Society for Psychical Research, *vol. 46, Part 151, 1940.*

Mbiti, J. S., *African Religions and Philosophy,* London, Heinemann, 1969.

Mbiti, J. S., *Introduction to African Religion,* London, Heinemann, 1975.

Mitchell, Janet Lee, *Out-of-the-Body Experiences, A Handbook,* London, McFarland & Co., 1981.

Moody, Raymond, *Life after Life,* New York, Mockingbird Books, 1975.

Moody, Raymond, *Reflections on Life after Life,* New York, Mockingbird Books, 1977.

Moore, E. Garth, *Survival, A Reconsideration,* London, Society for *Psychical* Research, 1966.

Moses, Rev. W. Stainton, *Spirit Teachings,* London, Spiritualist Press, 1949.

Moss, Thelma, *The Probability of the Impossible,* London, Granada, 1969.

Muldoon, Sylvan and Carrington, Hereward, *The Projection of the Astral Body,* London, Rider, 1929.

Murray, Gilbert, *Five Stages of Greek Religion,* London, Watts, 1935.

Myers, F. W. H., Human Personality and its Survival of Bodily Death, *London, Longmans, 1927.*

Naville, Edouard, *The Old Egyptian Faith,* London, Williams & Norgate, 1909.

Neumann, Erich, *The Origins and History of Consciousness,* London, Routledge & Kegan Paul, New York, Bollingen, 1954.

Onians, R. B., *The Origins of European Thought,* Cambridge University Press, 1954.

Ornstein, Robert E., *The Psychology of Consciousness*, London, Penguin, 1975.

Osis, Karlis, *Deathbed Observations By Physicians and Nurses*, New York, Parapsychological Foundation, 1961.

Parrinder, Geoffrey, *African Traditional Religion*, London, SPCK, 1973.

Parrinder, Geoffrey, *The Indestructible Soul*, London, Allen & Unwin, 1973.

Pearce-Higgins, J. D., and Stanley Whitby, G., *Life, Death and Psychical Research*, London, Rider, 1973.

Penfield, Wilder, *The Mysteries of Mind*, Princeton University Press, 1975.

Petrie, Sir Flinders, *Religious Life in Ancient Egypt*, London, Constable, 1924.

Piaget, Jean, *The Child's Conception of Causality*, London, Kegan Paul, 1930.

Piaget, Jean, *The Child's Conception of Time*, London, Routledge & Kegan Paul, 1969.

Pitcher, George, *Berkeley*, London, Routledge & Kegan Paul, 1977.

Plato, *The Last Days of Socrates*, London, Penguin, 1954.

Plato, *The Republic*, London, Penguin edn, 1955.

Plato, *Timaeus and Critias*, London, Penguin edn, 1965.

Plato, *The Laws*, London, Penguin edn, 1970.

Plotinus, *The Enneads* (ed. Stephen Mackenna), London, Faber & Faber, 1962.

Polanyi, Michael, *The Study of Man*, London, Routledge & Kegan Paul, 1959.

Popper, Sir Karl, *The Logic of Scientific Discovery*, London, Hutchinson, 1959.

Popper, Sir Karl, *Conjectures and Refutations*, London, Routledge & Kegan Paul, 1969.

Popper, Sir Karl, *Unended Quest*, London, Collins/Fontana, 1976.

Popper, Sir Karl, and Eccles, Sir John (q.v.), *The Self and its Brain*, Heidelberg, Springer International, 1977; London, Routledge & Kegan Paul, 1984.

Pribram, Karl, *Languages of the Brain*, London, Prentice Hall, 1971.

Price, H. H., Survival and the Idea of Another World, *London*, Proceedings of the Society for Psychical Research, *vol. 50, Part 180, 1953*.

Pringle-Pattison, A. S., *The Idea of Immortality,* Oxford, Clarendon Press, 1922.

Radhakrishnan, Sir S., *Eastern Religions and Western Thought,* London, Oxford University Press, 1939.

Radhakrishnan, Sir S., *An Idealist View of Life,* London, Allen & Unwin, 1961.

Randall, John, L., *Parapsychology and the Nature of Life,* London, Souvenir Press, 1975.

Randall, Neville, *Life after Death,* London, Hale, 1975.

Rawlings, Maurice, *Beyond Death's Door,* London, Sheldon, 1979.

Ring, Kenneth, *Life at Death,* New York, Coward, McCann & Geoghagan, 1980.

Roberts, Jane, *Seth Speaks,* London, Bantam, 1974.

Rogo, D. Scott, 'Aspects of Out-of-the-Body Experiences', London, *Society for Psychical Research, Journal,* vol. 48, pp. 329-35, 1976.

Rohde, Erwin, Psyche, The Cult of Souls and Belief in Immortality among the Greeks. *London, Kegan, Paul, Trench & Trübner, 1925.*

Rowell, Geoffrey, *Hell and the Victorians,* Oxford, Clarendon Press, 1974.

Russell, Bertrand, *The Analysis of Mind,* London, Allen & Unwin, 1921.

Russell, Bertrand, *The Scientific Outlook,* London, Allen & Unwin, 1931.

Russell, Bertrand, *History of Western Philosophy,* London, Allen & Unwin, 1946.

Russell, Bertrand, *Human Knowledge – Its Scope and Limits,* London, Allen & Unwin, 1948.

Russell, Bertrand, *Portraits from Memory,* London, Allen & Unwin, 1956.

Russell, Bertrand, *Why I am not a Christian,* London, Allen & Unwin, 1967.

Ryle, Gilbert, *The Concept of Mind,* London, Peregrine, 1963.

Salmond, S. D. F., *The Christian Doctrine of Immortality,* Edinburgh, A. and C. Black, 1899.

Sabom, Michael, *Recollections of Death,* London, Harper & Row, 1982.

Schiller, F. C. S., *Riddles of the Sphinx,* London, Swan Sonnenschein, 1891.

Schiller, F. C. S., *Humanism*, London, Macmillan, 1903.

Schmidt, R. R., *The Dawn of the Human Mind*, London, Sidgwick & Jackson, 1936.

Schmithals, Walter, *An Introduction to the Theology of Rudolf Bultmann*, London, SCM Press, 1967.

Schopenhauer, Arthur, *Essays and Aphorisms*, London, Penguin, 1970.

Schumacher, E. F., *Guide for the Perplexed*, London, Cape, 1977.

Schweitzer, Albert, *The Decay and Restoration of Civilisation*, London, A. and C. Black, 1923.

Schweitzer, Albert, *An Anthology* (ed. Charles Joy), London, A. and C. Black, 1952.

Sheldrake, Rupert, *A New Science of Life*, London, Granada, 1983.

Sherrington, Sir Charles, *Man on his Nature*, Cambridge University Press, 1942.

Sherwood, Jane, *The Country Beyond*, London, Neville Spearman, 1969.

Shibles, Warren, *Death*, Wisconsin, Lang Press, 1974.

Smythies, J. R., *Analysis of Perception*, London, Routledge & Kegan Paul, 1956.

Smythies, J. R. (ed.), *Brain and Mind*, London, Routledge & Kegan Paul, 1965.

Smythies, J. R. (ed.), *Science and ESP*, London, Routledge & Kegan Paul, 1923.

Steiner, Rudolf, *Theosophy*, London, Rudolf Steiner Press, 1922.

Steiner, Rudolf, *Goethe the Scientist*, London, Rudolf Steiner Press, 1950.

Steiner, Rudolf, *Occult Science*, London, Rudolf Steiner Press, 1963.

Stephen, Sir Leslie, *English Thought in the Eighteenth Century* (2 vols), New York, Harbinger Books, 1962.

Stevenson, Ian, *Twenty Cases Suggestive of Reincarnation*, New York, American Society for Psychical Research, 1966.

Stout, G. F., *Mind and Matter*, Cambridge University Press, 1931.

Streeter, B. H., *Immortality*, London, Macmillan, 1917.

Swedenborg, Emanuel, *Arcana Caelestia* (12 vols), London, Swedenborg Society, 1909.

Swedenborg, Emanuel, *Heaven and Hell*, London, Swedenborg Society, 1958.

Swedenborg, Emanuel, *Spiritual Diary* (6 vols), London, Swedenborg Society, 1962.

Swedenborg, Emanuel, *Divine Love and Wisdom*, London, Swedenborg Society, 1969.

Taylor, A. E., *Elements of Metaphysics*, London, Methuen, 1924.

Taylor, A. E., *Plato, The Man and his Work*, London, Methuen, 1948.

Tertullian, *De Resurrectione Camis* (tr. A. Souter), London, Macmillan, 1922.

Thakur, Shivesh C. (ed.), *Philosophy and Psychical Research*, London, Allen & Unwin, 1976.

Tolstoy, Leo, *The Death of Ivan Ilyich*, London, Penguin edn, 1969.

Toynbee, Arnold, *Experiences*, Oxford University Press, 1969.

Toynbee, Arnold, *Surviving the Future*, Oxford University Press, 1971.

Toynbee, Arnold (ed.), *Man's Concern with Death*, London, Hodder & Stoughton, 1968.

Toynbee, Arnold (ed.), *Life after Death*, London, Weidenfeld & Nicolson, 1976.

Toynbee, Arnold and Ikeda, Daisaku, *Choose Life*, Oxford University Press, 1976.

Trotter, Wilfred, *The Instincts of the Herd in Peace and War*, London, Benn, 1916.

Tylor, Sir Edward, *Primitive Culture* (2 vols), London, John Murray, 1903.

Tyrrell, G. N. M., *Apparitions*, London, Duckworth, 1953.

Underhill, Evelyn, *Mysticism*, London, Methuen, 1911.

Underwood, Peter, and Wilder, Leonard, *Lives to Remember*, London, Hale, 1975.

Vesey, G. N. A. (ed.), *Body and Mind*, London, Allen & Unwin, 1964.

Voltaire, François-Arouet de, *Lettres Philosophiques*, Oxford, Blackwell, 1946.

Voltaire, François-Arouet de, *Dictionnaire Philosophique*, Paris, Garnier, 1967.

Wagner, August H. (ed.), *What Happens When You Die?*, New York, Abelard-Schuman, 1968.

Wallis Budge, Sir E. A., *The Egyptian Book of the Dead*, London, Routledge & Kegan Paul, 1969.

Wambach, Helen, *Life before Life*, London, Bantam, 1979.

Wambach, Helen, *Reliving Past Lives*, London, Hutchinson, 1979.

Watson, Lyall, *Supernature*, London, Hodder & Stoughton, 1973.

Watson, Lyall, *The Romeo Error*, London, Hodder & Stoughton, 1974.

Weatherhead, Leslie, *Life begins at Death*, London, Denholm House, 1969.

Whately, Archbishop Richard, *Rhetoric*, London, 1841.

Whitehead, A. N., *Science and the Modem World*, Cambridge University Press, 1928.

Whitehead, A. N., *Adventures of Ideas*, New York, Collier Macmillan, 1967.

Whiteman, J. H. M., *The Mystical Life*, London, Faber & Faber, 1961.
Wilber, Ken (ed.), *The Holographic Paradigm*, London, Routledge & Kegan Paul, 1983.

Williams, Paul V. A., 'Myths, Symbols and the Concept of Immortality among some Amerindian Societies', *Folklore*, vol. 84, Winter 1973.

Wilson, Colin, *Mysteries*, London, Granada, 1979.

Wittgenstein, Ludwig, *Tractatus Logico-Philosophicus*, London, Routledge & Kegan Paul, 1961.

Zaehner, R. C., *Mysticism Sacred and Profane*, London, Oxford University Press, 1961.

Zodiac, *The Zodiac Messages*, London, Greater World Association, 1975.

INDEX OF CASES

Paperbacks also available from
White Crow Books

Elsa Barker—*Letters from
a Living Dead Man*
ISBN 978-1-907355-83-7

Elsa Barker—*War Letters from
the Living Dead Man*
ISBN 978-1-907355-85-1

Elsa Barker—*Last Letters from
the Living Dead Man*
ISBN 978-1-907355-87-5

Richard Maurice Bucke—
Cosmic Consciousness
ISBN 978-1-907355-10-3

Arthur Conan Doyle—
The Edge of the Unknown
ISBN 978-1-907355-14-1

Arthur Conan Doyle—
The New Revelation
ISBN 978-1-907355-12-7

Arthur Conan Doyle—
The Vital Message
ISBN 978-1-907355-13-4

Arthur Conan Doyle with
Simon Parke—*Conversations
with Arthur Conan Doyle*
ISBN 978-1-907355-80-6

Meister Eckhart with Simon Parke—
Conversations with Meister Eckhart
ISBN 978-1-907355-18-9

D. D. Home—*Incidents in my Life Part 1*
ISBN 978-1-907355-15-8

Mme. Dunglas Home; edited,
with an Introduction, by Sir
Arthur Conan Doyle—*D. D.
Home: His Life and Mission*
ISBN 978-1-907355-16-5

Edward C. Randall—
Frontiers of the Afterlife
ISBN 978-1-907355-30-1

Rebecca Ruter Springer—
Intra Muros: My Dream of Heaven
ISBN 978-1-907355-11-0

Leo Tolstoy, edited by Simon
Parke—*Forbidden Words*
ISBN 978-1-907355-00-4

Leo Tolstoy—*A Confession*
ISBN 978-1-907355-24-0

Leo Tolstoy—*The Gospel in Brief*
ISBN 978-1-907355-22-6

Leo Tolstoy—*The Kingdom
of God is Within You*
ISBN 978-1-907355-27-1

Leo Tolstoy—*My Religion:
What I Believe*
ISBN 978-1-907355-23-3

Leo Tolstoy—*On Life*
ISBN 978-1-907355-91-2

Leo Tolstoy—*Twenty-three Tales*
ISBN 978-1-907355-29-5

Leo Tolstoy—*What is Religion
and other writings*
ISBN 978-1-907355-28-8

Leo Tolstoy—*Work While
Ye Have the Light*
ISBN 978-1-907355-26-4

Leo Tolstoy—*The Death of Ivan Ilyich*
ISBN 978-1-907661-10-5

Leo Tolstoy—*Resurrection*
ISBN 978-1-907661-09-9

Leo Tolstoy with Simon Parke—
Conversations with Tolstoy
ISBN 978-1-907355-25-7

Howard Williams with an Introduction
by Leo Tolstoy—*The Ethics of Diet:
An Anthology of Vegetarian Thought*
ISBN 978-1-907355-21-9

Vincent Van Gogh with Simon Parke—
Conversations with Van Gogh
ISBN 978-1-907355-95-0

Wolfgang Amadeus Mozart with Simon
Parke—*Conversations with Mozart*
ISBN 978-1-907661-38-9

Jesus of Nazareth with Simon Parke—
Conversations with Jesus of Nazareth
ISBN 978-1-907661-41-9

Thomas à Kempis with Simon
Parke—*The Imitation of Christ*
ISBN 978-1-907661-58-7

Julian of Norwich with Simon
Parke—*Revelations of Divine Love*
ISBN 978-1-907661-88-4

Allan Kardec—*The Spirits Book*
ISBN 978-1-907355-98-1

Allan Kardec—*The Book on Mediums*
ISBN 978-1-907661-75-4

Emanuel Swedenborg—*Heaven and Hell*
ISBN 978-1-907661-55-6

P.D. Ouspensky—*Tertium Organum:
The Third Canon of Thought*
ISBN 978-1-907661-47-1

Dwight Goddard—*A Buddhist Bible*
ISBN 978-1-907661-44-0

Michael Tymn—*The Afterlife Revealed*
ISBN 978-1-970661-90-7

Michael Tymn—*Transcending the
Titanic: Beyond Death's Door*
ISBN 978-1-908733-02-3

Guy L. Playfair—*If This Be Magic*
ISBN 978-1-907661-84-6

Guy L. Playfair—*The Flying Cow*
ISBN 978-1-907661-94-5

Guy L. Playfair —*This House is Haunted*
ISBN 978-1-907661-78-5

Carl Wickland, M.D.—
Thirty Years Among the Dead
ISBN 978-1-907661-72-3

John E. Mack—*Passport to the Cosmos*
ISBN 978-1-907661-81-5

Peter & Elizabeth Fenwick—
The Truth in the Light
ISBN 978-1-908733-08-5

Erlendur Haraldsson—
Modern Miracles
ISBN 978-1-908733-25-2

Erlendur Haraldsson—
At the Hour of Death
ISBN 978-1-908733-27-6

Erlendur Haraldsson—
The Departed Among the Living
ISBN 978-1-908733-29-0

Brian Inglis—*Science and Parascience*
ISBN 978-1-908733-18-4

Brian Inglis—*Natural and Supernatural:
A History of the Paranormal*
ISBN 978-1-908733-20-7

Ernest Holmes—*The Science of Mind*
ISBN 978-1-908733-10-8

Victor & Wendy Zammit —*A Lawyer
Presents the Evidence For the Afterlife*
ISBN 978-1-908733-22-1

Casper S. Yost—*Patience
Worth: A Psychic Mystery*
ISBN 978-1-908733-06-1

William Usborne Moore—
Glimpses of the Next State
ISBN 978-1-907661-01-3

William Usborne Moore—
The Voices
ISBN 978-1-908733-04-7

John W. White—
The Highest State of Consciousness
ISBN 978-1-908733-31-3

Stafford Betty—
The Imprisoned Splendor
ISBN 978-1-907661-98-3

Paul Pearsall, Ph.D. —
Super Joy
ISBN 978-1-908733-16-0

All titles available as eBooks, and selected titles available in Hardback and Audiobook formats from www.whitecrowbooks.com

CPSIA information can be obtained
at www.ICGtesting.com
Printed in the USA
BVHW070547170323
660514BV00006B/976